Praise for the new edition of *Living in Balan*

"The Leveys are engaged in work that has great prospects for bringing the inner sciences to a wide section of people who may not under ordinary circumstances come in contact with the inner technologies of mental development and transformation."
— The Dalai Lama

"As a great cookbook gets dog-eared with years of use, this comprehensive mindfulness and life-tuning guide could become like the Be Here Now of the early twenty-first century — but "with legs" for the long haul. This book is a rich time-release resource which leaders, young people, skeptics, spiritual seekers, parents and family members alike will find to be life-giving and useful in the crafting of beauty and harmony in our lives and in our world."
— Kolin Lymworth, Banyen Books

"*Living in Balance* is an absolute treasure, filled with an abundance of insights and practices that lead the reader into depths of peace. But with all these riches, I was most affected by the love, compassion, and wisdom Joel and Michelle present in every page. Their embrace of the reader is the best testimony that these practices lead to lives of wholeness and harmony."
— Margaret J. Wheatley, author of *So Far from Home*, *Perseverance*, and *Leadership and the New Science*

"*Living in Balance* is a global priority. Joel and Michelle skillfully highlight the inner dimension to international crises. Through modern science and ancient wisdom traditions, they offer insights and practical tools to help us find and maintain balance in daily life — so we can contribute to creating a more peaceful and environmentally sustainable world."
— Philip M. Hellmich, Director of Peace, The Shift Network; author of *God and Conflict: A Search for Peace in a Time of Crisis*

"Today more than ever modern society makes demands on the individual for which evolution has not prepared us. *Living in Balance* gives each of us tools that not only will allow us to navigate through a complex world but allow us to thrive. By gaining insights into ourselves and learning techniques that fundamentally allow one to rewire their brain, Joel and Michelle have given us a wonderful gift... the gift of transcendence."
— James R. Doty, M.D., founder and director of Stanford's Center for Compassion and Altruism Research and Education; clinical professor of neurosurgery at Stanford University

"A vital compass for navigating our way through this era of chaos and possibility. *Living in Balance* guides us on a deep and expansive journey, flowing with transformative wisdom. Lucid and engaging, it is a tonic for the heart, mind, body, and the world we inhabit."
— Angeles Arrien, PhD, author of *The Four Fold Way* and *Living in Gratitude*

"*Living in Balance* invites us to return to the inner source of serenity and wisdom within. Never before have we so urgently needed the clear, compassionate teachings that are so lovingly described in this book."
— Larry Dossey, MD, author of *Healing Words*; executive editor, *Explore*

"In this book, Joel and Michelle offer us all that we need to create a meaningful and balanced life. Anyone who follows these practices and teachings will become a blessing to others, a refuge for all beings. The revolution we seek must always come from the inside out."
— NOAH LEVINE, author of *Refuge Recovery, Dharma Punx*, and *Against the Stream*

"The benefit of *Living in Balance* is in the skillful weaving of the personal, interpersonal, and ecological perspectives with the fields of wisdom, faith traditions, daily life, and science. It's a pleasant combination of practical advice and inspiration that is very helpful as we seek to develop wiser relationships with ourselves, our community, our technology, and our world."
— BILL DUANE, senior manager, Well Being and Sustainable High Performance Development Programs at Google

"A vital compass for this era of chaos and possibility, *Living in Balance* guides us on a deep and expansive journey, flowing with transformative wisdom. Lucid and engaging, it is a tonic for the heart, mind, body, and the world we inhabit."
— NOVA AMI AND VELCROW RIPPER, award-winning filmmakers, Fierce Love Films

"Joel and Michelle are not just experts in this field, but two of the most balanced people I have ever met. In *Living in Balance*, they offer not only cutting edge science and their own experience, but wisdom from the ages on living wisely and well. A must read for all of us seeking calm in the chaos of our times."
— M.J. RYAN, author of *This Year I Will* and *How to Survive Change You Didn't Ask For*

"This book is both a practical and inspirational resource for living our lives to the fullest while also encouraging and impacting those around us — whether it's a single family, a workplace environment or an entire community of citizens. *Living in Balance* offers wisdom and depth gleaned from innovative, entrepreneurial, and compassionate thinkers and doers; it is thoughtful, well researched, and immensely valuable in bringing balance and productivity to the increasingly complex, challenging, and global world we live in."
— GREG FISCHER, mayor of Louisville, Kentucky, an International Model City of Compassion

"Wonderful! A radical yet simple approach that can save our sanity and the world! The timeless wisdom and modern science in this book offer critical insight for everyone working to rebalance their lives or engaging in social change. The mindfulness practices share essential skills for keeping calm in the midst of today's raging storms. I recommend this book to everyone and return to its quotes and passages often."
— RIVERA SUN, author of *The Dandelion Insurrection*

"I've known and admired the work of Joel and Michelle Levey, and have witnessed firsthand the loving wisdom and depth of their teaching. This book elucidates and enlivens their work and makes it accessible to anyone who is on the journey to find more peace, joy, and fulfillment in life. The Leveys affirm the many strategies we might embrace to find our way. This book is to be treasured and read until dog-eared and damp with sweet tears of deep recognition."
— KAREN GUZAK, mayor, City of Snohomish, Washington State

LIVING IN
BALANCE

LIVING IN
BALANCE

A Mindful Guide for Thriving in a Complex World

Joel Levey & Michelle Levey

Foreword by His Holiness The Dalai Lama

DIVINE
ARTS

Published by DIVINE ARTS
DivineArtsMedia.com

An Imprint of Michael Wiese Productions
12400 Ventura Blvd. #1111
Studio City, CA 91604
(818) 379–8799, (818) 986–3408 (Fax)

Cover design: JohnnyInk www.johnnyink.com
Interior design and layout: Howie Severson www.fortuitouspub.com
Copyeditor: David Wright

Printed by McNaughton & Gunn, Inc., Saline, Michigan
Manufactured in the United States of America

Library of Congress Cataloging-in-Publication Data
Levey, Joel.
 Living in balance : a mindful guide for thriving in a complex world / Joel Levey and
Michelle Levey ; foreword by His Holiness the Dalai Lama. — [Revised edition].
   pages cm
  ISBN 978–1–61125–029–9 (paperback)
1. Conduct of life. 2. Quality of life. I. Levey, Michelle. II. Title.
BF637.C5L46 2014
158.1—dc23
                           2014014689

Printed on Recycled Stock

This book is dedicated to all those
who yearn for balance,
and to the spirit of harmony and wholeness
awakening within us all.

Contents

Foreword by His Holiness The Dalai Lama

THE DALAI LAMA

Humankind has always been faced with problems, and in different parts of the world, at different times, people have come to varying conclusions about the nature of these problems and how to tackle them. One of Buddhism's most relevant lessons is the avoidance of extremes. It teaches that freedom and happiness will not be found in the extremes of either sensual indulgence or mortification: a middle way must be found.

Today there is an overemphasis on the external world. Science has rapidly extended our understanding of external phenomena, and technological advances have contributed to improved health and physical comfort. Yet even in the most developed countries we do not find a corresponding increase in peace and happiness; if anything, there is even greater anxiety and stress. Fear stimulates the need for terrifyingly destructive weapons systems, while greed gives rise to damage and pollution of the environment, putting the very existence of humanity at risk.

These trends are symptomatic of the dangers of pursuing external progress alone. What is missing is a corresponding inner development. To redeem the balance, our new frontier should be inner worlds, and not outer space. If the mind is explored with the same stringent scrutiny applied in other branches of science, it will certainly be of immense benefit not only to individuals but to society as a whole.

Within the world's contemplative traditions can be found numerous methods for investigating and training the mind. This book summarizes why the adoption of such "inner science" is necessary now, and how interest has grown in the search for compatibility between contemporary needs and ancient techniques. It presents an array of methods for transforming the mind. These methods may seem relatively simple, but to be effective they must be applied steadily in a rigorous, rational way—much as a physicist or a chemist conducts his experiments—so that the inner scientist may both test and become familiar with them.

This book will be of use to anyone interested in exploring and transforming the mind. As more people achieve some degree of mental calm, insight, or the ability to transform negative emotions into positive ones, there will be a natural reinforcement of basic human values and consequently a greater chance for peace and happiness for all.

—THE DALAI LAMA

Authors' Preface
to the New Edition

This book that you hold in your hands is a weaving together of many streams of energy, information, and inspiration. Distilled within are wisdom teachings we have received from many respected teachers from around the world...who received them from their teachers... who received them from their teachers....This newly revised and expanded edition comes to you in partnership with our publisher, Divine Arts, with a vision and dedication to bringing *Living in Balance* to readers around the globe in response to the emerging needs of this evolutionary time.

The theme of *Living in Balance* is a universal theme with deep roots in verified evidence-based science, the ancient wisdom traditions, and indigenous cultures throughout the world. As our world becomes ever more complex and stressful, developing our capacity for dynamic balance in our lives, work, and relationships becomes ever more vital to understand and embody in our own lives and to model for others whose lives we influence.

What does living in balance look like in the digital age? Is such a thing even possible during this time of unrelenting complexity, accelerating demands and pressures on our resources and energy, genetically modified and engineered foods, acidification of the oceans, species extinction, and other unbalancing changes in our climate and ecosystem? How do we learn to recognize early warning signs that we are moving away from balance and what can we do at these times to move back in the direction of harmony and wholeness? What kinds of enhancing "pings" and "alerts" can we create and discover to help us wake up, shift gears, and recalibrate?

These are some of the challenges, strategies, and tools we invite you to explore and bring to life as you read this new edition. Some of these challenges and methods are evergreen and universally relevant

"We clasp the hands of those who go before us,

and the hands of those who come after us;

we enter the little circle of each other's arms,

and the larger circle of lovers whose hands are joined in a dance,

and the larger circle of all creatures,

passing in and out of life,

who move also in a dance,

to a music so subtle and vast

that no one hears it except in fragments."

—Wendell Berry, "Healing"

to being in a human body on planet Earth, and some of them are unique to this particular period of rapid change, global interconnectivity, and uncertainty.

As you read this book, remember that we are not teaching that there is a state of static, enduring balance to be realized and maintained — but rather that moment to moment and day to day, you have the capacity to be mindful if you are moving towards harmony and balance or away from harmony and balance, and that through this awareness you have the capacity to make a conscious choice to continue on the path you are on — or — to change your attitude and direction as you so choose. The real key to this is to remember: "Choice follows Awareness!" Mindfulness is truly the portal to living in balance!

As many-dimensional human beings, there are a myriad of principles and practices offered for your consideration and experimentation in this book. As you read *Living in Balance* we encourage you to be mindful of which ideas are most resonant and meaningful for you, and then to experiment with weaving these into your life as practices that you actually embody and bring to life.

We live in what many global leaders refer to as "VUCA times" — times of unprecedented change and upheaval characterized by global Volatility, Uncertainty, Complexity, and Ambiguity. These VUCA times offer both great chaos and uncertainty in our lives and world, as well as a great upwelling of emergent new expressions of creativity, entrepreneurial spirit, and innovative life-affirming, grass roots, community, corporate, and global initiatives to encourage more sustainable ways of living in harmony and balance together in our world. Such times bring out the best and the worst of people resulting in stresses, strains, and emerging opportunities that stretch our limits and call us to develop our extraordinary capacities for living in harmony and balance — and helping others to do the same.

Living in Balance is written to help you to develop the wisdom, compassion, creativity, resilience, and discernment necessary to become ever more Visionary, Understanding, Confident, and Adaptable in response to these VUCA times. Interestingly, in the Zulu language, the word vuca means "to wake up" — a practice that is essential for learning, wisdom, compassion, and creative adaptation to cope with VUCA consequences!

Living in Balance is a book that offers inspiration and practical advice for people from all walks of life.

For leaders, *Living in Balance* is a guide to developing the wisdom and methods required to develop the capacity of people and organizations

"It is the worst of times because it feels as though the very earth is being stolen from us, by us; the land and air poisoned, the water polluted, the animals disappeared, humans degraded and misguided.... It is the best of times because we have entered a period, if we can bring ourselves to pay attention, of great clarity as to cause and effect. Because we can now see into every crevice of the globe and because we are free to explore previously unexplored crevices in our own hearts and minds, it is inevitable that everything we have needed to comprehend in order to survive, everything that we have needed to understand in the most basic of ways, will be illuminated now."

—Alice Walker

to thrive and be sustainably successful and adaptable in rapidly changing times.

For young people, it is a primer to develop personal life-skills needed to enjoy a long, healthy, fulfilling, and meaningful life, and to helping many others along the way.

For skeptics, it offers a variety of experiments to run in the laboratory of your own lives to offer proof that it truly *is* possible to be successful at creating more balance and wellness.

For spiritual seekers, *Living in Balance* offers a wealth of inspirations, affirmations, and contemplations to inspire your journey of Awakening.

For parents and family members, *Living in Balance* provides insights and inspirations for developing greater harmony, deeper connections, and more meaningful relations with loved ones.

Our hope is that each person who reads *Living in Balance* will discover his or her own unique mix, or "play list" of meaningful insights, practices, and ways of living to awaken to greater harmony, wholeness, wisdom, and balance. As each of us comes to live more in balance, we will become less of a troublemaker sharing our confusion and stress with others, and we will become a more tuned-in, empathic, wise, helpful, compassionate, and inspiring presence in the lives of all we touch along The Way.

We offer our deepest gratitude to the many people whose love, vision, leadership, and dedicated work have inspired this new edition in coming into being, and we hope that you will take these teachings on living in balance to heart in ways that bring blessings to your life and to the lives of others.

"We are in the midst of an awakening. At no time in history has Mother Earth needed her children to care more than at the present. Ancient prophecies from every culture around the world warn of dramatic global change. It's time to believe we can make a difference. If we have hope, there is potential for extraordinary change. The Elders teach us if we return to harmony in our lives, melting the ice in our hearts, reconnecting with one another, we will survive."

—Angaangaq Angakkorsuaq, Big Ice Wisdom Keeper, Greenland

"The New Pioneers." © 2010. Used by permission, Mark Henson, www.MarkHensonArt.com

"In this era, to become a spiritual inquirer without social consciousness is a luxury that we can ill afford, and to be a social activist without a scientific understanding of the inner workings of the mind is the worst folly. Neither approach in isolation has had any significant success. There is no question now that an inquirer will have to make an effort to be socially conscious or that an activist will have to be persuaded of the moral crisis in the human psyche, the significance of being attentive to the inner life. The challenge awaiting us is to go much deeper as human beings, to abandon superficial prejudices and preferences, to expand understanding to a global scale, integrating the totality of living, and to become aware of the wholeness of which we are a manifestation."

—Vimala Thakar

Staying Centered
in Challenging Times

THROUGH THE JOURNEY OF WRITING THIS BOOK WE HAVE BEEN BRING-
ing the question of what it means to live in balance in today's world into
our every day, in our work and travels, and into our meditations and our
dreams at night. What we have discovered is that no realm of experience exists outside of this theme of "balance"! In fact, dynamic balance
seems to be a central organizing principle of every living system in the
universe. Is it any wonder, then, that as our lives become more complex,
with increasing demands and less time to meet those demands, that the
challenge and value of balance is looming large in our collective psyche? From boardrooms to bedrooms, in health care, education, and
global forums, people are seeking to bring more of this elusive quality
into their lives.

In our own lives, as a husband-and-wife consulting team to a wide
spectrum of organizations, we witness, on a daily basis, the escalat-
ing longing for greater balance emanating from people everywhere.
Feeling this need resonating within ourselves as well, we wanted to
respond to this general malaise of our time, to reach out to people's
feelings of being overwhelmed and out-of-balance within themselves
and with others. From our own experience, we have found many strategies and perspectives that can help restore and maintain a sense of inner
and outer balance—even if you can't simplify your lifestyle, quit your
job, or run away from home! We want to share this essential wisdom
with you, and to offer you the knowledge and reassurance that balance
can be cultivated and enjoyed.

Rather than try to write the definitive, exhaustive (and exhausting!) book about balance, we decided that the wisest course would be
to acknowledge the immensity of the issue up front, and then focus on
providing you with some practical, easy-to-integrate techniques to
bring the living reality of balance and inner peace more alive for you,

and for all whose lives you touch. We've been deeply inspired to see that the practices we ourselves use to keep balanced on the waves of our own busy lives work as reliably for the folks we've introduced them to. Those who have taken our approaches to heart and integrated them into their day-to-day lives have shown us that applying the wisdom of balance can truly save your health, your sanity, your relationships, your job, the quality of your life, and even your life itself!

Pause for a moment now to appreciate where you are in the journey of your life, and to wonder at the miracle of your being. Some decades ago, through the merging of two cells in perfect harmony and balance, a doorway into life was opened to you. Myriad experiences, lessons, breakdowns, and breakthroughs later, you find yourself sitting here with this book in your hands, questioning, yearning, and wondering.

This book comes to you likely at just the right time and at an appropriate stage of your pondering of your life with all its opportunities and challenges. In that spirit, we invite you to take the ideas and methods that you find here to heart. Listen deeply to the many voices that will speak to you through these pages; look for the value, meaning, and practical applications of what you discover here for enhancing the quality of your life and your influence in the lives of others. Much of what you find here will be new, and much will remind you again of things you once knew, but may have forgotten. Please take from these pages the inspiration you need to nourish and sustain yourself at this time in your journey.

LIVING IN BALANCE — NOW MORE THAN EVER

In decades past, when living-in-balance practices like mindfulness, yoga, meditation, and healthy living first began to emerge in popular culture, they were generally regarded as optional, though highly recommended, practices for easing stress, offering peace of mind, enhancing well-being, or becoming enlightened.

But in today's complex, fast-paced, insanely stressful and overloaded times, for any sensible person who is aware of what is going on, and what is likely coming, who has an interest in personal and global sustainability, staying healthy, being successful, raising a healthy family, making wise decisions, or making a meaningful difference in the world without crashing and burning out, these principles, practices, and disciplines for living in balance are no longer optional — they are essential. The quality of our lives and world depends on our learning these lessons now more than ever.

> "Courage is contagious. If you take a courageous step as an individual, you will literally change the world because you will affect all sorts of people in your immediate vicinity, who will then affect others and then affect others. You should never doubt your ability to change the world."
>
> —Glenn Greenwald

> "There are those who are trying
>
> to set fire to the world
>
> We are in danger.
>
> There is time only to work slowly,
>
> There is no time not to love.
>
> —Deena Metzger

Never has the theme of living in balance been so universally relevant in our world. Wherever we turn we find individuals, couples, families, organizations, communities, cities, societies, and our global civilization seeking for ways to thrive in today's world and be well, stay strong, and become more resilient in embracing what the future may bring.

Different forces inspire and compel us to take an interest in living in balance. On one hand, we live at a truly unique and pivotal moment in human history, when a perfect storm of complex circumstances and global crises are emerging and converging to sweep away many established social structures, institutions, norms, ways of life, and cherished yet increasingly irrelevant misconceptions that billions of people have relied upon for meaning and direction for many generations. With global climate conditions becoming increasingly erratic and unpredictable, crops and water supplies are failing, sea levels are rising, inequity and injustice are extreme, economies are crashing, and the dreams so many have of the future are increasingly uncertain and unsettling.

Yet, at the same time, a myriad of profoundly sensible, sustainable and life-affirming new sciences, technologies, health practices, lifestyles, alternative economies, building practices, energy sources, and wiser and more compassionate ways of living are also emerging that offer great promise and potential for people, families, organizations, communities, and cities around the globe.

We have crossed the threshold now where we have a virtual mother-lode of compelling evidence-based research extolling and confirming the profound value and practical advantages for individuals, teams, and whole organizations of adopting ways of living and working that promote greater harmony and balance as core success strategies. This is truly a golden moment of opportunity to invest ourselves in deepening our personal and collective wisdom, becoming more resilient, and developing our most extraordinary capacities in order to ride through the big changes and challenges on the horizon.

These are indeed the best and worst of times. What is at stake is no less than the present and future quality of life for humanity and the integrity of every life-support system of our precious and fragile planet — the only place in our known universe that will be our home for generations to come.

> "To live in this world, you must be able to do three things: to love what is mortal; to hold it against your bones knowing your own life depends on it; and, when the time comes to let it go, to let it go."
>
> —Mary Oliver

> "All this systems stuff has no meaning without understanding that we're part of something larger than ourselves... If our work has an impact, it will bring us back into the natural order of things."
>
> —Peter Senge

A GREAT TURNING

This is both an exciting and terrifying time to be alive as things are getting better and better and worse and worse, faster and faster, in more and more places around the globe. It takes great courage and capacity to stay open to the torrents of information that each new day, text, tweet, email, or download streams our way.

This age is being called the Anthropocene—the age when human influence is irreversibly altering the critical feedback loops of the self-regulating life-support systems of the whole planet, affecting the lives of virtually all beings living now or ever to come. For the most part, humanity's collective influence on the life-sustaining and balancing forces of our world is rife with "unintended consequences"—each of which gives rise to a host of complex and interrelated global crises that reflect a lack of wisdom, care, or political will to make decisions necessary to maintain healthy balances in our world.

For example, "fracking" for natural gas to free America from reliance on foreign oil poisons aquifers and people, and releases immense amounts of methane into the atmosphere accelerating global warming. Mismanaged nuclear power plants intended to free Japan from dependence on importing fossil fuels led to meltdowns that contaminated their country, much of the Pacific Ocean, and a legacy of nuclear fallout across the northern hemisphere. No one planned for this, no one really knows how to manage for this, and the impacts will endure for millennia.

This is also fittingly called the time of The Great Turning—a time when the "industrial growth society" that has flourished by exploiting natural and human resources for the past three hundred years is now so depleted, mismanaged, and corrupt that it is rapidly disintegrating due to a lack of capacity (or willingness) to wisely evolve, balance, govern, and transform its powerful influence in our lives and world for the good of all. The resulting upheavals and imbalances in global economies, climate, and societies are leading humanity to make a great turn toward remembering, discovering, and establishing more sustainable, life-affirming, and just ways of living, guided by deeper wisdom, compassion, and alignment with the laws of nature.

Coincident with this Great Turning toward more sustainable ways of living is the Great Unraveling of a myriad of outdated and increasingly irrelevant social systems and structures, institutions, and belief systems that have long served as enduring pillars or norms of our civilization. The daily news offers a litany of stories of how these overstretched, destabilized systems and structures are imploding, and the host of challenges and opportunities that are emerging as a result.

It's been nearly fifty years since the Apollo 8 mission when William Anders snapped his epic "earthrise" photo of our home planet, which gave humanity its first look in the mirror of its unity and fragility as a single spaceship we call Earth floating in space. It's profound to remember that we live in the first generation of global connectivity where we can reach out to be instantly seen and heard, "friended" "or "liked" by people in vast social networks that encompass the globe. For the first time in history, we can witness and reflect upon global events real-time as they are unfolding, and activate our local and non-local networks to respond.

We witnessed this firsthand on March 11, 2011, when we received a phone call from Civil Defense informing us of a massive earthquake and tsunami in Japan, and activating us as Community Emergency Response Team members in our rural community on the northern tip of the Island of Hawaii. We logged on to Twitter and the web and watched with amazement as more and more people around the globe tuned in and began to respond to what was unfolding in Japan. With a sense of awe, we monitored both of our laptops as a few posts appeared, then dozens, hundreds, and thousands followed, in a rapidly growing tsunami of tweets, posts, videos of the destruction, prayers, and humanitarian responses flooding into cyberspace from and through hearts and minds broken open and bearing witness around the globe.

Turning toward each other, individuals, families, organizations, and communities around the globe are now able to connect, to question and reflect on their ways of life, explore options, and reorient toward ways of living that embody deeper wisdom, compassion, resiliency of spirit, and balance. *Living in Balance* is a handbook for bringing this "Great Turning" to life.

There is a general consensus in the global networks of solutions seekers and facilitators of which we are a part, that while we really do not know for certain what the future will bring, we are likely in for a turbulent ride through many decades and generations to come. From our travels, time with global leaders, researchers, and wisdom teachers, what *is* clear is that developing our personal and collective wisdom, compassion, resilience, and balance is absolutely the most wise and timely investment and commitment that any of us can make in these times.

Working in medicine, hospice, palliative care, and meditation training, we often have people call us, saying, "I've been diagnosed with a terminal illness. Can you teach me how to meditate?" We

"When we seek for connection, we restore the world to wholeness.

Our seemingly separate lives become meaningful as we discover how truly necessary we are to each other."

—Margaret Wheatley

"It is time to be insane together! It is time to violate consensus reality...

We are all holding each other in an emerging story that will restore and regenerate our hurting world."

—Charles Eisenstein

> "We live in a moment of disruption, death, and rebirth. What's dying is an old civilization and mindset of 'me.' What is being born is less clear but in no way less significant... It's a future that requires us to tap into a deeper level of our humanity, of who we really are, and who we want to be as a society. It's a shift that requires us to expand our thinking from the head to the heart. It is a shift from an ego-system awareness that cares about the well-being of me to an eco-system awareness that cares about the well-being of all, including myself."

—Otto Scharmer

> "Another world is possible, this very moment when we choose to live it. It begins with our very next breath. As more and more of us choose an uncompromising life, a life that is truly lived, the more attainable that world is for everyone else. The field of possibility expands exponentially each time one of us chooses to step up to the plate and shine."
>
> —Velcrow Ripper

usually reply "of course," and we also comment to each other, "How sad that they didn't seek out this kind of learning earlier in their lives so that when they really needed this kind of inner strength, wisdom, clarity, and peace of mind, they would already have that empowering wisdom, confidence, and skill set fully loaded and online for them." The same applies to many people, organizations, and situations in this day and age, where we look at each other and say, "Oh, that they would have learned and practiced these methods for years, so they'd have the confidence, skills, neural integrity, and depth of presence in place to surf the waves of change that come sweeping through their lives."

In this spirit, we have written this updated and revised edition of *Living in Balance* as a timely and mindful guide for curious, courageous, and committed people seeking to awaken and live in greater harmony and balance, to thrive and help others thrive too, in these VUCA times.

As we've lived through the changing cycles of the seasons over the course of writing this book and contemplating deeply the profound permutations, awesome implications, and vast dimensions of this mystery called balance, our lives have been blessed and transformed. Through this deep immersion into the world of balance, we've seen that the lessons of balance abound everywhere when we begin to look for them. Writing together as co-authors, our shared creativity has shown us the balance between structure and emergence, and the balance of our unique styles. Through it all, we have grown in our appreciation and love for each other, and for this we are most grateful.

May the words on these pages help bring balance alive for you in new and meaningful ways, and may the turning of the seasons remind you that it is always the season for balance.

"Another world is not only possible,
she is on her way.
On a quiet day, if you listen carefully,
you can hear her breathing."
— Arundhati Roy

"Humanity is taking its final examination.
We have come to an extraordinary moment
when it doesn't have to be you or me.
There is enough for all.
We need not operate competitively any longer.
If we succeed, it will be because of youth, truth and love."
— Buckminster Fuller

An Inside-Out Approach to Balanced Living

"To know how to wonder and question is the first step of the mind toward discovery."

—LOUIS PASTEUR

IT'S EASY TO SEE THAT MANY OF US ARE LIVING OUT OF BALANCE. PEOPLE ARE working more and enjoying it less, and the effects of such an unbalanced work/life are manifesting everywhere. For example, numerous studies indicate that the majority of Americans are suffering from a severe sleep deficit and are currently getting 60 to 90 minutes less sleep per night than is necessary for optimal health and performance. Many of us have no choice about where we spend our time — or at least we feel we don't. As one young father said to us recently, "Either I can spend time with my family or I can support them — not both."

If you are reading this book, obviously you are feeling the need to examine this issue in your own life. So take a few minutes right now to consider these questions:

- What indications are there in your life that you are living more or less in balance?
- What indications are there in your life that your life is out of balance?
- What beliefs, values, and assumptions led you to your answers?

There will be time to examine your answers to these questions later. Right now, just hold onto what you learned as we look at some ways to begin thinking about balance itself.

"If you look for the
truth outside yourself,

it gets farther and
farther away.

Today, walking alone,

I meet him
everywhere I step.

He is the same as me,

yet I am not him.

Only if you
understand it
in this way

will you merge with
the way things are."

—Tung Shan

The story of balance in our personal lives unfolds within a larger context of wholeness, but it begins from the inside out. That's why, in Section One of *Living in Balance*, we begin by building the foundation for understanding this bigger picture. Here you will learn the number one skill for cultivating a balanced way of living. This indispensible skill is an inner awareness called mindfulness. Developing mindfulness gives you an internal guidance system that helps you know when you're heading off the course of balance, so you can self-correct and find your way back on track. It's like having an inner compass or radar, advising you of your present reality and the direction you're heading in, then lighting your way home. With this foundation to guide and support you, you are ready to begin the journey of turning toward balance — the most crucial journey of our time.

"Only she who is ready to question,
to think for herself, will find the truth.
To understand the currents of the river
he who wishes to know the truth
must enter the water."
— Nisargadatta

chapter one

It's All About Balance

A human being is part of the whole called by us the Universe.
He experiences himself, his thoughts and feelings as something
separated from the rest — a kind of optical delusion of his consciousness. This delusion is a kind of prison for us, restricting us to
our personal desires and to affection for a few persons nearest us.
Our task must be to free ourselves from this prison by widening
our circle of compassion to embrace all living creatures, and the
whole of nature in its beauty. Nobody is able to achieve this completely, but the striving for such achievement is, in itself, a part of
the liberation and a foundation for inner security.

— ALBERT EINSTEIN

THOUGH OUR YEARNING FOR BALANCE IS A DEEPLY PERSONAL QUEST, IT
is truly a journey of universal proportions. While at an individual level,
we may be feeling overwhelmed with trying to juggle our jobs, family,
and social engagements, it is helpful to remember that every thing at
every level and dimension of the universe is constantly in search for
balance. Indeed, it is the yearning for balance that keeps everything in
our universe in motion, while the motion itself provides balance for the
dimensions of reality that dwell in stillness.

Science and spiritual teachings have converged to remind us that,
in truth, nothing is separate. Nothing can be sensibly studied in isolation from its environment. Within seamless wholeness, the fields and

flows of energy that we label as "living beings" or natural resources or "mysterious forces" all interact in perfect balance and harmony. In the dance of life, the currents of oppositely charged particles flow. Electrical, biochemical, chemical, and mind fields all interact and weave together. To truly understand anything, you must see it as a point of perfect balance, a reflection of everything else in the universe that converges in that moment and place to support the involvement of you, the observer and the observed. In the natural world, pressures build and are released, balance flows within natural limits that define the game of life. The earth spins, ever so steadily, moving through space at tens of thousands of miles per hour, yet nothing shakes apart and no one falls off!

In our own lives, balance emerges through the dynamic interplay of inner and outer forces. In order to get a feel for it, sense or imagine yourself sitting here now at the center of your universe, like an endless ocean of information and inspiration. Within you and around you myriad strong and subtle forces dance together in a movement of constant change to maintain the dynamic balance that weaves the amazing fabric of your life. Within you, each pulsing cell and organ maintains its integrity, form, and function by finding an active balance of energy and information flow within and across the permeable membranes that define the realms of "inner" and "outer." With the inhale and exhale of each breath, we affirm the life-giving flow of inside to outside and outside to inside. Breathing consciously with awareness, we begin to sense the flow and change that is at the heart of our experience of life, and in each moment, each interaction, each day well lived, we learn that balance is to be found in the flow of life.

As you approach this inquiry into the theme of balance in your life, you may discover, as we did, that everything will become a teacher for you. You will find lessons of balance in the rhythms of your breath and pulse, in the rising and setting of the sun, in the turning of the seasons, in the cycles of change that weave birth and death, activity and rest, work and play, and alone time and time with others into the wholeness of your existence. Viewed in this way, your whole life will become a wonder-land in which the ongoing inquiry into the nature of balance unfolds.

By learning to be more fully present and aware of this process, your learning will increase and you will recognize many more possibilities and choices. As your insight deepens, you will see more clearly what paths in your life lead you toward and away from the balance you yearn for.

"The only dream worth having is to dream that you will live while you are alive,

and die only when you are dead. To love, to be loved. To never forget your own insignificance. To never get used to the unspeakable violence and vulgar disparity of the life around you. To seek joy in the saddest places. To pursue beauty to its lair.

To never simplify what is complicated or complicate what is simple.

To respect strength, never power. Above all to watch.

To try and understand. To never look away. And never, never to forget."

—Arundhati Roy

THE WAVES AND THE OCEAN

Balance can also be sensed in terms of the waves and of the ocean. Just as waves have a beginning, development, culmination, disintegration, and end, balance in our life is found in the flow of periods of activity and rest, paying attention to others and to ourselves, work and play, wakefulness and sleep.

Yet at a deeper level, the changing tides of such "waves" are balanced by the profound reality of an unchanging "ocean" within you. Just as the ocean is the water that forms all waves, the ocean within you is the universal reality or essence that dwells within all beings. Its presence is so deep, clear, and transparent that, like a fish in the sea, your whole life may go by without your ever really noticing it. Yet if for a moment you discover it, your life will never be quite the same. Discovering this ocean is vitally important for the discovery of balance because it provides a place of peace for you to return home to despite all the chaos of the day. You can discover the ocean within you right now.

Sit up and feel your feet touching the floor. As you breathe in, know you are breathing in. As you breathe out, know that you are breathing out. Just do that for one minute. Smile to yourself. Awareness of the Self is as simple as that. Just as waves rise out of and dissolve back into the water of the ocean, awareness pervades the changing flow of forms that weave the ever-unfolding patterns of your life. And the smile of balance keeps you from trying too hard, or getting too self-critical, or taking this marvelous discovery of yourself too seriously.

"The same stream of life that runs through the world runs through my veins night and day and dances in rhythmic measure. It is the same life that shoots in joy through the dust of the earth into the numberless blades of grass and breaks into tumultuous waves of flowers."

—Rabindanath Tagor

WALKING THE TIGHTROPE OF DAILY LIFE

We find it helpful to view our journey through life as a walk on a tightrope stretched across the vastness of space. Life, in this sense, is a learning laboratory in which to learn how to walk in balance. Believing in a responsive, compassionate, and often playful universe, we notice that the width or narrowness of the rope appears to be adjusted to help each walker optimize his or her learning. For a real beginner, it might be 10 feet wide with handrails. As your skill and confidence grow, the rope narrows and becomes more challenging to walk. Ideally it is still just wide enough to keep you in the upper end of your "learning zone" rather than moving off into danger.

In thinking about balance in this way, there are a few helpful things to keep in mind:

- There are two primary states of being. One is walking in balance, i.e., staying on the rope. The other state is tumbling, i.e., mindless, fearful, and out of control. We are always either walking mindfully and fully present on our rope or we are to some degree mindlessly tumbling.
- The moment you are mindful that you are tumbling, you are already moving back toward balance and you land back on the rope. Boing! People who have yet to learn this, tumble — and because they are tumbling, they get more stressed about being distressed, or become more anxious when they notice they are anxious, ad infinitum. These strategies, however, only lead to becoming more dangerously out of balance and feeling out of control.
- It's as important to know when you are tumbling, or about to tumble, as to know when you are in balance. That is, the real accomplishment — the deeper balance — is having the presence of mind to recognize when you are in balance and when you are not.
- The more you struggle to stay in control or in balance, the less you are. Real control, real balance, emerges as a state of naturalness. For people who play stringed instruments, this is easily understood by the analogy of a well-tuned instrument. For the richest, most beautiful, most harmonious sounds, the strings must be neither too tight nor too loose. Learning to listen for when you are in or out of such a state of optimal tuning is in itself a fine art.
- Remember, it is all about learning, not about being perfect. The key is not to tumble about having tumbled, or to get more mindless about being mindless.

When we developed and instructed the once-secret Ultimate Warrior (aka "Jedi Warrior") program for the U.S. Army Special Forces troops prior to deployment, one of our primary axioms was "Choice follows awareness." In corporate settings we sometimes express this as "You can only manage what you monitor." Either way, it is only when you know that you are moving out of balance that you can take the necessary steps to move more toward balance — and remember, the recognition is in itself the first step of a return toward balance!

It's also important to recognize that walking on the rope means being more or less in balance. There are some of us who walk in a very tight, controlled way. These are the folks who are paranoid of falling, so afraid of the forces that might challenge them that they are easily knocked off balance. When they fall, they tumble for a long time, snarled in the net of frustration and blame. Though they tend to be very critical of others, they are especially hard on themselves. This attitude keeps them tumbling most of the time.

Fortunately, there is an alternative. Through awareness and practice, your confidence can grow to a point where your terror of falling fades away. For people in this league, the obstacles they encounter are viewed as welcome opportunities to further develop their skills and strengths. In those moments when they do fall, they pay more attention to how gracefully they can fall, and even learn how to glide through space with grace and ease. For these folks, falling ceases to be a "failure" and tumbling becomes an exercise in creative gliding.

You can learn to walk the tightrope of life this way. And the better you get, the more you will discover that walking and gliding become the same. As the tightrope gets finer and finer in response to your increasing skills, the more your walking begins to resemble flying. Each moment, each step, becomes one of joy, wonder, discovery, or creative expression. Are you ready to hop on the rope together now, and explore this balancing adventure further? Here we go!

"Sometimes you reach a point of being so coordinated, so completely balanced, that you feel you can do anything—anything at all. At times like this I find I can run up to the front of the board and stand on the nose when pushing out through a broken wave; I can goof around, put myself in an impossible position and then pull out of it, simply because I feel happy. An extra bit of confidence like that can carry you through, and you can do things that are just about impossible."

—Midget Farrelly, champion surfer

chapter two

Glimpses of Wholeness

We are part of the earth and it is part of us...
The perfumed flowers are our sisters,
    the deer, the horse, the great eagle,
    these are our brothers.
The rocky crests, the juices of the meadows,
    the body heat of the pony, and human beings
    all belong to the same family...
The shining water that moves in the streams and rivers is not just water
    but the blood of our ancestors...
The rivers are our brothers, they quench our thirst...
    The air is precious to the red man, for all things share the
    same breath—
    the animal, the tree, the human, they all share the same breath...
    The air shares its spirit with all the life it supports. The wind that
    gave our grandfather his first breath also receives his last sigh...
What are people without animals?
    If all the animals were gone, humans would die from a great
    loneliness of spirit.
For whatever happens to the animals soon happens to the people.
All things are connected. This we know.
The earth does not belong to human beings;
    human beings belong to the earth. This we know.
All things are connected
    like the blood which unites one family.
All things are connected.

Whatever befalls the earth
befalls the children of the earth.
We do not weave the web of life,
we are merely a strand in it.
Whatever we do to the web, we do to ourselves.

—ATTRIBUTED TO CHIEF SEALTH

LESSONS FROM ALOHALAND ON LIVING IN BALANCE

Over many decades we have lived at least part-time in Hawaii. Through these years we have been very fortunate to work and study closely with many beloved *Kumus*, or keepers of the Hawaiian wisdom traditions. The Hawaiians have a unique view of living in balance that is rooted in thousands of years of an oceanic voyaging culture. Through its deep wisdom, ingenuity, intuition, and high valuing of sustainable living and resource management, it spread across the Pacific Ocean and populated a geographical area far vaster than any other civilization on planet earth.

There is an ancient saying from the island voyaging tradition that means: "My canoe (*wa'a*) is my island (*moku*), and my island (*moku*) is my canoe (*wa'a*)." The voyaging people deeply understood that they would need to cherish and care for (*malama*) their resources if they were to survive. Setting off on journeys of discovery across vast oceans, they carried with them on their small boats all the resources, plants, animals, and supplies that they would need to settle and sustain themselves on a new island *if* they were fortunate enough to read the subtle signs of the seas and find new lands. Once they did find and settle a new island home, these few precious resources they had cared for at sea in their canoes would now need to be nurtured and cared for as they developed their new home so that the plants and animals they brought with them would propagate to provide food, fiber, shelter, and sustenance for their people and for generations to come.

When Captain Cook and the first Westerners arrived in Hawaii in 1778 they noted in their journals that in all their travels around the world they had never seen a culture that was able to so bountifully provide for and sustain themselves. They marveled at the deep wisdom

"Zugunruhe, 'migratory restlessness,' is a term we first learned from Janine Benyus, author of the best-selling book, *Biomimicry*. Within a society of animals on the move, Zugunruhe always begins with those who are most attuned and environmentally aware. When animals enter Zugunruhe they become agitated and alter their habits, gathering and conserving energy leading up to the big journey to come. In these times of the Great Turning, Zugunruhe is being used to describe the restlessness and activation of those of us who are seeking to transform our lives and our society to be more in harmony and balance with our natural world."

—Joel and Michelle Levey

and attunement to managing and caring for their natural world that allowed these people to live in harmony and balance with the streams of natural resources that were available to them on their islands.

Our Hawaiian teachers remind us that our earth is both our island and our canoe, and that if we are to survive, we must learn to better nurture and care for the precious and limited resources that we steward here together. In the voyaging tradition the vital bond between people who journey together is regarded as a sacred trust and each person has a *kuliana* — a sense of responsibility to the community (*ohana*) at large — and each is regarded with respect for their roles within the community. Such wisdom is echoed in the teachings of countless First Nations peoples in indigenous cultures around the globe who sustained themselves for millennia with traditions rooted in living in harmony and balance with their natural world.

THE LOKAHI TRIANGLE

Centered at the heart of Hawaiian teachings for living in balance is the core value of *Lokahi* — the seamless unity and interconnectedness that embraces and gives rise to all things and all beings. As a practice for daily life, you orient yourself to living within the "Lokahi Triangle," whose three points of reference and reverence attune you to continually checking in on your relationship to Nature, Community, and Spirit. One uses the Lokahi Triangle as a navigational aid or inner compass for charting one's course through life in harmony and balance with all creation.

Taking this practice to heart as a way of life cultivates a quality of continuous mindfulness regarding the vital resources that sustain your life, and encourages you to closely monitor and carefully manage the quality of relationship you have to each of these dimensions of experience. One frequently pauses to reflect and assess:

1. What is the quality of my relationship to my natural world, the biosphere, and the land (*aina*) that sustains me? Am I "*pono*" (i.e., living in harmony and balance) with my natural world? If so, how can I deepen into this quality of balance? If not, then how can I most skillfully return to a *pono* relationship with the land and natural world?

2. What is the quality of my relationship to my community (*ohana*) — friends, family, colleagues — with whom I share my life? Am I in

"The true state of affairs in the material world is wholeness. If we are fragmented, we must blame it ourselves."

—David Bohm

"We are here to awaken from our illusion of separateness."

—Thich Nhat Hanh

right relations with these people and in harmony and balance in relation to each of them? If so, how can I best nurture and care for this harmony and balance? If not, how can I best restore harmony and balance in relation to them?

3. What is the quality of my relationship with Spirit, Mystery, the ground of all being (*Keakua*), the powerful, subtle, essential dimension of all that is true and sacred? Am I *pono*, in harmony and balance with these subtle yet profound dimensions of Spirit? If so, how can I nurture and refine this attunement and alignment? If I am out of alignment and balance with Spirit, then how can I restore this vital harmony and balance to be *pono* in relation to Spirit?

Such simple, profound, and essential wisdom teachings provide a valuable, accessible, and coherent set of practical tools for monitoring and managing the quality and health of our lives, communities, relationships, ecosystems, and society. They offer a glimpse of the potentialities available to us if we were to individually and collectively dedicate ourselves more fully to living in a more *pono*, balanced way of life together within the Lokahi Triangle of wholeness.

The universality of this wisdom offers inspiration for anyone in any way of life, organization, or culture seeking to go beyond mere sustainability in order to thrive, flourish, and become ever more wise, helpful, balanced, and resilient in the face of the complex changes and challenges of these times. Even contemplating the potentialities we have for living in balance, i.e., living a more *pono* life, and being committed to staying more mindful of when we stray from balance, and disciplined about taking steps to restore harmony and balance in relationship to these three essential domains, is a profound step toward living in greater harmony and balance.

The most essential lesson here is that living a *pono*, balanced, and harmonious life is about learning to live with a view of wholeness and the dynamic field of interrelationships so essential to our lives and well-being. How could we ever come to live in harmony and balance as a solitary being, isolated from the world, other beings, and the Mystery?

As John Muir reminds us, "When we try to pick anything out by itself we find it hitched to everything else in the universe." Taking this wisdom to heart, whenever we align and attune ourselves in harmony and right relations with Spirit, Nature, and Humanity, it sets up a resonance in the web of life that affirms this innate potential within ourselves and within the shared depths of all beings.

> "Our individual well-being is intimately connected both with that of all others and with the environment within which we live. It becomes apparent that our every action, our every deed, word, and thought, no matter how slight or inconsequential it may seem, has an implication not only for ourselves but for all others too."
>
> —The Dalai Lama

BEACONS OF BALANCE

To understand the deep yearning for balance in our own lives, let's take a giant step back and look at the search for balance from a more universal perspective. For millennia, a wealth of clues reminding us to live in balance have been offered in the sacred symbols of the world's great religious traditions. The balanced crossing of the lines of the Cross; the interpenetrating triangles of the Star of David; the complementarity of the swirling halves of the Tai Chi symbol; the harmony of the Islamic kismet of crescent moon and star; the Buddhist lotus or wheel of dharma; the ancient winged, double helical staff of the Greek caduceus used today as the symbol of the medical profession; the shri yantra of the Hindus; and the medicine wheels, mandalas, and sacred circles of many indigenous peoples of the world—reflect the marvelous sense of harmony, balance, and unification of complementary opposites that weave the fabric of the whole we call the universe. Through them we are continually reminded how to harmonize the forces of heaven and earth, the universal and the personal, in our everyday lives.

Properly understood, each of these sacred symbols serves as a beacon to help us find our way home to the center of all centers. By finding a balance between the personal and universal dimensions of ourselves, we can return to the harmony and balance of ourselves, inseparable from the whole of creation. In the realm of science, the equations of mathematicians and physicists can also be understood to symbolically represent this intrinsic balancing nature of the universe.

THE COINCIDENCE OF OPPOSITES

Balance is essentially about the wholeness in which all dualities, polarities, and complementary forces find their resolution. The wisdom traditions of the world, whether religious or scientific, remind us that the closer we come to truth, the more we encounter paradox. Nicholas de Cusa once described God as the "coincidence of opposites"—a description very much in keeping with the views of most scientists regarding the nature of the universe. Discovering wholeness and balance in our life brings us into an ongoing awareness of this coincidence of opposites. The ancient Hindu Upanishads puts it this way: "What is within us is also without. What is without us is also within." Or, as the ancient Greek sage Herakleitos puts it, "To live is to die, to be awake is to sleep, to be young is to be old, for the one flows into the other, and the process is capable of being reversed."

"Almost every wise saying has an opposite one, no less wise, to balance it."

—Santayana

"The human mind recognizes things only in contrast to other things. We know 'I' only in relation to 'Thou,' good only in relation to evil, right only in relation to left, up only in relation to down. The human mind rarely sees beyond these opposites to the Greater Unity that necessitates them. But the mind can awaken to Greater Unity, and in this lies the purpose of Creation and of humankind."

—Reb Yerachmiel Ben Yisrael

In search of balance, it is helpful to think of everything — every quality, action, or object — as inseparable from its opposite: male and female; night and day; inside and outside. No matter how much you might like to have only the positives in life — freedom, peace, love — if you are seeking that static state, you will always be disappointed. For every thing also contains its opposite and both sides must be balanced: form and space, creativity and receptivity, activity and rest, growth and decay, manifest creation and the unmanifest source of all creation. The good news is that, as your sense of balance grows, you'll find it easier to integrate the other side, "the negatives," into your life; you'll discover the clarity in the midst of confusion, the stillness at the center of motion, and the love that waits behind fear and anger. If you can learn to dance with the innumerable paradoxes of your life while staying anchored in an extraordinary suppleness and flexibility, you will create the stability necessary to actually find balance in your life.

"When you make the two one, and when you make the inner as the outer and the outer as the inner and the above as the below, and when you make the male and female into a single one—then shall you enter the Kingdom."

—Jesus in the Gospel of St. Thomas

Stillness and Motion in Balance

Here's a practice to help you discover the exquisite balance that comes from holding a sense of both stillness and motion in your mind at the same time. Be aware that, while the ordinary mind tends to focus on objects in motion, the universal mind is rooted in the stillness that gives rise to all motion. As you observe stillness and motion you will learn that every motion begins with stillness and ends in stillness, and that at every moment along the way, stillness and movement interweave.

Begin by mindfully observing the world within and around you. Let your attention notice everything that is changing in the world around you: the breeze that comes and goes against your cheek, the dance of shadows against the roof of your house.

After a while, shift your attention inward and notice everything that is changing within you. Feel the myriad changing sensations and vibrations within you. Begin with the easily noticeable flow of your breathing. Then deepen your awareness to sense the more subtle beat of your pulse. Then shift your attention to sense the reverberations of the pulse as it echoes through even the tiniest part of your body. Notice the ebb and flow of vibrations and sensations as they constantly change.

Now ease your attention back to the world around you. In the midst of all of this noticeable change, search out stillness. Identify everything that is more or less unchanging. Notice how the buildings, lampposts, pavement, and fire hydrants remain still. Notice how the rocks, earth, and mountains are still, while the winds move the clouds and the trees. Notice the stillness of the space in which the trees sway.

"The mystery, the essence of all life is not separate from the silent openness of simple listening."

—Toni Packer

Then, inwardly search out the stillness within you, even amid the million tiny changes. As you learn to find stillness in the midst of motion, a profound sense of balance, peace, and power can emerge for you. With practice, and with grace, you will learn how to discover this sublime sense of stillness even when you are actively moving through the world.

Balancing Sound and Silence

Our friend Rick is an inspired and compassionate teacher who works with inner city youth in Seattle. He was out on the playing field with the kids one day when suddenly he yelled out, "What was that?" The kids were silent, looking around and trying to figure out what he was talking about. Somewhat sheepishly Rick said, "I think that was a moment of silence. I don't know if we've ever had one of those in this class before."

Cultivating an integrated awareness of both silence and sound is another simple key to balance. Our ordinary habits of mind tend to pay attention to sounds and not pay much attention to the silence. But every sound arises out of silence, lasts a while, and then dissolves back into silence.

To notice this, sit and listen, really listen, to the world around you. Notice how many sounds you can hear. Notice how some are clear, close, and distinct, while other sounds are more faint and distant. Let your listening awareness reach out into the space around you. Sense yourself here at the center of your universe, bathed in sound vibrations, listening.

Next, turn your listening awareness inward, and listen for myriad often unnoticed, subtle, but present sounds: the inner gurgles in your belly, the sounds of your breathing and your pulse in your ears, the click of your jaw as you swallow. Hear also the conversations, inner mental voices, or sounds that you can "hear" as you listen. Smile to yourself, as you tune in to discover what is always going on.

Now, as you listen to these inner and outer sounds, try to feel the silence. Ah... Train your ear to listen to that space of silence that precedes every sound, surrounds every sound, absorbs every sound.

Notice how silence and sound dance together, and balance each other to weave the fabric of your experience. They are inseparable and make no sense without each other. Let your awareness open to the exquisite balance that can embrace both sounds and silence equally. In each moment they are inseparable from each other. Training your attention to embrace these two profound realities is another powerful way to find balance in every moment of your life.

"The temple bell stops

But I still hear
the sound

coming out of
the flowers."

—Basho, Japanese
    Zen poet

THE BALANCE OF NATURE

We have seen how stillness is meaningless without motion and sound is meaningless without silence. Likewise male and female, light and dark, birth and death, summer and winter, full moon and new moon all have meaning only in their interdependence.

These and other complementary and inseparable realities unfold through four nodal phases of balance. For example, we see that from the darkness of midnight, light gradually grows until the dawn. Dawn matures into the brilliance and warmth of noon time. The brightness and warmth of noon gradually diminishes until sunset. As light fades and darkness increases, we return again to the time of greatest darkness — midnight. In a similar way, the four seasons also exhibit the same waxing and waning. Following the dark, cold, starkness of winter, there is a time of warming, emergence and blossoming that we call springtime. And springtime matures into the fullness, warmth and brilliance of summer. The peaking of light, activity, and warmth in summer gradually diminishes into autumn, until once again we return to the darkness, stillness, and coldness of the winter solstice. The same theme is found in the lunar cycle, a human life, and mirrored throughout nature.

Miraculously, the balance and flow of the seasons is mirrored in the heavens. At the lightest, brightest time of summer, the summer solstice, the sun is farthest to the north in the northern hemisphere. At the winter solstice the sun is farthest to the south (or to the north if you live in the southern hemisphere). At spring and autumn equinoxes, the times of celestial balance, our sun is directly above the equator. For additional proof that balance is really an integral part of the larger cosmic dance, keep in mind that in the winter, when the days are short and dark and the sun is farthest from our part of the world, the moon is actually more directly overhead. So when we see the sun the least, the light of the moon is more available.

Though the moon is a thousand times smaller than the sun, it is a thousand times closer to us. And miraculously it is in orbit in such a way as to perfectly balance the sun, giving rise to the indescribable splendor of a full solar eclipse. When the moon perfectly covers the face of the sun, it reveals the true radiance of the sun's streaming corona, which is too bright to see at any other time.

Add to this the miracle of how steadily the light of the moon waxes and wanes, giving rise to an endless succession of full moons and new moons. Think also of the continuous rising and falling of the planetary tides, inseparably linked to the invisible pull of the moon's gravity, as

"Sixty-six times these eyes beheld the changing scenes of Autumn.

I have said enough about moon light.

Ask me no more.

Only listen to the voice of the pines and cedars

when no wind stirs."

—Ryo-Nen

the earth spins and the moon moves more slowly than the earth turns. Without these eternal rhythms, our ancestral forms of life would never have emerged from the sea to find dry land.

You and I, being physically composed of more than seventy percent water, are moved and touched by the same powerful and invisible forces of the moon. And we are also affected, more subtly of course and thus less noticeably, by the movements of the sun, the planets, and every heavenly body in the vastness of the universe.

In cultures where people live in tune with the natural world, people naturally rise and sleep with the changing cycles of the day. Women in these cultures often menstruate at the time of the full moon, so the women of a village will commonly have their monthly flow and times of fertility at the same time as each other. Even today with the hectic pace of our modern lives, most women have experienced how common it is for their periods to come at the same time as the other women in their dormitories or houses. This in turn sets up cycles and rhythms of interactions between men and women, and ripples out in natural ways into the formation and regulation of human societies.

And at our deepest core, we are connected and encoded in the most fundamental cyclic wisdom of the circadian rhythms that govern our waking and sleeping, our times of activity and rest, mental clarity and dullness. Thus our yearning for balance is completely natural, for our bodies seek only to live in harmony with the rhythms of the world around us.

THE DANCE OF GAIA AND CHAOS

Another way to look at the task ahead of us is to look at a Greek creation myth. Before time, at the very beginning, according to one story, was Chaos, the endless, yawning void empty of form or pattern, a state of complete unmanifest potential. The partner of Chaos was Gaia, the mother of the earth, who brought forth the form and stability of the earth and all manifest worlds. To the ancient Greeks, Gaia and Chaos were inseparable partners representing two primordial forces whose dynamic dance generates everything that we know in our world.

Our ability to live in balance in today's modern world depends on our ability to bring both Gaia and Chaos more consciously alive in our lives. In each moment that we give shape, form, and meaning to our world, Gaia is present, alive, and expressive. In each moment that we move in the powerful realm of potentials, chaos surrounds us, embraces us. Finding the balance of Chaos and Gaia in our lives means learning to dwell in a lucid, clear, fully present quality of mind that can witness

"When we look deep into the heart of a flower,

we see clouds, sunshine, minerals, time, the earth,

and everything else in the cosmos in it.

Without clouds there could be no rain, and there would be no flower."

—Thich Nhat Hanh

"Nothing is finite which doesn't include the infinite. The finite is the byproduct of the infinite as such becomes the outer form, the mirror of the infinite, its external revealing image. Essence and form are inseparable. Essence is the eternal Being. But living form is its constantly ever new manifestation —everlasting revelation... I try to learn from the finite sciences the lessons of the infinite."

—Arthur Young

how we weave the limitless, unbroken wholeness of Chaos into the limited forms and ideas that allow us to live, work, and communicate effectively in the world.

Both Chaos and Gaia have their light and dark sides. We can be unconsciously lost and confused in Chaos. Or we can rest with an awake, appreciative, open mind in the ocean of Chaos and simply marvel at the presence of this profound reality in our lives. While the light side of Gaia is to manifest and express the potentials of Chaos by giving order and meaning to our experience, we are also in danger of slipping into the dark side of Gaia by holding our creations as being too rigid, too real, or by mistaking our wonderful ideas for being the absolute truth. A healthy balance is found in learning to live fluidly and to adapt where chaos and order meet.

This is hard enough, but it is even more of a challenge for those of us living in a culture with a longstanding fear of Chaos. We humans have a tendency to distrust the unknown and to believe in shallow and untested ideas. Many of us tend to believe that our concepts adequately describe the nature of reality; we ignore the raw intensity and uncertainty of our actual experience. We stubbornly fixate on things without recognizing that they are only relatively, not absolutely, the way things are.

As technology enables us to look ever more deeply into the mysterious foundations of our universe, a whole new science of complexity and chaos theory has arisen to describe what is observed. The deeper we look, it turns out, we find that even in the most subtle recesses of reality that are beyond our ability to adequately measure, there are exquisitely meaningful patterns and ordering principles at play. At the threshold where we are able to glimpse the emergence of these patterns into measurable forms, what we see is merely an extrapolation of an exquisite order that lies hidden in the heart of chaos. Properly understood, this profound insight tells us all, scientists and lay folks alike, that we can live with faith and trust and set aside our fear and anxiety, because we really do live in a universe that at the deepest level does make sense, even though we cannot fully fathom it.

Understanding the dance between Chaos and Gaia is essential in our lives, because to truly experience the quality of balance we seek, we must shift from focusing merely on the forms and structures in our lives — "If only I could figure out how to do my job, have time for my exercise class, and my husband and kids," — to becoming more aware of and sensitive to the flows of these energies as they present themselves in our lives. We have such trouble finding balance because we think it is about cleaning our desk or getting up an hour earlier in the

"Each day of human life contains joy and anger, pain and pleasure, darkness and light, growth and decay. Each moment is etched with nature's grand design—do not try to deny or oppose the cosmic order of things."

—Morihei Ueshiba O'Sensei

"The spiritual gift on the inner journey is to know that creation comes out of chaos, and that even what has been created needs to be returned to chaos every now and then to get recreated in a more vital form. The spiritual gift on this inner journey is the knowledge that in chaos I can not only survive, but I can thrive, that there is vitality in that chaotic field of energy."

—Parker J. Palmer

morning. These may indeed be useful strategies, but not unless we first begin to have a deeper understanding of balance as an interplay of forces and energies. Balance is not a static state that we find once and for all by the perfect fine-tuning of our daily schedules.

Equilibrium is defined by Webster's as, "1. A condition in which all acting forces are canceled by others, resulting in a stable, balanced, or *unchanging* system. 2. Physics. The condition of a system in which the resultant of all acting forces is zero...."

The dynamically active quality of living balance presents a very different picture, in which we

- learn to listen to and trust our internal guidance system;
- notice whatever strong or subtle impressions are offered by our senses;
- observe the inner movements, attitudes, directions, and intentions of our hearts and minds;
- notice the dances and struggles at play in relationships;
- discover what feels right, true, and on purpose in living our life.

THE DANCE OF MASTERY AND MYSTERY

Setting your intention to live in balance will invite and challenge you to learn to work and dance with both Mystery and mastery in your life. Embracing mastery and Mystery, knowing and uncertainty, we return to wholeness.

The inner alchemy that weds mastery to Mystery is sometimes described as the marriage of heaven and earth, the harmonizing of yang and yin, creative and receptive, the unification of masculine and feminine, or balancing intellect and intuition. True mastery is realized only when our discipline has become so wholehearted and sincere that it carries us to the threshold where, to go any further, we must surrender our sense of certainty to Mystery. The union of mastery and Mystery is a path toward wholeness, a dynamic state of being as natural as inhalation and exhalation, the pulse and stillness of each heart beat, or the striding balanced rhythm of our two feet carrying us along life's path.

As we develop our capacity to live more in balance, we increase our mastery as well as our capacity to sustain the intensity of embracing the mysterious realities of our lives that defy our full comprehension. We participate in the self-renewing revelation of creation described by the great mystics of the world, and we drink from the wellsprings of our deepest nature at the heart of all creation. As our meditative insights

"There is in all visible things... a hidden wholeness."

—Thomas Merton

And I have felt a presence that disturbs me with the joy

Of elevated thoughts; a sense sublime

Of something far more deeply interfused,

Whose dwelling is the light of setting suns,

And the round ocean and the living air,

And the blue sky, and in the mind of man;

A motion and a spirit, that impels

All thinking things, all objects of all thought,

And rolls through all things."

—William Wordsworth

deepen, we unify mastery and Mystery, and open the inner depths of our being to discover a stream of inspiration rising forth and flowing through us as a blessing to our lives, and the lives of all we meet. Mastery reveals Mystery and is truly guided by Mystery, and each breath becomes a journey weaving our countless dimensions into a unified wholeness.

"Physicists explore levels of matter;
mystics explore levels of mind.
What they have in common
is that both levels lie beyond
ordinary sense perception."
— Fritjof Capra

Pause for a moment and reach out with both hands. Imagine that in one hand you can hold everything that you fully understand and have certainty about or mastery over, and in your other hand hold or touch everything that is still mysterious and defies your full comprehension or control. Sense the relative balance in what you hold in your two hands. Ponder what this means for how you live your life, set your priorities, and creatively weave the fabric of your life.

"For those who are awake the cosmos is one."

—Heraclitus

Our home and organic permaculture farm on the Island of Hawaii is a magical realm of great beauty and abundance. While some associate Hawaii with *mai tais* on the beach and lovely hula dancers, the Island of Hawaii has nearly all of the climate zones on planet Earth, boasts the two tallest mountains on earth measured from base to summit, and is home to not only the most active volcanic vent connected to the molten core of the earth, but also an array of high-tech celestial observatories that look deeper into the fabric of space and time than any other place on our planet.

Living in this dynamic mix of cultures and microclimates, we have become active in the vibrant astronomical community here and attend many of the public talks and presentations they offer. One of the most profound revelations from the farther reaches of cosmology and astrophysics is the notion that only five percent of the energy and information in our universe is measurable, and that ninety-five percent of what exists defies our grasp or definition. It is mysterious and immeasurable. This ninety-five percent is referred to as "dark energy" and "dark matter" but at this point their actual nature remains a "mystery."

In the world of business management, Edward Deming, father of the Total Quality movement that relies on intensive measurement of complex dynamic systems, similarly observed, " ninety-eight percent of what is important cannot be measured."

Mystery is present even within the dimensions of the universe that we can measure. Within the "measurable" spectrum of energy and information spans fifty octaves of radio waves, microwaves, infrared radiation, visible light, ultraviolet, x-rays, and gamma rays which weave the multi-frequency fabric of the universe. Of this vast spectrum, the universe of visible light is merely a tiny one of these fifty octaves, meaning that we are virtually blind to seeing or comprehending the full scope of measurable reality without extending our senses with technology.

Similarly, we can only hear frequencies spanning ten octaves of audible sound and are deaf to the other forty octaves of resonance and vibration in the electromagnetic spectrum. It is humbling to consider how little of the known measurable universe we ordinarily see or hear or sense, compared to the richness of energy, vibration, and mysterious forces that comprise the full dimensions of our body, life, and world.

THE POWER OF OPENNESS

"If your mind is empty, it is always ready for anything; it is open to everything.

In the beginner's mind there are many possibilities; in the expert's mind there are few."

— SHUNRYU SUZUKI ROSHI

The wisdom necessary for living in balance is not found in certainty, but in what our colleague Elizabeth Mathis Namgyal describes as "the power of an *open question*." The aspiration to live in balance invites us to cultivate a great sense of openness, wonderment, and a "high tolerance of ambiguity." This tolerance of ambiguity protects us from leaping to premature conclusions or the illusion of certainty. In addition, research indicates that our creativity is directly related to the level of our tolerance for ambiguity. Cultivate the little voice that continually whispers "are you sure?"

Soen Sa Nim, a Korean Zen master with whom we have studied, taught a classical practice that strikes deep toward the heart of balance, challenging and inviting us to simultaneously hold mastery and mystery, knowing and not knowing, certainty and uncertainty all together. We often suggest this contemplative practice to people we work with to help them move from fixation into flow, and to focus this flow into clarity. This is how it works:

As you inhale, think to yourself:

"Each element of the cosmos is positively woven from all the others... The universe holds together, and only one way of considering it is really possible, that is, to take it as a whole, in one piece."

—Teilhard de Chardin

"The great thing about science is that the questions are so much more important than the answers. Almost any scientist can find an answer if he/she can only find a good question. I think that theology tends to make the mistake of straining for answers, even answers that claim to be final. Science lives with the questions. All its answers are tentative, and breed further questions. The really great questions—those a bright child might ask—are never finished answering."

—George Wald, Nobel Laureate, Biology

"Clear mind, clear mind, clear mind…"
And then as you exhale, mentally say:
"Don't knowwww…………"
Breathing in, "Clear mind, clear mind, clear mind…"
Breathing out, "Don't knowwww………"

Each inhalation focuses the mind, brings you to calm and clarity, and affirms a sense of control, certainty, and a stable place to stand. And then, just let it all go and let it all flow and trust to step into the free fall—open to Great Mystery—that underlies everything we think we know for certain. With each breath, there is both an invitation to focus and to flow. Stand strong, and then surrender control. With each breath you focus, coalescing like a particle, and then expand, opening into the mystery of your waveform nature. Each breath invites you to stretch between "clear mind" and "don't know"… certainty and uncertainty… particle and wave… clarity and trust… control and surrender. With each breath we learn to touch the earth, and then the heavens. We learn to straddle the abyss of extremes and be wonder-struck by the wisdom revealed in paradox.

We personally know of many people who use this method on a daily basis to help them focus, center, and find balance throughout the day. Some use it to clear their minds between meetings or sessions with clients. Others to keep a light heart and open mind as they walk through crowded streets, watch the news, contemplate complex circumstances in our world, or attend important meetings. For others, this balance and centering technique is a focus for quiet contemplation. For many it has been the source of tremendous insight.

This method can have a very direct effect on putting things into perspective and to bringing your life into balance. It fiercely anchors and frees your attention by reminding you to find a balance between knowing and unknowing, and to welcome everything that comes to you with fresh clear eyes and a deep bow of respect. Lao Tzu, that great Taoist master and proponent of balance, sagely writes,

"In the pursuit of learning, every day something is acquired.
In the pursuit of Tao, every day something is dropped.
Less and less is done
Until no-action is achieved.
When nothing is done, nothing is left undone.
The world is ruled by letting things take their course.
It cannot be ruled by interfering."

"The truth is, going against the internal stream of ignorance is way more rebellious than trying to start some sort of cultural revolution…

The inner revolution will not be televised or sold on the Internet. It must take place within one's own mind and heart…Waking up is not a selfish pursuit of happiness, it is a revolutionary stance, from the inside out, for the benefit of all beings in existence."

—Noah Levine

Living in the spaciousness of an open mind and open questions allows us to regard the vaporous stream of experience like a magical display of impressions, dancing clouds in the sky, shimmering images and colors, like a rainbow in the sky or bubbles in a stream. This powerful openness of creative potential is sometimes framed in the Buddhist teachings as the wisdom of "emptiness." Not emptiness as an utter vacuity or nothingness, but emptiness as an infinite expanse of interweaving interdependencies within which any fragment that one grasps is regarded as merely an incomplete waveform in a dynamic field of possibilities.

INTENTION AND VALUES: THE "STRANGE ATTRACTORS" THAT BRING BALANCE TO OUR LIVES

In modern times, scientific studies of chaos theory have revealed more of chaos' mysterious qualities. Using computers to simulate the marvelous feedback loops that led to living systems emerging out of chaos, scientists can replicate and visually display in a very short time the trillions of moments of a system's evolution coming into form.

To get a feeling for this, imagine being able to take a composite photo of your journey through life from the moment of your conception until your death. Imagine that this sequence of images unfolds as a stream of light that traces pathways of light through space over time. Though at first the patterns may appear somewhat chaotic, as you watch over time meaningful patterns gradually begin to emerge. There would be the loops and patterns that you trace by getting up and going to bed, and to and from school or work. Your habits and values also organize the shape of your life as you weave in patterns of travel to shop at your favorite stores, visit your parents, yoga studio, or daycare center. Over time, an exquisite, complex, and beautiful image would appear, revealing an elaborate and meaningful tapestry of self-repeating patterns that offer a glimpse of some of the deep organizing principles and values that guide your life.

Like your own life, in the early stages of the computer simulations, it seems that only the unpredictability of chaos rules, with points lighting up on the screen as if at random. But, over time, these points weave into lines, and the lines weave themselves into webs and patterns of breathtaking beauty, revealing an order that emerges literally from the heart of chaos. No matter how chaotic the fluctuations begin, a strange ordering principle inevitably emerges, giving form, beauty, and meaning to the chaos. This invisible ordering principle defines what are called

"Until one is committed there is hesitance, the chance to draw back, always ineffectiveness. Concerning all acts of initiative there is one elementary truth, the ignorance of which kills countless ideas and splendid plans: That moment one definitely commits oneself, then providence moves too. All sorts of things occur to help one that would otherwise never have occurred. A whole stream of events issues from the decision, raising in one's favor all manner of unforeseen incidents and meetings and material assistance, which no one could have dreamt would have come one's way."

—W.N. Murray

"strange attractors." Strange attractors are like guiding force-fields that define a basin of attraction within which the elements of a system are magnetically drawn into an observable and meaningful pattern.

One of the fascinating understandings from these computer simulations is that when even very tiny fluctuations are introduced into a system, especially early on in its evolution, dramatic changes in its evolving form will result. When the equation that gives form, meaning, and direction to the unfolding of chaos into order is changed even minutely—on the order of even a zillionth of a degree—the future of the pattern will be dramatically altered within a very short time. This is good news for us because it shows how we can influence the pattern of our lives by what we might consider to be a minor change. Thus, achieving the balance we are longing for is not as hard as it might first appear. It begins by looking at intention. For our intentions define the strange attractors that set the patterns for how our lives unfold.

THE POWER OF INTENTION:
IS MY LIFE'S JOURNEY "ON PURPOSE"?

Intention is a power that sets our trajectory as we initiate a path of action. If I set sail from Seattle in a boat, for example, my intention will determine where and how I go. (And if we set sail together, our shared intent will likewise determine the course that we take.) My intention may be to sail across the sound to visit friends on Vashon Island, or to sail to Orcas Island in the San Juan Islands, or to San Francisco, Honolulu, or Amsterdam. My intention may simply be to have the experience of a wonderful day on the water with my friends, and I may not be particularly concerned with making progress toward some outer destination. Or I can simply set sail for the pure joy and intent of discovering what the winds have in store for me, and be open to receiving and learning from the gifts of experience that I encounter along the way.

In life, if I "set sail" unclear of my intention, I tend to drift around, have pleasurable or frustrating experiences, driven by the winds of my unconscious inclinations. If at some point along the way I am mindful enough to notice that my intention is not clear, I may stop to ask, "Why am I here? Where am I going? How do I want to make the journey?" When I am clear on the answers to these questions, I can take up the helm again and sail consciously and intentionally in the direction of my choosing. If the force of my habit is strong, it is likely that now and then I lapse into mindlessness, and that once again my freedom and control will be taken over by the force of my unconscious habit. Yet

"Ask and it shall be given you;

Seek and you shall find;

Knock, and it shall be opened to you. For whoever asks, receives;

and he who seeks, finds;

and to him who knocks, the door is opened."

—Jesus, in Matthew 7:7:8

over time, if I am intent on becoming more in control of my journey, I quickly notice when old habits have asserted themselves, and I gently but firmly take the helm of my life again. With practice, I lose my intention less and less often, and if it is lost, I find it again quickly.

To the degree that I am clear on my intentions, I am more likely to stay on course in my journey, to travel "on purpose," and to be able to make healthy choices about how I want to spend my time. In this analogy, intention is the compass that I use to keep my life in balance. With intention, I will be more mindful of the direction that I am sailing and alert to when the winds and currents are supporting or challenging me in my journey. With clear intent in mind, I will check often to see if I am on course, on purpose, and will generate further intentions that lead to the actions that make subtle course corrections frequently along the way.

The more important my initial intention, the more likely I am to pay careful attention to how my journey unfolds. If I intend to move swiftly, I keep an eye on the sails and keep them filled to move me along. If I am intent on traveling in harmony and helpfulness with my crew members, I will likely have many moments to practice patience, and offer some helpful coaching or words of encouragement to them.

Or perhaps I'm just out sailing by myself, and my intent is to cultivate greater balance of mind, to stay alert, yet relaxed, or to cultivate a sense of the richness of my experience: the rudder in my hand, the cool breeze in my hair, the salt spray on my face, and my thoughts coming and going like so many clouds in the sky of my mind. If my intent is to be fully present in each moment of my journey, I will be more aware of my mind wandering and I will gently bring it back into focus. I will also notice when I am tired: perhaps I need to drop anchor for a while, set the autopilot, or turn the helm over to a crew mate while I rest or nourish myself. As a fully present sailor, I am aware of the way I relate to my crew members and the quality of interaction that I have with them.

So in the search for balance, whenever you begin to feel off track or overwhelmed, the first step is to stop and rediscover your deepest intention for what you are doing. You may discover you are right on track, or you may find it necessary to change course in order to keep to your purpose.

It's also important to recognize the state of being your intention is rooted in. We all know from experience what can happen when we act out of fear or caring, greed or selfless service. Not only are the outcomes often different, but our own inner experience during the process is also deeply affected. We may sow the seeds of satisfaction, gratitude,

"The winds of grace are always blowing, but it is you that must raise your sails."

—Tagor

"We must have a pure, honest, and warmhearted motivation, and on top of that, determination, optimism, hope, and the ability not to be discouraged. The whole of humanity depends on this motivation."

—The Dalai Lama

or we may sow the seeds of frustration, sadness, or guilt that may grow like weeds and plague us for a lifetime. Checking our intentions before we launch into action can help us to live and work with a much greater sense of balance and well-being. The more we are mindful of our intentions each moment along the way, the more likely we are to arrive at a destination that we feel good about.

Remembering that even minute changes in the equations of a system can make a dramatic difference in its character, we can understand how making even subtle shifts in our intentions can create extraordinary changes in the quality of our lives.

KNOWING WHERE HOME IS

"Anyone can hold the helm when the sea is calm."

— PUBLILIUS SYRUS

In the wisdom ways of the voyaging peoples of the vast Pacific Ocean, the profound arts of navigation are revered as a sacred and subtle science. Reading and sensing the subtle interphase of winds, converging and reverberating wave forms, cloud and wind patterns, ocean currents, and life forms in the sea, the navigators must remain constantly awake, in a state of refined and expanded consciousness, mindfully attuned to their natural world in order to know moment to moment where they are in the vast ocean.

The navigators say that it is essential not only to have a clear read and bearing on where they are at any given moment in time, and a clear sense of their intended purpose and destination for their voyage, but that most important thing is to stay in touch with where home is and to never, ever lose that point of reference. Navigator Chad Paishan is one of a small group of Pacific voyagers who hold the title of "Po"—a navigator holding the oral lineage of voyaging traditions who is entrusted with the commitment to "feed his people," nourishing them not only with an abundance of food, but also with love and with wisdom teachings for living in harmony and balance with their natural world and with each other.

We are always inspired to hear Chad speak and love to hear him teach: "We can go anywhere in this world because we know where home is." If we lose our bearings, our sense of knowing where our true home is—our deepest grounding, security, nourishment, purpose, and identity—then we are surely lost.

"When personal mastery becomes a discipline... it embodies two underlying movements. The first is continually clarifying what is important to us... The second is continually learning how to see current reality more clearly...

People with high levels of personal mastery are continually expanding their ability to create the results in life they truly seek. From their quest for continual learning comes the spirit of the learning organization."

—Peter Senge in *The Fifth Discipline*

In his poem, *Lost*, David Wagoner echoes teachings from the First Nations people of the Northwest coast of the Americas, giving voice to an oral tradition of advice to children regarding what to do if they become lost or disoriented in the forest.

> "Stand still.
> The trees ahead and the bushes beside you are not lost!
> Wherever you are is called Here.
> And you must treat it as a powerful stranger,
> must ask permission to know it and be known.
> Listen… the forest breathes… It whispers,
> "I have made this place around you.
> If you leave it you may come back again, saying "Here."
> No two trees are the same to Raven.
> No two branches are the same to Wren.
> If what a tree or branch does is lost on you,
> then you are surely lost.
> Stand still.
> The forest knows where you are.
> You must let it find you!"

This advice is clearly relevant for all of us who similarly, from time to time, wander far from "home," lose our way, and stray from balance. We are well advised to be mindful of the choices we are making and clear on the directions we take for each leg and activity we choose on our life's journey. Like the children in the forest, we too would be wise to be disciplined to be mindfully present, awake to reading both the strikingly evident and more subtle wave forms of energy and information that flow to us and through us as we move through the world. To develop a deep sense of where our true home is, being grounded in our true nature and identity is essential. This helps us be vigilant so that we do not become lost, disoriented, or out of touch with who we truly are and tumble out of balance. Zen Roshi Joan Sutherland offers the following pithy insight on this:

> "Enlightenment is our true nature and our home, but the
> complexities of human life cause us to forget. That forgetting
> feels like exile, and we make elaborate structures of habit,
> conviction, and strategy to defend against its desolation. But
> this condition isn't hopeless; it's possible to dismantle those
> structures so we can return from an exile that was always
> illusory to a home that was always right under our feet.

For many of us, there is something that pushes us and something that pulls us. We're pushed by our own pain and the pain we see in the world around us; we're pulled by intimations that there's something larger and more true than our ordinary self-oriented ways of experiencing life. Here's a tradition that says, 'Yes, we understand that, and there are ways to make those intimations not simply a matter of random chance but readily and consistently present. It's possible to make ourselves available, in all the hours of our days, to the grace we so long to be touched by, and to spread that grace to the world around us.'"

> "Live in the present, launch yourself on every wave, find eternity in each moment."
>
> —Henry David Thoreau

Whenever we see an icon of the Buddha reaching down to touch the earth, or of Jesus touching his blazing heart, or someone making a peace sign or *shaka* sign to us, these are images of touching and affirming the noble, innate qualities of the true ground of our being, our true home, and most essential identity. In other sacred gestures, or *mudras*, an awakening being may have one hand at their heart, connected to the essence of their true home and beingness, and one hand reaching out in a gesture of lovingkindness or protection that flows forth from this deep connection to our true nature.

Having been on this journey consciously for over forty years, it seems increasingly more common to meet people from all walks of life and orientations, who in some way are exploring or cultivating their "homing instincts" and seeking out the inner navigational skills necessary to stand still, listen deeply, and find their way home. One of the most treasured results for us of having dedicated so many years of our own lives to inner practices, and having devoted a year to silent, contemplative retreat, is that it has really opened our access to a deep, inner sense of "home" that is ever accessible and virtually never out of reach.

During these unsettling times, more than forty-five million people around the globe are grieving the loss of the place they call home, the lands sacred to their families and their people, the neighborhoods, gardens, groves and orchards planted by the grandparents, marsh lands and mountains they tramped in their youth, the low lying islands washing away in the rising seas, the once abundant and now depleted coral reefs and fishing grounds, and verdant forests that they and their ancestors called home.

Our grief and sorrow for our world is also our strength, deep ecologist Joanna Macy reminds us: "Our sorrow is the other side of love, for we only grieve what we deeply care for."

> "My home was at Cold Mountain from the start,
>
> Rambling among the hills, far from trouble.
>
> Gone, and a million things leave no trace
>
> Loosed, and it flows through the galaxies
>
> A fountain of light, into the very mind
>
> Not a thing, and yet it appears before me:
>
> Now I know the pearl of the Buddha-nature
>
> Know its use: a boundless perfect sphere"
>
> —Han Shan (Translation by Gary Snyder)

With home in mind, our colleague Glenn Albrecht, Professor of Sustainability and Environmental Studies at Murdoch University in Western Australia, has brought forth the word "Solastalgia" which is so relevant for our times. "Solastalgia: A combination of the Latin word *solacium* (comfort) and the Greek root — *algia* (pain). Solastalgia is "the pain experienced when there is recognition that the place where one resides and that one loves is under immediate assault...a form of homesickness one gets when one is still at 'home.'"

The meaning of Solastalgia is further illuminated by understanding the word "Soliphilia," which is "the love of and responsibility for a place, bioregion, planet, and the unity of interrelated interests within it." Soliphilia is the psychological foundation for living in balance.

A REVOLUTION IN CONSCIOUSNESS

These rapidly changing, complex, and wildly unbalancing times offer many compelling examples of why living in balance is so important. Einstein brilliantly diagnosed the core problem when he wrote: "The world we have made as a result of the level of the thinking we have done thus far creates problems that we cannot solve at the same level (of consciousness) at which we have created them... We shall require a substantially new manner of thinking if humankind is to survive."

Some years ago, on the steps of the Capitol building, Vaclav Havel, then president of the Czech Republic, eloquently encouraged this to the U.S. Congress, saying, "Without a global revolution in the sphere of human consciousness, nothing will change for the better in the sphere of our being as humans, and the catastrophe towards which this world is headed — be it ecological, social, demographic or a general breakdown of civilization — will be unavoidable.... The salvation of this human world lies nowhere else than in the human heart, in the human power to reflect, in human meekness and in human responsibility." As more and more people are beginning to wake up and seek wiser responses to our global predicaments, more and more people are joining this revolution.

In his famous letter to a bereaved father whose daughter had died, Einstein offers clear and essential guidance regarding where and how this revolution in human consciousness should be focused, saying, "A human being is a part of a whole, called by us 'universe,' a part limited in time and space. He experiences himself, his thoughts and feelings as something separated from the rest... a kind of optical delusion of consciousness. This delusion is a kind of prison for us, restricting us to our personal desires and to affection for a few persons nearest to us. Our

> "Within each of us, in the ground of our being, powers reside for the healing of our world.
>
> These powers do not arise from any ideology, access to the occult, or passion for social activism. They are inevitable powers. Because we are part of the web of life, we can draw on the strength— and the pain—of every creature. This interconnection constitutes our 'deep ecology': it is the source of our pain for the world as well as our love and appetite for life."
>
> —Joanna Macy

task must be to free ourselves from this prison by widening our circle of compassion to embrace all living creatures and the whole of nature in all of its beauty."

WHEN I AM IN BALANCE . . .

Deep wisdom for living in balance is found in an ancient psalm. In Hebrew the verse reads, "Shiviti Adonai L'negdi Tamid," (Psalm16:8). One way of translating this into English is, "I balance myself and God is before me always." Taken to heart, this prayer can be the seed of a profound contemplation on balance that can accompany you into every activity of your life. Reciting this prayer, in English or in Hebrew, let your mind grow more calm, clear, and balanced. Held in the same light and intention, reciting the rosary, the Lord's Prayer, or the Shema prayer, or chanting a Sufi zikr or the Tibetan mantra of universal compassion, *Om Mani Pedme Hung,* can offer similar results.

When we take a sacred verse like to this heart, we align and attune ourselves to the deep meaning and spirit of that pearl of wisdom. Sitting quietly... resting in the natural flow of your breathing... allow your contemplation or recitation of this prayer to carry you more and more deeply into a clear, lucid, loving, radiant peace and presence. Looking out from deep within, let your eyes truly be windows for your soul, and behold the world with wonder as sacred and vibrantly infused with living spirit.

Sitting, walking, driving, talking, alone or with others, allow your sense of inner balance to deepen and behold the sacred mystery, majesty, and presence of the world's deep radiance shining forth and expressed as the myriad of appearances that comprise the worlds of your inner and outer experience. Regard all things and all beings as the

"As we deepen in understanding, the arbitrary divisions between inner and outer disappear. The essence of life, the beauty and grandeur of life, is its wholeness. Life in reality cannot be divided into the inner and the outer, the individual and social. We may make arbitrary divisions for the convenience of collective life, for analysis, but essentially any division between inner and outer has no reality, no meaning.

The total revolution we are examining is not for the timid or the self-righteous. It is for those who love truth more than pretense. It is for those who sincerely, humbly want to find a way out of this mess that we, each one of us, have created out of indifference, carelessness, and lack of moral courage."

—Vimala Thakar

"As soon as there is awareness of wholeness, every moment becomes sacred, every movement is sacred. The sense of oneness is no longer an intellectual connection. We will in all our actions be whole, total, natural, without effort. Every action or nonaction will have the perfume of wholeness."

—Vimala Thakar

radiant display of the infinite potential of indwelling creative spirit. As you do this, anchor this experience with a soft and gentle smile, by reaching up and touching your heart, and if you like by gently sighing with the sound, "ahhh"))). Appreciate how close this sacred view of reality is, and how accessible this can be if you were to only slow down to the speed of life, open your wisdom eyes, look beyond superficial perception, and behold the deeper, subtler dimensions of all that is. With practice you will learn to live ever more closely attuned to this expansive, illuminated state of being and living in balance.

RIPPLES

We live in a responsive universe. If you drop a stone in a pond, it both sends out and draws in ripples. Through heartfelt prayer, the energy of our intent expands, creating a reverberation in our deep psyche that reaches out to the Mystery and draws back the inspiration and blessing energy that may help us to deepen or accelerate a shift in the patterns of our life. The way living systems return to balance is by continually expanding to encompass more of the whole. While fear may cause us to constrict, separate, or withdraw, this is not the path to healing and balance. Courage and love guide us to step out, meet and befriend what we fear, take it inside of ourselves, and learn from it in order to transform and heal ourselves. That is the true balancing act of our lives.

chapter three

Life as a Learning Expedition:
A Model for Balance

The essence of health is an inner kind of balance.

— DR. ANDREW WEIL, M.D.

EARLIER IN HIS LIFE, JOEL WAS DEEPLY INVOLVED WITH PSYCHOPHYSI-
ological research at the University of Washington, exploring the inner
nature and workings of the human mind, brain, and spirit. In those
days, he used to dream about what the "ultimate experiment" might
be to answer to the "ultimate questions." As he has grown older, wiser,
and explored many disciplines, he has come to believe that he is living that ultimate experiment. Joel calls it "the learning expedition of
my life. As I awaken, in the morning, and throughout the day, I often
reflect to myself, 'I wonder what the learnings will be today?' Stepping
out into the world my heart's prayer is a simple one: 'Teach me.' And I
do my best to respond in an inquisitive way with whatever arises."

As you continue to tune in more mindfully to the learning expedition of your life, you will find that paradox is a great teacher. For example, you will learn the most about living in balance during times when
you are out of balance. In the process, you will discover a greater balance that grows through holding both the experience of being in balance and that of being stretched out of balance. Once this new balance
is defined, it invites a further expansion of learning in a never-ending
cascade of dimensions of learning. Seeing that balance is really a
verb—something you must constantly do—you open yourself to this

balancing process as a continuous learning adventure. Morihei Ueshiba O'Sensei, regarded by many to be the greatest martial artist in modern times, deeply understood the larger flow of balancing. O'Sensei, the founder of the martial art of aikido, was once asked by his students, "How do you keep your balance all the time?" The master laughed and said: "The art is not in trying to keep your balance, but in losing it and seeing how fast you can regain it. The reason you don't see me out of balance is because I regain it so quickly!"

Embracing life as a learning expedition is the first step toward realizing balance. To understand this, it is helpful to understand the difference between living in your *comfort zone* and in your *learning zone*. Your comfort zone is what you are familiar with, what you already know so well the knowledge is almost automatic. Your learning zone is anything that stretches you beyond that, challenging you to learn new skills, new ways of relating. Ultimately, when we take to heart the lessons in our learning zone, we create for ourselves an expanded comfort zone, one far larger than we began with. In a sense, all of our lives are a pattern of rest in the comfort zone and then stretching and learning in the learning zone. Then we rest again in the new, expanded comfort zone.

The journey toward balance begins by becoming mindful of the invisible walls, boundaries, conditions, and mindsets that define your current personal comfort zone, and then exploring the new frontiers of learning that are your learning zone. As one of our clients observed, "I have never learned anything in my comfort zone!" So, with awareness, step out and meet reality, and let it teach you. Once you step through all the invisible membranes of your fears, excuses, and self-limiting beliefs, and begin to befriend a larger world, you will have performed the miracle of expanding your comfort zone to previously unimaginable proportions. A mind once stretched to new dimensions will never return to its original size. And the learnings of a lifetime, and beyond, will never end.

The model on the following page has been very useful for individuals, teams, families, and communities to assess the quality of balance in their lives and to identify the needs and opportunities for learning. On your journey, it is helpful to be mindful of your passage through five zones of experience.

From top to bottom these are:

* The Burnout Zone
* The Upper Learning Zone
* "The Zone" of Optimal Performance (which is embedded within the heart of the Learning Zone)

"Growth has not only rewards and pleasures but also many intrinsic pains, and always will have. Each step forward is a step into the unfamiliar and possibly dangerous. It also means giving up something familiar and good and satisfying. It frequently means a parting and a separation with consequent nostalgia, loneliness and mourning. It also means giving up a simpler and easier and less effortful life, in exchange for a more demanding, more difficult life. Growth forward is in spite of losses and therefore requires courage and strength in the individual, as well as protection, permission."

—Abraham Maslow

- The Lower Learning Zone
- The Rust-out Zone

Practicing the art of balance in an ever-changing world requires continuous learning. However, as you are probably aware, the glory of yesterday's hard won learning quickly pales as we encounter the next wave of new realities and challenges of our customers, kids, or environment. As the pace of change and challenge increases, anxiety grows and we are increasingly more motivated to discover and rapidly learn new skills. After these new capabilities are mastered and integrated, however, the danger of relapsing into boredom or complacency often occurs. Suspended between these "killing fields" — the danger zones of extreme intensity and challenge, and the realms of immobilizing boredom and depression, the circumstances of life compel us to search for balance. This crucial balance is found by avoiding the painful extremes of burnout and rust-out, and living with vitality in our Learning Zone. The stakes are high, and only the best learners will survive! In the journey of your lifetime, you have traversed each of these zones countless times. Let's visit each of them briefly and see what they have to teach us about balance.

As we discussed earlier, life in the universe survives within certain limits. When conditions go too far above or below those limits, or stay that way for too long, life is endangered. Thus, there is much wisdom in learning to manage your own life within "learningful limits." The Upper and Lower Learning Zones extend beyond "The Zone" into realms of both increasing and decreasing challenge. Here we stretch ourselves, and integrate our learnings in the never-ending cycles of learning that we call our lives. Beyond these reasonably tolerable Learning Zones, lie the forbidding and dangerous extremes of Burnout and Rust-out, both of which may be visited for a time, and can contribute much to learning, but neither of which may be lived in, in a balanced way, for long.

At the heart of the Learning Zone (which includes the Upper Learning Zone, "The Zone," and the Lower Learning Zone), between the extremes of overwhelming distress and the inertia of boredom, lies a realm of extraordinary or peak performance. This quality of being is characterized by a state of individual and team performance that delivers the most energy-efficient, exhilarating, and fulfilling experiences of human learning and potential. In the vernacular of sports, moments such as these are often described as being in "The Zone," a state of grace marked by effortless ease, power, precision, flow, ecstasy, certainty, or invincibility. Individuals or teams working in the The Zone are

"The world we have made as a result of the level of the thinking we have done thus far creates problems that we cannot solve at the same level (of consciousness) at which we have created them...We shall require a substantially new manner of thinking if humankind is to survive."

—Albert Einstein

"More than any time in history. Mankind faces a crossroads.

One path heads to despair and utter hopelessness,

the other to total extinction.

Let us pray that we have the wisdom to choose correctly"

—Woody Allen

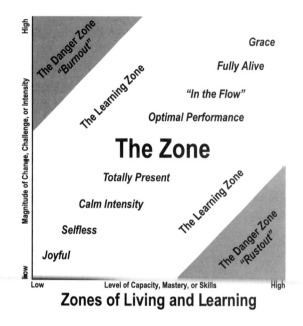

Zones of Living and Learning

confident, highly efficient, and equipped with skills adequate to meet the demands of their situation. When we are in The Zone, we feel in balance, in harmony with ourselves and the world around us. Challenges are neither too strenuous as to create anxiety nor too routine as to create boredom. Though for the novice The Zone is elusive and difficult to enter, true masters in any field have learned to live and work in or near The Zone for much of their lives. These rare and esteemed leaders remind us that if we are willing to accept the learning challenge to live in balance with ourselves, we and others will benefit.

In psychology, this dynamic balance is often regarded as being "in the flow," a self-fulfilling state of optimal performance, extreme fulfillment and well-being, and remarkable brain performance. In the great spiritual traditions, such precious moments of grace are moments when we feel the Presence, Intelligence, or the Love of Divine and Universal proportions manifesting in a deeply moving personal way in our lives. They offer us a glimpse of our true nature and of our potentials, which may spiritually nourish and deeply inspire our whole lives. In many domains of our life, these special times of balance are regarded as times of peak performance, extreme efficiency, or total quality moments when everything just clicks into place with no wasted energy or effort.

"There are moments of glory that go beyond the human expectation, beyond the physical and emotional ability of the individual. Something unexplainable takes over and breathes life into the known life. One stands on the threshold of miracles that one cannot create voluntarily. The power of the moment adds up to certain amount of religion in the performance. Call it a state of grace, or an act of faith...or an act of God. It is there, and the impossible becomes possible...The athlete goes beyond herself: she transcends the natural. She touches a piece of heaven and becomes the recipient of power from an unknown source.

The power goes beyond that which can defined as physical or mental. The performance almost becomes a holy place—where a spiritual awakening seems to take place. The individual becomes swept up in the action around her—she almost floats through the performance, drawing on forces she has never previously been aware of."

—Patsy Neal, Basketball Hall of Fame

⌒

Regardless of which frame of reference, or reverence, you choose, it is in these indelibly memorable moments that you catch a glimpse of the extra-ordinary balance that it is possible to realize and to weave more deeply into the fabric of your life.

Reflect for a moment on the times in your life when you were in "The Zone." During the moments of being "in the flow," times of grace, peak performance, or experience,

"When she danced the Blue Danube, her simple waltzing forward and back, like the oncoming and receding waves on the shore, had such an ecstasy of rhythm that audiences became frenzied with the contagion of it, and could not contain themselves, but rose from their seats, cheering, applauding, laughing and crying... We felt as if we had received the blessing of God."

—Margherita Duncan watching her sister-in-law, Isadora Duncan, dance

* How did it feel to you?
* What was happening within or around you?
* What circumstances supported you or triggered your experience?
* What strategies did you, or could you, use to enter "The Zone"?

Taking the time to look deeply into those special moments of flow and grace in your life, and asking yourself specific questions like these, can provide you with important clues into avenues of balance for you. Become a connoisseur of your own peak moments of balance, and learn what makes you "click"!

ANXIETY AND BEYOND:
THE UPPER LEARNING ZONE

Beyond The Zone is a realm of less grace and more taxing learning. As the challenges in your life increase, you will find yourself moving from The Zone into the Upper Learning Zone, where heightened difficulties and distress stimulate your learning. If the challenges increase further still, you are in danger of passing into the upper danger zone called The Burnout Zone.

Pause for a moment to remember what it was like and how you felt at times when you began a new job, changed your first diaper, were asked to take on new responsibilities at work. Each of these situations gave you important feedback regarding the level of your skills and provided the opportunity to develop yourself. If you were able to rise to the occasion and learn what you were being asked to learn, the distress matured into the euphoric stress of mastery and accomplishment.

Joel remembers an example of this from his own experience. "As a teenager I was out skiing at Steven's Pass with some of my buddies. Most of them had been skiing for quite a bit longer than me. As we reached the top of one of the lifts, a friend said, 'Hey, have you ever skied Seventh Heaven?' 'No,' I said, 'What's it like?' 'Come on,' he said, 'I'll show you.' Not knowing what I was getting into, I followed him down a small slope and, to my surprise, onto a second chair lift. Before I knew it, I was heading nearly straight up a sheer face where I could look down at the chair below me between my legs. My heart sank and my mind began to race, wondering what I was going to find when I reached the top. When I got off the chair at the top, the slope was equally steep going down the other side, only this time people were skiing down it! How did I feel? Distressed—to put it mildly! More like panic, fear, in danger, dread, embarrassed, fearful, out of my league. Well, suffice it to say that I managed to skid my way down without hurting more than my ego. It was clear that there was some major learning yet to be achieved. And learn I did. Returning to the scene a few years later, my distress had transformed into joyful exhilaration and a sense of accomplishment. An experience that with lesser skills had put me way out of my Zone into anxiety and danger, was now one of sheer joy and delight. What had changed? I had learned skills that lifted my level of confidence. In the process, the bar went up on the intensity of challenge that I could meet and be in my Zone." Now ask yourself, what words best describe how you felt at those times when you were in the upper end of The Learning Zone? The following words are often used to describe how people have felt when they were in this zone: anxious, stressed, fearful, out of control, embarrassed, inadequate, suffering from low self-esteem.

The anxiety of being in The Upper Learning Zone is only natural, and it is still a place to learn when approached with awareness, wisdom, and respect. Learning here compels us to search for the resources

"Seek above all for a game worth playing. Play as if your life and sanity depend on it because they do!"

—Robert de Rop

"I discovered the middle path of stillness within speed, calmness within fear and I held it longer and quieter than ever before."

—Steve McKinney, when he set a new world downhill ski speed record of 130.4 mph in 1987.

and skills we need to develop greater self-mastery. As we grow through learning, we again experience the grace of returning to The Zone — only this time, having increased our knowledge, strength, and capacity, we enter at a higher level.

SKILLS FOR THE LEARNING ZONE

What does it take to do well in The Learning Zone? Many people are asking themselves these questions today, especially as the stakes for "learning how to learn" are becoming higher than ever and their sense of imbalance is consequently increasing.

A few years ago, our friend Peter Parks conducted a study on brain function and creativity at the Menninger Foundation in Kansas. First, he ran a battery of psychological tests to determine the "baseline" creativity level of each participant. Next, he trained the group to learn how to recognize and increase specific frequencies of brainwaves in the theta frequency band (between 6 and 9 cycles per second) that are associated with enhanced creativity and intuition. After the training, he once again administered the creativity tests to see if there was a correlation between how successful people were in increasing their prevalence of theta brainwaves, and increasing the factors associated with creativity. One finding in particular stood out. There was a clear and strong correspondence between people's tolerance for ambiguity as measured by the psychological tests and the level of their theta brainwave activity. Interestingly, as people learned through feedback to increase their theta frequency brainwaves, they also showed an increase in their scores for tolerance for ambiguity associated with enhanced creativity.

Peter's ingenious study provides us with valuable insights that are helpful in our search for balance — particularly how to get the most out of The Learning Zone. Unless we can tolerate ambiguity and the unknown, we will have great trouble in The Learning Zone. As the great Nobel Prize winning chemist Ilya Prigogine once said, "The more rigid a system is, the more likely it is to collapse under pressure." In nature, rigid objects break or wear away, while more flexible and adaptable things learn, grow, and evolve. In contrast to those who cling to certainties, people with a high tolerance of ambiguity are more flexible and expansive in their thinking. Similarly, tense people quickly exhaust themselves, and people with "psychosclerosis" (rigid mindsets) who suffer from a "hardening of the attitudes," often isolate themselves or cut themselves off from meaningful relationships and learning.

"Be brave enough to live creatively. The creative place is where no one else has ever been. You have to leave the city of your comfort and go into the wilderness of intuition. You can't get there by bus, only hard work, risking, and by not quite knowing what you're doing. What you'll discover will be wonderful: yourself!"

—Alan Alda

To the degree that we are intolerant of ambiguity, we are prone to perceive situations as threatening rather than promising. When we lack information or encounter uncertainty, we are likely to feel uncomfortable and out of control. Yet as our lives grow more complex, three sources of ambiguity become more common: novelty, complexity, and insolvability.

Learning to develop our tolerance for ambiguity, rather than trying to avoid it, is an essential skill for living a balanced life in modern times because it creates flexibility. The more flexible we are, the better equipped we are to adapt to The Learning Zone, deal with stress, and learn from the surprises in our lives. These principles are, so to speak, "the rules of the game," and people who understand this are less likely to exhaust themselves struggling with life and more likely to live in harmony and balance.

THE ZONE OF BOREDOM AND FRUSTRATION

At times in our lives it is only natural that we want to drop out of the flow and effortless grace of The Zone into The Lower Learning Zone. Quieter times such as these afford us a welcome opportunity to rest, recuperate, and integrate our learnings from more intense times. Yet after a while, we begin to feel a bit bored and underutilized; we might want to stir things up, seek more adventure or challenge.

Pause for a moment to reflect on times in your life or work when you dropped into the lower reaches of The Learning Zone. Here, you were likely well equipped, possibly over-equipped, with the knowledge, skills, and confidence necessary for the levels of challenge in your life at that time. The unemployed, people in boring, repetitive jobs, and elderly housebound, are all likely dwellers in this domain. From our time as clinicians working with people with stress-related illnesses, we're convinced that as many were suffering from Rust-out as from Burnout.

Thinking back to times in your life and work when you were in this domain, what words describe how you felt? Bored, frustrated, unproductive, unmotivated, wasting time, and suffering from low self-esteem?

These indicators tell us that it may be time to seek out the challenges and opportunities that we need to stretch ourselves. As we step out of The Comfort Zone and reach toward greater heights, once again we find ourselves in the sweet flow of The Zone. Are you starting to get a sense for the rhythm of this dance of learning?

"I will not die an unlived life.

I will not live in fear of falling or catching fire.

I choose to inhabit my days, to allow my living to open me,

to make me less afraid, more accessible, to loosen my heart

until it becomes a wing, a torch, a promise.

I choose to risk my significance;

to live

so that which came to me as seed

goes to the next as blossom

and that which came to me as blossom,

goes on as fruit."

—Dawna Markova

DANGER ZONES: THE EXTREMES OF
BURNOUT AND RUST-OUT

While optimal learning takes place in our Learning Zone, times of crisis, tragedy, and breakdown are also part of the learning journey. We humans cannot survive for long in the frigid polar regions or the scorching deserts, in the deep ocean, or highest mountain peaks, but a brief visit there with the right survival gear may be a powerfully transformative ordeal in our lives — that is, if we survive.

To optimize our learning as well as a sense of balance, we need to increase our vigilance and mindfulness as we move farther and farther out of The Zone into the nether regions of increasing or diminishing intensity or challenge. Generally speaking, only the most crazy, dull, and stupid among us will willingly put themselves in danger and stay there. Remember the story of the boiled frog who didn't notice that the water was slowly heating up? How easy it is to forget, especially when we are surrounded by other "frogs" with their heads down, working hard, hell-bent for... are they even sure what?

The truth is, we humans are simply not bioengineered to live in the Burnout zone for sustained periods of time. Your body is equipped with the resources it needs to mobilize itself for brief "sprints" in that zone, but thinking you'll live there is as short-sighted as building your house on the slope of an active volcano. Your body is wiser than that. It will shut down by itself, either temporarily or permanently, depending on how extreme your situation gets.

If you study the physiology of balance in terms of biochemistry, you'll find that adrenaline and norepinephrine are the self-generated drugs of choice for brief periods of "fight or flight." But when you stay in a distressed or overwhelmed state for prolonged periods of time, your adrenal glands exhaust themselves, and the elevated stress levels of hormones actually begin to eat away the insides of your blood vessels, making them weaker and more liable to explode. Look how many people are taken out each year from the inside out with a stroke or a heart attack; nearly one-quarter of deaths! They are potent reminders of the dangers of imbalance.

Such conditions do not occur overnight, but are symptomatic of lives lived out of balance. Many of these people have lived too long in the Burnout zone and did not know — or did not care to learn — how to shift out back into learningful limits. As pressure mounts, miles of tiny capillaries, constricted due to the stress of battling against an overstretched

"Healing is embracing what is most feared; healing is opening what has been closed, softening what has hardened into obstruction, healing is learning to trust life."

—Jeanne Achterberg

heart, pump harder and harder with increasing pressure to get enough blood, oxygen, and nutrients to your exhausted body. Add to this the habit and poor judgment of a mind, mindless and exhausted, clouded by distraction and confusion, which habitually elevates the stress hormone levels in the blood. Add to this the exacerbating influences of caffeine, sugar, and nicotine, plus arteries clogged from a high-fat diet, and you have the all-too-common makings of disaster. Is it any wonder that heart disease and strokes are the most common killers?

Fortunately, there are plenty of alternatives. All of them involve taking the initiative and developing the skills necessary to take more control in our lives and to live in a more sanely balanced way. As part of a self-regulating system, your energy output needs to be matched with your ability to renew and refresh yourself. When you cross the line and the quality of healthy, homeostatic balance begins to slip, you quickly lose strength and vitality and slip into a potentially dangerous state. In this state of disintegration, the harder you struggle, the more exhausted and out of balance you become. After prolonged periods of unceasing distress, your resources are depleted, you are exhausted, your bloodstream is toxic rather than life-refreshing, and you are in danger.

Those chronically caught in the Rust-out zone are as much at risk as those chronically caught in the Burnout zone. Suffering from extreme frustration, exhaustion, and low self-esteem, they often lapse into life-threatening despair or lash out in angry violent ways. Some feel despair about living in such a state, and in a disintegrating spiral of increasing self-depreciation, they may decide to take their own lives — over the course of many years or impulsively in a moment — affecting all who share their lives.

Understanding the gravity of such extreme states of imbalance, and the equally tragic missed opportunities to discover, develop, and express the incredible potentials of our lives, we often urge people who learn this model to not only apply it to their own lives, but to share it with the people they live and work most closely with. Just imagine how many lives might be saved or improved if each person reading this book were to be a little more mindful of the people in their lives who may not have even considered the possibility of living more in balance.

Life in the Learning zone encourages a healthy balance between times in our lives when we are challenged to learn in order to meet a goal, and times when we are in a mode of rest, renewal, and integration. Living a healthy, balanced life means that we become aware where we stand on the Zone map, and to recognize when we are approaching the

"Security is mostly a superstition, it does not exist in nature, nor do the children of men as a whole experience it.

Avoiding danger is no safer in the long run than outright exposure.

Life is either a daring adventure or nothing at all!"

—Helen Keller

danger zones. Remember: Life is about balance. It's about breathing in and breathing out, action and rest, intense learning and reflective integration; even waking and sleeping are allowed!

THE BOTTOM LINE

The wisdom of living and working in The Zone can be succinctly articulated as follows:

- Moment to moment, you are either moving toward or away from The Zone of optimal performance.
- In moments that you are mindful and aware, you have the choice to either move toward The Zone, or away from it. Since you can only manage what you monitor, in moments that you are mindless, your unconscious habits run your life.
- The closer you come to living and working in The Zone the more your health, vitality, productivity, and effectiveness will be optimized.
- The farther you allow yourself to drift from The Zone, the less you accomplish, the greater your distress and anxiety, the more mistakes you make, and the more in danger you are of your health being compromised.

Here's how this translates in terms of action and productivity:

- Working a fourteen-hour day at twenty percent efficiency would result in 2.8 hours of productivity.
- In contrast, working closer to The Zone with greater wisdom and mindfulness, an 8-hour day at 90 percent efficiency would result in 7.2 hours of productivity.

"A man of knowledge chooses a path with a heart and follows it and then he looks and rejoices and laughs and then he sees and knows. He knows that his life will be over altogether too soon. He knows that he as well as everybody else is not going anywhere. He knows because he sees...a man of knowledge endeavors and sweats and puffs and if one looks at him he is just like any ordinary man, except that the folly of his life is under control."

—Don Juan

If you understand the essence of high-performance science, it's clear that being a highly motivated, intensely driven, success-oriented, exhausted, depleted, stressed out person is a "winning formula" only for decreased efficiency, reduced productivity, diminished intelligence, likely compromised relationships, compromised personal sustainability, and potential stress-related illness or untimely death. The bottom line is that maximal effort does not yield optimal performance. Working long and hard at minimal efficiency is unwise, unsustainable, risky, and taken to an extreme, deadly. As Arianna Huffington once noted, "We have a lot of leaders with high IQs in politics, business and the media making terrible decisions. This is not because they are not smart, but because they are disconnected from their own wisdom and best judgment. They are too stressed and tired."

LIFELONG LEARNING

The learning adventure of our lives continually reminds us that balanced living is achieved by seeking challenges when we are bored, and cultivating skills when we are challenged. It's an ongoing dance.

Imagine that you have exactly the skills and capabilities that you need to meet life's challenges. Things couldn't be better and you are in the Zone. And then, inevitably, things change. The pressures and demands upon you increase. What's the strategy to re-enter the Zone? You learn and develop new skills to meet the challenge. Take a class, get some coaching from a mentor, ask a peer to train you on that computer program you haven't learned but need for the project. As you learn, you find yourself moving back into the Zone. The challenges may remain the same for a time, but as your skills continue to grow you're likely to slip into boredom. This is no fun, and the work or way of life here is not very fulfilling. What's the strategy to move back toward "The Zone"? Easy, seek out more challenge. Take on some new responsibilities, challenge yourself to learn how to do something you've always wanted to learn, take that martial arts class that you've always wanted to take.

Balance, properly understood, is a cyclic dance of learning, meeting challenges, more learning, more accomplishments. At each step, you are able to bring a higher order of understanding to handle a greater degree of complexity in the challenge. Now, how long do you think these cycles of development and accomplishment go on? *Forever!* Lifelong learning is a way of life, not just a nice idea. As long as we keep on learning and seeking out new experiences, our brain keeps growing rich in making more and more complex connections. But if we stop learning and get stuck in the familiar, the integrity of our nervous system diminishes, like a once-strong muscle that weakens after a period of disuse.

If you look at the development of human culture over the past tens of thousands of years, you will find an ever-increasing intensity of challenge, complexity, and learning. Despite the comforts of our modern lives, the complexity and choices that we must face in a single week may exceed those that your great-great-grandparents faced in their entire lifetimes. And what about your children, and the world they will inherit?

"Each man has only one genuine vocation—to find the way to himself...His task was to discover his own destiny—not an arbitrary one—and live it out wholly and resolutely within himself. Everything else was only a would-be existence, an attempt at evasion, a flight back to the ideals of the masses, conformity, and fear of ones own inwardness."

—Hermann Hesse

In such a world, we need to cultivate awareness, to help us choose which zone we move toward. So, at different times throughout the day, pause to ask yourself:

* What zone am I in?
* What zone would I like to move toward?
* What do I need to do or not do to move in the desired direction?

Even at times when you feel totally overwhelmed or out of control, you can move toward your Zone simply by having the presence of mind to pause and reflect on these questions. The important question is not "Am I in the Zone?"; rather, it is "Do I know what zone I'm in and am I heading in the direction that I want to go?" The choice, as always, is your own.

Finding a fulfilling balance in your life may require that if you are really stressed at work, you look for opportunities to enrich yourself outside of work. Likewise, if you are bored at work, the challenge that gets you back in the Zone might be found by doing something in your community or with your kids. When in doubt, take one small step to improve your current situation. This may mean that you stop investing so much time and energy in activities or relationships that are unfulfilling, and begin to reprioritize your attention toward ones that are more rewarding to yourself and to others. Whatever you do to improve your situation can serve to generate the energy in your life necessary to create more overall balance. This doesn't mean that you don't explore possibilities to create more balance at work or at home, or wherever you need more challenge or development. It *does* mean you understand that the shift needed at any given time may be one on the inside, a change of heart or attitude, rather than a change in your job or relationship. Be sensitive to your needs, and ever-welcoming of deeper insights.

> "The outward work can never be small if the inward one is great, and the outward work can never be great if the inward is small or of little worth… All works are surely dead if anything from the outside compels you to work. Even if it were God himself compelling you to work from the outside, your works would be dead. If your works are to live, then God must move you from the inside, from the innermost region of the soul—then they will really live. There is your life and there alone you live and your works live."
>
> —Meister Eckhart

Living in The Zone: A Self-Test

The following practice will invite you to look deeply into the presence or absence of balance in the various arenas of your life. It is an exercise worth giving some quality time to, and may unfold as a sequence of contemplations over some days, or as an hour of more focused reflection.

First make a list of all the roles and identities that comprise your sense of yourself. You may want to list them on a piece of paper, or even write them down on Post-its, one statement per Post-it. To some you are a parent, to others a child. To some a follower, to others a leader. To some you are a friend, and to others a lover or a mate. You are a worker, a professional, an athlete, a musician, a writer. You are a physical being, a spiritual being, a deeply feeling and passionate being, an intellectual being. A member of a church or temple, of your neighborhood, professional societies, clubs, community, or the Rotary, a coach for the soccer team, a member of the golf league. You are a global citizen and a universal being. You are a great Mystery. Make as complete a list as you can of all the different elements of your identity that comprise the whole constellation of your Self.

On a separate piece of paper, draw the Zone diagram, with the Burnout and Rust-out zones, the upper and lower realms of the Learning zone, and the Zone of Optimal Performance running diagonally up the middle. If you used Post-its you might want to map out the Zone diagram on a big piece of paper, or even use a window or a door. Pause to consider all the roles or identities that you just wrote down, and write or map those words onto the Zone diagram in the region that best describes where you stand on that particular quality of your life at this time.

Then step back and scan this "big picture" of your life. What does this say to you? Does it look like you are a burned-out boss? A rusting-out lover? A peak performer in the mom or musician category? Does it seem that there is too much or too little going on to live a truly balanced life? Notice what areas of your life are way out of balance and calling for your attention to make some changes. Notice in what areas learning is really going on. Then continue by reflecting on the following questions:

- What areas in your life are most out of balance and calling for your immediate attention to make some changes?
- In which areas of your life are you most "overextended"?
- In which areas of your life are you most "underdeveloped"?
- In what areas in your life is the most learning going on?
- In which do you feel most challenged?
- In which do you feel like you need to raise the bar and challenge yourself more?
- In which areas of your life are you in your Zone?
- What activities, roles, or qualities of your self are the sources of your greatest joy, satisfaction, or sense of accomplishment?
- Which aspects of your life are you most grateful for?
- Which do you have the most grief about?
- Which areas have you been ignoring that call for your attention?

- What elements of your wholeness have you left out and forgotten to even write down here?
- What strategies would help you to move toward the Zone in the areas of your life that you feel most out of balance?
- What are your top five priorities to give time and attention to in order to live your life in a more balanced way?
- What are the first steps you can take toward living in greater balance?

IT'S ALL ABOUT LEARNING!

Many of our friends from other cultures have commented that people in the modern West tend to be incredibly self-critical and unforgiving toward themselves. An exercise like the one we've just completed invites you to look deeply enough to really catch a glimpse of a deeper insight into who you are, how you live, and what is truly possible. It may reveal ways in which you are living that you are truly grateful for and proud of. It may also remind you of choices that you have made, or paths you have chosen that you now regret or have some grief about. Welcome to the learning expedition of a lifetime!

It is helpful to keep in mind that this is really *all about learning!* When you are aware of the forces that shape your life, you have a choice and things can improve. When you live in a mindless way, the habits you have internalized rule your life. With this in mind, observe how the patterns of your life experience are shaped by your actions; your actions are guided by your intentions; your intentions reflect your values; your values are shaped by your beliefs; and your beliefs are shaped by your experiences and by the quality of insight or confusion with which you interpret them.

Making the changes necessary to improve the quality of your life requires a fierce commitment to continuous learning. And learning, whether about yourself, about others, about the ways of the world, or about the immensity of the mysterious universe, requires considerable courage.

COURAGE, PATIENCE, AND FORGIVENESS

In the early '80s it was reported that more than twice as many men and women died of suicide after returning from the war in Southeast Asia than died in combat. The only way these veterans knew to turn off the

"Life behaves in messy ways...continuously exploring systems bent on discovering what works are far more practical and successful than our attempts at efficiency. Such systems are not trying to reduce inputs in order to maximize outputs. They slosh around in the mess, involve many individuals, encourage discoveries, and move quickly past mistakes. They are learning all the time, engaging everyone in finding what works. The system succeeds because it involves many tinkerers focused on figuring out what is possible. Could we begin to appreciate that this kind of tinkering is efficient?"

—Margaret Wheatley

war inside was to take their lives. People in the Pentagon were stunned and many felt considerable grief at having contributed to such a deep wound in the world.

One day, shortly after the report was released, we received a call requesting us to help design and deliver an "Ultimate Warrior Training Program" for the U. S. Army Green Berets. Our hearts raced, and we definitely felt stretched way out of our Zone. This was a level of challenge that dramatically exceeded our perceptions of our capabilities. It also challenged many of our most deeply held values. Yet, after considerable soul-searching, we realized that we'd feel safer knowing that the next wave of troops had learned some of the kinds of lessons we are offering to you here in this book. We accepted the assignment, with promises of support from many of our mentors, whose guidance would be necessary to take on such an immense project.

Over the next three years, the government paid us to travel far and wide, and to talk soulfully with many incredible people from diverse traditions and professions about what they thought should be included in such a monumental program. Talking one day with Zong Rinpoche, the profoundly wise elder abbot of one of the largest monastic universities in Tibet, we explained that the men we were planning to train might well find themselves in a position to avert or trigger the next world war. The stakes were huge, and our hopes were that the team we'd put together would be able to impart some skills that would help these warriors to make wiser choices.

We asked the respected elder, "What do you think is the most important thing to teach these men?" He thought deeply for a moment, and then through his interpreter he replied, "Most of all it is important to teach them courage." "Us teach courage to the Green Berets?" we asked, taken aback. "How are we supposed to do that?" "Just teach them courage and everything will turn out for the best" was all he had to say. We lived with this conundrum for a number of years. Then one day we mentioned Rinpoche's advice to a friend who was a translator for the Dalai Lama. He laughed with delight and said, "Oh, that's so perfect. Did you know that in the Tibetan language, the word that we usually translate as *courage*, could also be translated as *patience*, compassion, *forgiveness, or 'heart power'?*" Upon hearing this, something deep inside of us burst open: *Teach them courage…teach them patience…teach them forgiveness…teach them compassion…teach them to find the power of their hearts!*

The moral of this story is that to make changes in our own lives, we all need to develop our courage, patience, forgiveness, and compassion for ourselves, and for the many other out-of-balance people whose

"Gandhi talks about meditation being as important to the nonviolent soldier as drill practice is to the conventional soldier. Nonviolence doesn't just happen. You don't just suddenly walk into the middle of conflict and know what to do.

I've discovered that the people who impress me with their nonviolent behavior in violent situations are inevitably people who have trained themselves and been involved in nonviolent strategies for a while. You can't do it in a weekend workshop…one must accept nonviolence as a form of fighting, and that's very hard for people to understand. However, compassion and joy can be as contagious as war fever."

—Joan Baez

mindless actions can cause so much grief. And this we can only learn when we have the courage and balance of mind to contemplate these two questions:

- What is really working in our lives?
- What is really not working?

We often say to clients, "You have to reward yourselves for making mistakes. If you don't take risks, if you are too self-protective and fearful about failure, then you will never step out of your comfort zone and into your learning zone. You will never realize what is possible. Not only will the quality of your life, work, and relationships suffer, but you honestly may not survive. A mistake is only a mistake if you fail to learn from it, or if you don't make those learnings visible to others who may benefit from your own learnings." This advice applies equally to individuals, to relationships, and to organizations searching for survival, sustainability, and for a more balanced way of life. Remember, learning is fed by feedback and led by questions:

- What feedback delights you?
- What feedback disturbs you?
- What feedback do you ignore?
- What questions are unconsciously driving your life?
- What questions would help you to focus your efforts to learn how to live a more balanced life?

You do not need to know the answers to these questions yet. By carefully observing the workings of your own mind and body, you will discover many clues for how to live in greater balance. We begin by stepping through the gateway of mindfulness.

"Wealth, position, and power become tiresome if the spiritual nature is not satisfied in its quest for meaning. As life progresses, the value of meditation and the cultivation of qualities of joy, equanimity, compassion, and love which give life its nobility and value will become more important. Amidst gain and loss, fame and defame, praise and blame, happiness/pleasure and sorrow/pain, the Awakened One urged us to keep a balanced mind. Only in this state can deep understanding arise, and the heart attain peace."

—Rina Sircar

chapter four

Mindfulness:
The Gateway to Balance

With an eye made quiet by the power of harmony and the deep
power of joy, we see into the heart of things.

—WILLIAM WORDSWORTH

LOOK OUT THROUGH YOUR EYES RIGHT NOW, NOTICING THE WORDS ON
this page, and recognize that you are "seeing." Feel the contact of the
book in your hands, noticing its texture, weight, and form, and know
you are "touching." Watching the thoughts floating in your mind, wondering what will come next, know that you are "thinking." This lucid
presence of mind that simply, effortlessly notices what is true for you
in the moment is called mindfulness. This dynamic state of attention
is a deep, direct awareness of the present moment. It is your natural
capacity and most crucial tool for discovering and sustaining balance.

Mindfulness is a presence of mind that we bring alive one moment
at a time, right here and now. It brings clarity to our lives because the
moment you realize that you have been mindlessly lost in your thoughts,
you are awake again and back at the center of your life. Mindfulness
allows you to recognize when you are out of balance and then to come
back into balance, because it is the part of your mind that can notice
what's happening. You've stopped falling off the tightrope—or at least
you are aware of falling and can figure out how to get back on.

Because of the spaciousness that mindfulness creates around any experience—you aren't just noticing something, but you are aware that you are noticing it—it creates balance in the mind without grasping things too tightly, pushing them away, or confusing them with what they aren't. When we are mindful, we meet the moment completely, without being driven by our unconscious prejudices, assumptions, and conditioning. In this way, every moment of mindfulness becomes a moment of freedom that liberates us from mindless habit. That's why it is the cornerstone for creating balance in our lives.

THREE ESSENTIAL POINTS

The practice of mindfulness is essentially the cultivation of present-moment awareness. Mindful awareness arises through intentionally paying attention in an open, accepting, and discerning way. In the cultivation of mindfulness, there are three essential points to "dial in" and keep in mind. These are to optimize the quality of the attention, intention, and attitude that you bring to being mindful. Let's look at each of these in more detail:

Attention: Attention is the quality of mind that observes the ever-changing contents of experience in the present moment. To anchor and activate attention, reach up and touch your heart, in a gesture of rebooting and affirming your mindful clear presence, connecting with yourself, and embracing your experience with awareness in this present moment.

Intention: As you begin, clarify your intention, and anchor that intention by being mindful of the flow of your breathing. Allow each breath to help you focus your attention in the ways that you choose.

Attitude: To optimize your attitude, gently smile to yourself with a self-reflective smile that knows that you are awake to this moment. Allow this gentle inner smile to anchor an attitude of lovingkindness and acceptance, protecting you from trying too hard in your mindfulness practice, and activating a sense of open-heartedness, curiosity, and compassion in discerning the flow of life experiences that you attend to.

Throughout your session of any mindfulness practice, continue to mindfully monitor and fine-tune the quality of your attention, intention, and attitude.

"The more and more you listen, the more and more you will hear. The more you hear, the more and more deeply you will understand."

—Dilgo Khyentse Rinpoche

TIPPING POINT TOWARD MINDFUL BALANCE

In a mountain resort in the east Alps of Switzerland, more than 2,500 of the world's elite business, government, and thought leaders with key roles in shaping civil society gathered for the annual World Economic Forum (WEF). What brought these global leaders to Davos was less about the formal meetings and presentations and more about the emergent spirit of global community in dialogue and inquiry regarding themes that matter to humanity and its potential for perishing or thriving with the world. While it was only two years before that mindfulness was discussed at Davos, mindfulness reached full ignition at the 2014 conference which was entitled The Reshaping of the World: Consequences for Society, Politics, and Business—with over twenty-four venues offering teachings related to mindfulness, mindful leadership, and mindful governance to overflowing audiences.

Mindfulness, the intentional cultivation of moment-to-moment awareness, is both the gateway to living in balance and one of the most swiftly growing global trends. To inform and inspire your practice, we'll share some examples here to illustrate how this trend related to living in balance is playing out across different sectors of modern society in these times.

According to JWT Worldwide, one of the world's largest marketing communications companies, "mindfulness" is one of the top ten trends that will shape the world in 2014—and beyond. In its February 3, 2004, issue, *Time* magazine affirmed this growing trend in its cover article titled, "The Mindful Revolution."

"Mindfulness is part of a much larger trend we've been observing called mindful living," Ann Mack, director of trend-spotting at JWT, told the *Huffington Post*, "It's kind of a counter-trend to the past decade of overly stimulated, ADD-afflicted, tech-saturated culture that we've been living in. What was once the domain of the spiritual set has filtered into the mainstream as more people are drawn to this idea of shutting out distractions and focusing on the moment."

All signs are that this global interest in mindfulness is not a passing fad, but a key indicator of the maturing of global consciousness and the enduring responsiveness of humanity seeking greater balance amidst the emerging crises and opportunities of these times. Mindfulness has staying power because as our world becomes ever more complex and fast paced, and our use of technology continues to overwhelm our capacity to keep up, people are highly motivated to seek out empowering tools and develop finer capacities that will

"Choices in a meditator life are simple:

Do those things that contribute to awareness.

Refrain from those that don't."

—Sujata

help them to optimize their health, balance, and peace of mind, while interacting with their rapidly changing world. Mack explained, "We're reassessing our relationship with technology. Over the last decade, we've allowed technology to rule us. Now we're trying to be more mindful in the way we use technology and find more balance."

Upon reflection, is seems that nearly every single global crisis facing humanity has its roots in personal and collective mindlessness, denial, ignorance, and delusion that mindfulness can help to antidote. In search of greater survivability and thrivabilty, increasing numbers of entrepreneurs, leaders, and innovators in the high-tech arena are gravitating toward mindfulness and related mind-fitness disciplines. Wisdom 2.0 has become high-tech's "mindfulness Woodstock," convening a series of conferences in Silicon Valley and the Bay Area to sold-out audiences of thousands of high-tech innovators, leaders, educators, researchers, and entrepreneurs who are savvy to the value of mindfulness-related practices for these stressful, fast-paced times. Innovations stemming from mindfulness-related programs in high-tech have reached millions if not billions of users worldwide.

Stanford University's Center for Compassion and Altruism Research and Education (CCARE) is expanding on the theme of mindfulness to also offer lectures, courses, and conferences exploring Compassion and Technology, Science of Compassion, and related topics which bring together presenters and participants from many high-tech organizations in dialogue with leaders in neuroscience, contemplative science,

~

"Mindful awareness is fundamentally a way of being—a way of inhabiting one's body, one's mind, one's moment-by-moment experience. It is a natural human capacity. It is a deep awareness; a knowing and experiencing of life as it arises and passes away each moment. Mindful awareness is a way of relating to all experience—positive, negative, and neutral—in an open, receptive way.

This awareness involves freedom from grasping and from wanting anything to be different. It simply knows and accepts what is here, now. Mindfulness is about seeing clearly without one's conditioned patterns of perceiving clouding awareness, and without trying to frame things in a particular way.

It is important to learn to see in this way because how a person perceives and frames the moment generates one's reality."

—Shauna Shapiro

and high-tech development. Loic Le Meur, a serial tech entrepreneur from Silicon Valley, remarked in an interview for the *New York Times*, "It's funny, everyone I know has started meditating. In the Valley, there's a real social pressure on you [to do it]. Six months ago I gave in and started my own daily practice."

As early pioneers in mindfulness practice, research, and education, we remember the days when people doing any kind of mindfulness practice were very rare in the West, and we have watched this trend in mindfulness retreats, research studies, and organizational programs grow steadily over time. This is a global trend that will continue to grow, especially as stress, complexity, and the rate of change increase in the years to come. According to the National Institutes of Health, mindfulness-related programs represented a four billion dollar industry in 2007 alone. Can you imagine where this is going?

Mindfulness-based capacity development programs have been offered with inspiring results for thousands of employees at: Google, Facebook, Twitter, AOL, Apple, Aetna, Travelers, Cisco, Huffington Post, Eileen Fisher, Intel, Hope-Lab, Hewlett-Packard, QUALCOMM, Sun Microsystems, Mail Chimp, Silicon Valley Bank, Honeywell, Boeing, Ford, and the World Bank. In our own work, we've taught mindfulness in hundreds of organizations to thousands of people, with universally positive and often enduring measurable benefits ranging from better health and performance, to improved communications, more empathic relationships, and greater self-mastery and self-confidence.

Mindfulness in medicine is growing with over forty universities belonging to the Consortium of Academic Health Centers for Integrative Medicine, where mindfulness is given a premium role in training medical students. We ourselves have offered programs and training related to mindfulness in medicine for physicians and nurses from hundreds of medical centers. Through an N.I.H. grant that ran for nearly ten years, we taught mindfulness related programs for hundreds of medical students from nearly every medical school in North America. Mindfulness in Law programs are being offered at a growing number of law schools, and practice groups of mindful or contemplative professionals are emerging in more and more cities around the globe.

In education, mindfulness is now a key element in many excellent programs focused on "social and emotional learning" or SEL. One Bay Area–based program called Mindful Schools offers online mindfulness training to teachers, instructing them how to teach children to focus better in classrooms and to deal with stress. Since their launch in 2010, Mindful Schools has reached more than 300,000 students, and educators

"The every-man-for-himself model cuts against what all of our great religions have taught us; it also goes against what our great scientists are teaching us, and it denies what we know in our hearts. It's time for compassion to come front and center in our public discourse. We need to get away from worshipping at the altar of profit and markets as if they were flawless deities. If we care about each other, invest in each other, and put the well-being of human beings first, we will soften the rough edges of the market system and we all will profit more.

Mindfulness can help us slow down enough, and pay attention enough, to see clearly the basic human truth Darwin stated. We're not going to get this from the business talk shows: they will tell us that if we buy the right stock, we'll flourish. We won't get it from the news channels: they'll tell us that if we have a certain political view, we'll vote the right people into office, and then we will flourish as never before. We won't get it from the commercials telling us that the latest product will bring us deep satisfaction. We'll get it by slowing down and seeing how powerful compassion can be."

—Congressman Tim Ryan

in forty-three countries and forty-eight states have taken its courses online—and they are just one of hundreds of organizations offering similar programs.

Mindfulness is not just for nerds, tech gurus, and people with desk jobs. The historic Seahawks victory at the 2014 SuperBowl was widely attributed, in part, to mindfulness-related training as being key to the Hawks' success. Programs such as Elizabeth Stanley's Mindfulness-based Mind-Fitness programs touched the lives of hundreds of Marine Corps and Army troops, and first responders. Our once-secret Jedi Warrior Program for Special Forces equipped soldiers in harm's way to learn to "recognize and befriend their inner enemies and to stop the war inside." By developing the mental skills, neural circuitry, and attuned relationships as a team, these solders were able to show up for their missions with the presence, fine attunement, discernment, empathy, and wisdom necessary to make critical decisions in the face of unreasonable distress.

The month-long silent mindfulness "encampment" that we included in our Jedi Program's basic training was likely the longest, deepest dive into mindfulness practice taken by any military teams to date, and this training played a significant role in preparing one of our teams to be tagged as the most outstanding team in the NATO games following the program. Mindfulness training also equipped our troops with a depth of clear presence and self-mastery that enabled them to succeed in acing mission simulations that no other teams in previous history had been able to successfully complete. In a debrief after the encampment, we

"Mindfulness...is not for the faint-hearted, nor for those who routinely avoid the whispered longings of their own hearts. It is for individuals interested in the adventure and challenges of self-exploration and transformation, for those who wish to taste and explore new ways of knowing and new ways of being—not someone else's, but one's own moment-to-moment experience."

—Jon Kabat-Zinn & Saki Santorelli

discovered that while many of the men initially thought we'd been talking metaphorically about the nature of the mind and its powers when the program began, after thirty days of deep, silent, intensive mindfulness practice they realized that we were actually speaking quite descriptively.

In his book, *Mindful Nation*, six-term congressman Tim Ryan affirms that "a quiet revolution is happening in America. It's not a revolution fueled by anger. It's a peaceful revolution, being led by ordinary citizens: teachers in our public schools; nurses and doctors in hectic emergency rooms, clinics, and hospitals; counselors and social workers in tough neighborhoods; military leaders in the midst of challenging conflicts; and many others across our nation. This revolution is supported by the work of scientists and researchers from some of the most prominent colleges and universities in America, such as the University of Wisconsin, Stanford, UCLA, the University of Miami, Emory, Duke, and Harvard, to name just a few. At the core of this revolution is mindfulness."

THE MIRACLES OF MINDFULNESS

The value of mindfulness is a universal theme common to all Eastern and Western wisdom traditions. Now scientists are discovering what contemplatives have been experiencing for a long time, as the health benefits of bringing this kind of dynamic awareness to our daily lives are being widely studied at Harvard Medical School, University of Massachusetts Medical Center, Stanford, Emory, University of Wisconsin, Yale, and many other prestigious research centers. Although the benefits of effective stress reduction can be tasted almost immediately when one begins to live more mindfully, mindfulness taken deeply enough creates a profound state of inner balance that does more than reduce the harmful effects of stress in the body and mind. At its deepest levels, mindfulness ripens into the qualities of appreciation, love, and compassion. When this happens, we not only feel centered and good, but these positive states of psychospiritual caring and connectedness have immediate, measurable effects on enhancing immunological resilience, brain function, and the workings of the heart.

The rigor, objectivity, and insight gained through the practice of mindfulness have drawn thousands of scientists, psychologists, and researchers to this discipline in recent decades, and hundreds of studies have been launched to document the health and performance benefits of mindfulness meditation.

Mindfulness is a perfect practice for people who live and work intensely. This rigorous and subtle practice cultivates such mental and emotional faculties as vivid mental clarity, deep listening, calm intensity,

"Mindful practitioners attend in a nonjudgmental way to their own physical and mental processes during ordinary, everyday tasks. This critical self-reflection enables physicians to listen attentively to patients' distress, recognize their own errors, refine their technical skills, make evidence-based decisions, and clarify their values so that they can act with compassion, technical competence, presence, and insight....

As a link between relationship-centered care and evidence-based medicine, mindfulness should be considered a characteristic of good clinical practice."

—R.M. Epstein in *Journal of the American Medical Association* (JAMA)

and authentic presence. The faculties that can be developed in this way are very important in balancing the complexity, intensity, stress, and change of our busy lives. When compared with the many problems caused by mindless living, mindfulness has been demonstrated to:

- Improve focus, concentration, and precision.
- Enhance the quality of communications and relationships.
- Heighten the clarity of our thinking and intentions.
- Improve efficiency and safety.
- Deepen peace of mind and sense of flow.
- Master stress.
- Deepen insight and intuitive wisdom.
- Awaken more authenticity, heart, soul, and caring in our lives and work.
- Increase resilience to change.
- Strengthen self-confidence.
- Strengthen selflessness.

A wealth of clinical studies confirm that mindfulness training can lower cortisol levels and blood pressure associated with stress and anxiety, increase immune response, affect gene expression, focus attention, increase pain tolerance, enhance empathy and compassion, promote wound healing, reduce pain, increase empathy of health care providers toward their patients, and reduce stress and anxiety.

In corporate settings, mindfulness-based programs have been consistently demonstrated to: improve concentration, boost productivity, increase confidence, enhance teamwork and authentic, quality communications, and shift the "locus of control" toward feeling more empowered and able to influence situations that would previously have left people feeling victimized.

Most importantly, mindfulness gives you a still point to return to in chaos, and it helps you notice where your energy is being expended. By noticing what you are paying attention to, you have more freedom to choose. In every domain of human experience, our ability to make wise choices, influence situations, and move toward greater balance depends upon the awareness we bring to the moment. The more mindless we are, the less we are in control of our lives, and the more out of balance we feel. Increasing mindfulness, therefore, is an essential tool for living, learning, and working in balance.

Because it seems so simple, it can be hard to believe that mindfulness can be of any importance in finding balance in our lives. But if you

"Measurable changes in the function and structure of our brains, and in the expression of our genes is being shown from as little as ten hours of disciplined mindfulness practice. Reductions in burnout, anxiety, depression, and distress have been demonstrated lasting for over a year shown for physicians who received only a weekend training and two evening follow-up sessions in mindfulness practice. Mind training offer enormous returns on the time and attention invested."

—Joel Levey

practice mindfulness, you will be surprised at your ability to change, radically and dramatically. This is like the trim-tab effect, where a massive ship can be more easily turned by putting a small rudder on the larger rudder, which helps it to move more easily. The place of the greatest leverage in your life is to practice mindfulness. It will give rise to a qualitative shift in your attention that will then allow you to easily make positive changes in the quality of your life.

Remember, in the mathematics of chaos science even the tiniest change in an equation will, over time, create a dramatically different structure and form of appearance. Each insight that you come to through mindfulness, if taken to heart, has the potential to substantially transform and reshape the course of your life.

MINDFULNESS IN CONTEXT

It is helpful to regard mindfulness as a state of being on a continuum of consciousness:

* At one end is a state of complete ignorance and non-awareness.
* At the next stage we are in denial.
* As interest arises, there is a momentary registration or flash of conscious experience that quickly fades into distraction.
* Then, we learn to sustain attention through mindful presence. This sustained and deepening mindfulness indicates that we value or care about what we are attending to.
* As mindfulness fully ripens and matures, it is experienced as loving-kindness and compassion.
* As the love deepens, the boundaries separating the subject (lover) and the object (beloved) dissolve and melt away allowing the experience of true intimacy and selfless unity to emerge.

We often say that it requires courage to be mindful. As we muster the courage to show up fully for our lives, we will naturally become more intimate with the intensity, complexity, non-duality, and ever-changing flow of our experience. We will also realize waves of insight and discovery that reveal an infinite array of teachings regarding ways we can be more kind and helpful, more harmonized, attuned, and balanced to reduce the suffering, resistance, or problems that may present themselves.

As mindfulness matures and progresses, the wisdom it reveals liberates us from the illusions of a separate, solid, definable self, and

"In Asian languages, the word for 'mind' and the word for 'heart' are the same. So if you're not hearing mindfulness in some deep way as heartfulness, you're not really understanding it. Compassion and kindness towards oneself are intrinsically woven into it. You could think of mindfulness as wise and affectionate attention."

—Jon Kabat-Zinn

teaches us to stand strong, live in the power of an open question, and be more comfortable with the uncertainty and ambiguity of our lives. Mindfulness gives us the strength and presence of mind to be more resilient and adaptable in the midst of incessant, unpredictable change. It also gives us the power of presence to touch stillness in the midst of activity, find clarity in the midst of confusion, be peaceful within turbulence, and open our hearts to compassion in the presence of suffering.

At its core, mindfulness is not different than love, and love is the greatest healing force there is. By nurturing our entire nervous system with the healing power of mindfulness in this way, we can maintain balance in our emotional lives and keep our bodies and minds functioning with optimal integrity. Thus, mindfulness provides a psychophysical basis of stability, which in turn, provides the foundation for building stable and nurturing relationships.

THREE HIGHER TRAININGS

Mindfulness is regarded as intrinsic to a trinity of core practices called the Three Higher Trainings that are vital to balancing and transform our minds, our lives, and our world. As the practice of mindfulness has become increasingly secularized and even commodified, this essential triad has unfortunately been under-emphasized as a key set of guidelines for developing, maintaining, and realizing the fruits of mindfulness practice. These three core disciplines are: ethical discipline, concentration, and insight.

This triad mirrors the Wellness Triangle described in Chapter Five in that mindfulness plays a key role in optimizing the quality of our relationships, creates more harmony, balance, and integration in our nervous systems, and is essential for cultivating greater coherence, harmony, and balance in our minds.

"Ethics is how we behave when we decide we belong together."

—Brother David Steindl-Rast

Ethical Discipline

Classically, the first of these core practices vital to mindfulness is cultivation of ethical or moral intelligence necessary to discern whether or not our choices and actions related to how we manage the flow of energy and information in our lives is conducive to harmony, balance, or "right relations." These principles, practices, and codes of conduct are sometimes referred to as "mindfulness precepts." Developing a discerning intelligence helps us to distinguish those ways of living and relating that create disharmony, imbalance, and turbulence in our lives, and those that promote and assure greater harmony and balance. This is akin to the practice of the *yamas* and *niyamas* in the yogic traditions.

Classically in the mindfulness traditions, a set of five mindfulness precepts or guidelines was followed as a guide to help practitioners assure the progress of their practice. These five guidelines are skillfully expressed in the following way: "Aware of the suffering, imbalance, or problems created by...I deeply aspire to be mindful of..." For example, "Aware of the suffering caused by mindless speech, I deeply aspire to speak in ways that are true, kind, and helpful." Or, "Aware of the suffering created in my life, world, and relationships by harming others, I deeply aspire to be more kind to others."

While the classic mindfulness precepts provide a very helpful and fierce guide for optimizing the progress of mindfulness practice, we also find that this becomes more real, accessible, and useful in people's lives when they actually take time to deeply reflect on the wisdom of their own experience, and articulate their own set of "mindfulness precepts," using the basic structure of, "Aware of the suffering, imbalance, and problems resulting from/caused by...I deeply aspire to..."

One day when we were teaching a graduate program at Mahidol University in Thailand, a group of our students invited us to go on an outing to visit a local organic farm. Talking with the owner of the farm, we learned that her rural community had been in upheaval for many years with crime, aggression, and dishonesty.

A respected community elder finally called everyone together to discuss how to bring greater peace and harmony to their community and it was decided that they would all set the intention to live by the five mindfulness precepts that had been traditionally taught and practiced in Thai culture. These precepts are to be mindful of avoiding the suffering caused by: harming others; taking what has not been offered; mindless or harmful speech; sexual exploitation; mindless over-consumption of intoxicants, media, or resources. As people began to take personal responsibility for being more mindful in these ways, tensions within and between people began to subside, relationships began to improve in the community, harmony and trust was restored, and the community began to flourish and prosper as a beacon of inspiration for surrounding communities.

Just as a key success strategy for a business unit or manufacturing department is to establish a set of optimal parameters that are constantly monitored to assure the optimization of business operations, establishing a set of self-optimization "thresholds" in the form of personal mindfulness precepts or aspirations is a powerful transformational practice.

"We can use the precepts to train ourselves, to awaken ourselves and make our relationships more open and harmonious. When we are about to break them, the precepts are like warning lights and alarms signaling us to take a careful look at the mind state behind the action in which we are involved. If we look closely, we can usually discover where we became caught or confused and how we can let go and be free. Use the precepts. They are incomparable tools for changing ourselves and the world around us."

—Jack Kornfield

Living with this strong intention, your inner vigilance will "ping" you whenever you approach or cross the line with any of these precepts. In those moments you have the opportunity to make a conscious choice whether to stay true to your intended goals and best interests — or not.

While you may have high ideals, it is also essential to remember that for your practice to succeed and be sustainable, you need to manage your attitude to insure that you bring a generous amount of patience and self-compassion, as we all will inevitably encounter challenges and fall short of consistently realizing our highest goals. Without such patience, you are in danger of joining the ranks of the many discouraged people who bailed from their mind training only to be left with Zen décor, mindfulness beads, or yoga clothes, but having no enduring transformational practice.

This said, with ongoing practice you are assured of realizing success in reducing outer turbulence and tension in the field of your relationships with the world and your mind will naturally become calmer, clearer, more peaceful and powerful — opening the way for the second core practice which is the practice of concentration and the cultivation of the ability to focus our minds unwaveringly on whatever we choose.

With patience, practice, and discipline you'll find that you are able to gradually use this practice to bring your life into greater alignment with the values and principles you most deeply aspire to live by, and as a result experience greater harmony and balance.

Concentration

The second core mindfulness-related discipline balances the flow of energy and information streaming through our minds so that we are able to concentrate and focus our attention with little or no distraction. The practice of concentration helps us to transform mental dullness into mental stability, and harness the power of the mind to transform mental excitation into vivid clarity. As our practice of concentration progresses, we learn the subtle set of inner moves necessary to balance both stability and clarity of mind in order to maintain whatever focus of attention we choose, without fading into dullness and without drifting into excitement and distraction.

While this may sound like an accomplishment of mythic proportions, with practice, the wildly leaping, hyper-distracted monkey mind can actually become tamed, and an unwavering laser-like focus can be realized. This second practice is sometimes described as "making the mind fit for action." These practices of mental focusing teach us to balance the

"If anybody asks you what the Path is about....

It's about generosity.

It's about morality.

It's about concentration.

It's about gaining insight through focused self-observation.

It's about the cultivation of subjective states of compassion and love based on insight.

And it's about translating that compassion and love into actions in the real world."

—Shinzen Young

stability of mind necessary for continuity of attention with a vivid clarity of mind that is capable of seeing clearly. We learn how to shift the balance of energy and information in our minds from being so overly stable that we can lapse into drowsiness, and how to balance the energy and brightness of our minds into a vivid clarity free from excitement or distraction.

Some key advice for developing the power of your concentration is:

- Choose a focus of attention. Classically, this is to carefully attend to the flow of sensations of your breathing in a continuous and unbroken manner. You can also focus your attention on a flower... a star... an actual image or object, or a mental image. Whatever focus you choose, set your intention to keep your attention focused on this continuously.
- Remember the power of Attention, Intention, and Attitude, and set your intention to maintain your attention focused on purpose, with an attitude of patience, openness, and discerning acceptance.
- Be vigilant to notice whenever your attention wanders off toward any distraction and simply return to your focus.
- For best results, keep your practice sessions short to begin with, not more than five minutes without a short break. Let these short sessions be like little "mindfulness sprints" where you set a strong determination to keep your attention focused during this whole period without losing your focus. As your concentration develops, gradually work your way up to longer and longer sessions. When we sat our yearlong meditation retreat, our teacher instructed us to begin with five-minute sessions, take a short break of even thirty seconds to refresh the mind, and then focus again for another five minutes. Gradually we increased the length of our sessions until we were sitting for many hours at a time with strong, unwavering focus.
- Be patient with the process and realize that through this practice of taming your mind, developing greater mastery of attention is actually possible.

Appreciate that personal practices, be they conscious or unconscious, create the habit patterns that shape your neural circuits and the functioning of your mind. If your habit has been to let your mind wander, to be mindless, distracted, or mentally dull, then as you begin to practice, you will inevitably become hyper-aware of those unhelpful and imbalanced tendencies of mind.

"Concentrate, and listen not with your ears—

But with the heart.

Then, not listening with the heart, do so

With the breath.

The ear is limited to ordinary listening;

The heart (mind) to the rational.

Listening with the breath, one experiences

All things in purity."

—Chuang Tzu

Be heartened to realize that these powerful and dominating habits of mind are the result of decades of mindless habit, rather than conscious choice. Now, with the power of focused, intentional practice, you can shift the balance of your mind in the direction of greater clarity, stability, and mindfulness. Gradually, with patience and practice, you will progress along the path.

THE POWER OF MINDFULNESS

Through concentration and ethical discipline we bring peace, balance, and harmony to our minds and minimize intrusive distractions and mental dullness. This firm foundation assures progress in mindfulness. While the practice of mindfulness can create a host of wonderful and beneficial results such as reducing stress, increased focus, increasing wellness, reducing pain, enhancing peace of mind, empathy and compassion—the greatest power of mindfulness is the liberating wisdom and insight that is its ultimate fruit and highest purpose.

The following practices will guide and inspire you to develop and realize your potentials for mindfulness.

Being Awake

Have you ever stopped to consider how much of the time in your day you're fully present? For example, how much of the time are you really present when you're eating, and how much of the time is your mind wandering to memories of the past or fantasies of the future? How much are you really tasting the flavors and savoring the aromas of your meal, and how much of your attention is absorbed in watching TV, reading the paper, daydreaming, or talking with people as you put food in your body? When you're sleeping, how much of your energy goes into working out and wrestling with unresolved issues from the day, and how much of your energy is devoted to simply resting deeply and peacefully, restoring balance, and recharging your system? When you're talking with someone, what percentage of your attention is really present and listening, and what percentage is invested in thinking about other things or planning what you're going to do later?

There's an old Zen teaching story that speaks to this. The master is asked by his student, "How do you put enlightenment into action? How do you practice it in everyday life?" "I put enlightenment into action," replied the master, "by eating and sleeping." "But everyone sleeps and everyone eats," replied the student. "Quite so," says the

"Power properly understood is nothing but the ability to achieve purpose. And one of the great problems of history is that the concepts of love and power have usually been contrasted as opposites—polar opposites—so that love is identified with a resignation of power, and power with a denial of love. We've got to get this thing right. What is needed is a realization that power without love is reckless and abusive, and love without power is sentimental and anemic. Power at its best is love implementing the demands of justice, and justice at its best is power correcting everything that stands against love. It is precisely this collision of immoral power with powerless morality which constitutes the major crisis of our time."

—Martin Luther King, Jr.

master, "But it is a very rare person who really eats when they eat and sleeps when they sleep."

We are so often out of balance because we are not awake or, as we like to say, "no one is home." When no one's home, we are in a mindless trance, an all-too-familiar state of (un)consciousness where we are unknowingly lost in a fog of inner dialogues and daydreams that can lead us to miss our exit on the freeway, or miss an important communication from someone we are totally oblivious to—though they may be standing directly in front of us!

A classic example of this came from a woman who was in one of our corporate team training sessions. On her way home from work after the first day we had introduced the concept of mindfulness to her team, JoAnn picked up her young daughter from the local school on campus. Little Ana was sitting next to her, happily chirping away about all the exciting things that had happened to her in school that day. JoAnn was driving, preoccupied with things mulling around in her own mind, and she periodically mumbled, "Mmmmm…that's nice, dear…Uh huh…" in response to her daughter's animated tale and excited commentaries. After continuing on like this for a while, JoAnn suddenly felt a little hand tugging at her sleeve as they slowed down for a stoplight. "Anybody home, Mama? Anybody home?" came the piping little voice beside her.

"Wow, did I get the message, loud and clear," she told us the next day. "I really wasn't there for her, or for myself either, for that matter. I was just going through the motions like Mom on autopilot lost in the clouds of my thoughts. What a timely wake-up call that was for me!"

Why aren't we awake all the time? Is it even possible to be fully awake all of the time? Throughout the ages people have asked these questions and have experimented with various ways to increase mindfulness. We offer a few here.

MOTIVATION AND MINDFULNESS: LIBERATING THE SPIRIT IN OUR LIVES

In his novel *Island*, Aldous Huxley tells the story of an island utopia. Understanding the importance of mindfulness for building optimal human relations, the founder of the community had trained a flock of myna birds and then set them free. The myna birds would land on windowsills and fence posts and deliver their wake-up call to anyone around. Their message was "Wake up! Wake up! Pay attention…Attention… Here and now, boys, here and now, girls! Wake up! Wake up!"

"…the core capacity needed to access the field of the future is presence. We first thought of presence as being fully conscious and aware in the present moment. Then we began to appreciate presence as deep listening, of being open beyond one's preconceptions and historical ways of making sense. We came to see the importance of letting go of old identities and the need to control and… making choices to serve the evolution of life…Virtually all indigenous or native cultures have regarded nature or the universe or Mother Earth as the ultimate teacher. At few points in history has the need to rediscover this teacher been greater."

—Peter Senge, Otto Scharmer, Joseph Jaworski & Betty Sue Flowers

We've introduced the notion of the "myna birds of mindfulness"—simple reminders to wake up and be present in your life—in most of the organizations we've worked with. In some places, this has taken inspiring high-tech forms, such as in certain divisions of Hewlett-Packard where, after our training session, people created screensavers proclaiming in brilliant colors: "Wake up!" "Breathe...Smile...Relax..." "Present...Open...Connected." One employee had even found a sign saying "WHOA!" and placed it in the middle of a busy corridor to remind people to slow down, focus, and re-balance. Another woman had the ingenious idea of putting a can of beans on her desk. Whenever her eyes would fall on this anomalous item in the middle of her desk, it would remind her to take a mindful breath and return to the present moment. When she got used to having the can there, she would find something else anomalous to replace it with!

> "Understanding is the fruit of looking deeply...This present moment contains the past and the future. The secret of transformation at the base lies in our handling of this very moment."
>
> —Thich Nhat Hanh

One simple myna bird strategy is that if you wear a watch, shift it to your other wrist. Every time you check the time, you are reminded to breathe, smile, and return to the stillness at your center, even for just a moment. By interrupting a familiar and often unconscious way of doing something routine, like looking at your watch, you can create an opening to pause and check in on the level of your wakefulness at that moment.

If you carry a smartphone, there are dozens of fun apps with titles like "Mindfulness Bell," or "Zen Timer" that will allow you to set a random chime to ping you throughout the day, reminding you to "wake up," refresh your mental screen, and take a mindful breath. One physician friend who uses an app like this keeps the chime activated while she is seeing patients. If a patient asks, "What's that chime?" she'll take advantage of the teachable moment to explain how it's a tool to remind her to stay more focused and mindful throughout the day. This often opens an interesting and useful conversation regarding self-care strategies that may be useful for her patient. If patients don't inquire, she simply smiles to herself to clarify the quality of her own presence, and to fine-tune her attention, intention, and attitude as she streams on through her busy day.

> "Zen pretty much comes down to three things—everything changes; everything is connected; pay attention."
>
> —Jane Hirshfield

A variation on this method was suggested to us by one of our teachers from the Tibetan tradition, the venerable Gen Lamrimpa (Gen-la), when he first came to the West for a two-year research and training program on the mastery of attention that we helped to coordinate. Gen-la is a colleague of the Dalai Lama, and is revered as a national treasure for the Tibetan people in exile. He lived on a very modest stipend from the Tibetan government to be a professional meditator. In this way, he could keep the well-spring of their profound knowledge and realization vital as a living stream of tradition, rather than allow it to decay into fantasies about the miraculous mental powers of the ancient Tibetan yogis.

Having lived alone in a tiny hermitage in the Himalayas for nearly seventeen years, he didn't have much in the way of material possessions, and soon after he arrived, he asked if we could get him a wristwatch. When Gen-la made his request, he was explicit that he wanted a watch that could be set to beep once an hour, explaining to us that this would be an important aid to his meditation practice. We looked at each other somewhat quizzically, not quite understanding what he meant by this. Sensing our puzzlement, Gen-la explained to us that whenever he heard the beep, it would remind him that another precious hour of his life had just passed, and that his death was now an hour closer. Laughing, he explained that if he really took this to heart, he would stay more balanced and focused, be more loving and kind, and use every moment of his precious life to really make progress in his mental development and service to others. (In Tibetan, "mindfulness" means "not to forget the object of your meditation.")

In numerous organizations we have worked with, teams have adopted a bell or chime of mindfulness, rung at random times during the day as a reminder for people to take a moment to come back to themselves. Each day the bell is passed to another person in the office, and as the gently melodious sound of the bell echoes out through the floor, people are invited to take a deep breath, to focus their mind and let it shine.

This time-honored technique actually stems from Southeast Asia where, for centuries, the villagers have kept alive the tradition of the "bell of mindfulness." In many ways, our workplaces have become our modern villages because we spend so much of our time there and have so many community and social interactions organized around our jobs. So what better place to ring the bell!

There's a mindfulness poem that accompanies this practice that we learned from our teacher Thich Nhat Hanh. You can use it when you hear the bell or use any other "myna bird" to return to the present moment. It goes like this: "Listen, listen. This wonderful sound brings me back to my true self."

When you hear the bell, stop talking and thinking and just focus on your breathing with awareness for about three breaths, and enjoy your breathing. It seems so simple; it is hard to see how three breaths can help you find balance in your life. But the first step in achieving

"It is the power of a witnessing or reflective consciousness that provides the practical basis for building a sustainable future. Reflective consciousness will enable humanity to stand back from counterproductive behavior and choose more ecological ways of living."

—Duane Elgin

"Your intentions set the stage for what is possible. They remind you from moment to moment of why you are practicing . . . I used to think that meditation practice was so powerful. . . that as long as you did it at all, you would see growth and change. But time has taught me that some kind of personal vision is also necessary."

—Jon Kabat-Zinn

balance is to begin to see where your mind goes. Until you have awareness of where your attention is focused, you have little power to redirect your attention.

MINDFUL TRANSFORMATION

One very helpful way to approach the practice of mindfulness is to understand the four transformational powers of R.A.I.N. inspired by Jack Kornfield. Here is how we teach it:

R— **Recognition** allows us to clearly apprehend the nature of experience arising and passing in any given moment. Moment to moment we recognize what we are experiencing, "a joy…a sorrow…a hunger…a fullness…a fleeting pleasure…a pain…an experience of seeing… of hearing… of physical sensation… a memory of the past… a fantasy of the future…" Each experience is recognized simply for what it is.

A— **Acceptance** is the power of fully embracing each experience as it is without resistance of any kind. Especially when we appreciate that every experience is impermanent, flowing, and changing moment to moment, we can simply welcome whatever arises with an attitude of, "This sound is with me…this emotion is present…this pattern of thought is passing through my mind…Ahhh…" Each experience is clearly seen, deeply felt, and accepted just as it is like a cloud dancing through the clear sky of our mind.

I— **Investigation** is the capacity to apply mindfulness to look deeply into the nature of our experience in order to awaken insight. In this mode, mindfulness actively inquires, "What is this?" Mindfulness is not simply an open clear awareness here, but also allows for a lucid quality of investigation, discernment, and discovery. This analytical quality of direct, non-conceptual investigation illuminates how everything is constantly changing, and how every experience is interdependent with a myriad of other experiences and influences.

N— **Non-Identification** is the power of simply regarding experiences as they are in themselves without needing to personalize them as defining "me" or "mine." Through the process of identification we define ourselves by our experiences, while the power of non-identification opens a spacious freedom to simply regard experiences as mere experiences. With mindfulness we realize that we can simply rest in present moment awareness and witness the changing flow of life experiences like clouds arising and passing—dynamic appearances in the clear sky of being.

"What we observe is not nature in itself but nature exposed to our method of questioning."

—Werner Heisenberg

"I came to see that my suffering was not a result of not having control; it was a result of arguing with reality. I discovered that when I believed my thoughts I suffered, but that when I didn't believe them I did not suffer, and that this is true for every human being. Freedom is as simple as that. Suffering is optional."

—Byron Kathie

As emotions arise we notice them and note: "Ah…Anger is with me…sadness is with me…joy is with me…frustration is present in this clear open space of mindful awareness."—rather than identifying with the emotions as in "I am angry/sad/joyful/frustrated," etc.

Understanding these transformative powers of R.A.I.N. offers a useful way to calibrate and fine-tune our mindfulness to realize the true fruit of mindfulness practice. While the benefits of mindfulness certainly include a sense of calm, focus, presence, clarity, and peace of mind, the highest realization of mindfulness practice is transformational insight that cuts through confusions, liberating us from misconceptions and misidentifications, and inspires us to awaken ever more deeply and completely to the true nature of ourselves, our experience, and all things.

MINDFULNESS OF BREATHING

The greatest strategy we have to offer for whenever you're feeling particularly frazzled, scattered, and out of balance is simply to return to the awareness of your breathing. Like an anchor in the midst of a stormy sea, breath awareness is a balancing force for the mind, anchoring you in the present.

We are made to live in harmony and balance between our inner and outer worlds. The breath offers a vital key to understanding this dynamic relationship. In many of the world's spiritual traditions the words for breath and for Spirit are the same. In contemporary science, breathing is regarded not only as a vital balancing force in all mind-body functioning, but as the only function that can take place both unconsciously and also be very easily consciously controlled. If you take these ideas to heart, you will realize that the simple practice of mindful breathing actually teaches you to balance in the center of the gateway where your conscious and unconscious minds meet, where your inner and outer worlds join, and where your ordinary, limited sense of self encounters your boundless Universal Self.

Each breath teaches us many lessons about balance, reminding us of our interconnectedness with the whole world. Each breath also affirms that our life depends upon finding a balance between taking in and putting out, and reminds us that "inside" and "outside" are dancing with each other, and that they can be harmoniously reconciled as long as we can create the space and time for both inner and outer.

"When we see these creations of our own mind, as being solid, material, substantial—and then we take the next step and believe them to be real—at that point we say we have become deluded—as we are seeing phenomena as being real from their own side when it is our own mind that has created them. And to then endlessly enjoy all of those illusory creations as being something real—is what is called the round of rebirth within ordinary existence. This is the continuation of delusion—always taking what our mind has created as being real. Thus we must look to the nature of all phenomena and free ourselves from this delusion. 'All composite phenomena in their entirety are an illusion with many false designs, and beings are like a magician deceived by his own magic.'"

—Lama Tharchin

With each inhalation the lungs fill and the heart rate increases a bit to counteract the pressure of the lungs upon it. With each exhalation we release, relax, and our heart rate slows down. Similarly, we too can find greater balance in our lives when we can harness the energy, and exhilaration of initiating some course of action, and then, having given it our complete attention, we relax and let go into a joyful flow of awareness, action, and discovery.

If you carefully observe the flow of your breathing, you will discover that in the midst of constant change there are still points. These are revealed at the very climax of the inhalation before the exhalation begins, and at the bottom of the exhalation before the next inhalation begins. Taking this principle to heart, you may find the wisdom in pausing after you finish something and before you start the next thing to collect yourself, to fully focus your attention, or to get clear on your intention. With practice, you can learn to be more fully present with change by building frequent pauses into your busy day. These needn't be long in duration, but the more frequently we stop, scan, and tune ourselves toward a more balanced state, the more we will be able to bring greater flow, sensitivity, wisdom, and care into the moments that follow.

Building more still points into your life provides a welcome opportunity to harvest insights and to apply them. This is like pausing to push the clear button on your calculator after the computations have become so numerous that they are all getting confused. The blank slate allows you to begin again, fresh and clear.

The technique is very simple: As you inhale, know that you're breathing in...as you exhale, know that you're breathing out...as you watch your breath, mindfully experience the flow of sensations that come with breathing.

The more effortlessly and naturally you ride the waves of your breath, the more effective this technique will be. This is not an exercise to control or change your breath in any way. It isn't about breathing deeper or slower, or trying to manipulate the breath as in some yoga or deep breathing exercises. In fact, strictly speaking, this isn't even an exercise, but simply a focusing of awareness into what is already going on by itself. In essence, it's a letting go of trying to control, and allowing the power of awareness to do the balancing work by itself. Simply relax into the breath, feeling it just as it is.

Mindful breathing accomplishes one of the greatest miracles of life: It brings your mind and body into synch with each other and into focus, so that your mind-body-spirit can work together with balanced

"Breathing in I calm my body and mind,

Breathing out I smile.

Dwelling in the present moment,

I know this is the only moment."

—Thich Nhat Hanh

"Most men pursue pleasure with such breathless haste they hurry past it."

—Soren Kierkegaard

presence. Because your mental functioning and quality of consciousness are so closely linked to the way you breathe, mindful breathing can have a focusing, calming, and vitalizing effect for your whole mind and body.

As a technique for balancing energy, focusing on the rising and falling movement of your abdomen is especially effective. Follow your breath and simply notice the natural rising and falling sensations of the movement itself. Practiced in this way, mindfulness of breathing can become like a centering heartbeat, a focused and flowing pulse creating a wave of awareness that you can use to steady yourself as you ride through every activity of your life. With mindfulness of breathing as your home base, you can focus your attention and direct it to observe anything, or to perform any action, with greater presence and equanimity.

Some of our friends use this with their children. Whenever one of the kids is upset, overly excited, or about to have a tantrum, s/he is gently reminded to "go to your breath." How different an approach from being told merely to "go to your room!" Once the children have had a short while to calm and balance themselves with their breathing, they can then speak more clearly about what happened, how they feel, and what they need. Imagine how different your life would have been if this had been a family practice when you were growing up!

Beth, a client of ours, used mindfulness of breathing to handle a breakdown in communications with one of her customers. She was part of a team that provided technical support to other departments in a large insurance company. Keeping their information systems online and running efficiently was a high priority, because if one of their systems went down it could cost millions of dollars a day. One day a major breakdown occurred, and a very upset customer called, speaking abusively. Beth had enough presence of mind to say, "Look, we're both pretty upset about this situation. It would be easy for us both to get out of balance here and waste a lot of time. How about if we try getting focused first? Can you come over to my office and let's talk about this in person?" Her client agreed and came right over.

As they began to talk, Beth said, "I know that you're really upset, and I'd really like to see us figure this design issue out. Let's take a minute to cool our jets and get focused first, that way we can let our minds clear so we can think straight, OK?" The client had to admit that that was a good idea. "Look, it's real simple," Beth said. "Let's just be quiet for a couple of minutes and breathe together. Let your mind get focused with the breath, breathing in with full awareness and breathing out with full awareness...that's it." After a couple of minutes, Beth

"The best antidote to stress—besides altering your life so it's less stressful—is learning to manage it through mind-body methods such as meditation, mindfulness, guided imagery, and deep breathing. Recent Harvard studies have found that these techniques can successfully treat a host of... health problems."

—Dr. Alice Domar, Chief of Women's Health Programs at Harvard Medical School's Division of Behavioral Medicine and Mind/Body Medical Institute

said, "Wow, that really helped. My mind's a lot clearer now and I think I may have a solution to your problem." Her customer agreed that he was more focused and able to concentrate as well. Within a very short time they arrived at a very efficient solution to a complex problem, and got to work bringing the system back online.

Later that afternoon, the customer called Beth and thanked her for taking the time to get focused and centered. "By the way," the customer said, "Thanks for that breathing technique. It's really simple, but it sure works." The next day Beth learned that this customer had also left a voice message for her manager, and talked to the senior vice president of her department telling them what good service he'd received from her.

In a profound and simple way, cultivating a mindful awareness of the flow of the breath provides you with a continual reading on the overall status of balance and flow in your life.

If you learn to anchor your mindful awareness in the flow of your breath as a backdrop for all the experiences of your life, then refreshing your mindfulness is never more than a breath away.

So…whenever you're feeling frazzled and out of balance, come back to your breath.

MINDFULNESS OF YOUR BODY

The second base of mindfulness is to be mindful of your body. Right now as you sit here, become aware of your posture. Notice what the sensations of your hands are, and feel the sensations of your bottom touching the seat. Smile to yourself as you come out of the clouds of your thoughts and land with full awareness in your body.

Throughout the day, one of the simplest ways of getting focused and mastering stress is to become mindful of the position that your body is in. When you pay attention to your body frequently throughout the day, you recognize the accumulation of tensions and you're better able to let them go more easily and swiftly. As a result, you are less likely to accumulate a lot of tension and, therefore, less likely to develop stress-related illnesses. In this way, mindfulness is the basic foundation of preventive medicine.

There's a very simple, powerful method for weaving body awareness into your daily life. As you breathe, feel the rising and falling of your chest or abdomen. Feel the stream of sensations as the breath flows into and out of your nostrils. At the top of the inhalation, in the pause, tune in to a touch point: notice your bottom touching the chair, or the sensations of your hands or your lips touching. Then, ride the wave of

"Nothing stops the body's arrival in each new present, except death itself, which is intuited in all cultures as another, ultimate form of meeting. Nothing stops our ageing nor our witness to time, asking us again and again to be present to each different present, to be touchable and findable, to be one who is living up to the very fierce consequences of being bodily present in the world.

To forge an untouchable, invulnerable identity is actually a sign of retreat from this world; of weakness, a sign of fear rather than strength and betrays a strange misunderstanding of an abiding, foundational and necessary reality: that untouched, we disappear."

—David Whyte

sensations of the out-flowing breath, and at the bottom of the exhalation, tune again into a moment of mindfulness of your body.

AWARENESS SWEEP

Another way to strengthen body mindfulness is by sweeping your awareness throughout your body, part by part. Begin at the top of your head, and as you breathe, allow your inhalations to focus your attention in this region. Simply be aware of any sensations or vibrations that you experience here. Then allow your mindful attention to travel down, noticing any sensations or vibrations at the back of your head, on either side of your head, or around your face. Whatever you notice, you're simply aware of, with no judgments.

Now, allow your mindfulness to gently sweep down into your neck and throat...as you breathe, your mindfulness travels across into your shoulders. Then allow your mindfulness to move through your right **arm,** traveling down from the shoulder to the fingertips, and then down through your left arm to your fingertips. Become mindful of your chest and rib cage, and then your abdomen and back...and then gradually sweeping this wave of mindfulness down into and through your hips, buttocks, and genitals. And then sweeping it down through your legs one at a time or both together...being mindful of your thighs...and then of your knees...Don't forget your ankles and feet, and finally your toes.

When you reach your toes, smile, breathe, and focus your attention once again at the top of your head. Again let your awareness move and scan through your body, lighting up each part of your body with awareness.

As you sweep your awareness through your body, welcome whatever comes to your attention. If what you encounter is pleasurable or painful, let those feelings flow into and through your awareness of the present, ever-changing moment. Let your mindfulness pass through your body like a warm wave passing through an ice field, allowing any places of holding or tightness to release. Let your mindfulness sweep through your body like a magnet passing over a pile of jumbled iron filings. With each pass through your body, feel your energies beginning to align and to flow more smoothly and harmoniously. As you learn to listen to your body, it will reveal a treasury of insights to you.

NOTICING YOUR THOUGHTS

Having built a foundation of mindfulness with your breath and body, the next base of mindfulness to develop is that of thinking. According to

"Mindfulness is the practice of aiming your attention, moment to moment, in the direction of your purpose. It is called mindfulness because you have to keep your purpose in mind as you watch your attention. Then, whenever you notice that your aim has drifted off, you calmly realign it."

—Frank Andrews

"Awareness in itself is healing."

—Fritz Pearls

some researchers, the average person has nearly 20,000 thoughts each day and ninety percent of those thoughts are "reruns" of thoughts we've already had before!

You can learn to simply and heartfully watch the changing images and listen to the endless flow of inner voices, without needing to get involved in them. However, this is not as easy as it sounds. If you're like most people, you've spent your whole life identifying with these voices, and struggling with them without really considering that these thoughts are only thoughts, and they really have little power over you unless you give it to them. Your real source of balance lies in remembering that you are more than the chatter that you hear in your head. You are also the presence of mind that knows these thoughts, as well as the space of awareness in which all these many thoughts coalesce and dissolve. When we hold our thoughts lightly, like wispy cloud formations dancing in a deep clear sky of mind, we are able to see through them to the creative intelligence that underlies and sustains them.

You can choose which thoughts or voices to follow and which ones to merely let pass by with mindfulness and a compassionate, patient smile. This smile will protect you from taking any of these voices too seriously, trying too hard, or being too judgmental, as you learn to sit quietly by the stream of your mind. Here are a series of exercises to increase your mindfulness of thoughts.

Past, Present, and Future

Begin by sitting quietly, focusing your attention with a few moments of mindful breathing. Build the strength and continuity of your attention by breathing your mindful awareness into this moment, and letting it continue as an unbroken stream of awareness into this next moment. Stay fully focused and mindfully present with each moment and each breath.

Now, rest your hands on your knees, right hand on the right knee, and left on left. As you breathe, draw your attention to the stream of your thoughts. Staying mindful of each moment, whenever you notice a thought that's a memory of the past, tap gently with your left hand, indicating to yourself that you're aware of a special kind of thought called a memory. If you like, you can anchor it by saying mentally to yourself, *past*. And whenever you notice that you're having a thought that's a fantasy of the future, then tap on your right knee and if you like, mentally note *future*. Whenever your attention is totally focused here and now in the present moment, just smile to yourself and enjoy the ride.

"This being human is a guest house.

Every morning a new arrival.

A joy, a depression, a meanness,

some momentary awareness comes as an unexpected visitor.

Welcome and entertain them all!

Even if they're a crowd of sorrows,

who violently sweep your house empty of its furniture,

still, treat each guest honorably.

He may be clearing you out for some new delight.

The dark thought, the shame, the malice,

meet them at the door laughing,

and invite them in.

Be grateful for whoever comes,

because each has been sent

as a guide from beyond."

—Mevlana Jalaluddin Rumi

As thoughts arise, just view them as clouds floating through the sky of your mind, or as different taxi cabs racing here and there in the mind. Remember not to hitch a ride on any of them! Avoid the tendency to mindlessly climb aboard and get lost in those thoughts. Simply let the thoughts come and go. Stay mindfully focused, and keep tapping your left knee for thoughts of the past and your right knee for thoughts of the future.

After a few minutes, reflect to yourself. Has your attention been drawn more to memories of the past, to fantasies or plans for the future, or balanced more in the present? Objectively, learningfully, and without criticism, simply notice which ways your attention is most drawn.

As your powers of mindfulness grow, you'll gain more and more insight into how your mind works. Understanding more and more about your patterns of attention, you'll come to a clearer recognition of the patterns of mind that you'd like to strengthen as well as the patterns of mind that you'd like to reduce.

Pleasant, Unpleasant, and Neutral

Once again now, as you watch the flow of thoughts passing through your mind, be mindful of three kinds of thoughts. When you notice judging thoughts or disliking thoughts that feel unpleasant, mark them by tapping your left knee. And when you notice experiences that trigger appreciative, pleasant thoughts or acceptance, tap your right knee. When you're neither judging nor accepting, but are merely "neutral" and present, then just sit quietly and mindfully ride the waves of the breath.

Once again, avoid the tendency to dive in and get carried away or caught up with the content of your thoughts. Simply notice and be mindful that those tendencies are activated in your thinking process. Ultimately, you'll learn to be mindful of whatever you're thinking, and by being more mindful of what you're thinking you'll be able to direct your thinking as you wish.

MINDFULNESS BRINGS UNDERSTANDING AND UNDERSTANDING CULTIVATES BALANCE

When you practice mindfulness, you begin to see clearly what is really going on inside you. As you see more clearly, you find that you can just naturally come into balance. And as you do, you come to three very important realizations about how your mind works.

"Yesterday is but a dream,

tomorrow is but a vision.

But today well lived

makes every yesterday a dream of happiness,

and every tomorrow a vision of hope.

Look well, therefore, to this day."

—Sanskrit proverb

"The real work of meditation is not so much just to calm ourselves but to find a capacity to open to the sorrows and joys and the complexity and struggles and pains and beauty of our human life in a very immediate way. Spirituality really has to do more with our humanness than with anything extraordinary."

—Jack Kornfield

The contents, qualities, and states of your mind are constantly moving and ceaselessly changing. You can no more stop this flow than you can stop a powerful river or stop the wind. And if you could stop it, it would cease to be the river, the wind, or the mind.

Within or beneath this flowing movement of mind is a deep, quiet inner stillness that is completely undisturbed by all the movement. It is a quality of presence, like the open sky, completely undisturbed by the fierce winds of thoughts, images, and feelings that blow through the mind. This sky-like presence of mind can contain any experience; it is completely unstained by any of the contents of the mind. It is always clean, clear, and open to whatever flows through it.

The movement and the stillness are both present in your mind at every moment. you can't have movement without stillness or stillness without movement. You can't have silence without sound or sound without silence.

A very wise young friend of ours named Caton explained this difficult point quite simply to his mom on the way to daycare one morning when he was about five years old. Laurie, his mother, asked him if he knew where his thoughts came from. "The thoughts come out of the quiet in my mind, Mom," Caton said quite knowingly. Mom smiled, taking his wisdom to heart, and then asked him, "Well, then where do you think the thoughts go when you are done thinking them?" With a giggle Caton replied, "They melt back into the quiet of my mind, Mom."

THE WHEEL OF MINDFULNESS

The essence of mindfulness is to be aware of what you are sensing, feeling, thinking, wanting, and intending to do at any given moment. Like any other life skill, mindfulness grows with practice. As you learn to understand how your perceptions, feelings, thoughts, desires, and intentions influence your body, your communications, and your behavior, you will feel more confident and better equipped to guide the course of your life and find balance moment to moment, day to day. The Wheel of Mindfulness offers a simple yet powerful compass for charting the course of your life.

This navigation tool helps you to discover and to describe to yourself what is true for you in each moment in each dimension of your being. By knowing what is true for yourself in terms of what you are perceiving, thinking, feeling, wanting, and intending, you will be more likely to recognize options, make wiser decisions, and to honestly and accurately communicate your experience to others. For greater clarity

"Understanding is the fruit of looking deeply...This present moment contains the past and the future. The secret of transformation at the base lies in our handling of this very moment."

—Thich Nhat Hanh

"In the Native way we are encouraged to recognize that every moment is a sacred moment, and every action, when imbued with dedication and commitment to benefit all beings, is a sacred act."

—Dhyani Ywahoo

"One instant of total awareness, is one instant of perfect freedom and enlightenment."

—Manjushri

The Wheel of Mindfulness

I
Notice
"Perceptions"

I
Will
"Intentions"

Mindful Presence

I
Feel
"Emotions"

I
Want
"Desires"

I
Think
"Stories"

"The thought manifests as the word;

The word manifests as the deed;

The deed develops into habit;

And habit hardens into character:

So watch the thought and its ways with care,

And let it spring from love

Born out of concern for all beings."

—The Buddha

"In the beginner's mind there are few possibilities.

In the master's mind there are many."

—Shunryu Suzuki Roshi

in any situation, focus the beam of your mindfulness to illuminate each of the following five domains:

I notice... Mindfulness of Perception and Action. In this moment of experience what do you notice going on? What is the raw sensory data available to you directly through the doorways of your sense perceptions—what do you see, hear, smell, touch, or taste? What you are looking to discover here is the kind of objective information that a video camera or tape recorder would pick up if they were turned on to record this experience, with no overlay of judgment or interpretation.

I feel... Mindfulness of Emotions and Feelings. How does this experience make you feel? Do you feel anxious or at ease, happy or sad, mad or glad, depressed or excited? What words best describe the emotional tone of your experience in this moment? Be watchful of the tendency to respond by saying "I feel that..." Adding the word *that* after *I feel* probably indicates that you're moving into thinking and judging rather than staying with your actual emotional response.

I think... Mindfulness of Thinking, Thoughts, and Imagination. What are your thoughts or "internal conversations" about your experience? Are you creatively thinking about a situation, or are you merely replaying old thoughts? What is the story you're telling yourself about a situation—your thoughts, fantasies, and assumptions? Recognizing the old stories helps you to live in a more grounded way and liberates you from mistaking your thoughts and assumptions for reality!

I **want…**Mindfulness of Values, Intentions, and Desires. What are your values, intentions, and motivations? What do you really want or need? Having clarity on your values, desires, intentions, and motivations is essential for effective communication and action.

I **will…**Moving Mindfulness into Action. What action are you willing to take in this situation? What are you unwilling to do? What are you willing to stop doing? Bringing mindfulness across the threshold of awareness into the domain of conscious action is the key to transformation. When you consider and then communicate to others what you are and are not willing to do, you become a conscious co-creator of your experience, rather than being unconsciously enslaved to it. And remember, your actions and inactions speak more loudly than your words. Be mindful of the impact that all your communications have on others.

FOUR DIMENSIONS OF MINDFULNESS

One wonderful way of introducing mindfulness in organizational settings, presented in the next diagram, outlines four dimensions of mindfulness and seven steps or stages to the practice. Once you learn the architecture of this practice, your sessions can be very brief, moving through each stage rather quickly, or you can be very thorough, diving deeply into each phase, and giving each step a fuller amount of time.

The four dimensions of mindfulness are:

*   **1st Dimension:** Mindful of the flow of sights, sounds, and impressions from the world around you
*   **2nd Dimension:** Mindful of the flow of feelings and sensations in the body
*   **3rd Dimension:** Mindful of the flow of thoughts and mental images
*   **4th Dimension:** Resting in Awareness: Mindful Clear Presence

In teaching this mindfulness practice, we find it helpful to mark the transition between each phase of the practice by softly sounding the syllable "Ahhh))) ." This sound serves to note the shift in the focus of attention, while helping to open and relax the mind. The vocalization also anchors this mind training in our embodiment. As you move through this sequence of steps, abide in each step for as long as it is interesting and easy to maintain your mindfulness there, and then, when your interest or focus begins to wane, move on to the next step.

"Awareness is like a beam of light that shines endlessly into space. We only perceive that light when it is reflected off some object and consciousness is produced...Awareness is the light by which we see the world... We mistake the clear light of pure awareness for the shadows that it casts in consciousness... We forget that we are the light itself and imagine that we are the densities that reflect the light back to us."

—Stephen Levine

Step One: As you begin, reach up and touch your heart in a gesture of coming back to your senses. As you touch your heart, gently smile to yourself with mercy and compassion as you return again to the sweet territory of Mindful Clear Presence. With the sound Ahhh))), mark the initiation of this practice and open the field of your senses to welcome and embrace the flow of sights, sounds, and impressions from the world around you. Be mindful of how each sensory experience comes and flows, arises and passes within the clear open space of awareness.

Step Two: Ahhh))) Remaining deeply grounded in the awareness of the space around you, now open the field of your mindful presence to embrace the changing flow of feelings and sensations pulsing and streaming through your body. Notice how each sensate experience comes and flows, arising and passing within the clear open space of awareness.

Step Three: Ahhh))) Shift your mindful awareness now to focus on the movement of thoughts and mental images streaming in the clear space of your mind like so many clouds or winds passing through the vast sky undisturbed by their movement. Be mindful of how each of these mental experiences comes and flows, arises and passes, within the clear open spaciousness of awareness.

Step Four: Ahhh))) Simply rest here in the Clear Presence of Mindful Awareness, having arrived home to the most subtle, clear, and essential dimension of your being. This ground of awareness is your true home. Rest here for as long as you like. Be nourished, inspired, and renewed by touching this deep essential dimension of your true being.

Step Five: Ahhh))) Remaining deeply grounded in and connected to this dimension of mindful clear presence, as the active mind begins to stir, with an Ahhh))) open your field of awareness to once again welcome and embrace the arising and passing of thoughts and mental images within the clear open space of awareness.

Step Six: Ahhh))) Remaining deeply grounded in the dimension of mindful clear presence, as you expand your field of awareness to once again welcome and embrace the flow of sensations and vibrations within the body as they arise and pass in the clear open space of your awareness.

Step Seven: Ahhh))) Remaining deeply grounded in the deep ground of mindful clear presence, as you expand your field of awareness to once again welcome and embrace the flow of sensory experiences streaming to you and through you from the world around you. All these too simply arise and pass in the clear open space of awareness.

"If you just sit and observe, you will see how restless your mind is, if you try to calm it, it only makes it worse, but over time it does calm, and when it does, there's room to hear more subtle things—that's when your intuition starts to blossom and you start to see things more clearly and be in the present more. Your mind just slows down, and you see a tremendous expanse in the moment. You see so much more than you could see before. It's a discipline; you have to practice it."

—Steve Jobs

Dimensions of Mindfulness

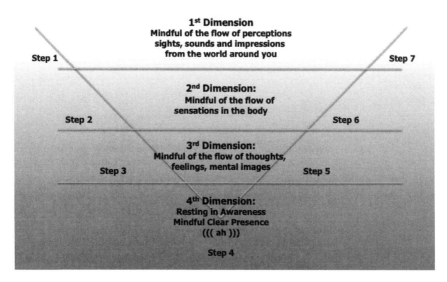

1st Dimension
Mindful of the flow of perceptions
sights, sounds and impressions
from the world around you

Step 1   Step 7

2nd Dimension:
Mindful of the flow of
sensations in the body

Step 2   Step 6

3rd Dimension:
Mindful of the flow of thoughts,
feelings, mental images

Step 3   Step 5

4th Dimension:
Resting in Awareness
Mindful Clear Presence
(((ah)))

Step 4

With this final Ahhh))) affirm the unity and integration of all of the dimensions of your being, embracing the full spectrum of your experience in all its many waveforms, frequencies, and nuances.

Also with this final Ahhh))) envision that you can expand the sphere of your influence to dedicate and share any of the positive feelings or qualities of being that have been cultivated, refined, and activated through this practice. Imagine that you can dedicate all this positive energy like streams of light or nectar that flow into the continuum of your being, that you might be more fully present as your journey of awakening continues. Envision that you can let the light of these positive qualities flow from your heart into the hearts of all your loved ones and friends, your colleagues and coworkers, and to beings everywhere that they too may live in greater harmony and balance and awaken to the full dimensions of their true being.

BALANCING CLEAR PRESENCE
AND GREAT COMPASSION

For some people the practice of mindfulness in and of itself can sometimes seem a bit sterile, stark, or dry. Many teachers recognize this and

"The human brain is a highly differentiated form through which consciousness enters this dimension. It contains approximately one hundred billion nerve cells (called neurons), about the same number as there are stars in our galaxy, which could be seen as a macrocosmic brain. The brain does not create consciousness, but consciousness creates the brain, the most complex physical form on earth, for its expression."

—Eckhart Tolle

emphasize that, properly understood, a deeper harmonic of mindfulness also brings forth the quality of great compassion.

Decades ago when we began inviting people to touch their hearts as a gesture of bringing more warmth and compassion into their mindfulness practice, there were no other teachers whom we had met who taught this way. In recent years we have noticed that this simple symbolic gesture of connecting deeply with ourselves is being more commonly integrated into mindfulness instruction by many other teachers now as well.

Here are two practices that we teach to balance mindfulness with heartfelt compassion.

The first is an integrative mindfulness practice that is inspired by our study with Joanna Macy, who calls this technique "breathing through." While the instructions are quite simple, the effects can be quite profound:

> Mindfully resting in the easy, natural flow of the breath, allow the stream of your experience to flow through, or be filtered through, your heart center. If you like, you can gently touch your heart as you begin in a gesture of affirming that you are in touch with the flow of your experience in a compassionate and open-hearted manner. In this way, cultivate and affirm the inseparability of clear mindful presence, compassion, and great love.

A second simple yet powerful method for practicing mindfulness with compassion weaves in three embodied anchors for mindfulness that are synchronized with three focusing phrases. The focusing phrases are:

Clear Presence...
Embracing the Flow of Experience...
With Great Compassion

In the practice, each of these focusing phrases is synchronized with the phases of the natural flow of breathing, and with the following three embodied gestures:

- Mentally thinking or saying, "Clear Presence," sense or touch your heart.
- Mentally thinking or saying, "Embracing the Flow of Experience," be mindful of the sensations of the natural flow of your breathing,

"In all the Asian languages, the word for mind and the word for heart is the same word. If you see the mind and heart are the same, then compassion is built right into it. Mindful attention is itself affectionate. It's open, spacious, curious, and in the seeing of the interconnectedness, then compassion arises naturally, as there is no separation. Wisdom is the knowing of no separation, and compassion is the feeling of no separation."

—Jon Kabat-Zinn

as well as any other physical or mental experiences that are arising and passing in the clear space of your awareness.
- Mentally thinking or saying, "With Great Compassion," open your heart to yourself with the gesture of an inner, heartwarming smile. Allow this gentle smile to be a gesture of balance that helps you keep your heart open and protects you from being too self-critical or judgmental. The combination of this phrase together with the smile invites a feeling of tenderness that can counteract a tendency to create physical and mental tension and imbalance by meditating with too much effort or in too tight a way.

As you practice in this way, each breath becomes an expression of

- Clear Presence (with the inhalation)
- Embracing the flow of experience
- With Great Compassion (on the exhalation)

Or even more simply,

- Clear Presence (inhaling)
- Great Compassion (exhaling)

We breathe in 21,600 times a day…and we breathe out…With each breath, this simple practice can deepen, affirm, and refine the balance of wisdom and compassion that we bring to our lives and our world. This can be practiced while sitting quietly or carried into action as you move with the breath throughout your daily life.

MINDFUL DIALOGUE: EXPLORING BALANCE THROUGH COMMUNICATION

So much joy and suffering comes through how we communicate, so learning to practice mindful dialogue is a vital skill for living in balance. It's also one of the best ways to develop and deepen your mindfulness practice. Since most people have dozens of conversations each day, engaging in some percent of those conversations in an intentionally mindful manner is a great way to develop and strengthen your mindfulness muscles. The spirit and practice of mindful dialogue can be understood through the following series of gestures and images:

First, reach out with both hands and imagine that this indicates that all of your attention is focused outwardly toward other people and

"It is only with the heart

that one can see clearly,

for what is essential

Is hidden from the eyes."

—Antoine de St. Exupéry

"We cannot do great things in life;

we can only do small things with great love."

—Mother Teresa

the world around you, and that in this mode you are not really in touch with or deeply listening to yourself.

Second, bring both hands to your heart in a gesture that indicates that you are really in touch with yourself, mindful of your thoughts, feelings, etc., but in this mode of internal focus your attention to what is going on with others or in the world around you is minimal.

Next, leave one hand at your heart as an anchor and affirmation of maintaining a deep mindful connectedness with yourself—you know what is true for you and what you are perceiving, feeling, thinking, wanting, and willing to do. And, with your other hand, reach out and imagine that this hand expands the radius of your attention out to be mindful of others and the world around you.

The key now is to hold this gesture of balance as you engage in a mindful dialogue with someone. Notice the tendency for your attention to be pulled out and become totally engrossed in what the other person is saying, or to implode into your own internal process. See which is stronger for you, and what it takes to find a balance to be present both for yourself and for your conversation partner. This gesture of balance and mindfulness invites you to explore what it is like to be in touch and deeply listening in a mutual and reciprocal way—both to yourself and to whomever you are talking with. As your conversation continues, practice maintaining this balance of mindful awareness of what is taking place inside you—what you are feeling, thinking, and wanting, etc.—while being completely present, open, connected, and attentive to your partner. Notice how and when you drift out of, and then return back to the interplay of this dynamic balance. Let this symbolic gesture of balance integrate mindfulness of your own inner experience, as well as a vivid, clear, deeply attuned mindfulness to the presence and flow of energy and information streaming from your partner. Also, keep in mind that the actual physical gesture is merely a tool to help you learn to remember and maintain this balance of inner and outer awareness. Once you have learned to tune your mindfulness in this way, then the actual physical gesture becomes an optional reminder in the role of an embodied metaphor.

Mindful dialogue can be practiced with others who share the intention to be fully present in this way, or you can simply set your own intention to be mindfully present in dialogue with anyone with whom you are talking, even if they aren't aware of your mindful intention. Odds are that even if people have no idea that you are practicing mindful dialogue, they will be grateful for the quality of your presence and deep listening.

"Do whatever it takes to contribute your gifts, talents, and skills not to 'saving the planet' but to awakening all beings to their true nature, and to their inherent goodness."

—Michael Bernard
 Beckwith

Here are some simple guidelines for your practice of mindful dialogue:

1. As you prepare to initiate a conversation, set your intention to be fully present and mindful with yourself and your partner.

2. As you engage in this exchange, stay attuned to the fine balance of mindfulness to your inner experience and mindful of your partner. You can also use the Wheel of Mindfulness as a guide to tune in more deeply to what you are Noticing, Feeling, Thinking, Wanting, or Intending in your dialogue, as well as the principles of R.A.I.N. to Recognize, Accept, Investigate, and Not identify with the flow of energy and information streaming to you and through you in this dialogue.

3. If or when your attention wanders, notice the excursion into distraction or mindlessness, and return to being mindful of yourself and your partner.

4. As your dialogue comes to completion, pause for a moment to mindfully notice the reverberations of this close encounter with "another myself," and appreciate how this experience lives in your body... the emotions that are most present and alive within you... and the thoughts or words related to this experience that are streaming through your mind...

Now that you know how to bring this extraordinary quality of mindful presence into your interactions with people, can you imagine how many opportunities you can find each day to deepen your experience of balance and expand your practice of mindfulness through conscious moments of mindful dialogue?

"If I want to transform what is happening globally, then I have to look within myself and see where I am separating myself from other human beings and from the earth. Where am I living in blame, in hate, in terrorism, in any negative capacity toward another being? For if I am not willing to clean up the fear or the disconnect that is within myself, then I am responsible for what is happening on a planetary level."

—Sean Corn

A Mindful Week in Review

Here's another useful technique you can use to help you stay mindfully in balance every day. First, pick one day a week to set aside some time for mindful reflection on the larger picture of your life. Even a few minutes with the following questions can make a big difference in restoring your sense of balance:

* What have I been paying the most attention to in my life this week?
* What elements of my experience are calling for greater attention?
* What specific activities do I want to bring greater awareness to?

- How will becoming more aware improve the quality of my life, my relationships, and my work?
- What indicators have reminded me that I had drifted off into mindlessness?

By giving yourself the gift of a few minutes each week to evaluate the level of awareness that you're bringing to the things that matter most to you, you'll be able to fine-tune and reset your attention patterns before you get too far off course. Then once a month, enjoy a special "day of mindfulness" celebration. On the day of the month that corresponds to your birthday, invite yourself to mindfully explore something new and different. Even for a little while that day, do something, in some way, that you've never done before. The freshness of mind that you bring to experiencing something for the first time is a good way to refresh your taste of mindfulness!

HARMONICS OF MINDFULNESS

While mindfulness teachings in the West are usually offered in a very secular approach, the value of mindfulness is a universal theme found in all Eastern and Western wisdom traditions.

In Western traditions, mindfulness is often associated with devotional practices in which we walk with God as our constant companion within us, or apprehend the presence of God. It has been described as looking at the world with the eyes of Christ's love, or as walking with Jesus by our side or within our deepest self at all times. In many Christian contemplative traditions, practicing the presence of God is a core and essential practice and an encouraged way of life.

In Jewish kabbalah the idea that creation is continually renewing itself moment-to-moment helps us bring a sense of wonder and awe into every moment, inviting each moment to be one of discovery and revelation. The experience of the Shechina, "the indwelling presence of the Divine," offers an intimate glimpse of the sacred nature of mindfulness as a means of dwelling or abiding within the presence of God.

In Islam, a key teaching is to be ever mindful of Allah, and the mindfulness of spiritual excellence is to shield oneself from heedlessness and distraction through complete turning to Allah Most High.

Each of these traditions offers a facet of the jewel of ancient, sacred harmonics of mindfulness that raise our level of consciousness and open our minds to behold our world in its infinite interconnectedness and dimensionality.

"In Western traditions, mindfulness is associated with devotional practices in which the Divine is a constant companion within us. In Christianity, the practice is having Jesus by our side at all times. In Judaism, the Kabalistic idea that creation is taking place in each and every moment brings an acute sensitivity to everything. All of these ideas can be practiced to raise our level of awareness and induce an entirely new perspective, seeing things 'as they really are.'"

—Rabbi David Cooper

VARIETIES OF MINDFULNESS PRACTICE

Just as there are many ways to make soup, there are a wide variety of ways to teach and practice mindfulness.

While the practice of presence is treasured and cultivated in all of the world's great wisdom traditions, the mindfulness practices that are most commonly taught and researched today have their roots in lineages of practice that come to the West from Thailand, Sri Lanka, and Burma.

Some traditions of mindfulness training use simple instructions to rest in "pure awareness" or "choiceless awareness" or "bare attention," or "clear presence."

Some mindfulness teachers or traditions use "focusing phrases" or "gathas" as an aid to strengthen concentration by coordinating these phrases with the rhythm and flow of the breath.

Some methods of mindfulness practice coordinate movements with the flow of breath and the flow of awareness.

Still other styles of mindfulness practice guide the practitioner to sweep awareness through the body part by part, or focus on a succession of different bandwidths of embodied experience.

Each of these approaches has its virtues and benefits for learning how to be mindful and how to live in greater harmony and balance. Each serves to balance the observing mind with the experiencing mind, and strengthen the integration of different functions of the mind, and regions of the brain that are vital to well-being and balance. Being familiar with a variety of mindfulness styles and practices provides a more expansive and balanced view of mindfulness training, and prevents one from becoming too rigid regarding what is the "correct" or "true way" to practice mindfulness. In practice, the key is to be clear about your intention in any given session, and to be clear regarding which of these many approaches you will engage in.

In the pages that follow, we'll offer a glimpse of some of our favorite and most universally useful mindfulness practices. We have taught these to tens of thousands of people in hundreds of communities, organizations, businesses, medical centers, military bases, sports arenas, and universities around the globe, and in each case people have affirmed the universal value to weaving such practices for living with greater wisdom, compassion, and balance into their lives. In this spirit, we invite you to experiment with each of these methods in the laboratory of your own life, work, and relationships, and to see for yourself which of these approaches are most resonant and useful for you at this time in your life's journey of living in balance.

"How do we know
if our practice is
a real practice?

Only by one thing:
more and more, we
just see the wonder.

What is the wonder?
I don't know.

We can't know
such things
through thinking.

But we always know
it when it's there."

—Charlotte Joko Beck

BRINGING THE MIND HOME

The cultivation of mindfulness is a lifelong process. Here are some useful distinctions to remember as you begin to integrate this essential practice for balance:

- Self-awareness is not the same as self-centeredness. When I am truly aware of myself, I am more in touch with everything around me, more available and sensitive. In fact, I can be more spacious and relaxed, and less self-protective.
- I can be aware of others only to the degree that I am willing to be aware of myself.
- Mindfulness requires being fully present, here and now. Because it is easy to drift into memories of the past or fantasies of the future, the pursuit of awareness in the "here and now" calls for practice and dedication. As we often say to our clients: "You can only manage the moment!" Every moment is an opportunity to increase your awareness.

A good place to begin is exactly where you are. So right now, begin by bringing your mind home from wherever it may be straying. When the mind comes home, it becomes present and peaceful. With mindfulness, right now, you are aware that you are seeing these words, and may even smile to yourself with delight as you know that you know. You are aware of the texture and weight of the book in your hands, or of the thoughts and associations triggered by reading these words.

Outwardly, be aware of your surroundings. Notice what you see and hear in the world around you. Then, drawing your attention inward, first tune into what's most real and true for you as a physical being right now. Mindfully sense your position and posture. Quietly observe the natural movement and flow of your breathing.

One helpful technique here, suggested by Vietnamese monk Thich Nhat Hanh, is to mentally add the words "arriving" as you breathe in, and "home" as you breathe out, silently letting these words guide you into a steady focus on the present-moment balancing of your own rhythmic breathing. Arriving...Home...Your mental energy will gradually begin to settle and stabilize in this way, with the calming, balancing effect of mindful breathing. Then direct your mindful attention to the flow of sensations and vibrations moving within and through your body.

Stress is caused by being 'here' but wanting to be 'there'."

—Eckhart Tolle

Next, open the focus of your attention to mindfully observe the flow of your thoughts, your internal conversations, and the emotional feelings that color this moment of your life. Simply, effortlessly, easily bring your mind home to focus and rest within yourself. Dwell in the calm, clarity, and peace of mind that's always here, mindfully observing the flow of experiences.

Having brought your attention back to yourself as home base, now you can open and expand your attention to reach back out into your world again. As you do this, maintain your awareness of your thoughts, feelings, breath, and body…mindfully present and balanced, focused and flowing from moment to moment.

Mindfulness is not some strange abstract or imaginary exercise. It's a proactive way to bring your life alive and in balance, and to discover what is real and true for you. As we have been saying, because you can change only what you're aware of, mindfulness lays the foundation for living in greater balance and harmony. With a clearer, more objective, and appreciative view of your current reality, you'll be better able to recognize and evaluate your options for moving forward. By helping you stay focused on what you are doing and thinking, and helping you recognize when you may be getting off track, the power of mindfulness helps continuously to counteract the tendency to get out of balance.

"This moment, clearly seen, deeply felt, opens a portal to infinite wisdom, compassion, and wonder."

—Joel and
   Michelle Levey

chapter five

The Science of Balance

"It is good to have an end to journey toward;
but it is the journey that matters in the end."

— URSULA K. LEGUIN

AS WE HAVE BEGUN TO SEE, WE ARE ALL LIVING SYSTEMS, COMPLEX interactions of energy-information that we freely and effectively exchange in relationship with our environment. As "open" living systems, we are also endowed with the capacity for homeostasis, which, like a thermostat, allows us to maintain balance within healthy limits. Derived from the Greek word meaning "to keep the same," the term encompasses the interplay of all the systems necessary to preserve and maintain the constant conditions of life.

The principle of homeostasis is evident in our bodies, our minds, and in the world in which we live. For example, as long as you are alive, the internal temperature of your body will remain at approximately 98.6 degrees Fahrenheit, through a complex system of energy conservation and dissipation. Though you may be subject to environmental temperature changes of more than a hundred degrees, unless you are ill, it is unlikely that your internal temperature will vary more than a degree or two. When you are hot, your pores dilate, you perspire and cool off. When you are cold, your body warms itself by shivering and physical activity. Every system of your body is balanced with homeostatic wisdom: regulating the chemistry of your bloodstream, the functioning of your digestion, the repair and replacement of old or injured tissue. Neurological, biochemical, and energy systems function interdependently to maintain the dynamic balance that you call your life. The good news is that we are made for balance—it's our natural state!

Balance in the world around us is maintained in a similarly miraculous way. Like any other "living being," the earth has its own homeostatic mechanisms. The Gaia hypothesis, formulated through the painstaking research of James Lovelock, has helped many people come to look upon the earth itself as a self-regulating, living system. (In Greek mythology, Gaia was the personification of the Earth, one of the Greek primordial deities.) By arranging a sensitive balance of atmosphere, oceans, and soil, and by absorbing and dissipating the energy of the sun, the intelligence of Gaia maintains the delicate planetary homeostasis necessary for life to thrive. A few examples will help us appreciate these exquisitely intricate balancing processes.

Though life can exist between the extreme ranges of 20 and 220 degrees Fahrenheit, it flourishes between 60 and 100 degrees. Gaia has managed to maintain this as an average temperature for hundreds of millions of years.

The mystery of balance upon the earth is also evident in Gaia's regulation of the amount of salt in the ocean. Despite eons of dramatic changes in weather patterns and sea levels, geological evidence indicates that the oceans have remained relatively constant at about 3.4 percent salinity. If this concentration were to rise to 4 percent, life as we know it would be much different. If it were to rise to 6 percent, even for a few minutes, all ocean life would be extinguished by the disintegration of cell walls at such a high concentration of salt. The oceans of the world would become as barren as the Dead Sea.

In physics, the second law of thermodynamics says that entropy tends to increase, so that ordered systems run down and become more chaotic and disorganized over time. Mountains wash to the sea, suns burn themselves out and explode, the energy potential of a rock at the top of a mountain exhausts itself as it rolls into the valley, buildings and bridges and books like this turn to dust over the ages. Though we might say that this entropic dissolution describes our life pretty well, the existence of life in the universe flies in the face of this "law." Living systems don't just run down. Entropy is not the only factor describing the evolution of systems in nature. Entropy and energy in the form of enthalpy together determine balance, which in chemical systems is called equilibrium. This balance is dynamic rather than static, as evidenced by a sugar crystal in water. A slight shift in temperature can favor dissolution or crystallization, but both processes are always occurring. Not all systems

"Gaia's main problems are not industrialization, ozone depletion, over-population, or resource depletion. Gaia's main problem is the lack of mutual understanding and mutual agreement... about how to proceed with those problems. We cannot reign in industry if we cannot reach mutual understanding and mutual agreement based on a worldcentric moral perspective concerning the global commons. And we reach that worldcentric moral perspective through a difficult and laborious process of interior growth and transcendence."

—Ken Wilber

"We are part of a vast web of interconnected species, that it is the biosphere, the zone of air, water and land, where all life exists. It's a very thin layer around the planet. Carl Sagan told us that if you shrink the Earth to the size of a basketball, the biosphere, the zone of air, water and land, where all life exists, would be thinner than a layer of Saran Wrap, and that's it. That's our home, but it's home to 10 to 30 thousand—30 million other species that keep the planet habitable. And if we don't see that we are utterly embedded in the natural world and dependent on nature, not technology, not economics, not science—we're dependent on Mother Nature for our very well-being and survival. If we don't see that, then our priorities will continue to be driven by man-made constructs like national borders, economies, corporations, markets. Those are all human-created things. They shouldn't dominate the way we live. It should be the biosphere."

—David Suzuki

attain equilibrium because the approach to chemical balance is too slow at room temperature. This is a blessing because equilibrium for us would turn our marvelously complex body mainly into carbon dioxide, water, and a small pile of ashes!

Living systems are miraculous in that they continually renew themselves by reaching out beyond themselves to take in the stuff of the universe and transform themselves. Through photosynthesis, plants take in sunlight, carbon dioxide, and nutrients from the soil, and create new forms and structures through their growth. Animals take in food, water, and information, then grow, learn, and transform themselves and their world. For life to exist, a circle of unimaginable complexity and subtlety must remain unbroken. Countless factors within and between living beings and their environment must continually adjust to the changing flow on many levels within the whole.

As living beings, we too are subject to this same flow and our lives depend on learning ways to respond and adapt to the unrelenting challenges of our world. To live we must maintain ourselves—our general shape, form, functions, and identity—while all the time adapting, taking in, and releasing information from our environment to adjust to the changing flow of life. Our health and vitality reflect our ability to manage both the intensity of such change in our lives—and how we assimilate it. We tend to forget, however, that the true nature of life is based in fluidity, interconnectedness, and mystery. To the degree that we live or think in terms of a static, separate, controllable world, our confusion sets us up for frustration and suffering. Considerable evidence suggests that the rate of change in our work is rapidly speeding up, which may account for some of our frantic, panicked, out of control feelings. As the rate of change increases, our harmony, health, sanity, balance, and safety are not to be found in holding on more tightly, or by becoming more rigid or controlling. Our ability to control the environment is limited, and the wise ones among us have learned to stop exhausting themselves by trying to control the river of change. Rather, they focus their efforts on increasing their mental, emotional, and physical capacities to harmonize with the intensity offered by their encounters with the outer world. Have faith that with practice, you can learn to do this too.

Looking deeply into the nature of our world today, we can understand how essential it is that we learn to raise the level of our personal and collective wisdom to bring greater balance to our lives. After decades of tolerating and justifying unwise practices of treating our oceans and atmosphere as a disposal site for pollutants that poison our world and destabilize our atmosphere, we have CO_2 in the atmosphere at over 400 parts per million and on the rise. Our climate is becoming increasingly chaotic and unpredictable, fueling a multitude of global crises. We can see how a myriad of complex and interrelated factors involving human consciousness, lack of wisdom, greed for profits to be made from continuing to pollute the atmosphere, disaster capitalism that profits from catastrophe, lack of political will to impose regulations and develop renewable and sustainable resources are all at play in unbalancing and shaping our world today.

BALANCE, INTEGRATION, AND WELLNESS

The complex circumstances and relationships of our lives constantly remind us that the path of living in balance is certainly not a solitary endeavor. People who are out of balance have a tendency to generously share their imbalances in ways that ripple out into the lives of other people in their lives and world. Similarly, people who are centered, kind, fully present, and living close to a healthy dynamic balance in their lives will generate a field of influence, benefit, and blessings for many people and other living beings.

To fully understand the primary dimensions of living in balance, a simple yet profound model integrating wisdom and insight from numerous scientific disciplines has been distilled through the brilliant work of Daniel Siegel, M.D., a pioneer in the field of interpersonal neurobiology at U.C.L.A. Siegel's "Triangle of Well-Being" has three deeply interrelated elements that are regarded as essential aspects of the whole:

* Coherent Mind—an emergent process that arises from within the system of energy and information flowing within and between people. The mind functions to regulate the flow of energy and information.

"Resilience is the maintenance of high levels of positive affect and well-being in the face of adversity. It is not that resilient individuals never experience negative affect, but rather that the negative affect does not persist.

—Richard J. Davidson

- Integrated Brain (including the extended nervous system spread throughout the whole body) — the structural, embodied mechanism of energy and information flow transmitted through neural nets and feedback loops throughout the whole body.
- Attuned Relationships — the ways we share energy and information flow.

According to Siegel, "the triangle depicts one unified complex system, the system of energy and information flow, as it passes through the mechanism of the body (brain), is shared (relationships), and is regulated (mind) across time." Integration — the linkage of differentiated elements — is the definition of a healthy system. A healthy mind, a healthy brain, and healthy relationships all emerge from such integration. As Siegel explains:

- The well-regulated brain coordinates and balances its function through linking and integrating its diverse parts.
- Healthy relationships thrive with empathic communication that honors differences and cultivates compassionate connection.
- Through embodied and relational integration, a coherent inner mental life emerges, and this further integration is reflected in greater resilience, mental health, and well-being.
- Health and well-being essentially emerge from a balanced and integrated brain, empathic and connected relationships, and a coherent, resilient mind."

We can also appreciate how when integration is compromised and vital connections are disrupted or prevented within us or between us, the quality of our mental and physical balance and interpersonal harmony quickly erodes and disintegrates. As we move away from balance we gravitate towards more rigidly locked down or chaotic states of being. Taken to extremes, such rigidity and chaos are associated with traumas in relationships or deficits in neural integration, and may manifest as psychiatric disorders such as neglect, depression, manic-depressive illness, schizophrenia, or autism.

Taken to heart, the wisdom of the Triangle of Well-Being can inspire you with optimism in moving toward greater healing, wholeness, and balanced integration. Viewing your life as a learning adventure you can empower yourself by actively seeking out and discovering new dimensions of freedom, expanded ranges of tolerance, and more easeful, balanced, and rewarding ways of life that enhance the integration, health, vitality, and balance of your mind, brain, and relationships.

Life should be touched, not strangled. You've got to relax, let it happen at times, and at others move forward with it."

—Ray Bradbury

As we apply these principles to our own lives and experience inspiring results, our confidence and skills will grow in expanding this learning to develop more integrative linkages with others in ways that can encourage the emergence of greater harmony and balance in our personal and professional relationships, our organizations and community, and our society as a whole.

Though each person has their unique challenges to health, harmony, and balance, each person also has an innate inclination or longing to gravitate toward greater integration, harmony, and wholeness. Though the approaches we take to this are sometimes misinformed, self-sabotaging, or counter productive, the potential for radical positive transformation is ever present. One of the most rewarding experiences we've had in all of our studies, travels, and work with people over the years has been witnessing the transformation and healing that has been possible for our friends, colleagues, and students who began their journey with seemingly insurmountable challenges. To see these same people years or decades later more balanced, happy, and whole, in good health and with loving relationships, has been a source of great joy and inspiration.

Translating the Triangle of Well-Being into how we view and live our lives, we come to realize that our minds emerge not merely from our nervous systems, but are fed and shaped by the streams of myriad of influences flowing to us and through us from our relationships and interactions with other people. The state and functions of our mind, and the structure and functioning of our brain/nervous system are shaped not only through these social interactions, but also by our built environment and our natural world. People who look at the night sky or spend time in nature each day, are generally happier and less stressed than people who are confined to indoor built environments, or glued to their personal devices.

We once received a call from a group of Japanese Employee Assistance Program professionals who provided emergency services to over a hundred thousand people in organizations throughout Japan. Their work was incredibly demanding and they themselves were burned out and in danger of *karoshi*, death from overwork. They had heard of our work and called to ask if they could fly to Hawaii for just three days to have a *Living in Balance* retreat for their team. We thanked them for their interest in our work and their sensibility in wanting to make time for such learning, rest, and renewal. We then took a firm stand and said, "No, you can't just come for three days. You'll be totally exhausted and after flying all this way, you won't have the time to dive deep enough into this work to realize the renewal that

"We perceive the environment and adjust our biology, but not all of our perceptions are accurate. If we are laboring under misperceptions, then those misperceptions provide for a misadjustment of our biology. When our perceptions are inaccurate we can actually destroy our biology. When we understand that genes are just respondents to the environment from the perceptions handled by the cell membrane, then we can realize that if life isn't going well, what we have to do is not change our genes but change our perceptions. That is much easier to do than physically altering the body. In fact, this is the power of the new biology: we can control our lives by controlling our perceptions."

—Bruce Lipton

you need. You need to come for longer." We finally agreed that they could come for five days and set about our preparations.

The night before their departure from Japan, the leader of the organization was admitted to the hospital with a "stress attack" and was too weak to join the team for this experience, so the rest of the team came without him. Once here with us on the Island, surrounded by natural beauty, orchards, bamboo groves, and vast views, each day allowed another layer of stress and tension to wash away. Walking barefoot in the grass...picking fruit from the trees...eating food harvested from the garden...gazing at stars in the night sky playing with our dog... for the first time in years these colleagues who virtually never saw the sky as they traveled from apartment building to underground transit straight into office buildings, witnessed firsthand the transformational power of the natural world.

We spent many hours in dialogue and reflection, connecting more deeply with ourselves, with each other, and with the natural world. Not only did we have amazing adventures exploring the beaches, mountains, and valleys of the Island, but we also offered a wealth of guidance and skills for exploring and discovering the value of taking more "time in" to reflect and connect more deeply with themselves. Through this process of connecting more deeply with themselves, with each other, and their world, vital linkages, appreciations, insights, and well-being naturally emerged. They realized that to really care for and serve the hundreds of thousands of people who looked to them, they really did need to care more wisely, deeply, and consistently for themselves.

At the end of their visit, they left transformed, balanced, optimistic, and well equipped with the integrative skills they would need to strengthen the coherence of their minds, the integration of the brains, and the attunement of their relationships. Our colleagues discovered that the key to living in balance was really to wake up and be more fully present, to cultivate a heartfelt gratitude for the gifts of their lives, to embrace challenges with greater curiosity and compassion, awaken a generosity of spirit that opened their hearts to greater kindness toward themselves and others, and then to expand this sphere of compassion in service by doing whatever they were able in order to improve the lives of other people and our world.

INTEGRATION AND COHERENCE

Our understanding of what living in balance means in today's world has been inspired by studies in complexity science and interpersonal

"Happiness is a state of inner fulfillment, not the gratification of inexhaustible desires for outward things."

—Matthieu Ricard

neurobiology, a field that combines insight from many disciplines. From these perspectives, living in balance is a high-function state of "integration" where the myriad of disparate elements of our lives are differentiated and then linked and harmoniously "attuned" to each other. This results in a highly adaptive, self-organizing, living dynamic system in which complexity is optimized and health, wellness, harmony, and balance can flourish. Integrated, balanced and attuned, living systems move in harmony with a sense of "coherence."

In complexity theory "coherence" means that the processes by which a system organizes and adapts itself are "emergent"—i.e., arising from within the complex system. Each self-organizing, open system incorporates the flow of energy and information in ways that allow the system to bring forth new creative, adaptive responses necessary for growth, change, and flourishing over time. Insight into what living in balance means is gained from a useful acronym for Coherence created by Daniel Siegel at UCLA: Connected, Open, Harmonious, Engaged, Receptive, Emergent, Noetic (a sense of knowing) Compassionate, and Empathic.

The integrated state of living in balance can be characterized by another of Dr. Siegel's acronyms—"FACES"—because in this state of dynamic flow we are naturally being...Flexible, Adaptive, Coherent, Energized, and Stable. When we are living in this way we are living in harmony and balance. A very helpful model from Siegel's work in interpersonal neurobiology is the "River of Integration" which provides a useful image of a complex, dynamic system in which the integrated FACES flow is the central channel bounded on either side by the two banks of a river — chaos and rigidity. With mindfulness, we can detect when we are moving out of a balanced, integrated state, losing our sense of harmony, flow, and well-being, and starting to move toward rigid or chaotic ways of thinking or acting. As our mindful awareness becomes more finely tuned, we'll be more likely to recognize the subtle indicators of imbalance before we are overcome by explosions of rage, locked down in terror, or drifting into other chaotic or rigid states of being that lie outside the River of Integration. As we learn to manage experiences of chaos and rigidity wisely, we are able to live with less distress and more natural ease.

From the view of psychopathology and mental health, each symptom of every syndrome listed in the Diagnostic and Statistical Manual of Mental Health Disorders (DSM-IV) is characterized by imbalanced and non-integrative states of mind that result in chaos, rigidity, or a combination of both, which results in impaired functioning, ill health, and human suffering. Likewise, states of health, wellness, balance, and vitality within our bodies and within the sphere of our social relationships

"The art of progress is to preserve order amid change. And to preserve change amid order."

—Alfred North Whitehead

are also indicators of how successfully we are living in the River of Integration and how well we are avoiding losing our balance by lapsing into chaos or rigidity.

At the heart of health and well-being is the state of deep dynamic balance, a state of integration that weaves the many different aspects, dimensions, and systems that comprise our being and field of relationships into a harmoniously balanced and integrative wholeness.

The cultivation of mindful awareness is the master key to learning how to live in balance at every level and dimension of our lives, because we can only manage or optimize what we monitor and attend to.

EXTRAORDINARY EXECUTIVE POWERS

Through our intentional cultivation of mindful awareness, the circuitry of our brain is stimulated by the focus of our attention to actually grow neuronal connections that link differentiated brain regions and functions to each other. Through the process of neuroplasticity, our minds actually sculpt and shape our brains by our choices, values, and focused attention. (This is truly a demonstration of mind over matter!) The focus and flow of mindful awareness stimulates the growth of vital neuronal linkages between different regions of the brain that increase our capacity for living in greater harmony and balance with ourselves and feeling greater empathy and compassion toward others.

Cultivating mindfulness also nurtures the neural development and linkage of key regions and functions within our brains to allow the emergence or blossoming of nine treasured "executive powers" which are the hallmark of extra-ordinary capacities of mental health, happiness, successful relationships, human thriving, and living in balance:

- **Body regulation:** Ability to balance and harmonize our nervous system for optimal health and performance.
- **Attuned communication:** Enables us to tune into others' states of being and communicate with authenticity and deep connectedness.
- **Emotional balance:** Ability to manage emotional intensity and maintain a balanced perspective.
- **Response flexibility:** Balance and capacity to pause before acting.
- **Empathy:** Considering the mental perspective of another person. Ability to put yourself in their shoes or their skin.
- **Insight:** Deep self-knowing, self-understanding awareness, and ability for "mental time travel" to compare current reality with past and possible futures.

- **Fear mitigation:** Balance to calm fear and to recognize, embrace, and investigate what scares us.
- **Morality:** The capacity to think of the larger good and act accordingly.
- **Intuition:** Being aware of the subtle wisdom and input of our body, especially information from the deep neural networks in our gut, heart, and subtler non-conceptual selves.

These nine, extraordinary, executive functions emerge as the result of neural integration that grows linkages between the middle prefrontal regions and insular cortex of our brain, and are realized through the practice of mindfulness. This set of qualities is integral for living in balance, mental health, and extraordinary well-being. They are the sweetest fruits of our humanity that have been treasured and cultivated by wisdom traditions throughout the ages.

NEUROPLASTICITY

A growing body of evidence for the "neuroplasticity" of the brain has demonstrated that the more total hours of practice a champion in a mind-body discipline has performed, the more pronounced are the measurable changes in her/his brain, mind, body, and performance. Studies of champion performers in a range of abilities—from chess masters and concert violinists to Olympic athletes and adept, long-term meditators—demonstrate dramatic changes in the pertinent muscle fibers and cognitive abilities that set those at the top of a discipline apart from all others.

The greater the number of hours of disciplined practice that these practitioners have engaged in, the more profound are the changes in suppleness, connectivity, and coherence of brain function associated with the regions they have been training in. Similar effects from practice occurs in mind-fitness, mindfulness, and meditation training which can be viewed from the perspective of cognitive science as the systematic effort to retrain and master attention, develop greater coherence of intention, engage in more complex thinking, and live with greater ethical and emotional intelligence and discipline.

You can have confidence that when you apply yourself to any practices for living in balance that the structure and functioning of your brain, mind, and body are being enhanced and empowered by your practice. Here is how it works:

"Our will, our volition, our karma, constitutes the essential core of the active part of mental experience. It is the most important, if not the only important, active part of consciousness. We generally think of will as being expressed in the behaviors we exhibit: whether we choose this path or that one, whether we make this decision or that. Even when will is viewed introspectively, we often conceptualize it in terms of an externally pursued goal. But I think the truly important manifestation of will, the one from which our decisions and behaviors flow, is the choice we make about the quality and direction of attentional focus. Mindful or unmindful, wise or unwise—no choice we make is more basic, or important than this one."

—Jeffry M. Schwartz

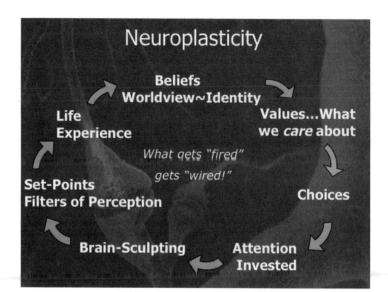

Neuroplasticity

Beliefs
Worldview~Identity

Life
Experience

Values...What
we *care* about

What gets "fired"
gets "wired!"

Set-Points
Filters of Perception

Choices

Brain-Sculpting

Attention
Invested

"The moment you change your perception is the moment you rewrite the chemistry of your body."

—Bruce H. Lipton

Our life experiences shape our beliefs, worldview, and identity.

Our beliefs inform our values, what we care most deeply about,

Our values determine our choices, and the habits and lifestyle patterns in our lives.

Our values and choices determine what we invest our attention in, and

Our patterns of attention shape and change our brain by activating the specific neural pathways related to our patterns of attending.

These neural circuits then filter the perceptions that color our life experiences, and

Our perceptions and interpretations of life experiences in turn reinforce or modify our beliefs.

"We have no idea how the subjective quality of consciousness emerges from the physical stuff of the brain."

—Richard J. Davidson

And so this cycle of mental and physical transformation continues moment to moment throughout our whole lives. Neuroplasticity assures that our mental beliefs and values will be embodied and hardwired into our brains. In moments when we are mindful and clear on intent, this process works to our advantage. In moments when we lose our balance and lapse into mindless habits, the results may be self-sabotaging.

Living in balance is a constant dance of monitoring and modifying the flow of energy, information, and activity that streams as our lives.

When we are mindful of a perception, a belief, a value, a choice, or how our attention is focused—in those precious moments of showing up fully for our life, we have the power of choice and self-determination to consciously craft our lives as our most exquisite creative masterpiece.

As our mindfulness continues to grow, we begin to recognize patterns that no longer serve us and naturally start making wiser, kinder, more compassionate, and life-affirming choices. In the process, many old, dysfunctional, and unbalancing habitual patterns in our lives simply fade away. A wealth of research demonstrates that both gradual and radical transformation is really possible in our lives, and our world, if we choose to dedicate ourselves to living in balance. Measurable changes can take place in the structure of our brains and the expression of our genes in only hours of mental training in mindfulness and other mind-fitness disciplines. With days, weeks, years, or decades of practice in these methods, our brains, minds, and lives become ever more well-tuned for living in harmony and balance.

STAGES OF THE JOURNEY

The journey of living in balance unfolds through a natural sequence of stages of development:

1. As we develop a more balanced and realistic view of ourselves, we come to take the contents of our mind and the patterns of our personality a bit less personally.

2. As we relax a bit around our personal identity, our identity naturally begins to expand beyond our skin to include and embrace more than our physical form, or the mere quirks of our conditioned personality.

3. As we become more balanced and at ease within our self, and in the presence of others, a natural sense of connection, relatedness, belonging, and intimacy emerges. We allow a lucid, yet more self-less awareness to awaken ever more deeply within us.

4. As our wisdom eyes open ever more widely we come to realize that "me" is actually a node receiving and radiating energy and information within a dynamic network of "we," and that we are constantly influencing and shaping each other through our interactions. Thich Nhat Hahn, a popular teacher of Zen and mindfulness, describes this wisdom view as "interbeing."

"Those who do not have power over the story that dominates their lives, the power to retell it, rethink it, deconstruct it...and change it as times change, truly are powerless because they cannot think new thoughts."

—Salman Rushdie

5. Dan Siegel reminds us, "Living a life of connection emerges from generosity, gratitude, and giving back, or what some simply call 'gifting' to others. This stance enables us to see how we move from 'me to we' and live as more than 'just me' to realizing that 'I am connected to you' and ultimately 'I am a part of we.' Integration is not the same as fusion; Embracing the reality of we does not involve losing me."

As you take this understanding more deeply, your view of living in balance expands and you come to view your relationship with each living being you encounter in terms of an exchange of energy and information filtered through highly sensitive, yet deeply conditioned, neural networks. This exchange of energy and information is then interpreted by our minds and ripples back out into our world as waves of energy, information, speech, or action that touch others.

We all know how the kind or harsh words of other people may comfort or distress us, impacting us through our nervous system and interpreted by our minds in ways that either increase our sense of ease or our tension. Yet as the Lokahi Triangle reminds us, the field of our relationships extends beyond our interactions with other human beings. Being licked in the face by your dog can lower your blood pressure. Likewise, the sight of a large wild animal may thrill or terrify us. In turn, the energy and information of our presence in their habitat will be registered by their nervous systems, interpreted by their minds, and lead them to approach us as a curiosity or avoid us as a threat.

A review of the research reminds us that meaningful and nourishing relationships are an essential element in determining our happiness, well-being, and even longevity. When our relationships are integrated, deep in connections, rich with empathy, compassion, kindness, caring, harmony, and balance, then our minds and bodies are also more likely to thrive in harmony and balance.

Mind-Body-Spirit

Harmony: Fine-Tuning Our Primary Instrument

> "Integrity implies an integration of soul, heart, mind and body.... It is humanity becoming all that we are.... A luminous thread in a seamless garment.... Integrity implies a new way of being—with others and in the universe. It implies caring; a quality of attention which involves a total commitment to looking, listening, feeling, sensing, intuiting, being..."
>
> —ANNE HILLMAN

OUR JOURNEY TO BALANCE IS TRULY ONE THAT INCORPORATES MORE AND MORE dimensions of our reality into a unified whole. Though we may think of body, mind, emotions, energy, and spirit as distinct dimensions, they are inseparably interrelated. Loss of balance in our outer lives reflects a cascade of inner imbalances: Imbalance in our behavior is often reflective of our emotional imbalance; emotional imbalance reflects imbalance in our biochemical and energy systems; these reflect the turbulence within our mind; and our mental imbalance is rooted in the conscious or unconscious confusion that arises when we relate to our world from a point of view of separation instead of connectedness, communication, and wholeness. The closer we come to knowing and living in a way that honors and reflects wholeness, at every dimension of our being, the greater will be the quality of harmony and balance that we experience in our lives.

In a sense, no aspect of ourselves can be separated from all the others. If we cut through confusion with a deep insight that beholds the wholeness of ourselves and our world more clearly, we will have greater peace. Inner peace puts us in touch with reality and brings a balance of mind that is less subject to conflicting emotions. As emotional turbulence subsides, and our emotions become more balanced, our biochemistry shifts to promote greater harmony throughout the body. As our body, emotions, and mind are in greater harmony and balance, we are more likely to see clearly, care deeply, and act wisely in bringing more balance alive in our own lives and in the lives of those we meet.

By learning to observe the changes of mind and body, we are able to consciously influence them. A well-known axiom in psychophysiological training comes from our friends and mentors, Drs. Elmer and Alyce Green, the grandparents of biofeedback. The Greens explained that "every change in the physiological state is accompanied by a corresponding change in the mental-emotional state, conscious or unconscious; and conversely, every change in the mental-emotional state, conscious or unconscious, is accompanied by a corresponding change in the physiological state." Simply put, this means that every change in the body is reflected in a change in the mind and vice versa.

If you carefully observe yourself, you will discover that these dimensions are actually inseparable. There are no hard and fast boundaries along what we call "body," "emotions," "thoughts," "energy," and "soul" or "spirit." Words, thoughts, and concepts are helpful for limited tasks, yet they exist purely in our minds; the living reality of our seamless wholeness is indivisible.

For the purpose of learning, it is important that we separate these concepts here in order to discuss each. But it is equally vital for a true sense of balance that we also learn to weave our body-mind-spirit into a unified whole. A simple way to do that is with the breath. For example, as you inhale, sense and feel your physicality and form, thinking or softly saying to yourself, "body." Resting in the silent pause at the fullness of your inhalation, feel and affirm your radiant luminosity, thinking, "mind." Exhaling, open your heart and mind to its unobstructed, essential wholeness, thinking, "spirit."

Inhaling... Stillness... Exhaling...
Body... Mind... Spirit...
Form... Radiance... Essence...

Understanding how this method works, you can change your contemplations to integrate and balance any trinity of concepts that you choose. If you anchor this balancing technique during quiet moments of undistracted contemplation, you will soon discover that you are able to awaken this same sense of balancing wholeness in the midst of your more active life. In this way, each breath — 21,600 times each day — becomes an opportunity to arrive home and to affirm your balance in wholeness.

Now, keeping the reality of wholeness in mind, we will take a look at the strands that make up the fabric of our selves.

chapter six

Physical Balance: Lessons from and for the Body

Body is that portion of Soul that can
be perceived by the five senses.

—WILLIAM BLAKE

DELPHINE'S SOFT, SMALL FIST WRAPPED FIRMLY AROUND MICHELLE'S thumb. Standing, wobbling, toddling forward, she took a step, and then another step. A smile of glee and delight burst forth and a giggle radiated from her joyful being as if to say, "Yahoo! I did it! I really did it! I took my first steps."

Delphine's experiment in walking continued throughout the day with more and more steps added. Her little body learned fast. The next day brought new triumphs. Climbing from the floor, up her mother's leg, she pulled herself up to a standing position. Balancing carefully, one hand on her mom's knee, she stepped out. The room hushed. Two dozen adult eyes watched. A small step perhaps for humankind, but a huge first untethered step for Delphine. Step...wobble...pause... wobble...center...breathe...then another step...then a moment to crouch... don't touch the earth... then standing and continuing. A wave of shared and sympathetic joy burst forth from big and little hearts around the room.

Our bodies, big and little, offer many insights into the nature of balance. As human beings we come fully equipped with myriad sensory systems. While we pay primary attention to the five senses that speak the loudest, there are other sensory voices that we rely upon so instinctively, such as balance, that are seldom brought to our full conscious awareness—that is, until they fail us.

In this chapter, we invite you to explore with us ways of bringing your life more into balance through nourishing yourself, exercising, and resting in wiser ways. We begin with some lessons that your physical body has to offer about balance.

MIRROR IMAGES

"Body and spirit are twins:

God only knows which is which."

—Swioburne

Sit or stand naked in front of a mirror to observe and discover the laws of form and balance revealed by your body. Informed we are balanced, more or less. The symmetry of left and right mirror images is apparent in your face, arms, torso, breasts, genitals, internal organs, legs, feet, and toes. Front side and back side, top and bottom, left and right, inside and outside... all weave together into the wholeness and perfect balance that we call our body. Even the dual lobes that form the left and right hemispheres of your brain show an amazing symmetry in both their form and function.

Those of us who are women have likely heard from our health care providers that our breasts should be nearly completely symmetrical with each other, "like the wings of a butterfly," as Michelle's doctor once told her, and that any lumps or bumps in one breast should be mirrored by similar ones in the location on the other breast. If they are not, they should be checked out more closely.

"Our bodies are our gardens—our wills are our gardeners."

—Shakespeare

Observing the functions of the body, balance is further revealed in the rhythms and cycles of activity over time. Breathing in, pause ... breathing out, pause...breathing in...and out....Activity...rest...agitation...sleeping...waking up! Hunger...eating...defecating....Thirst...drinking...satisfaction...urinating....Ovulating...menstruating...menopause....Youth...strength...elderhood....Wellness...illness....Births...deaths...births...deaths....

The body reveals balance and symmetry at every turn—seldom absolutely perfect, but always dynamic. Both structurally and functionally, balance reveals itself through the body in form and space, in movement and stillness, measurable and mysterious.

RHYTHM AND BALANCE

There is an intimate relationship between rhythm and balance. In Mickey Hart's *Drumming at the Edge of Magic*, the Nigerian drummer

Babatunde Olatunji describes the capacity of drumming to create realignment within the human system: "Where I come from we say that rhythm is the soul of life, because the whole universe revolves around rhythms, and when we get out of rhythm, that's when we get into trouble. For this reason, the drum, next to the human voice, is the most important instrument. It's very special."

Our need for and delight in rhythmic, bilateral movement has its genesis in the rhythms we experienced in the womb. From the first instant of our life, we are woven into form through the rhythms and pulsations of our mother's heartbeat and breathing, the rhythms of her walking and talking, her activity and rest, and the changing balance of biochemicals that flowed through our united veins. As our own heart began to beat, our form emerged as a dance between the harmonic waveforms and pulsations of our own internal rhythms and those of our mother, and of the environment in which she lived. From the moment of our birth, the dance that is our life has continued to be woven on a loom of many rhythms. Consciously or unconsciously, the balance or imbalance of our inner rhythms and outer rhythms work in harmony or disharmony to weave the fabric of our lives. Is it any wonder that such miraculously simple things as walking, sleeping, dancing, playing or listening to music, watching the sun rise or set, or making love bring us such joy and delight? They ground us in rhythms that carry us back to touch the wisdom and strength of our very source.

> "When you lose the rhythm of the drumbeat of God,
>
> you are lost from the peace and rhythm of life."
>
> —Cheyenne saying

Dancing and many forms of exercise can help you find a rhythmic doorway into the experience of dynamic balance, as can many of the following exercises. Notice how the theme of rhythm is woven into the deep fabric of so many exercises and principles in this book, and into the wisdom you naturally bring to living life in balance.

> "Mr. Duffy lives a short distance away from his body."
>
> —James Joyce

Rocking into Balance

Find a place to sit down where you have room to rock from side to side and from front to back. Now begin by rocking gently from side to side. Left and right ... left and right. If you like, you can synchronize your movements with your breathing. Gradually allow the movements to become more and more subtle, rocking closer to center with each rock. As the rocking becomes subtler, sense that you are coming into a finer alignment with a sense of balance. When you finally feel like you have arrived at the center of perfect balance, then quietly remain there with full awareness for a few moments.

When you are ready, rock gently forward and back. In the same way as before, allow the movements to become more subtle. As the movements become less and less, let your mindfulness also grow more subtle. Once again, feel yourself coming to a sense of balance. When you arrive at the center of this crossroads, savor the deep, sweet sense of balance that you find here.

For many people this simple exercise is a powerful tool for finding balance of both mind and body. Once you get a feeling for it, you can use this to find your center of balance whenever and wherever you like.

Cross Crawl

As human beings, many of our movements are bilateral, involving a coordination between both sides of our body. Walking, crawling, and swimming are good examples. Movements to the left are balanced by movements to the right, and vice versa. Notice how your arms swing in rhythm and balance with your footsteps.

In our workshops, we often invite people to stand up and do simple stretching exercises that are designed to promote balance in the body and brain. For example, begin with your hands touching right in front of you. As you inhale, let your right hand rise up and your left hand come down. As you exhale, let your hands come smoothly back to the center. Then as you inhale, let your left hand rise up and your right hand come down. Coordinate these alternating movements with your breathing, and allow them to be smooth and fluid in motion. For further effect, you can experiment with shifting your gaze from side to side in coordination with your moving and breathing. Once you have established a fluid pattern and rhythm of movement, then experiment to see if you can reverse it or do its mirror image. As you begin, a movement may be awkward and jerky, but with practice it will become more even and natural. Keep it simple at first, and experiment to discover what works for you.

As your familiarity with these kinds of exercises grows, you can begin to further enhance and expand the "cross-crawl" effects with your imagination. As your hands move upward, imagine them coming down. As you push forward, imagine pulling back. As you push upward, imagine drawing downward. As you step forward, imagine stepping backward. As you do these exercises, the contrast of these actual and mental movements acts to "depolarize" many habitual patterns of moving, perceiving, and thinking, and opens both your mind and body to new possibilities and a balanced freedom of movement.

"I believe that just being conscious of our ability to shift our rhythms within the fabric of a frenetic society will make our hours less anxious, our days less stressful, and our lives more complete. It will, simply enough, make us happier. Happiness has a rhythm, too. Happy people seem to live less frenetically. They have more time in their lives. They are more in the moment. This happiness is available to all of us."

—Stephan Rechtschaffen, M.D.

Side Switching

Another strategy that you can use to explore balance is an exercise in "switching sides." Each of us has a preferred side, a tendency to perform actions with one hand—for example, when brushing your hair, or answering the phone, or even wearing your watch. Ball players, skiers, skaters, and martial artists generally have a favored side for pitching, batting, turning, or rolling. Insight into balance can be enhanced by switching sides, such as switch-hitting in baseball, shooting baskets with the other hand, or brushing your teeth with your non-dominant hand. Even switching your watch to your other wrist for a day will offer many interesting insights into balance in the interplay of your muscles, eyes, and thinking. The novelty of side switching will intensify your attention to the subtle, usually unnoticed cues about balance from your body. The key insight of this exercise is in the intensified attention that comes when you introduce novelty by changing the "balance settings" in your life. If you look, listen, and feel for it, lessons on balance are available—all the time.

Contrasting Balance and Imbalance

Experiment with standing, sitting, and walking. First, simply be mindful of when you are balanced, and when you are not. When you are mindful of an imbalance, zoom in with your mindfulness and investigate how that feels. Perhaps even exaggerate the position a bit so you can really get a feeling for how that is in your body. In the same way, when you notice that you really do feel balanced, zoom in with your mindful awareness and explore what and how that is for you. If possible, fine-tune your position and your awareness and refine this sense of balance. See if you can make it even more perfect, and then notice how that feels. Continue to live in this experiment and continue to let the balance inherent in your body teach you.

BALANCE THROUGH NUTRITION

Not only can we learn about balance from the body, but we also need to provide the conditions of balance *for* the body—proper food, exercise, and sleep—so it can work in an optimally balanced way. Let's begin by taking a look at our food choices.

Some people live to eat. Others eat to live. We invest so much time, energy, money, and attention into feeding ourselves, yet health statistics indicate that nearly 90 percent of all disease is linked to unwise

"I have no doubt whatever that most people live whether physically, intellectually, or morally, in a very restricted circle of their potential being. They make use of a very small portion of their possible consciousness... Much like a man who, out of his whole bodily organism should get into a habit of using and moving only his little finger... We all have reservoirs of life to draw upon, of which we do not dream!"

—William James

choices in feeding ourselves. Food choices are deeply linked to many of the mindless habits in our lives.

From one point of view, eating is essentially a form of self-medication. We nourish ourselves but we also alter our biochemistry and thus our state of mind or consciousness each time we eat. If you doubt this, go without eating too long, and see what happens to your mental-emotional-physical state. We all know how eating some food leaves us feeling heavy, dull, lethargic, or sleepy, while eating other foods leaves us feeling more calm, balanced, or energized. At least three times a day, the food choices you make bring you more, or less, into balance. Being mindful of your food choices and how you feel after you eat different foods is an essential key to balance. Until recently, there has been little interest in our culture for learning about healthy food habits. Most doctors currently practicing have had less than an hour of formal instruction on nutrition, though they spent nearly a decade in medical school. But with growing concern over increasing health care costs, and the startling findings that so many of our diseases are linked to our eating habits and to the unwise practices used in growing food, many people are taking a greater interest in healthier nutrition and ways of growing food that are less harmful to our bodies and to the environment.

Simply put, your body is a walking, talking biochemical factory. What you eat directly and immediately affects your biochemical balance, the chemistry of your blood, and the ability of the countless sensitive biochemical processes in your body to function. The body is made to maintain health, to be effective at cleansing itself of elements that may cause disease. But if the immunological defenses of the body are overburdened trying to get rid of large amounts of imbalancing substances in the body, then our ability to maintain our health, restore our vitality, or to ward off disease is severely compromised.

We live in times that tax our bodies. Some say that the nutrition in our food is less than 10 percent of what it was a hundred years ago because the nutrients in the soil in which our food grows has been severely depleted by erosion, modern farming methods, and abuse of the soil with chemicals. Our food is so saturated with pesticides that the breast milk of every mother tested in the United States had higher levels of contaminants than would be allowable to sell in store-bought milk. Walking into a grocery store, we often have to balance two competing voices in our minds: one that says how tasty and attractive those foods are, the other that wonders how laden with pesticide and fertilizer residue they are, and what our risks are in eating them or feeding them to children who are in their formative years.

"When was the last time you had a glass of water and really drank it?"

—Thomas Merton

Choice follows awareness.

With balance in mind, consider:

Pounds of edible product that can be produced on an acre of prime land:

Cherries 5,000
Green beans 10,000
Apples 20,000
Carrots 30,000
Potatoes 40,000
Tomatoes 50,000
Celery 60,000
Beef 250

For better or for worse, the food you eat has very powerful bio-chemical consequences in your body. The good news is, with the right understanding and mindfulness, you can learn to control these consequences by the amount and types of food you choose.

Understanding that nutrition is a vast and complex field, we'd like to simply offer some information and a few guidelines here to help you make wise decisions regarding your food choices, which, in turn, will help you to create more balance in your life. If you are interested in learning more about nutrition, seek out a professional or read books to help you sort out a balanced nutritional strategy. There are many recent pioneering books advocating food choices based on new research, considering factors such as metabolic balancing, individual blood and body types, genetic ancestry, and mind-body interrelationships.

NUTRITION, STRESS, AND BALANCE

The ability of your body to maintain adequate reserves of energy against the impact of stress depends to a large extent on a well-balanced and nutritionally sound diet. The food you eat, and the way you eat it, plays a significant role in your total feeling of physical and mental well-being. A poorly designed and digested diet may counteract many of the benefits you could obtain from other strategies for balancing your life. Individual dietary needs vary a great deal. Read through the suggestions that follow and experiment to find your own optimal approach.

Relax at meals. The amount of nutrients you absorb from your food is partially determined by your eating habits. If you are tense and eat quickly, your food will not be properly chewed and mixed with saliva. This prevents your body from being able to extract all the necessary nutrients from your food, and adds additional stress on your gastrointestinal tract. Your appetite takes twenty minutes to register that you're full, so if you eat too quickly you may also eat too much. Slow your meal down by enjoying your surroundings and the conversation. Learn to enjoy the sensations of chewing your food. Begin to think of eating as a process that includes the preparation, tastes, aromas, textures, and environment, as well as the meal itself.

Set a meal schedule. A regular schedule for meal time is generally best for the digestive system. Snacking between meals and eating late at night is hard on your body. If you need to snack, try fruits, sliced fresh vegetables, nuts, or whole grain crackers. Plan your snacks ahead to avoid junk.

How often a child dies of malnutrition and starvation: *Every 2.3 seconds*

Number of children who die each day due to malnutrition and starvation: *3800*

Number of people who will starve to death this year: *20,000,000*

Number of people who could be fed if Americans reduced their intake of meat by only 10%: *100,000,000*

Listen to your appetite. Learn to listen to your body's needs. Are you truly hungry? Many people eat because of boredom, anxiety, or the need for oral gratification. Pay attention to what you're feeling as you reach for food. Because the same part of our brain that regulates our appetite is also linked to the control of our emotions and our sexuality, disordered eating often reflects unbalanced states of emotional distress, such as loneliness or unhappiness. If you feel you are eating more for emotional reasons than for physical nourishment, counseling may be helpful.

Eat simply. Read labels, know your ingredients, and avoid artificial additives and so-called "natural flavors." When food contains excessive fats, chemical preservatives, or byproducts from processing, the internal organs — stomach, liver, gallbladder, intestines, and kidneys — have to work harder at their specific tasks. Try to eat fresh, unprocessed whole foods as much as possible.

Eat organic foods as much as possible. Avoid foods that contain GMOs (genetically modified organisms) as there is mounting evidence that these cause great risk to our health and environment. Be discerning and keep in mind that often foods labeled "natural" may not be organic and healthful.

Avoid caffeine. Caffeine is a stimulant that triggers a stress response in your body, stimulating the nervous system, the heart, and the respiratory system. Headaches, nervousness, irritability, elevation of blood pressure, and stomach problems can occur even with doses as low as 200–500 mg/day. (Eight ounces of drip coffee contain 220 mg of caffeine; eight ounces of percolated coffee contain 175 mg. Cans of soda pop contain 35–50 mg.) Wake up in the morning with gentle exercise, stretching, or a cool shower and a glass of juice rather than coffee. Instead of a coffee break, try grain beverages and herb teas, or have a big glass of water. Take a short brisk walk and breathe deeply. Keep decaffeinated coffee to a minimum. It is not 100 percent caffeine-free and the most common decaffeinating process uses toxic chemicals to remove the caffeine.

Reduce sugar. Sugar is a stress-producing food in two ways. When you eat sugar, your body interprets the increased blood sugar level as a sign that you are in a "fight or flight" situation. Your whole body is stimulated and readied for action. This "sugar rush" throws your entire system out of balance, and may produce dramatic swings in energy and fatigue, often known as the "sugar blues." Reduce your intake of simple sugars as much as possible. If you can't eliminate sugar completely, try to avoid eating sugary foods by themselves, and have your sweets at the end of a meal rich in protein and complex carbohydrates. To counterbalance the harmful effects of sugar and to build your energy reserves, increase your intake of fresh whole vegetables, fruits, and grains.

Increase your fiber intake. Some people experience constipation when under stress. In addition to discomfort, this condition can cause fatigue and toxic buildup in the body. Exercise regularly, drink plenty of fluids, and eat a diet high in roughage. Supplement with bran, psyllium, or flax when necessary.

Drink plenty of fluids. Current research underscores the vital importance of drinking plenty of water each day. Your body is composed of more than two-thirds water, just like the planet, and every organ needs a sufficient amount of liquid to function properly. Sodium retention can be a stress response for some people, particularly when fluid intake is low. This puts an extra burden on your heart, lungs, kidneys, muscles, skin, and brain! To keep these vital organs in balance and working at optimal levels, researchers recommend drinking six to eight glasses of water each day.

Reduce salt. High blood pressure, or hypertension, is a disease that is often related to stress. Although some individuals may need medication to control this condition, others may find substantial improvement with lifestyle changes such as relaxation training and dietary changes. Lowering salt consumption helps hypertension in some people. If recommended by your doctor, and as a general preventive measure, reduce your salt intake to below five grams per day. Read labels of prepared foods to determine exactly what is in the food you are eating. Try herbs and spices for flavor instead. Once you have cut down on salt, you may find your sensitivity to other tastes increases.

Maintain a healthy weight. The majority of longevity studies indicate that ideal weights for a long life range from 10 pounds underweight up to 5 to 10 pounds overweight. Although many researchers believe obesity to be a health and stress hazard, weighing a few extra pounds is actually much healthier than continuously losing and gaining weight through fad diets. Once again, the best guideline here is to avoid extremes and cultivate the balanced middle way.

Get enough vitamins and minerals. Under conditions of high stress, the body uses increased amounts of some nutrients, particularly

"This food is the gift of the whole universe— the earth, the sky, and much hard work. May we live in a way that is worthy of this food. May we transform our unskillful states of mind, especially that of greed. May we eat foods that only nourish us and prevent illness. May we accept this food for the realization of the way of understanding and love."

—Zen Meal Blessing

"What is the use of planning to be able to eat next week, unless I can really enjoy the meals when they come. If I am so busy planning how to eat next week that I cannot fully enjoy what I am eating now, I will be in the same predicament when next week's meals become now."

—Alan Watts

water-soluble vitamins and certain minerals. Unless these nutrients are replaced, the body's supply can be rapidly depleted. Extra supplements of vitamin C, B-complex, calcium, potassium, zinc, and magnesium are often recommended for prevention and treatment of stress. Include in your diet on a regular basis those foods known to be naturally high in these nutrients, such as leafy green vegetables, sea vegetables, whole grains, wheat germ, nutritional or brewer's yeast, nuts, seeds, and fruits.

Be aware of allergies. Food allergies may be a hidden nutritional stress for some people. Even foods that are nutritionally sound for a majority of people may produce allergic reactions for specific individuals. Symptoms of food allergies might include bloating, nausea, headaches, skin irritation, or irritability. These symptoms may be mild or severe. Onset may occur immediately after eating the food, or may take up to several hours. In some mild allergic reactions, no symptoms will be experienced if the allergic food has not been eaten for three or four days, but will occur if the individual eats the food several days in a row. If you think food allergies may be a problem for you, observe your reactions to different foods and different combinations of foods and consult a physician who understands food allergies for further testing.

Get enough variety in your diet. To prepare your body and mind to effectively handle the accelerating stresses of daily life, a moderate, balanced diet with plenty of variety is the key. Any diet that emphasizes excessive amounts of any one food or type of food necessarily excludes a broad range of nutrients. Learn to listen to your body's needs, and plan your meals so there is plenty of variety. Include both cooked and raw foods; all colors of vegetables (be sure to include leafy greens); a variety of protein sources; nuts and seeds; and a variety of whole grains, such as brown rice, millet, bulgur, quinoa, oats, buckwheat, and whole wheat.

BALANCE THROUGH EXERCISE

You were made to move! For millions of years your ancestors roamed the savannahs, swam in shallow inland seas, climbed trees, ran, walked, rolled, and frolicked in the fields. They lived an active and embodied existence. Is it any wonder that it feels so good when you exercise and why you can feel so funky when you don't? Your body is not made to sit still in front of a computer monitor or TV for long periods of time, no matter what your boss or those little people in the TV say. To maintain a healthy sense of balance in life, it is necessary to get up and stretch or move at frequent intervals throughout the day.

"May this water
as it flows
through me
become medicine,

and strengthen the
earth and purify

and bring food
for people,

and renew the
people."

—Thundercloud's
Water Medicine
Prayer

Every tradition of exercise and physical development is, in essence, a discipline of balance: the balance of activity and rest, of contracting and relaxing, of integrating and balancing left side and right side, front and back, and of hundreds of subtle complementary moves and functions that are necessary for physical balance and health. Just go to a gym and watch the cycle of exercises or weight machines that a person follows in a well-programmed workout and you will see balance at work. Similarly, go to any well-conceived stretching or yoga, tai chi, or martial arts class, and you will see balance in action. Each move is followed by its mirror opposite, or by a movement or stretch that works the opposing muscle groups. Stretching backward is followed by stretching forward, reaching out to the left is balanced by a stretch to the right. As our understanding of optimal fitness expands, it is becoming more common to complement the high arousal achieved in an intense aerobics workout with at least five or ten minutes of deep relaxation at the end of a workout. Your body is made to move and to optimize its function through the dynamic balance of myriad exquisite components and functions. The more deeply and completely you understand your body, the more in balance you will live.

The topic of exercise is a deep, vast, and exciting one with much to teach us about finding balance in our lives. Rather than attempt to go into great detail in this book, we'd like to simply offer a few basic guidelines and some ideas on finding balance through exercise that you may not get from other sources. From here we encourage you to check with your health care specialists.

THE BASICS

- Exercise! Thirty minutes or more of moderate to intense physical actively most days of the week are recommended for optimal health by the USDA. You could also divide your time up into three to six ten-minute sessions throughout the day. This could involve walking, jogging, riding a bicycle, or working in the garden, and need not necessarily include more complex rituals that involve club memberships, costly equipment, or access to a locker room. Numerous studies show that just this much moderate exercise can produce dramatically enhanced immunological function, resistance to disease, and prolonged life, so take this advice to heart!
- Find an activity (or a variety of activities) that you enjoy. It is unlikely that you will sustain a exercise routine if you don't enjoy what you are doing. Experiment and find activities that work for

"We develop this sense of interconnectedness by acknowledging all that is eaten in its original form; envisioning the wheat that comprises the bread, the milk of the cow, the pod of the pea. The ocean of the fish. And the sun which feeds them all. We take in the sacred, the germ of life, like the Eucharist, in gratitude and respect."

—Stephen Levine

you: walking, bike riding, working out at a gym, yoga, tai chi, the list is almost endless.

* Take your pick: solo or social? Depending on your inclination, working out can be either a solo or a social ritual. For many of us, working out is not much fun unless we are connecting with and being supported by others. For others who are busy with people all day long, solo exercise time provides a welcome opportunity to integrate the experiences of the day, and for creative reflection and deep listening, which are so necessary for our lives.

* Make some of your exercise aerobic. Aerobic exercise increases the efficiency of your heart. While ordinary people have a resting heart beat of, on average, seventy beats per minute, trained athletes may have resting heart rates of less than forty beats per minute. For an average person, seventy milliliters of blood are pumped with each beat, while for an athlete it may go up to one hundred fifty milliliters. At rest your heart pumps five liters of blood per minute. During intense exercise it may pump up to **thirty** liters per minute — a bathtub-full every two minutes! Over the course of a lifetime your heart beats over 2,500,000,000 times. Reducing your resting heart rate with exercise by ten beats a minute would mean saving nearly twenty days of work for your heart over the course of each year.

Conditioning your cardiovascular system requires learning how to maintain your heart rate in your target zone for at least twenty minutes in a state that is not overly relaxed or overstrained. Your target zone lies between 60 and 80 percent of your maximal heart rate. For effective aerobic training, you must find and sustain a balance in this range; below 60 percent of your capacity you will achieve little fitness benefit, and above 80 percent there is little added benefit. The latest guidelines recommend that the lower and upper limits for your target zone can be determined with the following formula:

Your Maximum Heart Rate = 208 − (0.70 × age)

For example, if you are 40 years old, your maximum heart rate would be:

208 − (0.70 × 40) = 180 beats per minute.

Your lower limit would be 60% of your maximum heart rate:

0.60 × 180 = 108 beats per minute

"A smile can change the situation of the world."

—Thich Nhat Hanh

"When you walk, walk. When you run, run. By all means don't wobble."

—Zen poem

To determine if you are in your target zone, you must check your pulse immediately upon stopping exercise; once exercise is stopped or slowed down, your pulse changes very quickly. Ideally, find the beat within one second, and then count for ten seconds, and multiply by six to get your beats per minute. If you check your pulse and find it is below your target zone, then increase the intensity of your workout to get in your target zone. If the pulse is too high, balance that out by stepping down the intensity of your workout.

We call the ideal five-phase aerobic workout a WACSR:

1. Warm Up: Start out slow and gradually build the intensity of your workout.

2. Aerobic Phase: Maintain a balanced intensity in your workout that keeps you in your target zone for at least twenty minutes. Check your pulse as often as you need to, and adjust the intensity of your workout to stay in your target zone.

3. Cool Down: Gradually reduce the intensity of your workout, allowing your heart rate to slow down. Slow your pace and begin to feel the vitality and strength within your body.

4. Stretch: Take some time for balanced stretching. Breathe deeply and begin to savor the revitalization of your body.

5. Relaxation: To optimize the balance you gain through exercise, follow the natural wisdom of your body and take a rest. As you know from times of working and playing hard, or from making love and then snuggling up to enjoy the afterglow that follows, after a time of increased arousal, your body will naturally rebound into deep natural relaxation. When you work out, hit the shower, and then jet off to work without adding the relaxation phase, you miss the integration and deep balancing phase of your workout, and this is the best part.

"A pump when I picture the muscle I want is worth ten with my mind drifting."

—Arnold Schwarzenegger

To take advantage of this naturally balancing cycle, add an extra ten to fifteen minutes of deep relaxation to the final phase of your workout. Because your body may cool down as you relax, it can be helpful to have a blanket or a sweat suit handy. Lie down on a soft mat, kick back in the hammock, or sit comfortably and let the effortless and natural rhythms of your breath and the balancing wisdom of your body carry you into a state of deep relaxation. When it is time to return to activity, notice how intensely peaceful, calm, and alert you are. People often notice that they get as much deep rest and revitalization during fifteen minutes of this kind of relaxation as they get during hours of good sleep. Carry this calm intensity into whatever activity may follow.

Be strong, inside and out. To develop strength, weight or resistance training is suggested. Here balance is achieved through balancing the development of opposing muscle groups. Work biceps, then triceps. Push, then pull. Build the body in balance.

Develop flexibility. To find balance and move through the world with grace and power, we need flexibility. Follow stretches to the right by stretches to the left, and back bends by forward bends. Stretch deeply and comfortably in order to find an expanded range of motion.

Pick a theme for your workout. This may be a quality or strength that you would like to build in yourself through your training. It may be a question or theme that you would like to ponder. Make an agreement with yourself to let this theme be the primary focus for this time and agree with yourself to also remain watchful of traffic or aspects of your environment that you must attend to for safety.

Do a Dardick. Dr. Irving Dardick, founder of the Sports Medicine Council of the U.S. Olympic Committee, developed an unusual system of exercise that builds upon many of the insights into balance that you have been learning. From his extensive research with peak performers and with people suffering from chronic illness, Dr. Dardick discovered that people who built into their days frequent short periods of high-arousal activity followed by a period of deep relaxation were often able to dramatically improve their physical resilience. This usually resulted in a major upswing in their physical, mental, and emotional health, and an overall increase in the quality of balance in their lives.

From the perspective of balance, folks who are depressed tend to benefit most through exercise, while folks who are suffering from anxiety need to learn to slow down and meditate more. Alternating waves of arousal and waves of recovery through successive rhythms of both exercise and meditation or deep relaxation can provide immediate benefits from a preventive as well as a restorative point of view. "Doing a Dardick" can be very quick and simple:

1. Boost your activity level
   First, check your pre-activity heart rate. Then, launch into vigorous activity for one to five minutes: go run around the block, do some

> "Beware of a man who laughs and his belly does not jiggle, that is a dangerous person."
>
> —Confucius

> "We know a great deal more about the causes of physical disease than we do about the causes of health."
>
> —M. Scott Peck

push-ups, climb a few flights of stairs, or increase your activity in a way that works for wherever you are at the time.

2. Deeply relax

    Sit or lie down comfortably and mindfully ride the naturally slowing waves of your breathing and the slowing rhythm of your heart into a pool of deep revitalizing relaxation. Ideally relax until your heart rate has dropped to a rate slower than it was when you first began. As you relax, you might notice that you yawn or deeply sigh. These are often indicators that you are releasing accumulated tensions, so welcome them if they happen naturally.

3. Carryover

    Carry the calm vitality and sense of deep mind-body balance resulting from this brief time back into whatever activity will follow.

> "I never hit a shot, not even in practice, without having a very sharp, in-focus picture of it in my head."
>
> —Jack Nicklaus

You can repeat this Dardick cycle as often as every fifteen minutes, or at least a few times during the day. Especially on days when you are doing sedentary work, making time to move or stretch can be like stirring the soup so it doesn't stick to the sides of the pot and burn.

Go for a mindful bike ride, a run, or a walk. Make a mental commitment to be fully present from point A to point B in your workout. When you arrive, make a mental note of how fully present you were, and then pick the next "milepost" or marker. For example, give yourself the challenge to be fully present as you walk from your house to the corner. Notice how you did and then challenge yourself to stay mindful while you walk to the next intersection. Continue setting goals for yourself as you go.

Drift with mindfulness. Run or work out freely and simply witness where your mind wanders to. What do you notice in the world around you? What aspects of inner physical or mental experience call for your attention? What are the values, aspirations, or yearnings that work to organize and focus your attention? Just let your awareness drift where it wants to go without imposing any specific focus upon it. Simply follow the movements of your mind with mindfulness and see where it takes you.

> "If the heart wanders or is distracted, bring it back to the point quite gently... and even if you did nothing during the whole of your hour... but bring your heart back, though it went away every time you bring it back, your hour would be very well employed."
>
> —St. Francis de Sales

Exercise in nature. Whenever possible, get outside in nature and move. Though this takes some discipline to overcome your inertia, once you do finally get out into the fresh air, you will most certainly experience the benefits. We often suggest to people that one important strategy for living a balanced life is to spend an hour every day in nature. If you combine this with exercise, you will learn about balance from two great teachers, your body and the natural world. Let them teach you, and listen deeply.

SLEEP: THE GREAT BALANCER

As we work with thousands of people a year, we find that a large proportion of them have difficulty really sleeping well. Because information on nutrition and exercise are more commonly found than information on quality sleep, and because you will spend from one quarter to one third of your life sleeping, we'd like to take some time here to help you better understand the importance of quality sleep for living in balance. If you don't sleep well, you might find some lifesavers here, and if you do have good sleep habits, this section will affirm and clarify much of what you have intuitively learned.

National estimates are that 25 percent of the population has difficulty sleeping, and that as many as 00 percent of the population are sleep deprived. Being sleep-deprived also means that we're deficient in rapid-eye-movement (REM) or dream-time cycles, an important source of inner balancing and guidance. Twenty percent of doctor visits are related to exhaustion, and more than half of the burnout cases that find their way to a doctor's office are people suffering from sleep deprivation. And the vast majority of people who suffer from sleep deprivation are not even aware of it!

Pause for a moment to let this soak in. If sleep is so fundamental to our health that we spend nearly one-third of our life doing it, is it any wonder that, if so many people are not getting enough sleep, so many things in our world are so out of balance?

Sleep deprivation is due in part to the unrealistic expectations of our lifestyles that often drastically underestimate how much sleep we need—ideally seven-and-a-half to nine hours per night. It is also due to the fact that many people simply have trouble sleeping even if they have the time. In many cases, sleeping problems are stress related. People get so wound up, accumulate so much stress and tension, and drink so much caffeine during the day that they have difficulty unwinding and shifting out of a stress-arousal mode in order to fall asleep, and stay asleep. And often people's systems are so out of balance that they have developed physiological problems that contribute to the difficulty of getting enough sleep.

"Study the patient rather than the disease...

Observe, if he sleeps or is suffering from lack of sleep;

the content and origin of his dreams... one has to study all these signs

and to analyze what they portend."

—Hypocrites advice to physicians more than 20 centuries ago

NATURAL RHYTHMS OF REST

As you begin to rebuild healthier patterns of sleep, it is important, first of all, to understand that our natural waking and sleeping patterns are very different from the culturally imposed norms. The sensitive biological being that you are is made to awaken peacefully with the singing of the birds or the first gentle rays of the dawn—not with a screaming alarm. Second, as you may have noticed, your energy and alertness levels naturally wax and wane throughout the day with some periods of clarity and alertness, and other times when you are so drowsy and dull you can barely keep your eyes open. These rhythms and cycles of activity and rest are clues to your natural balanced state.

"Do few things but do them well, simple joys are holy."

—St. Francis of Assisi

Looking at the working and resting cycles of other living creatures, we gain some interesting insights into how out of balance we humans are. For instance, think of the intensity with which a hummingbird works, flapping its tiny wings with lightning speed and its little heart beating at hundreds of beats a minute. Yet the hummingbird spends 82 percent of its time resting, not flying around. A lion spends only 6 percent of its time on the prowl, and 75 percent of its time resting, while a walrus rests for 67 percent of the day. Observing our closer mammalian cousins, the spider monkey rests for 63 percent of its time, and the gorilla rests a full 51 percent of the day. In the case of each of these creatures unfettered by our societal expectations, periods of activity and rest weave naturally together into the balancing rhythms of each day.

THE IMPORTANCE OF SLEEP

Quality sleep is essential for a balanced life. During sleep, the body rests, cleanses, and purifies itself. It repairs, rebuilds, grows, and heals itself. During sleep, the stresses, strains, and tensions accumulated throughout the day are ideally released, and, in our dreams, to some degree resolved. In dreams, the mind is open to creative levels of the psyche, and we are able to tap the wellspring of deep inspiration, insights, and even premonitions that may profoundly inspire and guide our lives. And in deep sleep, our brain slows way down, and all the "mental programs" that we run cease to operate, allowing us to rest in a state of pure being. When our circuits are jammed with stress, and we tumble into bed exhausted and wake ourselves up with alarms, we are less likely to realize the full benefits sleep has to offer.

"Our truest life is when we are in our dreams awake."

—Henry David Thoreau

IMPROVING THE QUALITY OF YOUR SLEEP

A powerful key to learning how to rest effectively comes through understanding the stages of sleep and anticipating your own sleep cycles. The stages of sleep, each lasting about ninety minutes, have much to teach us about balance. When you first fall asleep, you pass through a brief period of intense semiconscious mental imagery and then spend a short while in dreams. Next you dive into a deeper, more peaceful and dreamless state. During this time, your brainwaves slow down into the delta frequencies of one to three cycles per second, and you rest in a state of deep, dreamless sleep. It is in this state, called "Stage IV sleep," where you get your deepest, most healing and harmonizing rest. In this dreamless stage, we are in a profound state of inner balance where our body rests at ease like a drop floating in harmony with the ocean of the universe.

After some time, your biological clock leads to a shift in your biochemistry and an increase in brain rhythms as they accelerate to a theta frequency of four to eight cycles per second. Once again you enter REM sleep, where you are likely to experience dreams. Though many people say that they do not dream, this is not because they aren't dreaming, but simply because they are unable to maintain enough mindful vigilance while they are in these more subtle states of mind-brain function to notice or remember them. As mindfulness grows in our waking life, we are more likely to be aware of our thinking and fantasies throughout the day. This lays a foundation of awareness necessary to begin to recognize and remember our nighttime dreams. As our waking mindfulness deepens, we may even learn how to "lucidly dream"—which is like becoming a virtual reality composer working with the limitless creative potentials of our own internal dreamscape. When mindfulness is perfected, this lucid, peaceful presence of mind can be maintained even during the most deep and quiet periods of dreamless sleep.

At about ninety minutes after falling asleep, we reach the most superficial stage of sleep. Here we are more likely to awaken or to be aroused by sounds or movements around us, or worries or pains within us. And then as the earth turns, the whole cycle begins again. Once again, we go deeply asleep, though likely not quite as deep as during the first sleep cycle. Then again we dream, and then move into a more superficial sleep where we are more likely to be awakened by sounds or movements around us. In this way, the sleep cycles continue throughout the night carrying us rhythmically through balancing cycles of deep sleep, dreaming, and shallow sleep. With each ninety-minute cycle our sleep is more shallow. At the end of each cycle we rise toward the waking state, until finally at the end of one and a half, three, four and a half, six, seven and a half, or nine hours we naturally pop through into ordinary reality and wake up.

Understanding these natural cycles of sleep, you can come to some very useful insights:

- First, your deepest sleep happens during your first sleep cycles and the amount of rest you gain is progressively less with later cycles. If you have only a limited amount of time to sleep, then plan to sleep for one-and-a-half, three, four-and-a-half, or six hours.
- Second, if you need to set an alarm, ideally set it to go off at the end of a ninety-minute cycle. If you wake up in the middle of a sleep cycle you are more likely to feel groggy and disoriented.
- For most of us mammals, our deepest, quietest metabolic time of the day is in the wee hours of the morning, an hour or two before dawn. If at all possible, this is a very wise time to stay asleep.
- You need to dream. Quality dream time is essential to living a healthy and well-balanced life. In studies where people are prevented from dreaming, they quickly become agitated, disoriented, and dangerously imbalanced. Next to breathing and drinking water, it seems that dreaming is the most essential vital function of our lives.

The healing, harmonizing, and balancing power of dreams can also be understood by realizing that the body is actually a biological oscillator embedded within the larger resonant fields of the earth. In dreaming sleep and in deep meditation, the predominant brain-wave frequency matches the rhythms of the pulse of the planetary electromagnetic field called the Schumann resonance field. Thus, when we sleep and dream, our little biophysical oscillator comes to rest and balance in sympathetic resonance with the rhythms of the larger planetary field. This, combined with the profound and miraculous biochemical changes accompanying sleep, results in our awakening feeling refreshed, renewed, and realigned.

HOW I LAY ME DOWN TO SLEEP

- People who know how to release stress throughout the day are often able to sleep more deeply and efficiently. In general it is always a

"In some aboriginal tribes the first thing a person does upon awakening is to wander alone into the bush or along the seashore and create a song based on the dreams of the previous night. The animals and birds, the Aborigines believe, hear the dream being sung and recognize that the singer is in touch with the innerworld, and therefore they assist him or her in daily hunting and gathering."

—Robert Lawlor

good idea to take some time to deeply relax when you first get into bed. Here are two simple methods you can use:

- Tense your whole body, hold it for a moment, and then completely relax. Then, tense again, half as much as the time before, hold, then relax deeply again. Then for a third time, tense half as much as the time before, hold it, and then deeply, completely relax.

- Imagine that your body is like an ice field, and that your mind and breath are like warm sunlight. Using your breath to help your awareness to focus and flow throughout your body, gently allow your awareness to travel through your body like a warm breeze flowing through the ice, warming and dissolving any places of tightness or tension. Continue to sweep the warmth of your awareness through your whole body until you are deeply relaxed or fall asleep. If your body quivers or twitches, or if you notice any deep sighs, ahhh…, recognize these as signs of tension being released.

"To my right (in the South) the angel Michael, "Who is like God"—lovingkindness;

To my left (in the North) Gabriel, Divine strength—courage;

In front of me (in the East) Uriel, Divine light:—vision;

Behind me (in the West) Raphael, Divine healing;

Above me (in the Center) Shekinah, Divine Feminine—She Who Dwells Within."

—A bedtime meditation, adapted by Michelle Levey from a Rabbinic Midrash

- Each of us is different and must learn to understand our own natural cycles and needs for sleep. Some people need nine hours of sleep to function optimally — even if they think they should get only five. One classic example is a woman who was a client of ours. She had a very rigid husband who insisted that they needed no more than six hours of sleep each night. When she came to see us for treatment, she was a nervous wreck. She hadn't slept more than six hours for many years and was suffering from many stress-related symptoms. As we worked together, we came to recognize that she was deeply exhausted. We offered her some suggestions for resetting her internal clock. As she got more sleep, her symptoms went away, and she felt much more energized, hospitable, and alive.

- Keep in mind that your biological clock is calibrated by your exposure to light. If possible, avoid the common practice of blasting yourself with bright lights — like when you turn on the bathroom lights to brush your teeth — for at least an hour before you plan to go to sleep. If possible, put dimmers on the lights in the rooms you spend time in prior to sleep, or simply use a soft night light rather than the regular lights.

- If possible, sleep in a quiet, dark room, with some fresh air at about sixty degrees.

- Use quilts or blankets and avoid electric blankets that create considerable imbalance in your body's own bioelectric field. In a pinch, use an electric blanket to heat up a cold bed and then unplug it during your sleeping time.

- Since your body is highly electromagnetically sensitive, avoid having any electrical devices such as cordless phones, clocks, radios or device players plugged in next to the head of your bed. If you use your mobile phone for an alarm, set it on airplane mode before you sleep to reduce the buzz in your field. If at all possible, turn off your wireless routers or put them on timers to be off during the hours you normally sleep. If you live in an apartment house, see if you can make some agreements with people in adjacent apartments to also turn off their routers at night — especially if theirs is just feet away from your head on the other side of your bedroom wall! Also, get informed on health risks of so called "smart meters" and if at all possible opt not to have one installed in your home, at least nowhere near where you sleep.

- Establish a regular sleeping schedule, but don't go to bed until you are sleepy. If you can't fall asleep within twenty minutes, get up and return when you are sleepy.
- A nightcap before sleep does not improve sleep. Though it may help you to relax and fall asleep, your sleep will be less deep and restful, and more easily interrupted.
- Avoid drinking caffeinated beverages for at least four hours before bedtime. And keep in mind that nicotine is also a stimulant that will interfere with restful sleep.
- If at all possible, avoid sleeping pills and learn skills to sleep more naturally. Sleeping pills can be addictive and should be used for very short periods of time only — never more than three nights in a row. They also lead to imbalanced sleep cycles and daytime fatigue that then is often worsened by using caffeine. Never combine sleeping pills with alcohol!

"A person is not a thing or a process,

but an opening through which the absolute manifests."

—Martin Heidegger

- Because the mind entering into sleep is highly suggestible to the images you feed it, avoid watching TV just before bed, or falling asleep with the TV or the radio on. Instead, we suggest that you either fall asleep quietly, or if you prefer, with soothing and uplifting music. You might also experiment with reading something that is inspiring or that nourishes your soul before you go to sleep. We often read to each other before bed, or give each other a foot rub or back rub to relax, and when we do, this is a very special time. You will be amazed at the balance this can offer to the frenetic pace of life and at the difference this can make in how well you sleep.

- Sleeping with your head to the north optimizes the quality of your rest. Your body is actually charged like a big bioelectric magnet. Your head has an electrical polarity similar to the north pole, while your feet have a polarity like the south pole. If you could imagine your body floating in a pool of water like the needle of a compass, your body would naturally come to rest in alignment and in synch with the geomagnetic environment when your head is toward the north and your feet to the south. Thus, sleeping with your head to the north aligns your body in a naturally balanced way with your larger environment. This alignment is more deeply restful than if you were to sleep oriented in another direction. If it is difficult to orient yourself to sleep with your head to the north, east is your second best choice.
- If you suffer from chronic or severe insomnia, talk to your doctor or make an appointment for an evaluation at a sleep disorder clinic.
- If you are so inclined, taking some time for prayer or meditation before sleep can greatly improve the quality and depth of your sleep
- Upon awakening, remember that a study showed that people who woke up with an alarm, leaped out of bed, and charged off to work were actually less productive during the day than people who got off to a slower and more mindful start. So, avoid checking your phone the first thing upon awakening, and take time to meditate, stretch, do yoga or tai chi, spend quality time with the people you love, go for a walk, and so on. In the long run, such "time-wasters" will actually enhance the quality of balance, effectiveness, and productivity you bring to a busy day at work. Once you have taken some "time in" with yourself, then go ahead and log in to your devices.

BALANCING CYCLES OF CLARITY AND DROWSINESS THROUGHOUT THE DAY

We all know how at times we can be so drowsy that we can hardly keep our eyes open or hold a pen in our hand. Then, twenty or thirty minutes later, we are again more clear-minded and focused. This is because these ninety-minute circadian cycles during sleep actually continue throughout the day. Understanding this, a number of insights are helpful in order to balance and optimize your energy levels throughout the day.

At times when your energy is naturally slumping, it's generally unwise to make a habit of reviving yourself with caffeine. Though it will artificially elevate your energy and alertness level for a short while, it also puts more strain on your body by overriding your body's natural balancing mechanisms. Caffeine simply makes your already tired body work even harder in order to make the shift in your biochemistry and energy level to get the rest it needs.

Fit your task to your energy and alertness level. If you are feeling drowsy and find it difficult to concentrate, this is not the time to balance the books or prepare a detailed spreadsheet. Instead, rouse yourself to do something more active like run some errand, walk materials across the office, or take a walk around the block. At least shift the focus of your work to tackle a project with which you can be in a more imaginative or creative state, such as brainstorming some design ideas or drawing a sketch. After a while, when your mind is more clear, you'll be better prepared to turn your attention to more focused work.

POWER NAPPING AND THETA TWITCHING

If your energy and ability to focus is on the wane, consider taking a brief nap. If you don't have time for a whole sleep cycle, you can practice a wonderful, quick method that we call "theta twitching."

Theta is the name of the brainwave states that are most predominant during dreams, deep relaxation, or in deep, lucid states of meditation. You likely know the feeling you have sometimes just when you're falling asleep, and the body jerks and sometimes wakes you or your partner up. This twitch is a signal that you have just released a big load of accumulated stress and tension as you crossed the waking threshold into theta.

So, to theta twitch on purpose, sit down at your desk after a good lunch, or later in the afternoon when you are feeling kind of drowsy. Rest your elbow on your desk or on the arm of your chair, close your eyes, breathe, relax, let sounds and thoughts float by, and drift deeply into sleep. As you doze off, you will lose muscle tension, and your arm will drop, most likely waking you up. When you do wake up, stay relaxed and mellow, and propping your arm up again, go for another round. See how easily and quickly you are able to drop again across the threshold of waking and into sleep After one or two twitches, check your energy and alertness level. Most people will notice that even after these few brief moments they feel refreshed and renewed.

"No account of the universe in its totality can be final, which leaves other forms of consciousness quite disregarded. How to regard them is the question—for they are so discontinuous with ordinary consciousness. Yet they may determine attitudes though they cannot furnish formulas and open a region though they fail to give a map. At any rate they forbid a premature closing of our accounts of reality."

—William James

LEARNING TO OPTIMIZE
YOUR ENERGY LEVEL

Understand that the quality of your life and work are determined in large part by how wisely you manage your energy. If you work a twelve-hour day at 20 percent efficiency, you may have worked hard but not really done much quality work. On the other hand, if you manage your energy more effectively and work at 60 or 80 percent efficiency, you may actually accomplish more working only six or eight hours. For people who are "knowledge workers," we know that in a half hour of inspired work, weeks or even months of more labored efforts can be achieved.

One of our teachers, Brother David Steindl-Rast, reminds us that lessons in balance are available in each moment if we only pause to listen to the wisdom of our heart. "The heart is a leisurely muscle," he says. "It differs from all other muscles. How many push-ups can you make before the muscles in your arms and stomach get so tired that you have to stop? But your heart muscle goes on working for as long as you live. It does not get tired, because there is a phase of rest built into every single heartbeat. Our physical heart works leisurely. And when we speak of the heart in a wider sense, the idea is implied that life-giving leisure lies at the very center... Seen in this light, leisure is not the privilege of a few who can afford to take time, but the virtue of all who are willing to give time to what takes time—to give as much time as a task rightly takes."

Understanding this, develop your personal skills and support those you work with in learning how to manage their energy levels throughout the day. Wise managers who understand the wisdom in this will support their people in taking breaks to eat, exercise, or even nap during the workday. They recognize that people should be rewarded not on the basis of the time they work, but on the quality of results they are able to produce. Because our rhythms and cycles vary, develop working relationships where you and your coworkers can cover for each other as you take care of your needs throughout the day, and help each other to be mutually successful.

chapter seven

Emotional Balance:
A Peaceful Heart

In this century, human knowledge is extremely expanded
and developed. But this is mainly knowledge of the external
world...You spend a large amount of the best human brain
power looking outside — too much — and it seems you do not
spend adequate effort to look within, to think inwardly...
Perhaps now that the Western sciences have reached down into
the atom and out into the cosmos finally to realize the extreme
vulnerability of all life and value, it is becoming credible, even
obvious, that the field of what we call "inner science" — dealing
with the inner things — is of supreme importance. Certainly
physics designed the bombs, biology the germ warfare, chemistry the nerve gas, and so on, but it will be the unhealthy
emotions of individuals that will trigger these horrors. These
emotions can only be controlled, reshaped, and rechanneled, by
technologies developed from successful inner science.

— THE DALAI LAMA

HAVING EXPLORED THE PHYSICAL DIMENSIONS OF BALANCE IN OUR
bodies, we now move to examine the closely related sphere of our emotional lives. The heart forms a good bridge linking these two worlds.
While still a physical organ, the heart also represents for many of us the
vital center of emotional tones and textures.

Day after day, year after year, your heart keeps beating, teaching you about balance with each pulse. With every beat, millions of sensitive cells work together in a complex rhythm that keeps things flowing through every moment of your life. Thirty-six thousand heartbeats a day, over 1,000,000 beats per month, add up to well over 2,500,000,000 heartbeats in a lifetime. The heart muscle represents the most intelligent and well-managed workforce in the world.

For your heart, as well as for your life, the secret to success is in finding a dynamic flowing balance between phases of working and resting, pulsing and resting, activity and receptivity, to be nourished so that it can pulse again. It's doing... and then pausing to just be. The heart is able to keep going strong and steady, without a break, for a lifetime because it knows how to focus and then flow, and it has the flexibility to adapt to each micromoment along the way.

There is a wisdom in our heart worth listening to for a lifetime. Though our thinking is useful for many things, we often confuse our thoughts about reality for the actual direct encounter with it. Learning to recognize when you are "in your head" or "heartcentered" is an essential skill for finding balance. The need for balancing heart and mind has been apparent to seekers of inner peace for a long time. From his meditative hermitage, over a hundred years ago, the Christian contemplative Theophane the Recluse shared his intimate insights into this subject. With careful observation he noted his awareness, advising us in the language of his day:

"For so long as the mind remains in the head, where thoughts jostle one another, it has no time to concentrate on one thing. But when attention descends into the heart, it attracts all the powers of the soul and body into one point there."

Decades of inspired global service work led our friend and teacher Ram Dass to witness and relieve considerable suffering in the world. Yet still so much remains. As he reminds us, "There are many levels of the heart. And the human heart will break because it empathizes. The deeper heart...looks at the universe, just as it is, in a nonreactive way and says, 'Ah so,' 'Yes'. And it includes your human heart which is breaking, but your identity isn't only with your human heart. Your identity is with a deeper, intuitive heart wisdom which is different. You don't deny the pain, but you don't get reactive to it."

"The hardest state to be in," he reminds us, "is one in which you keep your heart open to the suffering that exists around you, and simultaneously keep your discriminative wisdom...Once you understand that true compassion is the blending of the open heart and quiet mind, it is still difficult to find the balance. Most often we start out doing these things sequentially. We open our hearts and get lost in the melodramas, then we meditate and regain our quiet center by pulling back in from so much openness. Then we once again open and get sucked back into the dance. So it goes cycle after cycle. It takes a good while to get the balance...You have to stay right on the edge of that balance. It seems impossible, but you can do it. At first, when you achieve this balance, it is self-consciously maintained. Ultimately, however, you merely become the statement of the amalgam of the open heart and the quiet mind. Then there is no more struggle; it's just the way you are."

> "Our first teacher is our own heart."
>
> —Cheyenne saying

LIFE SIGNS

The heart is a powerhouse, a bioelectric miracle generating a bioelectric field that is 40 to 60 times stronger than the field generated by your brain. By biological standards, this is very strong. The bioelectric field generated by the heart ripples through your whole body and far beyond. If you could set up the right kind of sensitive scanning device across town from someone and zero in on him or her, you'd find that the information wave generated each time our hearts beat could be picked up for miles around you. Each time you enter a room, the beating of your heart announces your presence and informs other biological entities in the room as to how at peace or in conflict you are underneath your surface appearance.

The workings of the heart are influenced by the two branches of your autonomic nervous system: the sympathetic system that is associated with the stress-arousal response and the parasympathetic system that is associated with the relaxation response. These two work together to speed up and slow down your heart rate sort of like the accelerator and brake of a car.

> "Words that come from the heart enter the heart."
>
> —Moses Ibn Ezra

When we are anxious or stressed, the heart "drives" jerkily, like the car of a beginner driver who is unsure of himself and keeps stepping on the brake while he has his foot on the accelerator. Signals of stress, followed by signals of tentative comfort, then another surge of anxiety or doubt, and a moment of gentling reassurance—the interplay of these conflicting emotional reactions can wreak havoc on our poor heart, not to mention all the other physiological systems that go along for the ride. All the while, our internal turbulence broadcasts loud and clear to all those around us, affecting them negatively as well.

On the other hand, when we are in a more peaceful, balanced, loving, or appreciative mode, our heart purrs along like a car under the hand of a skilled driver on an open road. The heart rate is coherent rather than incoherent, steady instead of jerky, more musical in its waveforms than the noisy signals during stress. It is clear by the good vibes we are putting out that we are in harmony and balance, and likely we are safe to approach or depend upon.

You probably know from experience what it is like to walk into a room when there has been an argument: You can feel the tension in the air. Similarly, you may know what a "contact high" you can get when with someone who is truly peaceful, loving, kind, or joyful. Even if you are consciously out of touch with what's going on for you, your mind-body is belting out the broadcast for all to hear. To the degree that other people are stressed, imbalanced, or distracted, their ability to tune in, to be sensitive to you, or to empathize with you will be eclipsed. To the degree that they are present, balanced, and at peace with themselves, they'll be more likely to be sensitive to what is really going on for you. The following three-part sequence of heart-opening and stretching exercises will help you to live from your heart.

Heart to Heart

Imagine someone in front of you toward whom you feel much tenderness, friendship, love, or compassionate concern. This could be a loved one, a close friend, or even a pet. As vividly as possible, with your eyes closed, sense or imagine the presence of this being before you now. Allow yourself to get in touch with the genuine sense of love and care that you feel for this special one.

Now begin to focus on this person's heart, not the physical organ that pumps blood, but rather that center of love that lies at the "heart" of each person. Reach out now—actually raising your arms and reaching out with your physical hands—and imagine cradling in your hands this person's place of deepest feeling, really touching his or her heart. Imagine that as you breathe in, a feeling of love and care wells up within you and fills your own heart. As you exhale, this wellspring of love within you—visualized as streams of light or energy—flows from your heart out through your arms and hands, and pours gently into this person's heart. In a deep and silent way, offer this love and care, and imagine that it is being received in the way the person most needs at this time.

Now, imagine that this person reaches back to touch your heart. Imagine your eyes meeting in recognition, appreciation, and understanding. Imagine seeing each other with total love and forgiveness.

Let any memories that block your hearts be dissolved and healed in the joy of this heart-to-heart meeting. Imagine looking deeply into one another's eyes with heartfelt love and mutual respect. Feel the satisfaction and the intimacy of this flow between you.

Focus your attention again on the image of your loved one or friend. Visualize the image of this person condensing into a small bright sphere of light that you tenderly hold in your hands. As you breathe, gently place this luminous sphere in the center of your own heart. Imagine it shining brightly, like a gently glowing sun that shines with a light of love and peacefulness, dispelling any darkness within or around you.

Touching Your Heart

With both of your hands now, reach up and touch your own heart. As you breathe, imagine filling your heart with feelings of love directed toward yourself. Imagine what it is like to be here fully for yourself with the same love and care that you might offer to others.

Understanding that it is difficult to receive the care of others if you are unable to give love to yourself, breathe in the love now. Feel the sense of genuine self-love well up within your entire being. Use the natural cycles of your breath to circulate this feeling of love, moving from your heart out through your arms and hands and back into your heart again.

As you establish this flow between your hands and heart, begin to extend and circulate this feeling through your whole body now. With each breath, send ripples of love and care from your heart out to every cell and fiber of your body, to every nook and cranny of your mind. Fill yourself with love. Fill yourself with light. Let it move and flow and circulate through every dimension of your being. Send this loving light to those regions that are in pain or that cry out for attention. Let this love flow as light to dissolve any seeds of disease that may lie hidden in your mind or body. Imagine this light vitalizing and strengthening your undeveloped potentials for love, wisdom, power, and understanding.

Radiating Love and Light

Breathing gently now, imagine yourself filled with light and love. Begin to feel the power and the presence of this love and light within you. Begin to shine it out into the world.

"Just as a mother would protect her only child, even at the risk of her own life, even so let one cultivate a boundless heart toward all beings."

—Shakyamuni Buddha

"To know that we are loved by the whole universe is very important."

—Thich Nhat Hanh

Resting in this vitalized state, imagine beaming out your feelings of well-being and love to dispel any darkness or fear in the world. From your heart, send ripples of this loving light to your loved ones and friends, to all who live in suffering or fear, to all those leaders with the power to help or harm. Imagine this light as a beacon of love, a broadcast of caring that will be received by others in the way that they most need to be touched at this time.

Now simply rest in the flow of the breath. Effortlessly be filled, effortlessly extend who you are and what you have to offer, to yourself ... to others ... to everyone ... in whatever way they need it. Radiate your own love and light out into the world. Imagine it bringing light into darkness. Imagine it fanning the powerful flames of wisdom, love, and understanding in the hearts and minds of others.

Take a moment to appreciate how the inner changes you're making within yourself are touching the world in wonderful ways. Appreciate how these quiet moments of inner work have generated an atmosphere of greater harmony, balance, and well-being in the world.

EMOTIONS THAT KILL, EMOTIONS THAT HEAL

For human beings, one of the most powerful forces in shaping our world is the strength of our emotions. Our emotions lead to healing and to killing, to giving life or taking it. And only when we are aware of, understand, and know how to balance our emotions — along with our bodies, minds, and spirits — are we able to truly live in balance.

Most of us reading this book likely come from cultures that have little understanding of what Eastern wisdom traditions call the "inner sciences." As a result, most of us have inherited fairly primitive tools for working with the incredible power of our emotions, and thus we are emotionally way out of balance. Some people even pride themselves on not being very emotionally sensitive, joking that, "Oh, I had an emotion once and it went away!" When it comes to living, this is not something you want to brag about.

How intense does your emotional state have to be before you are aware of it and can put a name to it? How sensitive are you to noticing how your body is affected by your emotional states? How easy is it for you to put into words what you are feeling emotionally? How do you tell the difference between frustration and anger, happiness and sadness, fear or trust? Your answers to all of these questions are clues to whether you have alexythymia or not.

"...My joy is like spring, so warm it makes flowers bloom in all walks of life.

My pain is like a river of tears, so full it fills up the four oceans.

Please call me by my true names,

so I can hear all my cries and my laughs at once,

so I can see that my joy and pain are one.

Please call me by my true names, so I can wake up,

and so the door of my heart can be left open,

the door of compassion."

—Excerpt from Thich Nhat Hanh's poem, "Please Call Me By My True Names"

"Do not seek with cold eyes to find blemishes,

Or the roses will turn to thorns as you gaze."

—Sabistari

DO YOU SUFFER FROM ALEXYTHYMIA?

The term *alexythymia* was first used by Harvard psychiatrist Dr. Peter Sifneos in an attempt to describe a problem shared by a large proportion of patients suffering from various stress-linked medical disorders. Looking at the Greek roots for the word we discover that *alexy* means "no words," and *thymia* means "for feelings."

It's a dangerous state. If we have no words for our feelings, we are not in touch with our internal state until the subtle whispers have turned to painful screams within or around us. The more alexythymic we are, the further out of balance we get before we even have a conscious clue that something is not quite right. For this reason, alexythymia is regarded as a dangerous precursor to nearly every stress-related illness. Additionally, when we are out of touch with ourselves, we are far more likely to get stressed about being stressed, or to get anxious about being anxious, and to have small imbalances escalate out of control into major crises. Losing our balance, we are more likely to set off a whole cascade of problems in the lives of others, and the impacts may echo for generations to come.

For many people the first encounter with the notion of alexythymia is a fierce wake-up call. They immediately recognize people in their own lives who fit the description, and they often silently wonder to themselves, "How well does this describe me?"

Alexythymia is essentially a social disease that is most often transmitted to children from parents who are out of touch with their own feelings. It develops over childhood as we go to our dad, for example, saying that we are feeling hungry, and he negates our experience saying, "You can't be hungry! You just ate a sandwich!" or when we go to our mom feeling cold, and she responds by telling us, "You can't be cold, honey. It's eighty degrees in here and you have your sweater on." When our authority figures make a habit of ignoring or negating our own deeply felt experience, when they lack the patience, skills, or caring to help us figure out what was really going on, they put us in danger of developing alexythymia.

When this happens early in our lives, we begin to ignore our feelings, confuse our needs, distrust our interpretations of our own deep personal experience, and thwart our development of self-balancing skills necessary for knowing what we feel and describing what is true for us. Though we may come of age physically and assume our position as a "mature" adult in society, unless we heal this deficiency with ourselves, we are prone to be out of touch with what is going on within us and with

"Human capacity is equal to human cruelty: and it's up to each of us to tip the balance."

—Alice Walker

"Suffering is not enough. Life is both dreadful and wonderful. To practice meditation is to be in touch with both aspects. Smiling means that we are ourselves, that we have sovereignty over ourselves, that we are not drowned in forgetfulness. How can I smile when I am filled with so much sorrow? It is natural— you need to smile to your sorrow because you are more than your sorrow."

—Thich Nhat Hanh

other people, to unknowingly pass this condition on to our own children, and to be doomed to live our lives in a precarious, unbalanced way.

Though in many settings people scoff with disdain at approaches that they describe as "touchy-feely," there is considerable hard evidence to suggest that people who are out of touch with their feelings are especially vulnerable and at risk in the face of stressful change. And no matter how out of touch we may be, our warm, feeling bodies continue to be deeply affected by the experiences of our life, continue to pump out the biochemicals that heal or harm us, and keep broadcasting loud and clear the intensity of our feelings and needs, even if we choose to ignore them.

REVERSING ALEXYTHYMIA

Before you get too depressed, keep in mind that alexythymia can be cured. It takes some discipline, mindfulness, patience, and time. Here are some helpful guidelines. Keep in mind that emotional states are best described in a single word or an image. Remember, if you hear yourself saying, "I feel that…," then you are probably describing your thoughts and judgments about a situation, rather than an actual feeling (which is often experienced as a bodily sensation). With this in mind, and with a patient smile of mindfulness:

- Keep a log book next to your phone and make a note of how you feel each time you hang up the phone. How did that call affect you emotionally? Are you feeling anxious or relieved? Happy, angry, or afraid? Hopeful, doubtful, or confused?
- Make a similar written or mental note after each, or most, of the encounters you have during the day. How do you feel when you see your kids when you come home from work? After seeing your neighbor in the elevator? When walking out of that meeting?
- When listening to the radio or watching TV, after each segment, notice the emotional impact of that segment. Are you delighted or depressed when you hear someone talk about the election? Do you feel peaceful and loving, or agitated and disturbed after that last episode? Just as certain foods can balance or unbalance your body, your selection of media also has a direct impact on your biochemistry and your health. As you tune in and understand how the sensitive being that you are is being soothed, irritated, inspired, or drained by ingesting certain media, you may choose to change your "media diet" in order to optimize your chances of living a more balanced life.

"Emphasizing only happiness or only suffering to the exclusion of the other is limiting the experience. When you blend the good and the bad you learn to dance and flow with both expressions. Learning from both sides of the experience you become more whole and integrated. No event is all black or all white...Personally, I prefer not to dwell too much on the happiness without reaching into the misery."

—David Chethlahe Paladin

Understanding that your emotional responses are tied to your mindset, look behind your emotional responses in these situations to gain insight into the beliefs, values, expectations, or assumptions that lead you to interpret the objective raw data of your experience with the particular emotional charge that it has for you. Because the same situation may make one person happy, another person sad, and a third person angry, search for the factors that make your feelings uniquely your own, and remember that you can change your mind.

CLEANING UP TOXIC EMOTIONS

As we talk with people about times when they lost their balance in life, few people tell us about losing their physical balance, as in falling when skiing or riding a bike. Rather, they usually talk about getting emotionally upset. That is not surprising. Strong, roller-coaster emotions, be they positive or negative, do have a dramatic impact on our sense of balance, and strong emotions tend to drive us into behaviors that often create more imbalance in our own lives and in the lives of others.

Pause to reflect for a few moments on the times in your life when you have felt, and acted, most in or out of balance. How would you describe the predominant emotions during those times: Blind rage? Joy? Grief stricken? Head over heels in love? Wonderstruck?

There are numerous studies that draw a correlation between people's emotions and their physical health. One study conducted by Howard Friedman, professor at the University of California Riverside, analyzed a hundred different such studies. His analysis showed clearly that certain emotional states are absolutely toxic. The imbalance created by being chronically depressed, anxious, pessimistic, irritated, or critical actually doubles one's chances of developing a major disease! It's no wonder that in Buddhist traditions these negative mindstates are described as "afflictive emotions" or "mental poisons" believed to be at the root of a host of problematic human conditions.

To modern science it is clear that there are powerful links among the centers of the brain that regulate our responses to emotions and to immunological function and the cardiovascular system. These connections work powerfully to promote health and balance by boosting our defenses against disease when we are generating positive mental states such as love, appreciation, compassion, and empathy. Yet under the influence of stress hormones and other neurochemicals that are released when we are feeling negative emotions, these same connections hamper the ability of the immune system to protect us from diseases. Toxic

"If I told patients to raise their blood levels of immune globulins or killer T-cells, no one would know how. But if I can teach them to love themselves and others fully, the same change happens automatically. The truth is: Love heals."

—Bernie Siegel, MD

emotions and unbalanced states of mind create conditions in the body that make us vulnerable to developing serious illnesses such as cancer, heart disease, and diabetes. Toxic emotions also raise our blood pressure and cholesterol levels, and change our blood chemistry to leave more deposits that clog our arteries.

On the other hand, people who are genuinely optimistic, appreciative, kind, loving, and compassionate are far less susceptible to disease. Their hearts and brains exhibit far more balanced, coherent, and energy-efficient functioning. The biochemistry of a loving, positive mindstate promotes measurable balance, revitalization, and immunological strength throughout the systems of the body. Speaking on the new field of psychoneurocardiology at a large conference that we chaired for the Menninger Foundation and Life Sciences Institute, Dr. Miroslav Borysenko observed that "the brain is everywhere in the body!" There are special proteins, called neuropeptides, that are produced specifically for each emotion. Until recently it was thought that neuropeptides were manufactured solely in the brain, but scientists now have seen that neuropeptides are also made in our skin, liver, and other organs as well. As Dr. Borysenko says, "There's anger in your blood; there's compassion in your blood."

In short, loving mindstates feed us, while negative mindstates bleed us of our strength and vitality. The key to this, however, lies not in the words that people say or the affirmations they tell to themselves, but in the genuineness and authenticity of their attitudes and feelings.

IT'S UP TO YOU

If we felt total equanimity toward the experiences of our lives, we would be unlikely to ever feel out of balance. We would relate to everything that happened to us with a Buddha-like acceptance. But as long as we are human and experience preferences, we will be prone to tumble into emotional reactions of liking or disliking, attraction or aversion. We want something; we are afraid of losing what we have. The many subtle shades, intensities, and durations of our emotional reactions play upon the exquisitely sensitive instrument of our body.

As sensitive creatures, we are vulnerable to be wounded by the words and deeds of unkind, suffering people. Yet people often poison their own mindstreams and bloodstreams for decades, replaying simulations and frustrations over a minor insult of a person long dead. We have to ask ourselves, "Who is causing this suffering?" The only person who can turn your bloodstream into a toxic swamp or into a healing

"Knowing others is intelligence.

Knowing yourself is true wisdom.

Mastering others is strength.

Mastering yourself is true power."

—Tao Te Ching

"Our true nature is far more ancient and encompassing than the separate self defined by habit and society. We are as intrinsic to our living world as the rivers and trees, woven of the same intricate flows of matter/ energy and mind. Having evolved us into self-reflective consciousness, the world can now know itself through us, behold its own majesty, tell its own stories, and also respond to its own suffering."

—Joanna Macy

elixir of long life is you. No one can make you feel angry or happy. Moment to moment, your mental-emotional-biochemical-physiological state changes. And regardless of how kind or nasty anyone "out there" is to you, no matter how much you may blame others for how you feel, you alone determine the quality, intensity, duration, and direction of your response. Through mindfulness we can learn to be on the lookout for toxic emotions like aversion, hatred, and bitterness. Instead of making things worse by taking a negative situation personally and trying to push the pain away, we can develop a growing emotional equanimity that allows us to stay open to pain, understand it, and even generate a wholesome healing response such as compassion.

EMOTIONAL INTELLIGENCE:
WHAT IS YOUR EQ?

Walking down the aisles of the information systems area at Hewlett-Packard, we noticed a color copy posted on a cubicle. The words leaped out at us, "In the corporate world, it is IQ that gets you hired, and EQ, emotional intelligence, that gets you promoted." It was an excerpt from *Emotional Intelligence*, the bestselling book written by our friend Daniel Goleman, science editor for the *New York Times*.

Understanding the five dimensions of emotional intelligence is very helpful in cultivating a more balanced emotional state. These are:

* **Mindfulness or Self-Awareness:** Just what we've been saying—only when you know what you feel can you make decisions that will bring you happiness and satisfaction.
* **Managing Your Feelings:** In the absence of awareness, emotional reactivity and habits control your life. Learning to recognize and control emotional impulsiveness, to soothe anxiety and upset, to restore balance following stressful encounters, and to have anxiety or anger that is appropriate but not overblown requires a high level of mindfulness and skill.
* **Motivation:** Your attitudes and intentions will color your emotional response to difficult situations. Cultivating an attitude of optimism, trust, confidence, and respect goes a long way in boosting your EQ.
* **Empathy:** Your sensitivity to the unspoken and spoken feelings of others is another vital key to good relationships, whether in love or work.

"In the deeps are the violence and terror of which psychology has warned us. But if you ride these monsters deeper down, if you drop with them farther over the world's rim, you find what our sciences cannot locate or name, the substrate, the ocean or matrix or ether which buoys the rest, which gives goodness its power for good, and evil its power for evil, the unified field; our complex and inexplicable caring for each other, and for our life together here. This is given. It is not learned."

—Annie Dillard

- **Social Skills:** Faced with the intense and often imbalanced emotional reactions of others, developing the ability to stay mindful, centered, and at ease will help you to establish and maintain quality relationships.

Expanding on the practice of mindfulness, EQ has created a very powerful and effective "one-two punch" for helping many of our clients get a handle on the work they need to do on themselves to deal with stress more effectively and find greater balance in their lives. Once people take to heart that they alone are in control of their emotional reactivity, a path of learning opens up that is both humbling and exciting. The key is not to rate yourself on never losing your equilibrium, but on how often you lose it, how intensely you lose it, and for how long. If you measure your success in this way, you will find that with sincere practice, your emotional balance will improve.

GUIDANCE FROM AN EQUANIMOUS ELDER

In 1984, Michelle had the good fortune to study with a revered meditation master during a three-month retreat at the Insight Meditation Society in Barre, Massachusetts. The teacher was an old Bengali woman named Dipama, who lived in Calcutta, India, and taught in the Burmese tradition. A householder and mother herself, Dipama taught that even the simplest activities of everyday life, such as ironing or washing the dishes, could become the supports for developing mindfulness, equanimity, joy, compassion, and love. Many people came from all over the world to visit Dipama in her simple home in one of the poorest parts of the planet to learn the arts of mindful living from this humble master.

Dipama, whose name means "Mother of Light," was one of those rare people who embodied an abiding sense of peaceful equanimity. During one of the small group interviews Michelle attended at the retreat, a question came up about working with emotions. The young woman who had asked the question was desperately struggling with roller-coaster rides of intense emotions that were disturbing her meditative practice. After listening quietly yet intently, Dipama responded that a tendency to be emotional was not a hindrance to meditation practice. Emotions reveal the presence of a mind that is open and sensitive, or "soft," as Dipama put it ever so gently. "Just watch and don't identify with the emotions," she said. "Increase mindfulness of noticing and the concentration. Like everything else, emotions are impermanent. Watch them arise and pass away, like clouds in the sky."

The key to restoring inner emotional balance, Michelle learned, lay in not fighting with our emotions, but in simply accepting their being there as a natural expression of our minds, and not adding fuel to the fire of emotional turbulence raging within. By seeing our emotions simply for what they are, we allow them to settle back more easily and naturally into the clear inner openness from which they arise.

BEGIN WITH GRATITUDE

One day, we met a wise man from Chicago. He gave us a simple challenge that we took to heart and that has changed our life ever since. This is it: How often do you look for beauty in your world?

Can you imagine how your life would shift if you took this challenge to heart? What if, as you walk or drive down the street, you were to actually seek out beauty and things to rejoice in? As you sit and talk with other people, what if you were to decide to focus on what is beautiful about these people rather than being critical and judgmental? As you sit around your home or watch TV, what if you focused your heart and mind to notice the many blessings in your life and dwell less on the irritations? Such a shift can bring emotional balance to your life in a beautiful way.

"Thank you God for giving me the inspiration to thank You."

—From the Amidha, the central prayer of Judaism

In the wisdom ways of indigenous people, and in the annals of medical science, the balancing and restorative power of gratitude is deeply revered. Giving thanks was traditionally the first step for many indigenous communities whenever they gathered for meetings or ceremonies. Across the ages and across the globe, the intentional cultivation of an attitude of gratitude holds a central place in the daily practices of a wide variety of people and contemplative traditions.

〜໑

"The whole cosmos is being renewed moment by moment through sacrifice: brought back to its source through thanksgiving, and received anew as a gift in all its primordial freshness...To those among us who have entered into this mystery through faith it need not be explained; to others it cannot be explained. But to the extent to which we have given room in our hearts to gratitude, we all have a share in this reality, by whatever name we may call it. (It is a reality which we shall never fully take hold of. All that matters is that we let it take hold of us.) All that matters is that we enter into that passage of gratitude and sacrifice, the passage which leads us to integrity within ourselves, to concord with one another and to union with the very Source of Life."

—Brother David Steindl-Rast

Many of our teachers remind us that gratitude is an essential practice for living in harmony and balance. Some say that when we generate gratitude in our hearts and minds we complete the circle between ourselves and the source we are grateful for. With this sacred hoop of gratitude in place, it ensures that those circumstances causing us to feel grateful will continue to flow in our lives. On the other hand, if we don't generate gratitude for the goodness of gifts of our lives, we break this circle and the causes of gratitude will cease to flow. In these ways, gratitude opens our hearts and minds to a deeper sense of connection, deep, meaningful, nourishing relationships, and dynamic balance that allows us to thrive.

Gratitude infuses us with the strength to open our hearts more deeply in order to touch the vulnerability and suffering that may arise when what we love, value, cherish, or care about inevitably changes, decays, or fades away from our lives. This recognition opens our hearts to compassion. In this way, our beloved teacher Joanna Macy suggests that if we are seeking to embrace, understand, and wisely respond to the complex and challenging circumstances in our lives, world, families, or communities, that we should always "begin with gratitude." Gratitude anchors us in goodness and the precious, though fleeting gifts of our lives. In doing so, we release our tensions and calm our anxieties and fear. For a brief yet precious moment we can rest in wholeness, harmony, and balance.

Gratitude can be a way of life, a meditation, an attitude, or a practice. Since gratitude is such a direct path to experiencing a more balanced state, we'd like to offer a simple, yet powerful practice for you to take to heart and weave into your busy days. In our work designing and teaching the Mindfulness and Meditation Laboratory program for Google, we actually found that this meditation was the number one favorite of the Googlers, because it is direct, simple, can take as much or as little time as you wish to give it, and delivers immediate positive and stress-reducing results.

We teach this practice as a way to remember the many gifts and blessings of our lives worthy of our attention in the spirit of gratitude and thanksgiving. It has been shared by circles of friends, families, and communities around the world at times of thanksgiving, and we invite you to share this practice with your loved ones and friends as well. Here's how it goes:

As you begin, reach up, touch your heart, and gently smile to yourself with a tender sense of deep connection and deep reflection. Allow the

"To be alive in this beautiful, self-organizing universe—to participate in the dance of life with senses to perceive it, lungs that breathe it, organs that draw nourishment from it—is a wonder beyond words. Gratitude for the gift of life is the primary wellspring of all religions, the hallmark of the mystic, the source of all true art. Furthermore, it is a privilege to be alive in this time when we can choose to take part in the self-healing of our world."

—Joanna Macy

flow of your mindful clear presence to blend with the natural rhythms of your breathing, and allow yourself to simply settle into this state of open awareness and rhythmic, flowing sensations.

As you become more fully present now, bring your attention to your heart as you call to mind anyone and anything in your life that you are grateful for. As you inhale, gather whoever or whatever comes to mind into focus in your heart, reflecting upon your gratitude for them. Breathing out, let your heartfelt gratitude flow to them and through them as waves of blessings. Let your mindfulness savor and embrace the imagery, feelings, emotions, or sensations associated with this experience of gratitude for this person or this aspect of your life. Be mindful of how this presents itself to you. Rest in this contemplation as long as you like, and when you feel complete release your focus on this aspect of gratitude, and welcome whoever or whatever else next comes to mind that you are grateful for...gather them into your heart and radiate your gratitude and blessing back to them.

Let each unique experience of gratitude and blessings be taken to heart, one by one, like counting beads on a mala or rosary. Continue in this contemplation as long as you like, gathering anyone or anything that you are grateful for, radiating your gratitude and blessings to them. Taking your eyes, your ears, your hands, your intelligence, to heart, bless them in a similar way with the heartfelt radiance of your gratitude and appreciation. Whoever or whatever comes to mind, gather them into your heart, one at a time or all together.

You can rest in this contemplation for as long as you like or have time for, allowing each breath to bring to mind a loved one, a friend, or someone who has been kind to you, someone who is teaching you patience, or how to forgive, or any aspect of your life for which you are grateful. Allow each breath to shine from the depths of your being through the depths of their being in order to light up their life with your gratitude, love, and compassion.

Taking these many gifts to heart, complete and affirm the circle with gratitude, assuring that the stream of blessings and deep connections in your life and in the universe will be unbroken. This sense of deep connection and deep relatedness is the primary ground in which balance is rooted.

As we open our hearts to gratitude, we are better able to listen and sense more deeply into the tender dimensions of our hearts. As we open our wisdom eyes to see, sense, and commune with the deeper, subtler dimensions of our lives, we discern that even within gratitude, there may be overtones of sadness, disappointment, regret, vulnerability, or

"We turn logical with our gratitude because it is terrifying. The wonder of a moment in which there is nothing but an upwelling of simple happiness is utterly awesome. Gratitude is so close to the bone of life, pure and true, that it instantly stops the rational mind. That kind of let go is fiercely threatening. I mean, where might such gratitude end?"

—Regina Sara Ryan

grief that are all inseparable from our gratitude. Gratitude helps us to embrace all the many dimensions of our lives more deeply and gives us the insight and strength to open our hearts more fully to compassion for ourselves, and for others.

THREE REALITIES TO KEEP IN MIND

In every situation that you encounter, there are three levels of reality to be mindful of. Understanding each of these is essential to working effectively with emotions:

What is really happening, that is, what is "the truth"? Don't be fooled into thinking you can know the whole truth of a situation. Regardless of what you think, the Great Mystery is undoubtedly at work behind the scenes in this situation in ways too complex, too vast, too subtle, too deep for you to fully comprehend. Be wise enough not to be fooled by your limited perspective, and humble enough to wonder, "What is really going on here that I cannot comprehend?"

What do your senses tell you about this situation, that is, what you see, hear, smell, and so on? In seeing, what you see is only an image or interpretation in your mind. Likewise for all your other perceptions: hearing, just sounds in the mind; touching, only tactile sensations registering in the mind; in tasting and smelling, only tastes and touches. Your perceptions are only your perceptions! They are only mental representations of what is really going on. Before you get out of balance, pause to wonder, "What is really going on?"

What are your assumptions, interpretations, beliefs, and feelings about what is happening? Remember, your assumptions and interpretations are again merely mental constructs that help you to describe and explain your experience! They are stories you tell yourself to make sense of the world; they are not a direct experience of reality. Always pause to wonder what is really going on.

Emotional balance depends on how mindfully you are able to relate to each of these three realities—what is, what you perceive, and what you think—and to how they influence each other. When we confuse our thoughts or even our perceptions for what is really going on "out there," then we are in danger of losing perspective and tumbling into emotional reactivity. The balance of certainty and mystery is found in learning to regard each of these realities for what they are!

MANAGING EMOTIONAL ENERGY

Mindless emotional reactivity is one of the most powerful and destructive forces in the universe. So to live more in balance, learn to mindfully observe the interplay among your thoughts, emotions, and behavior. Experimenting with the following strategies will help you learn to better understand and deal with your emotions, particularly at times when you notice strong emotional states rising within you:

* Shift your attention from what is outwardly going on to focus on the internal pattern of physical sensations related to your emotional feelings.
* Ask yourself, what does this emotional state really feel like? Where and how do I feel this in my body? Befriend intense or negative emotional states by recognizing them; smiling to yourself; making a mental note: "Ah, this is anger (or fear, or jealousy)... of course!"
* Identify what thoughts and mental habits or "tape loops" are associated with the feeling. What are you telling yourself about the feeling? It is one thing to have a financial setback and experience fear. But is the fear coming from a story of utter doom that has you on the street as a bag lady in a matter of days, while the reality is that you will probably be able to cope just fine? Oftentimes we unconsciously make matters worse for ourselves by fantasizing the worst.
* Empathize with the feelings of other people and the circumstances that may have led to their suffering. Remember, when others act cruelly or insensitively, that no one can act that way unless they are suffering themselves.
* Painful emotional states may be intensified by getting angry about being angry or feeling guilty about feeling guilty. Learning to recognize and accept old, conditioned emotional reactions is the first step toward learning new, healthier ways of feeling and expressing your emotional truth.
* Develop emotional flexibility. Practice intensifying and diminishing your emotional intensity in different situations. Experiment with changing your emotional state and recognizing how much choice you really can have in how you respond to different circumstances.
* Learn from your experience. Analyze intense situations after they are over and clarify for yourself how you might learn from this situation in order to commit to a more effective and compassionate response next time.

"Sometimes I go about with pity for myself

and all the while Great Winds are carrying me across the sky."

—Ojibway saying

"Despair is often the first step on the path of spiritual life and many people do not awaken to the Reality of God and the experience of transformation in their lives till they go through the experience of emptiness, disillusion, and despair."

—Father Bede Griffiths

"We know finite disappointment,

but we know infinite hope."

—Rev. Martin Luther King Jr.

With a heart balanced by mindfulness, you can learn to:

- examine your current situation;
- examine your reaction patterns;
- examine your options;
- examine your ideal visions, goals, intentions, and desired outcomes; and
- make the wisest decision for moving forward.

When in doubt, choose a course of action that is either kind (will avoid causing harm to yourself or others), or helpful (bringing benefit to yourself and others in both the short and long term).

chapter eight

The Balanced Mindstate

Mind is the forerunner of all things.

— BUDDHA

BALANCE, AS WE KNOW IT, BEGINS AND ENDS IN OUR MINDS. TO FIND
true balance of mind, you must learn to balance mental agitation with
mental stability, and mental dullness with a vivid clarity of mind. As
you learn to do this, you'll experience an exquisite quality of peace of
mind, and the deep, steady concentration that allows you to understand life deeply.

Living a life of balance also means finding a healthy balance
between the functions of our active mind, such as thinking, intention,
and imagination, and the more direct and immediate experience of
reality offered by our receptive, open, or quiet mind, such as mindful
attention, a deeply felt sense of aliveness, and intuition. It's hard to
have balance when you don't even know one half of the equation!

Finally, to realize a truly balanced mind, we must know ourselves
in all our uniqueness and dimensionality. This means cultivating a spaciousness of mind that can hold the relativity of our ordinary identity,
the limited and partial "stories" we construct and keep telling ourselves about our favorite character — our self — and our "true nature" or
authentic Self which is infinitely more omnidimensional and Universal
in nature.

Gaining insight into these different states of mind is essential
as we gradually learn how balance is lost and can be regained in our

lives, moment to moment. Like many themes in your search for balance and wholeness, it is likely that you will have a better understanding of some of these dimensions of mind than of others. Learning to discover, develop, and balance these many facets of the jewel of your mind is part of living your life in an ever-evolving and dynamically balanced way.

ILLUSION, CONFUSION, AND REALITY

We often remember the advice offered to us by Gen Lamrimpa as we were about to embark on a year-long, silent retreat. With tender compassion and a peaceful smile, the Tibetan yogi reminded us, "As you look more and more deeply into your experience you will discover many dimensions and realities of yourself of which you were previously unaware." How true these words rang for us and should ring for you.

Keep in mind that as you peer into the depths of your own mind you will behold the appearance of many subtle images, thoughts, and patterns. Some of these mental experiences will be quite compelling, some will seem more like fragments of frantic cartoons, while still others will appear as ephemeral dream images. None of these has a concrete reality—all of them are like cloud formations that you imbue with your own meaning.

Just as the water in a pond will be moved and shaped into complex waves and images by the passing of wind or light, so too your remarkably sensitive mind/brain is bombarded by countless stimuli giving rise to a complex display of mental reverberations. Some of these mental appearances will please you, while others may displease, disgust, or even frighten you. Familiar and unfamiliar images will arise, abide momentarily, and then dissolve like so many wispy clouds in the deep clear space of your mind. But just as we saw with our emotions, these intangible inner appearances have tremendous power to influence your life, change your physiology, and compel you into action.

Again, we in the West have had little mind training. On his first trip to the West, a visiting Tibetan lama was amazed to see how little control most people in this culture seemed to have over their minds, and how strongly driven they were by the tyranny of their thoughts. After a full day of interviews, he turned to his translator in disbelief and exclaimed, "These people seem to be giving all their power away to their thoughts! When I want my mind to be focused on something, I put it there and it stays there as long as I want. If a thought comes to my mind that I do not wish to entertain, I simply do not dwell on it. These people have not yet learned how to do this...."

Remember that the more you come to center yourself in a stance of open-minded, open-hearted, quietly smiling, self-observing mindfulness, the better equipped you will be to find true balance by recognizing this ceaseless flow of mental images to be merely a passing show of changing appearances in the mind and not imbue them with so much power. Though these thoughts, images, or feelings may be easily confused with actual reality, they are truly insubstantial. Like images in a dream, they exist only as ephemeral shadows and flickerings that represent the unimaginably deep reality of yourself, others, and the world in which you live. The dawning of this realization is quite liberating for some, while for others it may be frightening at first to discover how illusory the dream fabrications of our own thoughts truly are.

"At the root of all war is fear."

—Thomas Merton

BALANCE FROM THE INSIDE OUT

Our inner and outer worlds reflect each other. When our minds are dominated by fear, anxiety, or preoccupation with ourselves, the world may appear hostile or threatening. When our minds are at peace, the world and the people in it are beheld as a source of wonder and delight. You likely know from experience that when your mind is agitated and unbalanced, the world appears to you as separate from or even antagonistic to yourself. In fact, the more unbalanced and agitated we are, the more separate, anxious, or alone we are likely to feel.

As we learn to relax, focus, and move more toward a deeper sense of balance, we become less tense, more peaceful, and begin to feel more trusting of and connected to the world. As the internal flow of energy and activity within us becomes more balanced, we begin to experience greater wholeness and harmony in relationship to others.

"A man with outer courage dares to die.

A man with inner courage dares to live."

—Lao Tsu

The key to this shift is the quality and depth of our mindful and caring attention. With practice we learn to turn scattered distraction into momentary concentration, and then to sustain that concentration as a flow of mindful awareness into action. The more wholeheartedly present we are with whatever we are doing, the more our mind will function in balanced ways. This translates into moving into and through our world in a more peaceful, powerful, energy-efficient, kinder, and wiser way.

Learning How to Stop the War

The summer Joel graduated from the University of Washington, he met Zen translator, author, and teacher Paul Reps, who touched him deeply.

"Since wars begin in the minds of men, it is in the minds of men that we have to erect the ramparts of peace."

—From the UNESCO Charter

"I was young, wide-eyed, and intent on exploring the further reaches of human potential. Having devoured nearly everything in print on the research in human consciousness and completed my first wave of research into the human mind-brain-spirit, I was filled with far more questions than answers, and had launched into the first of nearly four years of travel and study to seek the answers that my academic studies did not provide.

"I was offered a job setting up an international conference on consciousness research that was to be held at a beautiful contemplative center nestled on Kootenay Lake in the Canadian Rockies. Arriving two weeks early to prepare for the conference, I discovered a wonderful and eccentric companion in residence at the retreat center who, at first glance, appeared like an elder elf with bright eyes, deep gaze, and the presence of one deep in Spirit. We took a mutual interest in each other and Reps invited me to join him for tea and conversation every day at four.

"During our conversations, Reps a marvelous storyteller, would invite me into his memories, traveling through the Orient in search of the great wisdom masters who were still alive in the middle of this century. Reps, I discovered, was one of the first Westerners to travel to the East to study and translate the wisdom teaching of the Zen traditions. One day, over tea, he told me a story about the power of the tranquil mind.

"In the early '50s, Reps, who was then in his forties, had traveled to Japan en route to visit a respected Zen master in Korea. He went to the passport office to apply for his visa and was politely informed that his request was denied due to the conflict that had just broken out in Korea. Frustrated, Reps walked away from the counter and sat down quietly in the waiting area. He had traveled thousands of miles to a foreign land with the plan to study with this master in Korea. He was deeply disappointed, perhaps even angry, at being told he could not complete his journey. He realized that at that moment there was not only a war starting in Korea, but also another raging inside of himself. Recognizing that his internal conflict had the potential to erupt and create conflict in the world around him, he wondered what to do. Pausing for a few moments of mindful breathing, he then reached into his bag, mindfully pulled out his thermos, and poured himself a cup of tea. With a calm and focused mind, he watched the steam rising, swirling, and dissolving into the air. He smelled the fragrance of the tea, tasted its bitter flavor, and enjoyed its warmth and wetness. Finishing his tea, he put his cup back on his thermos, put his thermos in his bag, and pulled out a pen and paper upon which he wrote a haiku poem.

"Mindfully, he walked back to the clerk behind the counter, bowed, and presented him with his poem and his passport. The clerk read the poem, and it brought tears to his eyes. Looking up deeply into the quiet strength in Reps' eyes, the clerk smiled, bowed with respect, picked up Reps' passport, and stamped it for passage to Korea. Reps' haiku read:

"Drinking a cup of tea, I stopped the war."

Reflect for a moment on how this story speaks to you, and to the interplay of balance and imbalance, war and peace in your mindbody, relationships, and environment. Imagine living in the balance of mind that would allow you to recognize and befriend your own "inner enemies" and to make peace with the conflicts raging within your own mind. See yourself as a true and noble warrior, armed with the wisdom, inner strength, compassion, courage, and vigilance necessary to recognize and transform all of your inner enemies. Consider how you would like to be able to respond to the inner enemies who speak to you with the voices of irritation, frustration, disappointment. How would you like to respond to the stabs of doubt or self-judgment, or to the demons of resentment and fear, the plagues of pride or jealousy? Imagine or sense the inspiration you could draw from a deeper, more steady center of balance if you were to recognize and stop the wars when they are whispers, rather than waiting till they are screams, when they are tiny skirmishes, rather than raging atomic wars. Envision the peace and power you can find in your life when you learn to be more patient, tolerant, forgiving, and honest with what is going on within you so that your internal conflicts don't escalate and erupt into your outer relationships, causing grief and imbalance in the lives of others.

> "Breathing in, I know that anger is in me.
>
> Breathing out, I know this feeling is unpleasant...
>
> Breathing in, I feel calm.
>
> Breathing out, I am strong enough to care for this anger."
>
> —Thich Nhat Hanh

YOU CAN CHANGE YOUR MIND!

It is common for people just beginning to develop greater mindfulness to initially feel a bit overwhelmed at how wild and out of control their mind seems to be. But, if you have supportive friends, patient and insightful mentors, effective techniques, and the personal discipline necessary to put what you learn into practice, you can swiftly develop confidence in your ability to calm your mind.

Many of the people we've worked with are classic examples of people who are highly sensitive, stressed, or have been diagnosed with Attention Deficit Disorder (ADD). These people are usually high-intensity, high-energy sorts of people who are erratic, easily distracted, easily excited, or depressed. As a result, they often have a long history of frustration, poor self-esteem, and alienation from others who are impatient or uncompassionate toward them. What they learn when they calm their minds is that their personalities seem to change totally.

Lynn was an executive on the fast track in her telecommunications firm when she came to see Joel as a patient at the medical center. Her doctor had referred her for stress-related panic attacks, headaches, and stomach problems. Outwardly Lynn was attractive and highly controlled. Though she generally managed to keep a fairly cool and calm appearance, her internal turmoil was revealed as noticeable flushing of her face and neck, flared nostrils, perspiration beading at her brow, and a telltale racing pulse that was noticeable at her throat or temples. Inwardly she was prone to many swift and abrupt fluctuations in her thoughts and feelings.

As part of their work together, Joel and Lynn used a mirror and an instrument that monitored the changes in Lynn's skin temperature and skin conductance — two measures that are sensitive indicators of the level of physiological stress response. The mirror offered visual feedback on her furrowed brow, tense eyes, and **flushing**. The monitor showed decreases in skin temperature when she was stressed, and warming hands as she relaxed, as well as elevated skin conductance when her palms were sweaty under stress, and decreased readings when she relaxed. The mirror and monitor were visible to both of them, providing valuable feedback while they experimented with various techniques to help Lynn understand and master the intensity of her stress response. "On her first visit, it was clear by watching her physiological changes that her mental stress was strongly affecting her physiology," Joel comments. "The changes in her mental state were dramatically mirrored in swift, erratic changes in her body, as indicated by dramatic and abrupt increases and decreases in her skin temperature and skin conductance. At first these physiological changes seemed totally unconscious and out of her control. Yet as her mindful awareness developed, Lynn began to gain insight into how her mental stress tended to escalate. As she began to get more focused, and to bring more awareness into the interplay of her mental state, her pounding heart rate, her sweaty hands, and flushing neck, she recognized ways she could break the cycle and bring her stress response under control."

As Lynn learned and practiced new skills, she found that she could relate to her stress in a more spacious and playful manner. She learned to smile to herself as she tuned into her internal dialogue. She learned to make choices for how to respond to stressful situations that didn't intensify the distress. As the weeks passed, she learned to consciously control her stress responses. As she did, she maintained the same

"The unhappiness and suffering that we experience arise through our inability to control our own minds, and the happiness that we wish to achieve will only be achieved by learning to control our minds... You can use Inner Science to educate each individual to understand himself or herself, to control his or her negative emotions and distorted notions, and to cultivate his or her highest potentials of love and wisdom."

—The Dalai Lama with Robert Thurman

"I believe that any event from a person's past immediately becomes a myth (a personal story)."

—David Chethlahe Paladin

passionate intensity and breadth of responses, but was able to move between different states of mind and body in a much smoother, more balanced, and less erratic way. She began to feel more naturally calm, confident, and in control, and the frequency and intensity of her painful headaches and stomach problems diminished.

A year later, when Joel met Lynn at the market, she smiled and gave him a warm hug. "You know, that work we did together was the first stage of a long and wonderful journey," she said. "Since I last saw you I haven't had a single panic attack, and when I feel a headache coming on, I can usually relax it away. This has given me the confidence to finish my MBA and make some changes in my life and relationship that have been long overdue. I can't begin to thank you enough for holding up the mirror so I could see myself in a brighter light."

"What made the difference for you, Lynn?" Joel asked, knowing that something had made this work on herself a real priority. "You know, what really got me motivated to understand and change myself was seeing my five-year-old daughter begin to have worries, headaches, and stomachaches just like Mommy," she explained. "I realized that I probably picked up some of my strategies for dealing with stress from my Mom, and I made a commitment to myself to learn and model for my daughter some wiser, healthier, more balanced ways of dealing with the stresses that come with living in our modern world."

> "The human mind is a relational and embodied process that regulates the flow of energy and information."
>
> —Daniel Siegel, M.D. plus 40 UCLA scientists

STORIES WE TELL OURSELVES

The major cause of stress for most people arises from self-generated anxiety and worries. Because the body responds equally to mental images as to sensory ones, learning to monitor and sort through our thoughts can be a major step to finding greater balance.

Here's a "mindfulness of thinking" technique that comes from a tribe in Africa. From an early age, children there were trained to be mindful of their thinking. If a person became aware of a foreboding thought like, "Oh no, what if there is a lion hiding behind that tree waiting to eat me?" they learned first to recognize and then release the thought by saying to themselves, "This is a story that doesn't need to happen!"

We use this technique often. For example, one of us may be chopping vegetables with a sharp knife and the thought pops up, "I'd better be careful or I'll cut myself." Or we're in a rush driving on the freeway and the image of getting pulled over by the state patrol jumps to mind. The key is to first notice your thoughts and then, if they are harmful or unproductive, to say to yourself, "This is a story that doesn't need to

> "Why are you unhappy?
>
> Because 99% of the things you do, think, and feel are about your self.
>
> And there isn't one!"
>
> —Wei Wu Wei

happen." This technique is not about getting rid of negative thoughts or about the power of positive thinking. If a stress-inducing "doom and gloom" kind of thought comes to mind, you acknowledge it, you don't try to get rid of it, to hold on to it, or even analyze it. You simply honor it and let it go.

Balance is also found by recognizing that some of those stories that pop into our minds are ones we'd like to see happen. In response to a desirable thought like, "Maybe there is a watering hole over there," or "I hope the baby I am carrying will be healthy and a leader for the people," the members of the African tribe would add to themselves, "And this is a healing story!" In your life you might bless or energize thoughts such as, "I know I'll do a great job on that presentation," or "This meal is going to be delicious," or "This lump is probably benign," by thinking or saying, "Yes, this is a healing story."

In our work with leaders and teams, we often teach this technique as a way of strengthening mindfulness of our unconscious, and often self-sabotaging, inner dialogue. Many people have found it very simple and useful. For example, while out on his morning jog, the service manager for a medical instrument division we worked with in Australia noticed a worrisome train of thoughts racing through his mind, "Whoa!" he said to himself, "This is definitely a story that doesn't need to happen!" Immediately he felt his pulse rate slow down, his tension level drop, and his mind come into a more clear, focused, and balanced state. "It was amazing," he said to us over breakfast, "to see how immediate the effects of this applied self-awareness really are. I recognized that the mental scenario I was running was actually running me. The worries had a life of their own, and they were catapulting me in a direction that I would not choose to go. It's scary how much physical and mental stress I can create for myself through my own imagination. I would guess that most of the time I'm not aware of what I'm thinking, and that this is really the source of a lot of my stress and tension. In this case, instead of dwelling on the problem like I tend to do out of habit, my heightened self-awareness enabled me to think more creatively about the situation. When I got back from my walk, I made a few calls and then phoned the client who had a problem with our system. We worked out a solution that was really a "win-win" for their company and for ours. Over the long run, this will only increase their confidence in our ability to deliver and will increase our advantage over our competitors. Seeing how immediate of an advantage I could gain by recognizing and sorting out my thoughts is really a boost for my self-confidence and likely for my effectiveness on the job as well!"

"Worries are pointless. If there's a solution, there's no need to worry. If no solution exists, there's no point to worry."

—Matthieu Ricard

"Worryin' is just praying backwards."

—David Chethlahe Paladin

"The idea that biography becomes biology implies that we participate to some degree in the creation of illness. But...we must not abuse this truth by blaming ourselves or any patients for becoming ill. People rarely choose consciously to create an illness. Rather, illnesses develop as a consequence of behavioral patterns and attitudes that we do not realize are biologically toxic until they have already become so."

—Caroline Myss

Recognizing your flow of thoughts will help you smile to yourself and get playfully creative. For example, if you notice thoughts like, "I'll never get this done," "I'll mess this up," "They'll think I'm incompetent," or "My presentation will be a bomb," it may be helpful to smile to yourself and say, "This is a story that doesn't need to happen." And if you notice thoughts like, "My client will love this design," or "People are really going to love this idea!" anchor it by affirming, "And this is a healing story!"

ORIGINAL CONFUSION AND MISTAKEN IDENTITY

Imbalance in our lives is rooted in a fundamental mental confusion regarding who we really are. This confusion leads us to misperceive ourselves and our world, and leads to out-of-balance thinking and relating.

This original confusion is largely a case of mistaken identity. We know only a tiny fragment of the totality of ourselves and have lived our lives ignorant of our true nature. This is mainly due to habit. Who and what we call ourselves is based on a story that we keep telling ourselves over and over again. Over time, we forget that this story is only a story, and we come to believe and live in the story, rather than in the deep, vast, intense mystery of our totality. Research in the cognitive sciences suggests that we think tens of thousands of thoughts each day. Yet as many as 90 percent of these thoughts are thoughts that we thought yesterday — mindless reruns, cycling through our minds again and again and again: habit energies of the mind programming and reprogramming themselves into endless cycles of confusion, distortion, entropy, and dullness. If this is true for you, can you imagine how much creative potential and energy you could liberate if you were to live more wakefully?

Thoughts — good, bad, beautiful, ugly, new, or reruns — are merely thoughts. Stories. Descriptions. Abstractions. Reality is far more than a collection of your thoughts, far more than the volumes of descriptions and explanations that you generate. Wake up. Be mindful and amused by the passage of thoughts you take so personally and so seriously. Thoughts are thinking themselves. Look through them and discover reality.

If we take these ideas to heart, we realize that the limiting story we tell ourselves revolves around an imaginary and unquestioned identity that we come to know as our "favorite character" — our self. Over time, without even knowing it, we believe our personal myth, and forget that the story is only a story and not reality.

To find deep and lasting balance in our lives, we must learn to see our personal story as merely a story, and to expand our insight into the

"We are luminous beings. We are perceivers. We are an awareness. We are not objects.

We have no solidity. We are boundless. The world of objects and solidity is a way of making our passage on earth convenient. It is only a description that was created to help us. We or rather our reasons, forget that the description is only a description and thus we entrap the totality of ourselves in a vicious circle from which we rarely emerge in a lifetime. We are perceivers. The world that we perceive though is an illusion. It was created by a description that was told to us since the moment we were born."

—Don Juan

true depth and mystery of our self. As we do this, we discover that who we are is far more profound and extraordinary than we may have ever dreamed! Like the dweller in Plato's cave who had the courage to leave the familiar shadow world of his cave to step out into the vast, brightly colored world, our journey toward balance requires courage and may at times be both exciting and terrifying. The key teaching points to remember here are:

- Stories are stories.
- Reality is reality.
- Mistaking our stories for reality is a sure path to losing both perspective and balance.

TRUE NATURE

Years ago we discovered a wonderful radio series entitled *Moon over Morocco*, which is produced by the ZBS Foundation. Early on in this magical, mystical Raiders of the Lost Ark–style spoof, the hero, Jack Flanders, finds himself walking down a crowded street in Morocco. He is approached by a mysterious man who asks for a light. "Do you come to Morocco to seek the Mazamuda?" he whispers to Jack mysteriously. "Who are you?" asks Jack. "Do you know who you are?" the mysterious man asks Jack in return. "No . . ." stammers Jack. "You don't," the mysterious man chuckles, finishing Jack's thought.

So, what about you? Yes you, the one holding this book and looking out through your eyes at the words upon this page. "Do you know who you are?" If you are like most of us, this is a difficult question to answer. It is easy to list a variety of titles, roles, and vital statistics, but how much does that really describe who you truly are? Scientists and mystics will tell us that anything, or anyone, examined deeply enough reveals a profound indescribable mystery. As futurist Peter Russell reminds his callers on his answering machine, "Hello. This is not an answering machine; it is a questioning machine. The questions are: 'Who are you?' and 'What do you want?'. If you think these are trivial questions, consider that most people go through their entire lives without finding the answer to either one." Do you know who you are? If you think you know the answer, look again more deeply.

At the core of our self is a reality that is the very authenticity of our true nature. It is universal in nature, and the foundation of our ordinary personal self. Its nature is openness, wholeness, clarity, oneness, and

"There is the dual nature of self: The incomplete self and the complete self... As humans, we are seeing from the perspective of the incomplete self. This incomplete self is undoubtedly very important. But if we attach to this incomplete self, although this incomplete self is important, then we'll never be able to experience the complete self. We Zen people say, if you believe in God, this complete self means the same thing as God." That is it shares the same standpoint as God."

—Joshu Sasaki Roshi

peace. It is the source of all true love, healing, power, and intelligence in our lives. In essence it is not separable from your ordinary mind or sense of self any more than the water of the ocean is separable from the waves.

When, through mindfulness, the turbulence of our ordinary minds comes to balance, we discover what mind truly is when it is not busy fabricating and projecting illusions of separateness. We discover this deep true nature of mind in moments of peace, love, presence, clarity, calm, compassion, empathy, unity, or wholeness. Because it is the foundation and source of reality, it transcends separation and perceives wholeness. This awakened mind functions beyond the limitations of ordinary perception, and beyond the limitations of time and space. The awakened, universal, oceanic mind is the basis of all healing, the source of our intuitive intelligence, inspiration, and revelation. This is the medium through which prayer and extraordinary human faculties function. It also is the source of peace that the balanced state manifests.

Though the universal mind is immeasurable, invisible, and impossible to grasp, in every moment of mindfulness, patience, love, heartfelt appreciation, or compassion, the presence of this deep universal nature is present in our lives. The universal mind is grounded in reality, not in self-generated fantasies or stories. Its foundation is wholeness. As the ground from which all things spring, it is the essence of love that infuses all things.

Though our personal self is born and dies, the universal Self is birthless and deathless. Talking with respected leaders of many of the world's great spiritual traditions, there is a universal agreement that if we live our lives in such a way that we balance our personal self-importance with a deeper wisdom of our true self, we will be less afraid of death because we have already discovered our deathless nature. Many of our teachers have commented, "If you die (to the limited illusion of your personal self) before you die, then when you die, you won't die." According to "Holy Rascal" Rabbi Rami Shapiro, the wise Rebbe Yerachmiel ben Yisrael illuminated this point in a letter to his beloved spiritual son, Aaron Hershel:

"When we look at the world from the perspective of manifestation we see birth and we see death. But when we look at the world from the perspective of wholeness, there is no birth and no death. Manifestation and wholeness, being and emptiness, are poles of God's Greater Unity. Only God is whole and complete: Yes, Reb Yerachmiel ben Yisrael is gone, but the One who wore his face these many years is ever present. And that One wears your face, dear friend, as well. What we truly are is God manifest in time (Yesh) and eternity (Ayin). Know this, live well,

"You may imagine that there are many things you need to learn and realize in order to attain enlightenment. That's okay. But essentially, there's only one thing you absolutely must realize—the essential nature of your mind."

—Tharchin Rinpoche

and die easy. You have been a blessing to me beyond what words can convey. Remember, love is stronger than death (Song of Songs 8:6). Shortly I will be no more. Let our love grow ever stronger."

CREATIVE INTELLIGENCE: THE SYNERGY OF ACTIVE AND QUIET MINDS

The wisdom traditions remind us in countless tongues that just as balance is found in the presence of the all-embracing wholeness of the Universal Mind and its reflection as myriad personal minds, the presence of balance is similarly echoed within our personal minds as the dynamism of the active-creative-imaginative mind, which is complemented and balanced by our quiet-receptive-intuitive mind. Understanding and developing the vital balance between these two aspects of our personal mind is essential to living a healthy, balanced life. Let's take a closer look at the dynamic synergy between these complementary mental forces.

"I wanted only to live in accord with the promptings which came from my true self. Why was it so difficult?"

—Hermann Hesse

Using the power tools of intention, thinking and reasoning, and creative imagination, the active mind shapes thoughts and perceptions to give meaning to the fluid chaos of our experience of the world. These creative "doing" functions of your active mind are balanced by the quiet mind, whose faculties are the formless, receptive, and reflective qualities of mind—including mindful attention or presence, somatic intelligence (wisdom of the body), and intuitive intelligence. The quiet mind encounters reality deeply and directly, the way things are, without bias or distortion. The quality of our intuitive intelligence is a direct reflection of the mastery we have in developing our quiet mind skills.

Like everything else in nature, there needs to be a balance between our active and quiet minds. This can be hard, because we have been trained only to pay attention to (and be overinvested in) the active mind. But with mindfulness, you can begin to experience both. As you talk, also deeply listen. Notice how the active foreground display of your abstract thoughts or imaginings emerges and shapes itself against the backdrop of quiet mindful awareness. Within this deep stillness of the mind, experience how images arise, develop, and dissolve back into the open clear field of awareness. Observe and sense how images and associations cascade through the space of the quiet receptive mind like clouds forming and disappearing when warm moist winds pass over a ridge in the high mountains. As you learn to balance creative activity with reflective receptivity of your mind, you will discover the key to unlocking mental balance.

CREATIVE IMAGINATION

Imagery and creative visualization are universal mental functions common to every human being. Though they play a critical role in our psychological and physical health, performance, and creativity, these capabilities are poorly understood and are seldom developed to their full potential. By bringing these ordinarily unconscious mental processes into conscious awareness, we can learn to dramatically expand the scope of possibilities available to us.

It is helpful to distinguish between spontaneous mental imagery and creative visualization. Imagery rich in information is continually arising within the mind—fantasies of the future, memories of the past, dreams, visions, our own self-image, and myriad expectations we project upon our world. Properly understood, imagery is the stuff of revelation and intuition. Within the gestalt of a single mental image is encoded information that, when spun into concepts, words, or mathematical or musical formulas, could fill many volumes. Some mental images are experienced consciously; others are edited out by our belief system or are simply too subtle to be recognized.

Mindfulness of spontaneously arising mental imagery serves primarily a "read-out" function. Creative imagination and visualization is a more active function of the mind. With visualization we are intentionally engaged in generating and shaping the stream of mind-energy into prescribed mental images. Visualization equips us with a powerful tool for mentally simulating complex processes or possible futures beyond the scope of ordinary perception and thinking. "Imagination is more important than knowledge," said Einstein, who understood well the interdependence of creative vision and intuitive wisdom.

Understanding that every mental image directly influences our body, new dimensions of self-mastery or self-sabotage become clear to us. Although an actual or anticipated experience may last only a minute, our innate imaginative capacity to remember or anticipate the experience may trigger similar mental, emotional, and physiological reactions again and again. Bringing these emotionally charged images to conscious awareness, we can then learn to creatively and productively control our imagination, and not only master the psychosomatic symptoms associated with distress and anxiety, but also energize and strengthen positive, healing qualities of mind. As we learn to relax, focus, and move toward a deeper sense of balance, we become less tense, more peaceful, and begin to feel more trusting of and connected to the world.

"The Great Way is not difficult for those who have no preferences. When love and hate are both absent everything becomes clear and undisguised. Make the smallest distinction however and heaven and earth are set infinitely apart. If you wish to see the truth then hold no opinions for or against anything. To set up what you like against what you dislike is the disease of the mind. When the deep meaning of things is not understood the mind's essential peace is disturbed to no avail."

—Sengstan, the 3rd Zen Patriarch

"This pure Mind, which is the source of all things, shines forever with the radiance of its own perfection. But most people are not aware of it and think that the Mind is just the faculty that sees, hears, feels, and knows. Blinded by their own sight, hearing, feeling, and knowing they do not perceive the radiance of the source."

—Zen Master Huang-po

For example, if we imagine that we are feeling the warm rays of the sun, this may trigger a response that dilates our blood vessels, warms our hands, and lowers our blood pressure. Images of aggression can lead to the secretion of neurotransmitters associated with anger or fear, increasing heart rate, muscle tension, and blood pressure. Similarly, the image of biting into a tart, juicy grapefruit can cause saliva to flow; the memory of a tender embrace may fill us with the pleasant tingles of sexual arousal. When tested, athletes who mentally simulated shooting baskets each day out-performed others who had actually practiced for the same length of time on the court.

By calling forth a memory of a peak experience, we can awaken in the present moment those life-giving forces and character strengths that inspired past performance. Remembering the example of an inspiring teacher or role model or visualizing their presence can enable us to align our own thinking, will, and behavior with theirs.

FROM FIXATION TO FLOW

Though the deep natural state of mind is one of radiance and unimpeded flow of experience, the ordinary mind's habits of perception and thought tend to fixate and freeze the dynamic flow. In psychology this tendency is called reification. This tendency toward fixation leads us to misperceive and misconceive the appearances of ourselves, other people, and the various things in the world within and around us as solid, rather than beholding them as the ever-changing, fluid, radiant, and dynamic fields of energy that they are. This is what we mean when we say that people create "stories" about their experience — solidifying the meaning and making assumptions about the way things will turn out. However, by learning to find a balance between the tendency of the ordinary mind toward fixation and freezing the flow, and the universal mind's radiance and flow, we discover a natural freedom of mind that beholds the relativity of things and their appearance of solidity, while sensing or feeling their fluid, radiant nature at a deeper level of intuition. When we learn to do this, we are more able to respond to reality as it presents itself, rather than our ideas about it.

Feeling Fluid

To understand this, begin by sitting quietly. Because long-held patterns of thought tend to fixate in our bodies, focus first on your body. Notice the furrows in your brow, your posture and gestures as you talk, the hot

"Meditation does not necessarily make the craziness go away; it just makes it less personal. You just have more space and the less you identify with it, the less likely you are to get stuck in it. You 'demagnetize' so that all the stuff can arise in the mind, but the awareness does not implode and contract and become identified with all the stuff in the mind. But the stuff still arises..."

—Stephen Levine

spots where you hold tension around your eyes, in your neck or shoulders, or in your gut. As you become aware of these regions, tune into any of the patterns of mind—the attitudes, images, or feelings—that lead you to hold your body in these particular molds.

Now begin to use the flow of your breathing to help you to develop a balance between the focusing and flowing of your attention. Use your inhalations to help you draw your attention into any region in your body where you notice a sense of tension, holding, or fixation. Then as you exhale, allow the tension in that region to release, relax, and dissolve into a sense of radiance or fluidity. With each breath allow your awareness first to focus and then to flow within any regions of your body where you feel any tension, constriction, or fixation. In some regions you may need to linger for a number of breaths to allow these "ice fields" of tension to dissolve in the warmth of your penetrating awareness. In other regions you will find that one or two breaths will be sufficient to focus and dissolve fixation into flow.

As you continue to seek out and dissolve physical fixation points into flow, be mindful of any fixation points in your thoughts or feelings. These may be associated with regions in your body or simply points of tension or fixation in your mind. In the same way as before, as you breathe, allow the inhalation to focus your awareness within these regions of tension, constriction, or fixation. And as you exhale, allow the tension to relax, the constriction to release, and the fixation to dissolve into a sense of flow. Use the natural rhythm of your breathing to help you focus and flow. Continue in this way, seeking out any points of fixation in your body, thoughts, or emotions, and continue until your being feels deeply balanced, relaxed, vibrant, radiant, and open to the flow.

As you learn how to recognize and dissolve fixation into flow while you are sitting quietly, you'll better able to carry this same awareness into activity. For example, if you are walking down the street and you notice your mindbody go into constriction around some thought, simply smile to yourself as you recognize the target. Then, inhale and gently draw your awareness into the region of holding or fixation, breathe, and let it flow.

If you are talking with someone and you notice the constriction of your mindbody—associated with rising apprehension, self-consciousness, or stress—as you continue to talk and breathe, simply allow the breath to help sweep your awareness into and through that region and once again release fixation into flow.

The more you practice this simple, yet profound method of balancing yourself, the more confident you will be in any situation.

"During meditation one's mind, being evenly settled in its own natural way, is like still water, unruffled by ripple or breeze, and as any thought or change arises in that stillness it forms, like a wave in the ocean, and disappears back into it again. Left naturally, it dissolves; naturally. Whatever turbulence of mind erupts—if you let it be—it will of its own course play itself out, liberate itself; and thus the view arrived at through meditation is that whatever appears is none other than the self display or projection of the mind. In continuing the perspective of this view into the activities and events of everyday life, the grasp of dualistic perception of the world as solid, fixed and tangible reality (which is the root cause of our problems) begins to loosen and dissolves. Mind is like the wind. It comes and goes; and through increasing certainty in this view one begins to appreciate the humor of the situation."

—Dudjom Rinpoche

Beholding the Space Between

We learned an interesting lesson from one of our Chinese friends. "Hold up your hand and spread the fingers," he said. "Now, what number comes to mind that best describes what you see?" Most of us said five. He went on to say, "If you are like most Westerners, you will say 'five' because you see five fingers, or maybe you will say one, because you just see one hand." He laughed. "When you ask people in my country to do this they will most likely say 'nine,' because they see five fingers and they also see and value the four spaces between the fingers. Without the spaces, how can we have the fingers, and without the fingers, what sense does the space make? Just imagine how many other important things you Westerners overlook."

Look at one of your hands and spread the fingers apart a bit. Notice the hand as a whole, and each of the fingers, one by one. Then, shift your attention to notice the spaces between the fingers and around the hand. Focus back on the hand, then to the spaces. See if you can find the balance of mind that is able to hold both the form and the space equally at the same time. As you do this, what do you notice about your experience of the form and of the space?

Now, expand this exercise in balance by sitting quietly and observing the world around you. Notice trees, birds, people, buildings, cars, or telephone poles around you, and see each of them clearly and vividly.

After some time of noticing the forms, expand your mindful observation to notice the spaces within or around the forms. See the distances between trees, or between branches on a tree, or between the needles or leaves on a branch. Or notice the spaces above and between the buildings or the space that fills the hallways and rooms around you. Notice how the space between things actually connects everything, how the space between you and what you observe is a medium of connection, not of separation.

Now, see what it takes to attend equally to noticing the distinct and apparently separate objects, and at the same time to be sensitive to noticing the space that connects and pervades all things. Beholding this sense of infinitely expansive space that connects all things, can you view all objects as merely clouds of energy or standing wave forms filled with and floating in space?

This same principle can be applied inwardly to finding greater balance of mind. Notice how the objects of mind arise, change, and pass like clouds in the clear sky of your mind. Notice the tendency to observe only the thoughts or images and to miss the deep, clear sense of inner openness. You can anchor yourself in your thoughts or you can anchor

"What vistas might we see if we were to understand the full power of the human mind? The human consciousness may prove the most inspiring frontier in our history, an endless wellspring of knowledge, and our means of liberation from all limitation.... If we can find ways to awaken the full power of awareness, we could enter a new phase of human evolution and revitalize ourselves and our world."

—Tarthang Tulku

yourself in the mind's open field of awareness. Learning to balance these two perspectives can offer profound peace of mind.

Sense the infinity and the unity of inner space and outer space. Sense how the radiance in all things distributes itself in space into a state of perfect balance and harmony. Discover how all forms, inner and outer, arise out of and within space, last a while, and then through movement and change they exhaust themselves and dissolve back into space. Learn how this marvelous dance of form and space reveals a profound sense of balance that is fundamental to your deepest being.

THE BALANCED MIND/BRAIN STATE

Some of the most inspiring insights into how we can find greater balance in our lives can be gained by looking into how our brain works when our mind is in a balanced state. Over the years, we have had the good fortune to do extensive laboratory research using state-of-the-art technology to measure and observe the brainwaves of people while they were involved in a variety of self-mastery tasks.

One of the most amazing insights from our mind/brain research is that when the mind is in a balanced state, the brain functions in a measurably balanced way. As you watch the electrical activity of your brain displayed on a color monitor, you can see how moment-to-moment the mind/brain state flows in and out of balance. When the brain comes into balance, there is a "synching up" of the activity of both the left and right sides of the brain. It is like what happens when dozens of individual musicians stop tuning their individual instruments, or stop trying to drown each other out, and finally begin to actually play music together as one orchestra. This shift can be dramatic, instantaneous, and breathtaking, both for the person making the shift and for those of us in the lab watching the brain activity on the screen. By way of analogy, this shift from ordinary, distracted, turbulent mental activity to a more coherent, powerfully balanced mind/brain state is like watching the jumbled carbon atoms in a lump of coal organize and transform themselves into the coherent arrangement of the same atoms that we know as a bright, shining diamond. This shift toward a more balanced mind/brain state could also be described as like seeing a dim ten-watt lightbulb reorganize its energy into the coherence of a laser beam in which those same ten watts would have tremendous power.

Some examples of balanced mind/brain states were first recognized in rare and spontaneous moments that people describe as peak experiences, religious or mystical rapture, epiphanies, or illuminations. For many of us, these moments occur unpredictably and by chance

"When you are practicing Zazen meditation, do not try to stop your thinking. Let it stop by itself. If something comes into your mind, let it come in and let it go out. It will not stay long. When you try to stop your thinking, it means you are bothered by it. Do not be bothered by anything. It appears that the something comes from outside your mind, but actually it is only waves of your mind and if you are not bothered by the waves, gradually they will become calmer... Many sensations come, many thoughts and images arise but they are just waves from your own mind. Nothing comes from outside your mind... If you leave your mind as it is, it will become calm. This is called Big Mind."

—Shunryu Suzuki Roshi

at moments when we are wholeheartedly present with what we are doing—when we are filled with love, appreciation, or compassion; when we are cracked open in crisis; or when our attention is captured by beauty. For people who are well versed in meditation, prayer, martial arts, or other self-balancing practices, these powerful moments of profound grace and balance occur much more frequently and easily than for people who have invested little discipline in learning about themselves in a deeper way.

In terms of the brain power and performance of people in the laboratory, there is a striking difference between people who are highly disciplined in mental or spiritual disciplines as compared to others who have lived their life with little investment in personal development. Those who have trained in a disciplined way have measurably more brain power, greater concentration and mastery of attention, greater mental stability, enhanced tolerance for ambiguity, greater creativity, flexibility, and graceful fluidity in their mind/brain functions than those who have neglected to discipline and develop their minds. (Most of these qualities are ones we've been describing as useful for balance!)

When this unusually balanced brainstate was first discovered, numerous researchers attempted to identify the key method necessary to bring it about. After thousands of experiments, the data analysis revealed that the single most important element was an open focused quality of mind, sometimes described as "panoramic attention" or as "mindfulness of space." In this state of panoramic attention, the mind is balanced, peaceful, open, clear, and powerfully present. Brain activity is balanced left to right and front to back in a highly integrated, organized, coherent, and nearly superfluid state of responsive functioning.

Studies of people who are competing in extreme endurance sports show that when they are able to shift into an open-focused quality of mind, they are able to significantly increase their endurance and decrease their pain, when compared with competitors who are performing in a more narrowly focused and effortful way. Other studies show that open-focused people in stressful situations are able to think more clearly, make wiser decisions, process complex information more efficiently, and minimize stress when they are able to maintain a more panoramic or open-focused state.

The good news is that you don't need a brainwave machine or fancy techniques to do this for yourself. With practice, you can learn how to shift into this balanced mind/brain state whenever or wherever you like, even in the most stressful of situations.

The shift to an open-focused state does not happen by trying to make it happen. Trying just creates more tension, noise, or turbulence in the mind/brain. The shift toward balance takes place by simply relaxing and allowing the quality of mind and attention to rest naturally in its lucid, receptive, and alert state. You have already experienced a bit of this in the mindfulness practices in Chapter Four. Here are some steps to discover this balanced mindstate:

1. Because it is easier for the mind to open, equalize, and balance when your body is relaxed, take a few deep and easy breaths and release any tensions you may become aware of. To help you with this, imagine that your breath is like a warm and gentle wind. As you breathe, allow your inhalations to focus your awareness and breath into regions of tension or pain. Allow this warm and gentle breeze of the breath to melt any of the ice fields of tension or to soothe any pain. Then, as you exhale, allow the flow of the breath to help you to dissolve the tension, and to leave those areas feeling more internally spacious and open. Allow the natural flow of the breath to help you to focus as you inhale and to flow as you exhale. Take a few minutes to scan through your whole body and to let the breath help you to draw your awareness into any regions in your body that are calling for your loving attention.

2. Deepen this same technique to help you focus your awareness into any sticking points of tension in your mind. Breathing in, focus in a deep and spacious way within the center of any thoughts. Breathing out, let the energy of that thought flow or dissolve like a cloud melting into the deep clear sky.

    As you continue now, remember to smile to yourself so that you don't take this too seriously or try too hard to get this right. Also, let your eyes remain soft and relaxed. Everything up to this point is preparation.

3. Next, sense and feel your whole body like a big balloon that is completely open, unobstructed, and hollow inside.

4. Now, as you sit here, sense yourself sitting right at the very center of your universe. Consciously open and expand the field of your awareness to become aware of your unique place in space. Sitting here, allow the internal sense of openness and spaciousness to expand. Allow your attention to reach out now in an expansive way like a broad beam of panoramic awareness to see, sense, or feel everything that is in front of you. Let it reach out and become aware of whatever is behind you. Allow your peripheral vision to

"The faculty of voluntarily bringing back a wandering attention is the very root of judgment, character and will. No one is really in control of themselves if they do not have this. An education which would improve this faculty would be the education par excellence."

—William James

naturally expand and to effortlessly include everything to your left … and then to your right…. Allow your field scanners to reach up to see, sense, or feel whatever is above you, and to reach down to sense and discover whatever is below you.

5. Now allow yourself to effortlessly maintain this evenly hovering, open awareness that attends equally to the flow of both inner and outer experiences. Find the balance of mind necessary to equally attend both to the things or people around you, as well as to the spaces between these things. Delight in dwelling within the equalizing spaciousness of balanced awareness. As your spatial acuity deepens and expands, regard space itself as a medium of communication. Space, properly perceived, connects and unifies everything and everyone. Space pervades and supports all things; it doesn't separate them. It holds all things together. Remember that the new physics teaches that if you could expand the spectrum of your senses, the open spaces around you would be sensed as full of information waves. If you doubt this, turn on a radio or TV and remember how much invisible information bombards you all the time.

6. As you deepen and expand this quality of panoramic attention, effortlessly include the resonance of all the sounds filling the space within and around you. Balance this by including in your experience how these sounds emerge from silence … how they fill and move through space … and then how sounds dissolve again back into silence. In a similar way, sense everything within and around you that is in motion … and balance this with the mindful awareness of everything that is still and unmoving. Rest in this balanced awareness, allowing the flow of each breath to remind you to find a fluid, dynamic balance between focus and flow, forms and space, motion and stillness, silence and sound. Let this awareness extend equally to include all the experiences within and around you.

This deceptively simple practice for balancing the mind requires little or no effort. With panoramic attention, you simply rest at ease in the flow of experience while remaining lucidly aware. The benefits of using it, however, are far-reaching, profound, and extensively documented. One key finding of studies shows that while ordinary focal attention is commonly associated with tension and fixation, this effortless quality of "panoramic awareness" shifts your mindbody/brain into a state that is often described as being transparent to stress. When you are balanced in this quality of mind/brain function, stress and tension don't "stick to

> "The Way is perfect like vast space where nothing is lacking and nothing is in excess. Indeed, it is due to our choosing to accept or reject that we do not see the true nature of things. Live neither in the entanglements of outer things, nor in inner feelings of emptiness. Be serene in the oneness of things and such erroneous views will disappear by themselves. When you try to stop activity to achieve passivity, your very efforts fill you with activity. As long as you remain in one extreme or the other you will never know Oneness."
>
> —Sengstan

you." Instead, the intensity of your experience and the flow of information is smoothly processed in an easy and effortless way, free of tension, fixation, and the accumulation of distress. Though the tendency of most people when under stress is to tense, narrow, or constrict their focus of awareness and to "try harder," you will find extra clarity, strength, efficiency, and endurance by shifting into this more panoramic state of effortless awareness. Many people when faced with new information shut down or become more stressed and effortful. Those who know how to shift into a more openly focused mindset are better able to accelerate learning, integrate more information, and access intuition more easily.

PREVENTING INFORMATION FATIGUE

Enmeshed in this information age, we are bombarded with more information in a day than our ancestors received in years. Indeed, it is said that an average Sunday edition of the *New York Times* contains more information than the average person at the beginning of the twentieth century encountered in their whole lifetime! In our craving for knowledge and intellectual stimulation, it is common to devour vast helpings of sumptuous written and electronic material—only to wind up with a bad case of mental indigestion. When we take in more than we can absorb and integrate, the information drips off our minds like water off a duck. Few of us stop to soak on the ideas and implications of what we experience and get really "wet." Distracted and mentally moving fast, we don't have or make the time to be fully present, to ponder things deeply, or take our studies to heart.

In a report entitled "Dying for Information," 50 percent of managers surveyed reported feeling overloaded by information and worried about the stress-related problems associated with information overload. Respondents cited three factors in this overload: 1) They don't understand all the information they receive and don't have the time to figure it all out; 2) They worry about how to manage the sheer volume of information; and 3) They worry that they might put themselves at a disadvantage because they might miss important information.

For people working under these pressures day in and day out, it is common to experience a constellation of symptoms that has come to be called information fatigue syndrome. Symptoms include:

- increased sense of frustration
- increased irritability that acts like a corrosive acid eroding the quality of working relationships

"In a knowledge economy, digital information can flow fast and free. When everyone has the same digital information, value is created not necessarily by knowledge but through insights about that knowledge. In this new economy, human connections, and the conversation especially, is becoming a lost art that is ripe for a rebirth."

—David Rock

- inability to solve problems or make decisions
- tendency to panic, resulting in poor judgment, foolish decisions, and problematic consequences

Do these symptoms sound familiar to you? Take heart. If these factors are plaguing you, you can find greater mental balance in the following ways:

1. Increase your comfort and skills in working with information technology.

2. Increase your skills in accessing data through your eyes if you have the habit of subvocally reading information to yourself.

3. Learn to sort out the "urgent" from the "important" information by developing greater skills in prioritizing the flood of information in your life.

4. Build times to "unplug" or push your "clear" button. Remember the lessons from nature—waxing and waning, filling and emptying. If you want to develop the capacity to manage information overload, you need to periodically do an "information fast." Set aside times when you turn off the TV and radio, put aside your reading, and turn off your devices. Be content to simply, quietly, deeply be with yourself and those who share your life. Ideally, take an information fast during a time when you can be in nature and let yourself bask in the wave forms of your natural world.

5. When it is time to once again enter the information highway, begin mindfully and selectively. Be keenly aware of the impact of the intensity and volume of information that streams your way, and choose wisely which information you give priority to. As you re-engage in the many sources of information that are a part of your life, make a conscious effort to balance the information that you open yourself to. Challenge yourself to seek out as much good news as bad news, to harvest as much beauty as pain, and as much peaceful, soothing, harmonizing input as violent, agitating, and disruptive input. Realize that just like food, you do have a choice for what information you consume, and discipline yourself to turn off negative media that does little but disturb you.

6. Strengthen your intuitive intelligence by cultivating the strength of your quiet mind skills—mindfulness, attention, deep listening,

"Most everybody is overwhelmed. And they respond with various defense mechanisms. Denial, isolation, increased greed (I'll get it while I can"), righteousness (It's their own fault). There are a whole set of mechanisms that people use to keep from being open, because the quality of the human heart uncontrolled by the mind is that it will give away everything... We have to find ways to exercise the compassion of our hearts, and at the same moment learn how to know what the limits are and be able to say no without guilt."

—Ram Dass

and the physically felt sense of your aliveness. As you learn to trust your intuition, you will tap the wellspring of spontaneous and profound wisdom that is available to the open mind in a state of "not knowing." Most situations in which we want to be successful call more for the authenticity and spontaneity of our authentic presence, rather than the rote recitation of memorized data. Increasing your access to intuitive intelligence equips you with the skill, confidence, clarity, and peace of mind necessary for enhanced learning and creativity.

BALANCING DOING AND BEING:
DON'T JUST DO SOMETHING, SIT THERE!

Do you live your life more as a "human being" or as a "human doing"? Many of the people we meet comment that they have been so busy being a "human doing" that they have lost touch with their human beingness. They are often weary, and wound so tight that they exhaust themselves.

The business of doing takes many forms. We live in a culture where we are heavily conditioned to be uncomfortable with ourselves and to feel like we have to have something or do something to be a good, worthy human being. This leads us to be compulsively driven into doing things because we are so uncomfortable just being who or how we are. You will notice that some people are so out of balance that they are uncomfortable sitting still for more than a moment before they have to do something. You notice them tapping their feet, fidgeting around, chewing gum, smoking a cigarette, jumping up to get something to eat, anything but just simply being with and enjoying the moment without having to complicate it. Even if we are more or less physically still, it is likely that our mind will be agitated and busy doing—thinking, imagining, or otherwise complicating the simplicity of the moment. When we can't tolerate it any more, we space out or fall asleep.

Begin to recognize and appreciate when you are simply being and when you are necessarily, or unnecessarily, complicating things by doing. Gradually increase your capacity and tolerance to simply be with what is going on without having to change it. When it is time to shift, be mindful of shifting from being to doing, or from doing to being. Seek for the quality of internal strength and balance that ultimately allows you to maintain the integrity of your mindful presence of being, even while you are busy doing things.

"A mind once stretched by a great idea or new understanding will never fully return to its original dimensions."

—William James

"If you want to be truly understood, you need to say everything three times, in three different ways. Once for each ear... and once for the heart. The right ear represents the ability to apprehend the nature of the Whole, the wholeness of the circumstance, the forest. The left ear represents the ability to select a sequential path. And the heart represents a balance between the two."

—Paula Underwood Spencer

chapter nine

Catching the Waves: Balancing the Harmonics of Subtle Energy

Because energy is defined as the capacity to produce effects,
love may be referred to as an energy; it is subtle, not because its
effects or subjective impact are subtle, but because it is ineffable
to science, or so it has seemed.

—JUDITH GREEN AND ROBERT SHELLENBERGER

JUST AS MUSICAL NOTES HAVE THEIR PRIMARY NOTE AND THEN A HOST
of exquisitely subtle and beautiful overtones, the complex instrument
of your human body has its physical structure and a host of subtler harmonic dimensions along a seemingly infinite spectrum of energies and
frequencies. While novice musicians may not have developed the refined
attention necessary to consciously hear, appreciate, and produce such
exquisite tones, or may even lack the faith that they even exist, truly
great musicians are able to not only hear such harmonic overtones, but
to fine-tune their instrument to produce sublimely sweet music using
such tones. The same is true for the subtle energies within and around
us. We may not yet be able to sense them, but they are there and as we
learn to tune into them, we are naturally better equipped to live a more
beautiful, balanced, and creative life.

Insight into the world of invisible energies is offered by Buckminster Fuller, whose engineering genius inspired countless inventions and discoveries that have helped millions of people to live in greater balance upon the earth:

"The fact that 99 percent of humanity does not understand nature is the prime reason for humanity's failure to exercise its option to attain universally sustainable physical success on this planet.... When I was born in 1895, reality was everything you could see, smell, touch, and hear. The world was thought to be absolutely self-evident. When I was three years old, the electron was discovered. That was the first invisible. It didn't get in any of the newspapers; (Nobody thought that it would be important!) Today 99.99 percent of everything that affects our lives cannot be detected by human senses. We live in a world of invisibles.... I am confident that humanity's survival depends on all our willingness to comprehend feelingly the way nature works."

For many people, the notion of energy is an enigma. The greatest scientists of the world will readily admit that even energies that are taken for granted—electricity and gravity, for example—are still mysteries defying our full comprehension. The energies that we are talking about in this chapter are, at one level, related to subtle fields of life force that are bioelectromagnetic in nature and can be measured with a host of medical practices including X-rays, MRIs, CAT scans, electrostimulation, and acupuncture. There are also frequencies or qualities of energy that are more subtle and elusive in nature. They can be directly sensed, or even generated, with a high degree of precision by a sensitive person, and many of their effects can be measured. But the energies themselves are simply too subtle to measure with existing measurement technology, just as most ordinary electromagnetic energy was less than a century ago.

Every culture with a deep wisdom tradition has terms describing these subtle energies: life force, vital energy, or bioenergy; *prana* in Sanskrit; *chi, qi,* or *ki* in oriental medicine and martial arts; *lung* (pronounced 'loong') in Tibetan medicine and meditation; and *ruach* in Hebrew. In an excellent article recently published in *Bridges,* the Magazine of the International Society for the Study of Subtle Energies and Energy Medicine, Roger Jahnke, a doctor of oriental medicine, illuminates the nature of subtle energy from the perspective of the healing discipline of Qigong:

"One description of Qigong is as a discipline to 'refine the body of pure energy.' When ... the Qi develops and circulates ... it spills out into all of the channels and circuits. This is called the circulation of the light.... As the practitioner's attention is fixed on the body of light, the

"At the heart of each of us whatever our imperfections there exists a silent pulse of perfect rhythm, a complex of wave forms and resonances, which is absolutely individual and unique, and yet which connects us to everything in the Universe."

—George Leonard

dense body of substance becomes secondary. Rather than a physical body with a resonating energy field, the individual, from this perspective, is an energy field that has a small dense body of flesh at its center.

"Thousands of years ago, Chuang Tzu asked, 'Is it Chuang Tzu asleep dreaming he is a butterfly? Or is it the butterfly dreaming he is Chuang Tzu?' In the Qigong of transcendence it is asked, "Is the practitioner of the deep Qigong state a person in a moment of transcendent energetic experience, or is his manifestation in a physical body actually a brief exploration into substance by an entity whose normal state is one of highly refined resonating light energy?"

In recent decades, we have witnessed an increasing interest in the subtle energetic nature of human beings. This interest has been accelerating the evolution of medical science and fitness training to include progressively subtler and subtler dimensions of our human body. Gradually, we have come to recognize that within our physical structure are myriad vital biochemical, bioelectric, and subtle energy fields of influence that are essential to the state of dynamic balance that we call health. When the flow of energy at any of these levels is blocked, the quality of our health and vitality is compromised. Whenever the flow of energy at any or all of these levels is balanced, we move toward health.

The increasing awareness of subtle energies is due to a number of factors: the post-Einsteinian physics of the unified field has revealed that our world is composed of dynamic relationships of countless frequencies of energy. Advances in technology are revealing that our universe is indeed woven of myriad frequencies of energy, and that the health of living organisms is reflected in the flow of energy within them, and in the balanced exchange of energy between them and their environment.

The growing crisis in health care and the increasing density of electromagnetic fields in our environment are leading to advances in the number of studies related to life energy. Ultrasound, X-rays, MRIs, CAT scans, electrostimulation, acupuncture, and a host of modern and ancient approaches are increasingly being used in the diagnosis and treatment of disease and the promotion of health. Many of the hands-on treatments are proving to be highly effective, and free from the expense and side effects associated with pharmaceuticals or invasive technology.

As stress, complexity, and fragmentation in our modern lives continue to mount, more and more people are seeking knowledge and skills to restore their balance and to live with a greater sense of simplicity, connectedness, and wholeness. Increasing numbers of people are taking an interest in traditional and nontraditional spiritual pursuits, and are actively practicing various forms of contemplation, meditation and prayer, yoga, or healing and martial arts such as tai chi, chi kung (or Qigong), and aikido, all of which expand the spectrum of awareness to the natural flow of subtle energies within and among us. The effects of many of these ancient practices have been well documented in Western, Eastern, and indigenous traditions for thousands of years, and are now being confirmed by medical and scientific studies, increasing our collective faith in such pursuits.

BALANCE EQUALS HEALTH

Many medical systems in cultures around the globe regard health as the expression of balance. Unlike Western medicine, which looks at "fighting" disease with antibiotics of all sorts, other traditions — Tibetan, Japanese, Chinese, Ayurvedic, naturopathic, homeopathic, and bioenergetic, to name but a few — use nonviolent models that seek to restore health by restoring harmony within the living system as a whole. These medical systems understand that all parts of a living organism are necessary and important components of its wholeness. If there is illness, it means that one of the parts or systems is out of balance with the whole. Healing, then, becomes a question of recognizing where there is too much of one thing or too little of something else, and applying appropriate treatments to reduce the excesses or build up the deficiencies.

Looking through the lenses of the acupuncture tradition, Professor J. R. Worsley, president of the College of Clinical Acupuncture in the United Kingdom, explains that health is determined by the balance within the subtle energy called life force:

"The body-mind-spirit of every man, woman and child desires health so that we may be at one with the energy of the cosmos, both within us and without. When there is disunity the human life force signals its distress. We see then many different symptoms: continual anger, migraine headaches, sexual problems, emotional instability, ulcers, arthritis pain.... These life-force signals tell us that our balance is disturbed, that the energy is blocked and must be released to flow smoothly through the human system. Our drug-oriented and suppressive attitudes toward illness often create additional imbalance because we have not yet learned to place the emphasis on health as unity which brings wholeness to the human condition."

The law of the five elements in oriental medicine follows a basic cycle: begin with Fire, Earth, Metal, Water, Wood, and return to Fire.

"Heaven is my father and earth my mother and even such a small creature as I finds an intimate place in its midst. That which extends throughout the universe, I regard as my body and that which directs the universe, I regard as my nature. All people are my brothers and sisters, and all things are my companion."

—Chang Tsai

"From health stems harmony, balance, and unity. From disease we suffer discord, chaos, and disunity."

—J.R. Worsley, President, College of Clinical Acupuncture

"Energy medicine attempts to reconceptualize patterns of information flow in the body in ways that differ from those of biochemistry and molecular biology."

—Brendan O'Regan

This cycle describes the flow of life force energy, or chi, in every being and in the universe. According to this system of subtle energy balance, chi energy is characterized by its dual aspects of yin and yang, which form an inseparable wholeness. As Professor Worsley poetically describes it, "yin, the passive force—the negative, the night, the moon—is never separated from the yang—the creative, the positive, the day, the sun. The two are like poles of a battery. Without both poles, the battery will not function."

The five elements, like yin and yang, never stand alone. Each element governs and is governed by another. For example, according to this theory, Fire creates Earth and rules Metal, Earth creates Metal and rules Water, Metal creates Water and rules Wood. Water creates Wood and rules Fire, while Wood creates Fire and rules Earth. Each element is also understood to be related to a particular emotion, organ system in the body, and even season of the year and time of day. Learning to manage the energy of each of these interrelated elements is to participate in a dynamic dance of wholeness.

In practice, the cultivation of subtle energy awareness has to do with four areas of learning, each of which is related to balance:

1. Learning to relax and let go of unnecessary tension in the body or excessive turbulence and agitation in the mind.

2. Learning to balance the mind in order to access a state of intense calm and concentration without distraction (the panoramic mind-state described in Chapter Seven).

3. Practicing breathing exercises that link and balance the flow of mind/energy/body.

4. Learning to tap the wisdom and harness the power in rhythmic activity.

We have both done our share of traditional weight and aerobic training, and we've been amazed at the balanced power, strength, vitality, and suppleness achieved through the more subtle energy training. For nearly forty years now, Joel has practiced and studied various styles of tai chi, chi kung, and aikido. As he recalls:

"When I was in high school and college, I worked as a stock boy and then salesman for a lumber company. In my early days in that job it was not uncommon for me to stack more than a ton of lumber a day. As a result, I got really strong, but not in a particularly balanced or flexible way.

"Since Universe is Energy, part of the process of understanding, at least as I experience it, is to learn to "see" flows of energy and specificities of energy. Both are necessary. Because, you see, Universe is both Whole and Specific. Western science is beginning to understand this through explorations about particle and wave. Both particle/particularity/specificity of Universe and the wave/flow of Universe were aspects I was encouraged as a child to apprehend and understand. I was asked to "see" the dancing points of light and then to apprehend the shift from location to flow. Much of shamanic practice has to do with developing the ability to enter and use this shift."

—Paula Underwood Spencer

"Later, between my undergraduate and graduate study, I studied and practiced tai chi for nearly three hours a day for about six months. In those days I didn't have a car and I rode my bike to get around town. When I started doing tai chi, I was amazed how much stronger and flexible I became, even though the movements were so very subtle.

"Then, in preparation for an intensive six-month training program we did for the U.S. Army Green Berets, I did a lot of well-engineered weight training, plus internal energy training with aikido, a Japanese-style martial art that works with bringing 'the energies of heaven and earth into harmony within the human being.' This produced yet another quality of balance that served me well during the arduous training we did for the troops.

"And finally, when we did a year of contemplative retreat, my only real exercise was 60 to 90 minutes a day of chi kung, the Chinese Taoist energy balancing system, and a variety of yoga postures. This was a good balance for the quiet sitting practice that lasted from 14 to 20 hours each day. During the entire year, my health and spirits were excellent, and coming out of retreat I felt physically stronger than before and had amazing suppleness and endurance as I set out on a number of long hikes."

It seems that the more deeply we are able to cultivate inner balance, including energetic balance, the more dramatically it will be reflected in the "outer layers" of our lives. That's why we devote the rest of this chapter to energy practices.

Two Palms Talking

Palm to palm, rub your hands vigorously together as you breathe deeply for about a minute. Then, continuing to be mindful of your breathing, gently hold your hands about two feet apart and slowly bring them toward each other. Imagine that you are generating or gathering a spongy, luminous field of energy between your hands, and let your hands gently push in on this ball, and then bounce gently outward again. As you do this, remember to smile to yourself so that you don't try too hard, get too self-conscious, or take this experiment too seriously. After a short while, hold your palms facing each other and gently move your hands back and forth, noticing any subtle vibrations or sensations that may occur along your fingertips or palms. Maintain a sense of curiosity, and be open to discovery. Feel free to repeat stage one and to breathe and rub your hands together again if your sensitivity begins to fade. Experiment with the exercise at different times and see how your experience changes. Chances are you will have a direct experience of the subtle energies we are talking about.

"Convert the body into a luminous fluidity, surrendering it to the inspiration of the soul. This sort of dancer understands that the body, by force of the soul, can in fact be converted to a luminous fluid. The flesh becomes light and transparent, as shown through the x-ray—but with the difference that the human soul is lighter than these rays. When, in the divine power, it completely possesses the body, it converts that into a luminous moving cloud and thus can manifest itself in the whole of its divinity. This is the explanation of the miracle of St. Francis walking on the sea. His body no longer weighed like ours, so light had it become through the soul."

—Isadora Duncan

Heaven Meets Earth

Another dimension of subtle energy balancing is the weaving together of above and below, of heaven and earth. Your ability to reach to the heavens is dependent on how deep your roots are in the earth. One especially powerful method of staying present in your power throughout the day is to experience yourself as a conduit for the energies of the earth and heaven. Because the electrical conductance at your feet and at your head have inverse properties, there's actually a basis in the bioelectrodynamics of your body to support this practice. Variations of this method have been used in countless cultures around the globe for thousands of years.

As you sit or stand quietly, imagine or sense a spiral of energy rising from the earth up through you and opening into the sky. Just be with this image or sense for a few moments, allowing it to emerge as naturally as possible into your awareness. Breathe in and draw the energy of the earth up and into you. Exhaling, feel this flow of energy rising up through your body and opening upward into the sky. Draw the energy of the earth up and into yourself, and then offer it up to the sky. As you begin to do this, you may find it helpful to use one of your hands to make an uplifting spiral, reaching up from the earth and spiraling up to the heavens. As you breathe and continue this image, imagine that this rising vortex of energy spirals through you with a deep and powerful cleansing action, dissolving any blockages to the free flow of the energy of your bodymind, and leaving you feeling clean and clear, vitalized and keenly aware, as though your energy and vibration have bumped up a notch.

If this kind of visualization exercise is difficult for you, just relax and give it your best shot. It's important to remember that, as with most of these exercises, you'll find that the more effortlessly you hold the image and allow it to happen, the more vividly you'll be able to actually experience its reality.

As you breathe, simply allow the flow of earth energy to continue to rise and flow in the background. Now, as you inhale, imagine drawing a vortex of energy or light down into you from the heavens above. Use all the special effects you can to make the visualization as vivid or as deeply felt as possible. Imagine that you fill yourself with the energy of the heavens, and that as you exhale, it spirals down and through you into the earth. Drawing in the heavens, bring that energy or light down through you into the earth like a wave of blessings. Let this shower of light and energy wash through you, cleaning and clearing your body and mind of any energies that get in the way of the flow. Feel your

"All beings are embraced within one

All-encompassing great energy.

So I understood from the coolness

Of this morning's passing breeze."

—Yamada Mumon

body and mind sparkling clean and clear in this balancing flow. Let the descending wave smooth, balance, and ground your energy, and deepen your sense of stability and rootedness in the earth.

Once you have established the ascending and descending flows of energy, simply rest in the flow of awareness of both of these two spirals flowing through you at the same time. Allow this vitalizing, harmonizing, healing flow of energy to totally dissolve any remaining tensions or concerns. As you rest easily in this counterbalancing stream, any energy that's blocked or frozen within you simply dissolves and melts into the flow. Let any sense of denseness or solidity in your mindbody dissolve and find its dynamic balance as a higher order of stability and strength that is pure flowing energy and light.

Though at first you may just get the idea of what this image suggests, with practice this will become a concrete and powerful experience for you. Be patient, don't expect fireworks or anything special. Just let your mind move like a magnet over a jumbled pile of iron filings and know that as your mind moves, all of the energies and particles within you will begin to align. Allow the energy that's already within you to flow more smoothly through you.

As with many of the methods you're learning, its actual form is very simple, but the power and insight that can be generated through practice over time can be quite profound. Throughout the day, if it feels right to you, when you're sitting at your desk, on the bus, or walking down the street, you might activate your awareness of these spirals of energy and light flooding through you. As you do, awaken to and rejoice in your groundedness and connectedness to the strength, steadiness, and nurturing nature of the earth, and to the open, light, majesty, and vast potentials of the heavens. Realize that though you may not be aware of them, you're never separate from these realities even for an instant. Practicing in this way will quietly, powerfully, and invisibly equip you with a way of moving through the world in balance and in a way that leaves a trail of light, good vibes, and blessings wherever you go.

"When you walk across the fields with your mind pure and holy, then from all the stones, and all growing things, and all animals, the sparks of their soul come out and cling to you, and then they are purified and become a holy fire in you."

—Hasidic saying

Circle Breath

In this exercise we'll introduce you to one more extremely useful strategy for balancing and focusing the energies of your mindbody. We use this technique often when we're walking or sitting quietly for a few moments. Initially we learned this from bioenergy healer Mietek Wirkus, and later learned variations from numerous teachers from other disciplines. As a child in Poland after the war, Mietek would accompany the local doctor in his visits to people who were sick or in pain. The doctor had no medications and few supplies, but he had found that his patients would often get better just by having Mietek be with them for a while or hold their hand.

Through prayer and meditation, the healing love of Christ, and years of training with elders who had developed their own healing gifts, Mietek learned much about the balancing and healing energy of love. In 1982, when bioenergy therapy was approved in Poland to supplement ordinary medical work, Mietek became one of the first professional bioenergy therapists to work in the Polish medical centers performing detailed diagnoses and treatments for hundreds of people each week. In 1985, Mietek and his wife, Margaret, a journalist who assists in his work, emigrated to the United States. They settled in Bethesda, Maryland, and have offered classes for more than two thousand physicians, nurses, and other helping professionals.

Mietek has also participated in numerous research projects. We first met him at a special conference on energy medicine and healing at the Menninger Foundation, where Mietek was the focus of considerable interest. At one point, we were conducting an informal study on Mietek's brainwaves during a healing session. While he was working, one of the observing scientists stepped forward to get a closer look. "My God," the skeptical scientist exclaimed, "you can actually feel the energy he is generating." Stepping back and then moving forward with his hands outstretched in front of him, he excitedly pointed it out to the rest of us, "See right here, about four feet away from him, you can begin to feel the energy. It's like a very gentle breeze or an electrostatic field. And it grows stronger, or denser, the closer you approach. I've never experienced anything like this in my life." Intrigued by their notoriously skeptical colleague's discovery, dozens of other observers performed this simple experiment themselves, and most were amazed that they could actually sense a subtle and calming field of energy radiating from Mietek and his patient. One method that Mietek uses to keep his own energy balanced while he is working with people is the circle breath we're about to teach you. Here's one version of how the method we learned from him works:

Begin by becoming aware of your body and the natural flow of your breathing. As you inhale, draw your attention up along the back of your body, from the base of your spine to the top of your head. Then, as you exhale, allow your awareness to circle from the crown of your head down along the front of your body all the way to the base of the spine. Inhaling, again draw your awareness up from the bottom of your

"The healer must feel and be the heart chakra...Heart center vibrations relate to unconditional love, and to treating other beings with love, understanding and respect...It is not thinking the word 'love', it is not a visualization process, it is the real sensation of pure love which brings warmth delicate vibrations in your heart area."

—Mietek Wirkus

"The conclusion is always the same: love is the most powerful and still the most unknown energy of the world."

—Pierre Teilhard de Chardin

spine to the crown of your head; exhaling, allow your awareness to circle down along the front of your body to the base of the spine. The flow of the breath defines a circle rising up the back and then flowing down along the front of the body. The beginning and end point of the breath is at the bottom of your spine. At the peak of your inhalation, your attention is focused at the crown of your head for a moment. Practice until you establish an easy, effortless, circular flow of energy around this orbit. Once you know how to initiate this flow of balancing energy and awareness, you will be able to rest in this circulation of energy while you are engaged in other activities.

Like many other exercises that ask you to direct your attention and energy in unfamiliar ways, this may at first feel awkward. As with all learning, as you become more familiar with organizing your energy and awareness in this new way, it will begin to feel more and more natural, and unfold in more and more effortless and deeply sensed ways.

The Drop and the Ocean

Sitting quietly and comfortably now, allow the breath to freely come and flow, effortlessly releasing and dissolving thoughts and tensions into space. As you inhale, imagine a bubble of light filling you from within. As you exhale, imagine this bubble expanding and opening out into the space around you. With each in-breath, be filled by this luminous energy, and with each exhalation, imagine this sphere of light opening and expanding, moving freely through the space, the walls, the buildings, the earth around you. Let everything open. Let your small sense of self expand and open to your surroundings. Allow all of the feelings, sensations, and vibrations within your body to expand, open, and dissolve like a cloud melting into space. Use the breath to extend your sphere of energy awareness like the radiating circle of a pebble dropped into a still pool....

Ahhh.... Opening in all directions.... Filling the space above you.... Filling the space below you.... Expanding and opening out before you.... Behind you.... Opening and expanding as a sphere of energy life awareness all around you.... Opening and expanding with each breath....

Now as you inhale, allow this light energy to take on a pleasing color and a pleasant feeling quality — perhaps blue and peaceful, or red and warm, or any combination that feels right to you. As you inhale, allow this feeling and color to fill you deeply and as you exhale, allow this colorful, "feelingful" sphere to open and expand within and around

"Researchers of so-called energy medicine are a curious lot. We unearth ancient practices, dust them off, clean them with modern solvents, and study them under the lens of high technology. All the while, we seek to distill simple truths about health and illness."

—David Eisenberg

"...When you want to enter a different aspect of Life, you wait for the point at which Particle becomes Wave. And just at that split second before the Particle is gone and the Wave takes over, you enter between, and you become Energy. At that point where the wave becomes Particle again, you enter between and you re-become who you were or you make a different choice. Which is also possible. I think it is that space in which healing occurs."

—Paula Underwood Spencer

you. Imagine flooding the space around you with radiant waves of warmth and well-being. Imagine generating an atmosphere of peace, balance, and harmony that pervades the world around you. Sitting quietly, simply allow this wellspring of inner energy to rise within you and to open and expand so that everyone around is bathed in this light.

Now, having established this expansive sense of well-being, imagine that as your sphere of energy awareness opens, there is an echo from the universe at large. Imagine that as your nucleus of energy expands outward, a vast ocean of peace, or warmth, or love converges and pours itself into you. Sense the incredible feeling of balance that emerges as you simultaneously experience this expansion and convergence — your tiny mind-drop opening outward, dissolving into a vast spacious ocean, and this ocean of positive energy vibration flowing and converging into your drop. Allow all of your limitations, pains, thoughts, and cares to be dissolved into this free-flowing convergence, resting in wholeness, connected and belonging to the world.

The Nine-Part Breath

The last technique in this chapter is an important one to add to your energy balancing tool kit. It's called the "nine-part breath" because it has the powerful effect of focusing your mind/brain in just nine breaths! Because of its effectiveness in optimizing the functioning of your central nervous system, it's often used as a preliminary practice for any activity that calls for clear thinking and focused concentration.

It's been interesting in our research to see how many places we've encountered this technique. We've found it being widely taught in medical centers around the world, and when we were working with NASA it was being studied to see if it might be helpful in preventing lapses into the hazardous states of inattention that lead to high-speed plane crashes.

Many schools of natural healing describe cycles of energy changes that accompany each hour of the day. In acupuncture they are associated with the activation of different meridians and the physical, emotional, and mental functions associated with them. According to the natural body clock discovered by the Chinese, each meridian has its own two-hour period during the day when it is at its peak energy. For example, 11 p.m. to 1 a.m. is the time during which the gall bladder has slightly more energy than any other meridian. A person with an imbalance in the Water element often finds that their energy wanes during late afternoon beginning at about three o'clock, reaching a low ebb at about five o'clock. This is due to the bladder's dominance from 3 p.m.

"All things, material and spiritual, originate from one source and are related as if they were one family. The past, present, and future are all contained in the life force. The universe emerged and developed from one source, and we evolved through the optimal process of unification and harmonization."

—Morihei Ueshiba
   O'Sensei

to 5 p.m., and the kidneys' dominance from 5 p.m. to 7 p.m. Similarly, each of us has a time of day when we feel at our best or worst, depending on our unique life energy.

In the ancient Indo-Tibetan Kalachakra system of medicine and astrology, every second, minute, and hour of each day corresponds to subtle shifts in energy within the body and in the heavens above. The practice of meditation within this system is based on understanding the balance and harmony of these energies. Within the Judeo-Christian and Islamic traditions too, each section of the day has its own set of holy prayers and practices, reflecting an awareness of the different energies that each daily cycle brings. For example, in the Benedictine monastic tradition, monks and nuns observe a series of hymns, prayers, chants, rituals, and invocations for each hour of the day. The hours are regarded as the seasons of the day and are meant to be traversed in a mythical way in order to attune oneself to the elusive sacred mystery that lies beyond time. Until the crazed pace of modern life set in, many wisdom traditions encouraged a way of life that was slow enough to nurture balance, harmony, and deep connectedness to these energies throughout the many activities of each day.

One simple way to re-establish this balance is to cultivate a mindful awareness of the natural cycles of your breathing throughout the day. Not only does the breath flow in and out, but day in and day out, your breathing shifts back and forth on roughly ninety- minute cycles, alternating in its strength of flow between your nostrils like the ebbing and flowing of an inner tide. This natural cycle of energy flow is called the "nasal rhythm" in modern medicine.

Though outwardly this rhythm is reflected by the alternation of a stronger breath flow through one nostril or the other, inwardly the flow of the breathing affects, and is related to, shifts in dominance between the two hemispheres of your brain. At the mental level this cycle of alternating activation of the left and right hemispheres of the brain shows up as alternating periods of mental focus and mental diffusion throughout the day.

Learning to read your energy and to shift your energy from one state to another is an important key to personal balance. One of the most simple and direct ways to do this is to pay attention to the changing flux and flow of the breath from one nostril to another. Before we introduce you to two simple variations on this method, let's first do a little experiment to see how your brain is working.

When you begin, it's helpful to check and see which nostril you're breathing most strongly from. This can be done by simply observing

"We consist of and are sustained by interweaving currents of matter, energy, and information that flow through us interconnecting us with our environment and other beings. Yet, we are accustomed to identifying ourselves only with that small arc of the flow-through that is lit, like the narrow beam of a flashlight, by our individual subjective awareness. But we don't have to so limit our self-perceptions... It is as plausible to align our identity with the larger pattern, interexistent with all beings, as to break off one segment of the process and build our borders there."

—Joanna Macy

the flow of the breathing, or by putting a small mirror, like a compact, under your nostrils for a couple of breaths. Then you can look to see which nostril has left the largest cloud on the mirror. This is the nostril that you're breathing most dominantly through at this moment. If you don't have a mirror handy, you can just lick the back of your index finger and hold it under your nose as you breathe. Now, as you breathe on your finger, whichever side you feel the most air flow from is the dominant nostril at this time. So what does this tell you?

At the times when you're breathing predominantly through the right nostril, the mental functions associated with your left hemisphere are activated, and activity of the right hemisphere is cooled or subdued. What this means is this is a good time to focus your attention on tasks that require sharp, clear thinking and attention to details, such as writing a technical report or balancing your checkbook.

On the other hand, or brain if you will, if the breath is flowing most strongly through your left nostril, then the mental functions of your left hemisphere will be cooled and the functions associated with the right hemisphere will be activated or enhanced. This will facilitate the focusing of your attention on qualities that are more related to patterns and process. Thus, left nostril breathing reflects easy access to mental functions associated with right brain functions, such as creative planning and design. Functions like imagination, intuition, and relaxation are naturally enhanced when you're breathing through your left nostril and activating your right hemisphere. Researchers have also observed that the state of left nostril/right brain dominance is more conducive to receiving new ideas, while right nostril/left brain dominance is an advantage for speaking and giving a presentation.

If you watch carefully, you'll also notice that there are periods throughout the day when the breathing is naturally balanced between both nostrils. These points of balance occur at those moments of the "changing of the guard," when the breath flow is at the point of shifting from right side dominance to left side dominance or vice versa. At these times, there's an evenly balanced flow of breath through both nostrils. This translates over to an evenly balanced flow of energy and information processes between the mental functions of left and right hemispheres of the brain. So, whenever the breath flow is even between left and right you'll be better able to stay focused, and to balance alertness with relaxation, thinking with observing, and analyzing with creative imagination. Once you learn the nine-part breath, you'll be able to tune your system with your breathing so that you can balance your energy/brain/mind whenever you like.

"What we call mystical experience occur when there is a sense of oneness or harmony between the energy of power of our bodies, minds, and spirits and the energy of other beings and the universe itself."

—John Mack, Harvard psychiatrist

"You and I and everything in the universe exist as a part of the endless flow of God's love. Realizing this, we recognize that all creation is bound together by the same benevolence. To harmonize with life is to come into accord with that part of God which flows through all things. To foster and protect all life is both our mission and our prayer."

—Morihei Ueshiba

The first variation in this approach teaches you the basic mechanics of the process, which are really very simple. Once you gain some mastery over this technique, it may quickly become your favorite balancing tool. This method has been described by many of our clients as the closest thing they've found to "mental floss" for clearing the noisy mind! First, inhale through your right nostril and exhale through your left nostril. This can be done by using the index finger of your right hand to close the nostril that you're not breathing through. As you inhale, close the left nostril, and breathe in through the right nostril. Then shift your finger to close the right nostril and exhale effortlessly and easily through the left nostril. Repeat for three full breaths. Then inhale through your left nostril and exhale through your right nostril three times. Finally, resting your hands in your lap, inhale and exhale through both nostrils three times, breathing as evenly as you can. Check in with yourself and notice any subtle shifts that have occurred in how your physical and mental energy is flowing.

Though at first this method may feel awkward, once you learn the moves and get into the flow, it's really very simple. The most important point to keep in mind as you do this nine-part, alternate-nostril breathing is to breathe easily and naturally. Avoid trying to breathe too deeply or forcefully. What works best is to simply relax and merely guide the flow of the breath through the floodgates of your nostrils as you breathe at your own natural rhythm and depth. You may be thinking, "Sure, I can just see myself now, sitting at my desk doing this one. I can just imagine what people will think." Well, keep in mind that once you learn how this works and what it feels like, you can simply guide the breath flow through the power of your visualization and intention alone, without needing the aid of your fingers. This will allow you to do this practice anywhere without anyone having a clue what you're doing.

Many people find that this is a useful technique to have in their pocket, kind of like a polishing cloth to shine up their mind in a spare moment here or there. One of our colleagues does this to get balanced for the day while she's warming up her car in the morning. Others we know will use the nine-part breath to clear their mind like a reset switch between intense meetings with clients. As you get to know yourself and your own natural rhythm, you'll find many useful times to plug this one in.

Now that you have the basics, let's add a second variation. Continue to breathe in the same alternating rhythms and add a simple visualization. In the space in front of you, envision a shining sun or a radiant source of the purest light and energy that you can imagine. Imagine

"Mindfulness can unblock the flow of energy in the body... As the body becomes clear for the flow of energy and the impermanence and change of all sensations becomes more apparent, the focus of attention... moves to the region of the heart. Now mindfulness and concentration on the changing sensations, even the movement of the mind, are experienced as changing, as vibrations. Perception of the whole world, matter and mind, becomes reduced to various levels of vibration. The meditator continues applying his understanding and growing skill and applies his penetrating insight to directly experiencing the true nature of existence."

—U Ba Khin, former Secretary General of Burma

the streams of light/energy filling you and flowing through you like a shower of light that washes you clean and clear from the inside out.

As you sit quietly in the presence of this source of light, tune in and remember that you are in essence a living, vital, field of energy. And that the quality of your life and health depends on how successfully you're able to receive, transform, and release energy. As you breathe naturally, imagine or sense yourself as a field of energy and light resting in and infused by a larger ocean of energy and light. Imagine that as you breathe you're able to light up your personal energy field and wash it clean and clear of any darkness or disease.

Holding this image in mind, begin the nine-breath sequence again. As you do the first set of three breaths, imagine that you can inhale this light through your right nostril, and that as you inhale it flows down through the right side of your body. As you exhale through the left nostril now, imagine that this pure, clear stream of light rises up through the left side of your body, totally flushing away or dissolving any tensions in your body or any **agitation** or disturbances in your mind. Once again, the stream of light and energy flows in through the right nostril filling you with the purifying, vitalizing light, and as you exhale, it streams up and out the left, washing your energy, body and mind, clean and clear. One more time now, in right ... pure clear light ... out left ... flowing clean and clear. Yes!

In the second set, inhale and draw the light in through your left nostril, down along the left side of the body and then let it wash up and out through the right side of your body. Vitalizing, purifying, energizing light in ... washing the body clean and clear and dissolving any trace of dullness or sluggishness in your mind ... good. Once again, breathe in through the left, mentally guiding the flow down through the body, then exhale up and out the right, breathing away any fogginess in your mind or any fatigue in your body. And a third time now, energizing and vitalizing, dissolving and releasing.

With the last three breaths, imagine two streams of pure clear light streaming into you from the sun or your special energy source, filling you through both of your nostrils. The two streams of light come down through the left and right sides of your body to meet and flow together. As you exhale, imagine or mentally guide these streams of flowing energy together into a single stream that spirals up through the center of your body, filling you with a deep, bright, clarifying light. In through left and right, down ... merging and flowing up together to your crown and out through the mid-point between your two eyebrows ... lighting

"The Sioux idea of living creatures is that trees, buffalo and man are temporary energy swirls, turbulent patters....You find that perception registered so many ways in archaic and primitive lore. I say that it is probably the most basic insight into the nature of things, and that our more common, recent Occidental view of the universe as consisting of fixed things is out of the main stream, a deviation from basic human perception."

—Gary Snyder

up your body and mind in a deep and quiet way. Allow each breath to bring your mind and body into balance and into flow....

Pause for a moment now and scan through your circuits to check for any subtle shifts in your energy or awareness. Like any new set of physical or mental moves, this may seem complicated at first. The essence of the nine-part breath is simple: in left, out right three times; in right and out left three times; and then in and out through both three times. Once you get the sequence, you can experiment with adding the visualization. As always, remember to smile, relax, and allow the breath to flow naturally without any effort.

BE MINDFUL OF LOCAL FIELDS

Having taught classes in bioelectromagnetic fields and health, we would be remiss not to address some of the more mundane, but important, health balance issues related to energy. Remembering that choice follows awareness, we are moved to share the following energy health guidelines for your consideration:

As we mentioned in the last chapter, since your body is highly electromagnetically sensitive, it is wise to be mindful of how the fields generated by your devices may impact or imbalance the energy field, metabolism, and health for yourself, your family, neighbors, and coworkers. Standards in many other countries for electromagnetic fields of mobile phones, devices, routers, and transmitting antennae are much more protective of health considerations than in the United States, and device manufacturers are not generally enthusiastic about putting warnings on their products—even though some states and countries are now finally beginning to mandate this. This is a topic worthy of considerable research and we encourage you to be dubious about safety claims generated by those who profit from these industries.

In general, we encourage you to avoid carrying a cell phone that is powered up in your pocket next to your generative organs—especially if you hope to conceive a healthy child. Also avoid carrying your phone in a shirt pocket or bra next to your heart, or in your pants pocket, as it can interfere with healthy cell development. Whenever possible use your speaker or a headset rather than actually holding the phone next to your own head. Similarly, keep in mind that your "laptop" is actually not well suited for use sitting on your lap when it is receiving and transmitting information—especially if you'd like to keep a healthy sperm count! While electro-mindfulness practices may be inconvenient and require some discipline and creativity, there is wisdom in this advice!

"There is a vitality, a life force, an energy, a quickening, that is translated through you into action, and because there is only one of you in all time, this expression is unique. And if you block it, it will never exist through any other medium and will be lost."

—Martha Graham

With children in mind, please avoid having a small child hold a cell phone next to their head, and never talk on a cell phone that you're holding at the same time as you're holding an infant, since the penetration of the phone's electromagnetic field into the brain of a small child is many times deeper than it is for an adult's brain. Related cautions are called for in using many wireless baby monitors as they too can generate strong fields, and seldom carry warnings. If possible, locate your wireless router distant from where you sit or sleep, and far from your children's bedrooms. Also, be mindful of the locations of cell-phone antennae and "smart meters" mounted on buildings close to where you choose to live, work, or send your children to school or play. Unfortunately, the placement and calibration of such transmitters is often poorly regulated and can create imbalances that compromise both health and safety.

ENERGY PROTECTION

Often we meet people who are afraid of being thrown off balance by other people's energy. They fear that they will be drained by others, or that they will pick up on other people's negativity. Their fearful anxiety, and the tension and toxicity associated with it, is honestly more detrimental than any incoming effects from other people.

In order to protect themselves, some people stay home behind locked doors, carry guns, drive cars with bulletproof glass, or live in gated communities. Others wear surgical masks or rubber gloves when they go out in public. Some people wear talismans, chant prayers, give to charity, or sprinkle holy water in order to protect themselves. Although each of these strategies may well have their appropriate application, each may also subtly reinforce a fearful mindset in relationship to others that would tend to make one even more vulnerable and out of balance.

In his book *Aikido: the Arts of Self-Defense*, the great aikido master Tohei Sensei speaks of a different quality of protective energy that we can invite into our awareness, one that connects us with a greater level of balance:

> "Remember that you live always under the protection of
> some mysterious force. This force is nature. Therefore, true
> self-defense does not stop with defending oneself against
> others, but strives to make oneself worthy of defense by
> nature herself. It respects the principles of nature. True
> practice must be in consonance with the will of nature....

"This garden universe vibrates complete

Some may hear a sound so sweet.

Vibration reaching up to become light

And then through gamma, out of sight.

Between the eyes and ears there lie

The sounds of color and the light of a sigh

And to hear the sun, what a thing to believe

But it's all around if we could but perceive.

To know ultraviolet, infrared, and x-rays

Beauty to find in so many ways."

—Mike Pinder

When your mind and your acts become one with nature, then nature will protect you. Fear no enemy; fear only to be separated from the mind of nature. If you are on the right path, nature will protect you … and you need not fear anything. When an enemy wants to attack you while you are asleep, nature will awaken you. When an airplane has an accident, you will fortunately not be on that plane. Trust nature and do not worry. Leave both your mind and body to nature. Do not recognize friend or foe in your mind. In your heart let there be generosity as large as the sea that accepts both clean and unclean water. Let your mind be as merciful as nature that loves the smallest tree or blade of grass. Let your mind be strong with sincerity that can pierce iron or stone. Repay the forces of nature, work for the good of all and make yourself a person whom nature is pleased to let live. This is the true purpose of training."

The most effective protection field is to fill your heart with love and to let that love illuminate your world. For example, let the radiance of your heart reach out and bless people as you drive to work. Pray that they safely reach their destinations and find the happiness and fulfillment that they are looking for.

Seek to discover the natural radiance of this inner light of love within you. When you find it, then let it shine as a blessing to the world. Because this dimension of your being may be too subtle for you to sense at first, experiment with living as though it is really here within you and around you. Looking out into your world, begin to notice and sense the radiance of everything—how sounds, smells, and lights radiate out through space, how the wind blows, yet is invisible. Notice how sounds travel through space and can be heard but not seen. Warming your hands by a candle or a stove, catch a glimpse of the radiance that shines through all things, especially living beings.

As you move through the world, imagine that you trace a pathway of energy through space and time. Imagine that anyone passing through the field of influence you have generated is drawn more toward balance in their own life. At stoplights, or at crossroads, on mountaintops, in churches, or meeting rooms along the way, pause, breathe, focus, and intentionally generate a large bright field of blessing energy that will refresh or inspire all those who pass through that space for a long, long time to come.

"From a hidden place, unite with your enemies from the inside, fill the inner void.

That makes them swell outwardly and fall out of rhythm; instead of progressing, step by step, they stop and start harshly, out of time with you. Bring yourself back into rhythm within. Find the moment that mates with theirs—like two lovers creating life from the dust. Do this work in secret, so they don't know. This kind of love creates, it doesn't emote."

—Neil Douglas-Klotz (translation from the Aramaic of Jesus' words "Love your Enemies")

"Be lamps unto yourselves; be your own confidence.

Hold to the truth within yourselves as your own truth."

—The Buddha

"You are the light of the world."

—Jesus

chapter ten

Balanced in Spirit

There is something in all of us that seeks the spiritual ....The
spiritual is inclusive. It is the deepest sense of belonging and
participation. We all participate in the spiritual at all times,
whether we know it or not. There's no place to go to be separated
from the spiritual, so perhaps one might say that the spiritual is
that realm of human experience which religion attempts to connect us to through dogma and practice. Sometimes it succeeds
and sometimes it fails. Religion is a bridge to the spiritual — but
the spiritual lies beyond religion. Unfortunately, in seeking
the spiritual we may become attached to the bridge rather than
crossing over it.

— RACHEL NAOMI REMEN, M.D.

BEDAZZLED BY THE DIZZYING COMPLEXITY AND BREAKNECK PACE OF
our modern lives, our wobbly balance has exiled us from the vitality
of staying in touch with the deep core of our wholeness: a spiritual
connectedness with our world. Rushing to and from work, managing
our investments, taking care of our kids and our parents, many of us
become distracted. We forget what we're doing and why we're doing it.
We forget where we came from and where we are going. Having wandered far from our homeland, we may have a gnawing feeling that what
is most essential in our lives has slipped away. Yet no matter how far we
have wandered, still it seems that something deep within us is calling us

home. As the Sufi mystics remind us, the main form of spiritual practice is remembrance of the one reality in which all things have their being.

A story, attributed to Dan Millman, comes to mind about a little girl named Sashi. It reminds us that our search to remember, to find balance in spirit, may begin very young. Not long after the birth of her brother, Sashi began asking her parents if she could be alone with her new baby brother. Her parents were uneasy about this, worried that she might be jealous and might hurt him, so they said, "No." But Sashi was really a loving big sister and showed no signs of jealousy toward her brother. With time her pleas grew more urgent. Finally the parents consented. Sashi was overjoyed. She went into the baby's room, and shut the door. It didn't close all the way and was open a crack—just enough for her curious parents to listen in. What they saw was little Sashi walking quietly over to her brother's crib, putting her face really close to his, and saying, "Baby, tell me what God feels like. I'm afraid that I'm starting to forget."

TAKING REFUGE

We checked our maps as we crossed the Straits of Juan de Fuca to make the most direct crossing to a tiny bay where we could find shelter from the storm. Braving fairly heavy seas for nearly five hours through eight-foot swells and fifteen-knot winds, we bounded along on our twenty-four-foot sailboat. The three of us were a pale shade of green by the time we reached the southernmost of the San Juan Islands. Rounding the point into a tiny harbor sheltered from the wind, we were feeling extremely wobbly; it was all we could do to keep our balance while we pulled down the sails and dropped anchor for the night. We fired up the stove and brewed a pot of green tea to settle our stomachs. "A toast to safe harbors and shelter from the wind!" We raised our raku cups with a clink of sincere gratitude for our safe passage.

As we sat on deck talking under the stars that night, our conversation turned to our countless fellow travelers—people out in their tiny boats on the heavy seas of their life—who may be dizzy, disoriented, and fearful, feeling out of their league, alone, or in danger, or even blissfully unaware of how at risk they are. It seemed to us that we are all attempting to skillfully navigate our way across the great ocean that spans from birth to death, and that many of us are ill-equipped. "Where can people take refuge from the stormy seas in their lives?" we wondered aloud together.

"Another name for God is surprise."

—Brother David Steindl-Rast

"Now there are varieties of gifts, but the same Spirit; and there are varieties of services, but the same Lord; and there are varieties of working, but it is the same God who inspires them all in every one."

—I Corinthians 12:4–6

"We are spiritual beings having a human experience.

We are not human beings having a spiritual experience."

—Albert Schweitzer

On your journey across the changing seas of your life, where do you take refuge and seek balance? In your work? In your family? In your possessions or investments? In your network of support? In your faith in, and communion with, the Mystery, by whatever name you may call it? The notion of refuge is a universal theme throughout the world's great spiritual traditions. One of the most beautiful references to it is found in the Koran, in this translation by Lex Hixon:

"With each breath may we take refuge in the Living Truth alone, released from coarse arrogance and subtle pride. May every thought and action be intended in the Supremely Holy Name as direct expression of boundless Divine Compassion and Most Tender Love. May the exaltation of endless praise arising spontaneously as the life of endless beings flow consciously toward the Single Source of Being, Source of the intricate evolution of endless worlds. May we be guided through every experience along the Direct Path of Love that leads from the Human Heart into the Most Sublime Source of Love."

A survey of the world's spiritual traditions reveals a common grounding in a trinity of refuges: First is the living example of great teachers. Second is the inspired body of spiritual teachings that gives practical principles, techniques, and advice on how to live a truly righteous and balanced life. And third is the refuge found in fellowship in the spiritual community of kindred souls who walk along the path with you and who are a source of companionship and support along the way. The presence, or absence, of any of these three refuges has much to do with your success in finding balance in your life. With this in mind, ask yourself,

- How have the spiritual beliefs and traditions you encountered growing up contributed to the quality of balance in your life?
- Who are the people — living or historical — whom you hold as the most inspiring spiritual role models or mentors? What qualities lead you to have faith in or devotion toward these people?
- What wisdom traditions speak most deeply to your soul and nourish you spiritually? Where do you find the most reliable, relevant, practical guidance and inspiration for living your life in a wise, compassionate, and balanced way? What principles or precepts guide your life, and what practices keep you in tune with the larger whole?
- Who are the members of your circle of spiritual friends — those who live with the integrity and values that you feel most in tune with, who are most supportive of the ideals you aspire to hold, who inspire you to stay true to a path worth walking?
- What other sources of spiritual inspiration do you rely on?

"If for a moment we make way with our petty selves, wish no ill to anyone, apprehend no ill, cease to be but as a crystal which reflects a ray—what shall we not reflect! What a universe will appear crystallized and radiant around us."

—Thoreau

"Everyone who is seriously involved in the pursuit of science becomes convinced that a Spirit is manifest in the Laws of the Universe—a Spirit vastly superior to that of man, and one in the face of which we, with our modest powers, must feel humble."

—Albert Einstein

Reflecting upon and answering these questions may be the cause of either much heartfelt gratitude or grief. Many of us have busied ourselves with so many other pursuits that these supportive influences have been severely neglected, and their balancing presence is sorely lacking. If this is true for you, it would be a wise investment of time and energy to seek out or rebuild these connections.

A THOUSAND WAYS

We live at a time when the traditional religious fabric of our society is unraveling, leaving many of us looking for a way to put our piece of it back together. A large portion of the population who didn't really get much of a spiritual education growing up are unsure of how to balance their spiritual inclinations with the rest of their life now. For many, spirituality is found more through communion with nature, in the arts, or in love for family, than in conventional religious institutions or weekly services. You may be one of those who grew up in a religious tradition but never really felt spiritually nourished by your religious upbringing, or perhaps you were at some point deeply disturbed by the incongruities or abuses that you encountered in the name of the religion you were raised in. Whatever the reason, you may feel uneasy when it comes to stepping out of your comfort zone to explore unfamiliar spiritual paths, or are simply just turned off by organized religion, yet still thirsty for true spiritual inspiration.

"There are a thousand ways to kneel and kiss the ground!" said Rumi, the great mystic poet, and now this is truer than ever before. The intensity of spiritual yearning of our time is matched by a sometimes dizzying diversity of approaches to fulfill it. In our search for balance, we may somewhat timidly step out of our comfort zone to explore old traditions that are new and unfamiliar to us. Stepping out across these boundaries generates an energy that can be interpreted as fear or excitement, or some blend of the two. These days, on any given weekend you might go hear a Dharma talk, celebrate Mass at a parish different from your own, sit a Zen *sesshin* (meditation retreat), take a yoga class, or rock for Jesus at a jammin' Mega Church. You might teach Sunday school or attend a Bible study class. A friend might invite you to a Jewish Renewal Friday night Shabbat or Saturday Shabbat meditation at a local *shurch* (synagogue), where you might return on Sunday for Christian prayer, or come again on Wednesday evening for Dances of Universal Peace, or Sufi dancing with the local Whirling Dervishes. You may be drawn to a temple or church where people worship in a language different than

"Our discovery of God is, in a way, God's discovery of us. We know Him in so far as we are known by Him, and our contemplation of Him is a participation of his contemplation of Himself. We become contemplatives when God discovers Himself in us. At that moment, the point of our contact with Him opens out and we pass through the center of our souls and enter eternity."

—Father Thomas Merton

"The Light is One Though the lamps be many."

—Anonymous

your own, where they may sit in pews, on zafu meditation cushions, or on folding chairs. You may sign up for a meditation retreat at a Buddhist center, yoga ashram, Jewish community center, or a Catholic abbey; attend an interspiritual symposium with mystics from diverse faiths; join the ArtMonks at the Art Monastery; or attend services at a Unity church, a Church of Religious Science, a Unitarian Universalist Church, or Baha'i temple. Perhaps you'll drink tea or study medicine ways with a Huichol, Shipibo, or Siberian shaman, or participate in a sweat lodge prayer and purification ceremony with a First Nations elder, or one of the Thirteen Grandmothers from different clans, or engage in one of countless other paths of spiritual practice. Along the way, perhaps you'll visit one of the growing number of spiritual bookstores. Given the number of options to choose from, it is easy at times to feel confused or overwhelmed. In search of balance and spiritual renewal, you may simply choose to putter in your garden, talk deeply with your spouse or friends, really play with the kids, be blissfully alone for a day, go for a walk in the mountains, volunteer at a senior center, or meditate in the sweet simplicity of your own home.

Whatever path or paths you take up the mountain of Spirit will be learningful. If you do venture out in unfamiliar ways, go slowly, mindfully, and watch the signs. Don't rush. Walking in balance, feel the earth at your feet. Let your heart and mind stay open to seek the source of the light behind the many lampshades you see. Friendships with fellow spiritual travelers are most precious; they can go deep and last a lifetime. Ask many questions. Celebrate the humanity, sincerity, and aspirations that you share. Let your heart be inspired and uplifted through prayer, chant, and rituals. Find unity in sharing sweet silence. As you learn from and appreciate diversity, balance differences with searching for common ground. Take courage in knowing that you can always return to the familiar paths, more mature in your wisdom, enriched by your explorations, and having discovered some new ways to "kneel and kiss the ground."

If you find that you are the type who is easily confused or bewildered by exploring many paths or studying with many teachers, it may be wise to simplify your spiritual pursuits. If diversity overwhelms you, do research until you find a path that is spiritually satisfying for you, and then through study, practice, and contemplation, drill that well deep until you come to the heart of balance.

If you are by nature a weaver and synthesizer, your temperament may better suit you to seek inspiration from study and practice with a diversity of different traditions. Seek to find the common heart and core around which they come together and appreciate how each contributes to deepening your wisdom and love and strengthening your faith. If you are a mature practitioner with a clear sense of your path and tradition, there is little to fear and much to gain through inspiring encounters with multiple spiritual traditions. These will likely serve to clarify and deepen your faith and insight. Instead of digging many shallow wells, it is possible to dig one very deep well using many different tools.

Remember that true progress in spiritual awakening may have little to do with unusual or extraordinary experiences or epiphanies. The real fruits of practice are found in the quality of your daily life and interactions with others, and an expansion of your compassion and sense of intimate relatedness with all life. As your wisdom and faith deepen, you will begin to live with greater empathy, respect, patience, kindness, and compassion. Developing more harmonious relationships, you'll come to naturally live a more ethical and moral life, and as you do you will grow freer of the burdens of tension, fear, anger, resentment, hatred, pride, jealousy, and selfishness. Gradually, authenticity and inner peace, harmony and balance, appreciation for both unity and uniqueness, and selflessness with divine dignity will emerge ever more fully and brightly in your life.

THE INTERSPIRITUAL MOVEMENT

While some geographical regions like the "Bible Belt" may be steeped in traditional religious ways, other regions like Cascadia in the Northwest United States and British Columbia are characterized by a majority of people inclined to be SBNR, "Spiritual But Not Religious." A full 63 percent of the NW population self-report as "none" in terms of religious affiliation with only 37 percent claiming a strong bond with a faith tradition. According to a recent study by the Pew Research Center, one fifth of Americans check "none" on surveys of religious preference, and among young adults under 30, a full third check "none." Yet, nearly 70 percent of "nones" still report belief in God or a universal spirit. More than half say they often feel a deep connection with nature and the earth (58%), while more than a third classify themselves as "spiritual" but not "religious" (37%), and one-in-five (21%) say they pray every day. In addition, most religiously unaffiliated Americans think that churches and other religious institutions benefit society by strengthening community bonds and aiding the poor. While this may or may not be the story of the decline of formal "religion," it is clearly the story of the ascent of a more universal and unbounded "spirituality."

"The whole idea of compassion is based on the keen awareness of the interdependence of all these living beings who are all part of one another and all involved in one another... The whole purpose of life is to live by love."

—Fr. Thomas Merton

"There comes a
time in the spiritual
journey when you
start making choices
from a very different
place. . . And if a
choice lines up so
that it supports truth,
health, happiness,
wisdom, and love, it's
the right choice."

—Angeles Arrien

"In the spacious
mirror of reflective
consciousness we
begin to catch
glimpses of the unity
of the interwoven
fabric of the cosmos
and our intimate
participation within
the living web of
existence. No longer
is reality broken into
relativistic islands
of pieces. If only for
a brief moment at
a time, existence is
glimpsed and known
as a seamless totality.
To explore our gradual
awakening to the
aliveness and unity
of the universe...
awakens the
intuition that a living
presence permeates
the universe."

—Duane Elgin

In recent decades this trend has steadily grown giving rise to the emergence of a thriving global "interspiritual movement" that draws inspiration from many great mystical traditions who share a common sacred ground. With many historical precedents in the lives of many Sufis and mystics throughout the ages who proclaimed allegiance to the One God shared by all faith traditions, the interspiritual movement has been fueled by the Monastic and Interspiritual Dialogues hosted by Gethsemane, the Naropa Institute, California Institute for Integral Studies, and the "gatherings of the gurus" that began in the '60s. Countless people are drawn to this movement, with notable leaders including Brother Wayne Teasdale, Father Thomas Keating, Father Bede Griffiths, Archbishop Desmond Tutu, His Holiness the Dalai Lama, Reb Zalman Schecter Shalomi, Will Keepin, Cynthia Brix, and Kurt Johnson. Brother Wayne, who coined the term "interspiritual," describes the many facets of this movement as follows:

- The emergence of ecological awareness and sensitivity to the natural organic world
- A growing sense of the rights of other species
- A recognition of the interdependence of all domains of life and reality
- The ideal of abandoning a militant nationalism and recognizing our essential interdependence
- An evolving sense of community among the religions through relationships between individual members as well as a growing receptivity to the inner treasures of the world's religions
- A reverent openness to the cosmos, with the realization that the relationship between humans and the earth is part of the larger community of the universe

In his last book, *A Monk in the World*, Brother Wayne says, "Interspirituality is not a new form of spirituality, or an overarching synthesis of what exists, but a willingness and determination to taste the depth of mystical life in other traditions." The interspiritual movement is based on dialogue, reflection, and deep silent contemplation with followers of different traditions with the notion that the more Protestants and Catholics, Jews and Muslims, Hindus and Buddhists, indigenous medicine people and mountain yogis, mind scientists and sincere seekers come together in silence, prayer, meditation, sacred chant, reflective dialogue, mutual worship and celebration from which enduring friendships and sacred bonds would grow, auspicious alliances would emerge, and the Mystic Heart that is shared by all will be illuminated.

WHERE TO BEGIN

The spiritual journey toward balance begins with the first step: opening your heart to a sincere wish or prayer to renew the spiritual vitality of your life. Because it truly is a responsive universe, if you are sincere and keep your heart, mind, and eyes open, you will likely begin to see signs that point you toward your next step.

On your quest for wholeness, seek the wise council of those whom you respect or who inspire you with their authenticity and spiritual integrity. Ask them what paths they have taken, what churches, synagogues, or temples they are nourished by. Ask them what preachers or teachers they have found who live with the greatest integrity and spiritual vitality, and who offer the most practical wisdom, inspiration, teaching, and guidance. Ask what books, translations of scripture, and inspiring biographies have most deeply touched and inspired them in their lives. Seek out the company of well-grounded, sincere, and credible fellow seekers. If possible, meet once a week, or at least once a month with a circle of fellow seekers to share your discoveries and to discuss your questions.

As your search continues, remember that, in essence, you already have what you are looking for. The spiritual path is one of remembering the true depth of your wholeness. It is not about deserving, earning, or acquiring something you don't already have. Some say, "God loves you just as you are." Others express it as "All beings have the seed of enlightenment or full awakening within them," or "There is nothing that exists outside of God." How could you ever be separate from the wholeness that you are?

> "When you search for the Beloved,
>
> It is the intensity of the Longing that does all the work.
>
> Look at me and you will see a slave of that intensity!"
>
> —Kabir

PERILS OF THE PATH

"How do you know your mother is your mother?" No, this is not a Zen koan. This was Joel's high school physics assignment on his first day of high school. Joel's teacher was an intense, brilliant scholar and social activist who had also at one time in his life been a Jesuit monk. "Write a paper," he said, "showing me your reasoning and proofs for your assumption that your mother is truly your mother. Question your assumptions about reality. How do you really know what to believe and where to put your faith?" "In some ways," Joel reflects, "I feel like I am still working on this homework assignment, and it has helped me to continually uncover and examine my unchecked assumptions."

In search of balance through spiritual pursuits, there are many perils of the path. Keep your eyes open and your discerning wisdom keen. There are teachers and traditions that are rare and precious beyond belief. If you are fortunate enough to be able to spend time with them, your life will be truly enriched. And, there are teachers and traditions that, quite honestly, we don't send people to. We find this practical advice from the Buddha very helpful:

"Do not believe in what you have heard; do not believe in the traditions because they have been handed down for generations; do not believe in anything because it is rumored or spoken by many; do not believe merely because a written statement of some old sage is produced; do not believe in conjectures; do not believe in as truth that to which you have become attached by habit; do not believe merely the authority of teachers and elders. After observation and analysis, when it agrees with reason and is conducive to the good and gain of one and all, then accept it, practice it, and live up to it."

How do you know if you are pursuing an authentic spiritual path, or if you have met a good teacher? If you are looking for a balanced approach, watch for: impeccable ethical and moral integrity; service to others; compassion; respect for discipline; personal accountability of both leaders and community members; faith; embodiment; groundedness; respect; joyfulness; fellowship with, or at least tolerance for, people of different faiths; an inspiring lineage of practitioners whose lives have been enriched; a community of kindred souls that inspires your respect and admiration; love; celebration; humanity; respect for silence as well as questions; an honoring of the mythical and the mystical; a path of clear reasoning that welcomes debate; a balance of prayer, contemplation, study, and service in practice; a reverence for the Mystery, by whatever name.

Avoid extremes. While discipline is important, a well-grounded, gradual, and steady approach to practice is more likely to develop balance than an overly austere or intense spiritual fast track. The diversity of spiritual paths is designed to fulfill the spiritual maturing of individuals of different temperaments. For example, if you tend to be overly indulgent, a path that offers some discipline and austerity can be helpful. If you tend to be a "control freak" or rigid in your ways, a path with too much austerity or rigorous discipline may just add to your imbalance.

"God is at home... It is we who have gone out for a walk."

—Meister Eckhart

Spiritual communities, though potential havens, can also become escapes for the socially challenged. And teachers from other cultures, though masters in their spiritual disciplines, may lack the experience they need within their new culture to give realistic council to their students — and may even lose their own balance as they encounter the enticements of the West.

We wholeheartedly encourage you to keep your eyes wide open. Open-minded skepticism will help you to find a healthy balance between over-critical cynicism that may miss the real thing, and gullible naïveté that is easily duped into signing up for misleading or dangerous pursuits. Over the years, in search of a deeper understanding, our work, travels, and research have led us to encounter many different spiritual paths. Having also encountered many of the perils of the path — and having worked clinically with some of the casualties — we offer the following list of cautionary guidelines to check out before you "sign up" with a spiritual teacher or group. Though it is possible that you may find some of the following warning signs on an authentic path, they are often associated with less trustworthy situations. It is always wise to observe the integrity of people's behavior carefully, and ask yourself these three essential questions:

- Does what I hear make sense to me?
- Does it conform to the golden rule?
- What is the intention? Is it to harm or to help? Is it for limited self-interest — "self"-improvement — or service for the good of the whole and benefit to many for generations to come?

If you are looking for balance on the spiritual path, beware if you encounter any of the following "red flags":

- teachers or circles of practitioners on your journey who are out of integrity, or who don't practice what they preach
- scenes where questions are not welcomed or answered in straightforward ways, or where raising concerns about conduct or ethical violations is frowned upon — especially if you are told you are being too judgmental when you do raise honest concerns
- anyone who claims that they can give "it" to you, especially for a price
- anyone who claims to be the only teacher or path that can deliver the goods

The Four Reliances:

"First, rely on the spirit and meaning of the teachings, not on the words;

Second, rely on the teachings, not on the personality of the teacher;

Third, rely on real wisdom, not superficial interpretation;

And fourth, rely on the essence of your pure Wisdom Mind, not on judgmental perceptions."

—Mipham Rinpoche

- if the price of admission excludes people who are truly sincere
- if you are expected to purchase lots of expensive merchandise or paraphernalia to get on board
- slick, extravagant trappings or heavily marketed, empire-building enterprises
- discrimination or attempts to turn your heart against others
- hidden agendas
- fanatical, narrow-minded sects
- a heavily authoritarian, paternalistic, sexist, or militaristic scene
- practices that work with intense energy manipulation or forceful breath work without having first established a strong foundation in ethics and personal grounding
- teachers, paths, or seminars that seem ungrounded, make outrageous claims, use coercion tactics, or hustle you to get others to sign up

Be discerning if you encounter people who seem to display unusual or extraordinary powers. People easily confuse psychic sensitivity with spiritual maturity, deluding themselves and others. Channeling, clairvoyance, or other entertaining displays may have little to do with anything spiritual. If teachers claim to be channeling disembodied beings, enjoy the show, and see if there are any messages of value to you. When in doubt use common sense and, if you stay around, carefully observe the ethical integrity and behavior of your traveling companions. Because some teachers misrepresent themselves, claiming spiritual authorizations, realizations, or backgrounds that are downright lies, you may want to check references or question their authenticity. If the biography of a spiritual teacher heavily emphasizes their attainments in past lives (maybe, but who knows?) we suggest that you stay focused on the integrity of the one you can see sitting in front of you.

IN SEARCH OF WHOLENESS

We often hear people say that their wholeness as a human being is not welcome at work, and they are expected to leave their values, feelings, spiritual orientations, and even physical needs at home. These comments are as common from executives as from blue collar workers. To ignore or deny any of our many dimensions is foolish, dangerous, and unfortunately quite common in the institutions of our workaday world. What we ignore or disown we tend to waste or destroy.

"Blessed are the man and the woman who have grown beyond their greed and have put an end to their hatred and no longer nourish illusions. But they delight in the way things are and keep their hearts open, day and night. They are like trees planted near flowing rivers, which bear fruit when they are ready. Their leaves will not fall or whither. Everything they do will succeed."

—Psalm 1, translated by Stephen Mitchell

As living whole systems, we are endowed with miraculous capacities for sensory discovery of our world, creative physical movement and communication, a broad bandwidth of emotions, an inconceivable capability for creative imagination, intelligence, and thinking, and a nervous system with an extraordinary ability for intuitive discernment of systems dynamics at a far greater breadth and depth than mere thinking or ordinary perception can ascertain.

At our heart and core, inseparable from the rest, is a quality of radiant and receptive presence — a creative and compassionate intelligence that defies description. In the English language we regard this as "consciousness" in the psychological sense, or "Spirit," the animating force within all things, if we assume a more spiritual view. Being universal in proportions, it transcends the narrow confines of our personal identity. To say that there is no place for spirit, or consciousness, in a relationship or business is as foolish as saying there is no place for our body or mind. Let's get real. We are multidimensional human beings — all other arenas of human endeavor will be handicapped without drawing inspiration from the full spectrum of our humanity.

The truth is that we of course bring our spirituality everywhere we go, we just don't think of it in those terms. In his dissertation, "Spirituality and Transformational Leadership in Secular Settings," Dr. Stephen E. Jacobsen, a former business entrepreneur and now ordained minister, observed that though leaders in business had a difficult time clearly defining "spirituality," they still believed and spoke strongly about its vital importance in forming the values, ethics, and beliefs that they brought to work. This diverse group of business leaders of different genders, backgrounds, organizational settings, and locations shared a common belief that spirituality is at the heart of their business activity. They regarded spirituality as a means of integrating self and the world, and affirmed that life is a seamless whole system without boundaries between what is "spiritual" and what is "secular."

WHOLENESS: THE BALANCE OF DUALITY AND NON-DUALITY

Looking out into your world, imagine opening your wisdom eyes and seeing clearly the true nature of all things and all beings. From this view, regard each living being like an island rising out of the sea. Each one embodies and expresses itself in a unique way, having its own physical and psychological topography, boundaries, personalities, quirks,

> "Spirit... is the point of human transcendence; it is the point where the human is open to the Divine, that is, to the infinite and the eternal. It is also the point where human beings communicate. At that point of the Spirit we are all open to one another."
>
> —Father Bede Griffiths

unique views and experiences unlike any other island or living being in the vastness of the universe. At first glance, if we rely solely on our physical senses, we appear to be separate and independent from each other. Yet, upon closer examination as our wisdom eyes open, we discover that each of us is actually comprised of streams of shared elements. We have similar aspirations, hopes, and fears. Looking more deeply, we see that underlying the unique visible expressions emerging from the ocean, we share a common bond, unity, and interdependence with all beings whose existence emanates from the deep ground of earth we share at our roots.

This understanding is expressed by many languages of the world as in, for example, the Mayan word for "you," *inlakesh* which translates as *"another myself,"* or the Hindu salutation, *Namaste*, "I bow to the Divine presence within you that is the deepest identity of all beings," or in the South African term *ubuntu*, signifying that "I am because we are." Such insight may dawn within us as an idea or a possibility. It may also arise in rare and precious moments of clear, deep "seeing" confirmed through direct, non-dual realization in the more intimate experience of meeting, greeting, or embracing ourselves within another. Nobel Peace Laureate Archbishop Desmond Tutu offers the insight that, "A too highly developed individualism can lead to a debilitating sense of isolation so that you can be lonely and lost in a crowd.... *Ubuntu* is not easy to describe because it has no equivalent in any of the Western languages.... *Ubuntu* speaks to the essence of being human and our understanding that the human person is corporate. The solitary individual is in our understanding a contradiction in terms. You are a person through other persons. *Ubuntu* speaks about the importance of communal harmony ... speaks about warmth, compassion, generosity, hospitality, and seeks to embrace others."

Each of us is both one and many, individual yet interdependent. We are both an "I-land" and the whole world. Unique and individual, our life is intertwined with countless other beings and generations in the great body of life.

As we seek to fathom the depths of what living in balance really means, we see that our nature encompasses two primary dimensions. The first is the "ordinary dimension" of dynamic balance that is found in the flow of ever-changing moment-to-moment experiences and occurrences that stream through our senses, mind, and body. Through disciplines such as mindfulness and the cultivation of compassion, loving-kindness, contemplative inquiry, and deep reflection we become ever more adept at monitoring and managing these ever-changing

"That which is sacred and unknowable is called spiritual.... The spiritual way of heaven is inherent virtue, which includes the four qualities of eternity, happiness, selfhood and purity; like the four seasons, these are orderly. 'Using the spiritual way to establish education' refers to complete teaching that is in accord with essential nature; therefore it is ultimately accepted by those in all realms of consciousness."

—Buddhist I Ching
(Trans. by Thomas Cleary)

tides of experience in order to live in harmony and balance in relationship to them.

The second dimension exists at the level of Essence. While the ordinary dimension is comprised of an ever-changing flow of both gross and subtle sensations, mind states and mental images, the "essential dimension" of living in balance is more subtle and elusive. This essential dimension of being is formless, vividly clear, and knowing. It is of the nature of love and compassion, and is accessed or known through refining our intuitive wisdom. When we are in touch with this most subtle dimension of living in balance, we realize that in each and every moment and situation we stand on sacred ground inseparable from harmony and balance. It is ever-present, available to us and pervading us, and expresses itself as the dynamism and multiplicity of all things, all beings, and all experiences. Mystics often say that this essential dimension of our true being is closer to us than our own breath, or as Rumi puts it, "*It is the breath within the breath*."

As we refine and deepen in our capacity for living in dynamic balance we realize that this includes embracing the integration of all the many dimensions of our being: the ordinary and the essential, the relative and the absolute, the historical and the timeless, the particular and the universal. Physicists speak of this in terms of the inseparability of local particles and non-local infinitely expansive waves, the manifest material world and the quantum realm of infinite potentiality, the explicate manifest and measurable world, and the implicate immeasurable dimension of infinite unmanifest potential.

TWO PATHS

There are two paths of awakening to balance that are realized through spiritual practice. One path leads metaphorically from the periphery of our being to our center, from our ordinary, imbalanced, confused, deluded, alienated, exiled, and homesick state of being to the promised land of our "awakening," "liberation," or "enlightenment." Such a path of harmonizing and balancing, purification, accumulation of spiritual merit, and gradual awakening is said to be a long and often arduous journey.

The other path begins by affirming that in the deepest most essential truth, we have really never left home. We have never left the center or lost our balance — no matter how far we may have imagined or dreamed ourselves to have wandered in our mindless distraction. On this path we begin with a glimpsing or an epiphany that awakens a remembering

"The real work of meditation is not so much just to calm ourselves but to find a capacity to open to the sorrows and joys and the complexity and struggles and pains and beauty of our human life in a very immediate way. Spirituality really has to do more with our humanness than with anything extraordinary."

—Jack Kornfield

and an indwelling confidence or faith that we have never completely lost our balance or tumbled out of grace, but rather that we have merely lapsed into a temporary obscuration like when transient clouds cover the sun. This clouded state manifests as mindlessness, distraction, confusion, or some deluded mode of being that views the world in ways that are mistaken and out of congruence or phase with the actual way things are. Out of this adventitious imbalance and ignorance, we become confused and "miss the mark" (the original meaning of the word "sin" in Hebrew) creating a myriad of unintended problems for ourselves, others, and our world.

When we "wake up" out of this confusion, our view aligns again with the way things are and we realize that we are actually inseparable from the Beloved that we yearn to merge with. The clouds pass and we see that we are embedded within the holiness of being and stand on sacred ground. We remember that our most essential identity is truly noble and divine, and that we could never, ever in our wildest imagination be unworthy of this birthright, or cast out and exiled from this most sublime, divine, source that is at the sacred heart of our true universal identity.

Problems arise when we lose our balance and lapse into a dualistic mode of perception that reifies our selves, things, and beings as separate, independent entities rather than dynamic beings whose lives and identities are shaped and formed by a myriad of streams of energy, information, and influence from the many people in our lives, media, and natural elements. Regarding people, animals, and objects as other than ourselves rather than a part of ourselves, our misperceptions and misconceptions naturally give rise to desire, attachment, lust, and greed toward those things and relationships that we are attracted to, and various degrees of anxiety, fear, hatred, or aggression regarding those we are averse to. Our confusion leads us to believe we can commodify, subjugate, own, enslave, or exploit other people, animals, minerals, trees, and ecosystems, rather than act as responsible stewards who nurture and care for them as part of the whole ecosystem that nourishes and sustains all life. Given that this is the default mode of ordinary consciousness in which most people operate, is it really any wonder that so many circumstances in our world are problematic and out of balance? In the simplest of terms, the main culprit is our ego identity or self-centeredness, and this fundamental misperception occludes the view of wholeness and sacredness that is clear to us when, as the "shiviti" psalm proclaims, we balance ourselves and behold the Sacred before us always.

"The Clear Bead at the Center changes everything.

There are no edges to my loving now.

Some say there's a door that opens from one mind to another.

But if there's no wall, there's no need for fitting the window.

Or the latch."

—Mevlana Jalaluddin Rumi

TWO WAY TRAFFIC

When our minds are dominated by selfish concerns and we lapse into duality, we fall out of the grace-fullness of resonant alignment with the field of wholeness. Our thoughts, words, and deeds reflect this dissonance and imbalance so that as we think, speak, or act from a fragmented state, it is likely that our inner imbalances will ripple and spill out into our world in ways that convey our imbalance to others. Our sense of unity with all things devolves into heavily defended and polarized "me's" and "you's."

At other times our minds are dominated by wholesome qualities that come forth from the depths of our being. To help us strengthen and restore balance within ourselves by attuning to these most essential states and qualities of being, many wisdom traditions offer a wealth of practices. Through our dedication to living in balance, and to the personal practices that we rely upon, it's as though the strings of our physical, emotional, and mental being become tuned to the more refined resonances and harmonics of our most subtle or spiritual being. We can directly experience that ways of living that are honest, true, pure-hearted, kind, and compassionate actually make us feel happy. This is because such attitudes and ways of being are resonant with the deep integrity and truth of the reality of our innermost essential being. When we drift out of alignment and attunement with our most true and essential nature, we wobble out of balance. Living in confusion, lying or being harmful, feel bad because they are dissonant with the true reality of who and how we are. We feel anxious, agitated, and confused, and our lives reflect this disconnect. It's as simple as that.

Achan Amaro, a contemporary Buddhist teacher living in the West, writes: "When the heart is completely enlightened and liberated, when there's... nondual awareness, then the natural disposition of the heart is loving-kindness, compassion, joy, and equanimity. These qualities naturally radiate forth when the heart is completely free. This is not some 'thing' that 'I do.' This is the innate disposition of the pure heart. It's the same with the factors of enlightenment (mindfulness, contemplation of reality, energy, joy, tranquility, concentration, and equanimity). These are intrinsic qualities of the liberated mind, of the awakened and enlightened heart. They are the immanent manifestations of that transcendent reality." Amaro goes on to say, "What's 'outside' in terms of the conditioned is completely attuned to what is 'inside.' It's a practice and process that works both ways. As we practice loving-kindness, our heart automatically comes into accord with reality and we feel good.

"At a deep level, ecology merges with spirituality because the experience of being connected with all of nature, of belonging to the universe, is the very essence of spirituality."

—Fritjof Capra

And when our heart is awakened to reality, it automatically functions with lovingkindness, compassion, sympathetic joy, or equanimity. It's like two-way traffic on a highway between the conditioned and the unconditioned."

The Buddha taught that the "divine abodes" of limitless compassion, lovingkindness, joy, and equanimity regarding all beings are not distant or transcendent qualities, but are innate qualities ever-present in the depths of each being. This is echoed in Jesus' teaching that "the kingdom of heaven is within you," a teaching that was further amplified by Thomas when he wrote, "If you bring forth what is within you, it will save you. If you do not bring forth what is within you, it will destroy you." By engaging in practices that cultivate such qualities of being, we align and attune ourselves in ways that bring forth a resonant harmony and balance between our inner reality and our embodied reality. As we do, we refine our capacity to create harmony and balance in our lives.

When you set the intention to live in harmony and balance, and dedicate yourself to live true to whatever principles, practices, and ways of life are most meaningful and resonant for you to align yourself with this deeper, more universal ground of harmony and balance, the innate sacredness and interrelatedness of all things and all beings becomes ever more clear and accessible to you, and your presence in the world embodies and expresses it more and more fully.

As you align ever more deeply and completely with this essential pure dimension and cultivate positive qualities of being such as mindfulness, compassion, generosity, patience, or gratitude, you are simply attuning yourself with the natural integrity, strength, and essential power that are always present in the deep ground of your being and of all being.

When you are aligned and attuned with this innate, indwelling goodness that is your most essential identity, it becomes impossible to willfully harm any living being, to exploit them sexually or financially, to destroy or pollute our natural world or our bodies, or to relate to our world or living beings in harmful, deceitful, or greedy ways. We are protected from violating or dishonoring the deep natural integrity, balance, and order of things and are able to live in harmony and balance, to be *pono*, and live in right relationships.

Living in ways that are ever more aligned and attuned to the essential dimension of deep harmony and balance that underlies all things and all beings, we experience the upwelling of a radiant natural force of spiritual integrity that is like the inner breath and light that animates and enlivens all things and all beings. In the mystical intuition and

"Rigpa is a Tibetan word, which in general means 'intelligence' or 'awareness'. In Dzogchen, however, the highest teachings in the Buddhist tradition of Tibet, rigpa has a deeper connotation, 'the innermost nature of the mind'. The whole of the teaching of Buddha is directed towards realizing this, our ultimate nature, the state of omniscience or enlightenment—a truth so universal, so primordial that it goes beyond all limits, and beyond even religion itself."

—Sogyal Rinpoche

imagery of Hildegard of Bingen, each being is seen to be like "a feather on the breath of God." This brings to mind the image of living like one of those dancing windsock figures that you see in used car lots which gyrate and dance with the pulsations and rhythms of the air streaming from a big fan at their bases. Or, as the Ojibway wisdom-keepers poetically remind us, "Sometimes I go about with pity for myself and all the while Great Winds are carrying me across the sky."

As we engage in practices that balance our mind, body, and energy system our daily life becomes ever more finely balanced and in "right relationship" with the web of life and the global ecosystem. Our way of living is more true to spirit, in harmony with the Tao, the Dharma, the Way, the Truth, and more transparent for the clear light, presence, lovingkindness, and compassion of our true nature to shine through into our lives and world. As we practice living in balance, the illusions and confusions embedded within our limited stories of self-identity are reamed out, and the optical delusion of consciousness that occludes our clear recognition of nonduality dissolves to reveal the true, selfless dimensions of our essential, universal, or divine identity. Sister Bernadette Roberts, a contemporary mystic, observes: "Emptiness is two things at once: the absence of self and the presence of the Divine. Thus as self decreases, the Divine increases."

The process of aligning and attuning ourselves to the noble qualities that are most essential to our being allows a flow of grace, goodness, and purity to flow through the gross and subtler structures of our personality, ordinary identity, nervous system, and subtle energy system in ways that dissolve incongruities, dispel our mental obscurations and confusions, resolve cognitive dissonance, and generally purify us across the many dimensions of our being to be more receptive and transparent, allowing the inner light of our true self to shine forth bright and clear in our lives and world. As our teacher Kalu Rinpoche once said, "As you practice these holy teachings, slowing the clouds of sorrow will melt away and the sun of wisdom and true joy will be shining in the clear sky of your mind."

"In ancient times, various holistic sciences were developed by highly evolved beings to enable their own evolution and that of others. These subtle arts were created through the linking of individual minds with the universal mind. They are still taught by traditional teachers to those who display virtue and desire to assist others. The student who seeks out and studies these teachings furthers the evolution of mankind as well as her own spiritual unfolding. The student who ignores them hinders the development of all beings."

—Lao Tzu,
  Inner Chapters,
  Hua Hu Ching

SPIRIT AT THE THRESHOLD

In most traditional cultures of our world, the day begins and ends with some time of meditation, prayer, worship, or communion and thanksgiving that affirms a life of balance in relation to the larger whole. For those of us who make the time for such attunement on a daily basis, life takes on a different tone as we establish a reference point of deep balance to access throughout the turbulence of the day. Joel remembers witnessing his grandfather's approach to balance:

Each morning before work, my grandfather, who was Jewish, would take time with his prayer book and skull cap to *davin*—say his prayers. I think he started this on a daily basis after his own father died. While he was praying, I'd often play in the kitchen at dawn with the sun streaming through the windows as it rose majestically over the Cascade Mountains to the east of our home. When he'd finish, we'd talk and have breakfast together, often oatmeal, or eggs and toast, and then he'd set out with his pickup truck to his recycling business. Then again in the evening before bed, Gramps would read the Psalms and take some time in prayer. Though he never pressured me to follow in his example, in his wise and gentle way Gramps succeeded in transmitting an important message through his disciplined, reverent example: there is a larger reality worthy of my reverent supplication, and making time to commune with it on a daily basis is a wise way to begin and end each day.

Years later, sitting on his deathbed together as we weathered the last raging storms of his life, we took refuge in his faith and the confidence that he had indeed lived a good life. When I first arrived at the hospital, he looked at me, saying in a serious tone, "Son, something is really wrong, and I think I'm gonna die. And I'm just not sure what to do." After being with Gramps in the hospital more than a dozen times before, I took his tone to heart. "Well, I'll be here with you and we'll make this journey together, at least as far as I can go with you. And you know, you just can't do it wrong." For days, his condition worsened until, writhing and moaning in pain, Gramps started pulling out his intravenous tubes. He seemed like a woman ten-months pregnant—trying to give birth to himself. Weak and exhausted, he finally drifted off to sleep resting in my lap, and I sat with him on his bed. A deep quiet and peace seemed to radiate from his frail body, so unlike the unbearable turbulence and struggle of the previous three days.

Then after about a half hour, Gramps opened his eyes peacefully. He looked transformed, renewed, and refreshed with a clear gaze like a young child waking from a peaceful nap. His eyes were deep and steady, and he seemed to gaze out from a clear, deep, loving pool. His presence was radiantly peaceful and I felt like I was looking into the eyes of a saint. "Son," he said, bemused and with a tone of discovery, "My whole life has been a crazy *mashugana* dream!" (*mashugana* is Yiddish for "crazy"). Surprised by Gramps' radical transformation, I laughed, and replied, "It took you eighty-nine years to figure that out, old man!"

"When you're very young you're given your first feather because in being born you have died, you've left the safe womb, the home, to come out into the world of spirits that have manifested flesh and you have died. One of my friends has told me that when you die, you are more alive than you think you are when you're alive. The warrior shaman recognizes that that feather is a symbol of the breath that goes out.... Each time we breathe out, our breath touches the face of all humankind, all animals, all of our ancestors, all of our relatives. That is the warrior-shaman's vision. He or she knows that they have died and because of that, is one with everything."

—David Chethlehe Paladin

"Yeah, I guess so!" he chuckled as he continued, "My whole life has been a crazy dream, and ya know what?" "What?" I leaned closer. "I'm going to dream a happier dream next time!" he said. And then, with a twinkle in his eye of absolute wonder and amazement, he explained how he had just died and come back, and died and come back again and again, and that he was not afraid to die now and felt he knew the way.

Then looking around the room, he said, "You know, son, I know there is only you and me here in this room, but I've got to tell you there are so many others here with me. My ma, and my dad, and Molly, and all my brothers and sisters [who had all been "dead" for many years]. They're all here with me and I can see them so clearly. Can you see them too?" I absolutely believed what he was saying, and looked hopefully around the room. With some disappointment I had to admit that I was unable to discern any angelic presences, "No, I can't see them," I admitted. "But I absolutely believe that you are close enough to the threshold and that the door is open wide enough for you that you can see through."

The impact of Gramps' close encounter had a profound effect. After three days of unbearable pain, his agony vanished, his fear evaporated, and the radiance of his peacefulness and joyfulness became a blessing for all who entered the room. Everyone who came into his presence left feeling more buoyant and balanced. The doctors were amazed at his transformation and thought he actually might live, but it became clear that his body was beyond repair. Two days later, on the last Sabbath of his life, and too weak to say any formal prayers, I played some Jewish music for him. He began to hum along. "Gramps, do you know any Jewish songs?" I asked. He laughed and said, "Oh sure I do. I know lots of songs," and then he started singing. "On Friday afternoon," he began in Yiddish, and then translated to English, "We clean the whole house and everything is clear, bright, and beautiful, and when the Sabbath begins the whole house is happy!" he sang. "Yeah, it goes just like that," he laughed. As death approached, his peace, love, and joy deepened. The intense suffering and turbulence of the days before never returned. His strength and his breath gradually waned. At dawn on Memorial Day, his breath became more and more subtle until at last only his radiant smile remained. As the sun rose over Mount Rainier to the east and flooded the room, Michelle and I sat quietly and peacefully in meditation and prayer. What a beautiful end to Gramps' "crazy *mashugana* dream," and perhaps what a beautiful beginning to his next one!

"Rabbi Zusya used to say: My mother Mirl, peace be with her; did not pray from the book, because she could not read. All she knew was how to say the blessings. But wherever she said the blessing in the morning, in that place the radiance of the Divine Presence rested the livelong day."

—Martin Buber

"In a flash, the violent mind stood still;

Within and without are both transparent and clear.

After the great somersault

The great void is broken through.

Oh, how freely come and go

The myriad forms of things."

—Han Shan

GRACE: THE BALANCE THAT BRINGS
TEARS TO YOUR EYES

Can you remember those precious moments in your life when you felt so ecstatically whole and in balance that it brought tears to your eyes? The great poet Kabir says, "Between the conscious and unconscious, the mind has put up a swing; all earth creatures, even supernovas, sway between these two trees, and it never winds down. Angels, animals, humans, insects by the million, also the wheeling sun and moon; ages go by, and it goes on. Everything is swinging. heaven, earth, water, fire, and the secret one is slowly growing a body. Kabir saw this for fifteen seconds, and it made him a servant for life."

At rare and precious times in each of our lives, we catch a glimpse of the exquisite balance we call "grace." If you are an athlete, you might describe this experience as being in "the Zone." For others, such an event is regarded as a "peak experience." And for those with a more spiritual orientation, such rapturous moments of unity and wholeness may be reverently regarded as "moments of grace" or as "spontaneous communion with the sacred Source"—by whatever name you call it. These are times when balance is realized in its fullness across all dimensions of our being.

Kabir saw this for fifteen seconds, and each of us in our own ways—in the rare and precious moments in our lives—have also caught a glimpse of unity and wholeness beyond description. In one of our favorite accounts, Mary Austin remembers: I must have been five or six when this experience happened to me. It was a summer morning, and the child I was had walked down through the orchard alone and come out on the brow of a sloping hill where there were grass and a wind blowing and one tall tree reaching into the infinite immensities of blueness. Quite suddenly, after a moment of quietness there, earth and sky and tree and wind-blown grass and the child in the midst of them came alive together with a pulsating light of consciousness. To this day I can recall the swift inclusive awareness of each for the whole—I in them and they in me and all of us enclosed in a warm, lucent bubble of livingness....

"I remember the child looking everywhere for the source of this happy wonder and at last she questioned: 'God?' because that was the only awesome word she knew. And then, deep inside, like the murmurous ring of a bell, she heard the answer, 'God, God.'"

Can you remember a time when your tiny bubble of self cracked open, dissolved, or expanded, when your inner and outer worlds touched, communicated, and unified? Can you remember the exquisite

"It is as if God planted a great big kiss in the middle of our spirit and all the wounds, doubts, and guilt feelings were all healed at the same moment. The experience of being loved by the Ultimate Mystery banishes every fear."

—Father Thomas Keating

moments of love, peace, and wholeness when boundaries dissolved, and you beheld yourself and your world as radiant and alive with a sacred Presence?

* What stands out to you when you recall them?
* What qualities of being were most alive for you then?
* What inner or outer factors seem to make you receptive to this sublime balance?
* What inner or outer factors seem to reduce your availability to such grace?
* How have these timeless moments lived on for you or influenced how you have chosen to live your life?
* How did those experiences influence how you relate to other people or other living creatures?

Grace is found in both intense peace and activity. Polls tell us that fully one-third of us — your friends, family and coworkers — have had a profound or life-altering religious or mystical experience. In reality, this unnamable mystery is as close to us as water is to waves. Even if we don't talk about it, even if we don't have the vocabulary to discuss it, there have been moments in most of our lives when, for a timeless moment, the fabric of the story we tell ourselves dropped away to reveal that, in truth, we are both particle and wave, wave and ocean. As Saul demonstrated on the road to Damascus, and as countless others have experienced giving birth, playing sports, in nature, in love, or driving down the road on the way to work, we are utterly unable to protect ourselves from spontaneous moments of grace.

Often when we lecture on this topic, we will sometimes conduct an informal poll. "How many of you have experienced moments of grace when you were alone?" we'll ask. "How many have touched or shared

~~

"Contemplative prayer, rightly understood is the normal development of grace...it is the opening of mind an heart—our whole being—to God beyond thoughts, words, and emotions. Moved by God's preeminent grace, we open our awareness to God whom we know by faith is within us, closer than breathing, closer than thinking, closer than choosing—closer than consciousness itself. Contemplative prayer is a process of interior transformation, a relationship initiated by God and leading, if we consent, to divine union."

—Brother David Steindl-Rast

"... I was taking a walk in the garden by myself, I felt that a golden spirit sprang up from the ground, veiled my body and changed my body into a golden one...my mind and body turned into light. I was able to understand the whispering of the birds, and was clearly aware of the mind of God...the spirit of loving protection for all beings. Endless tears of joy streamed down my cheeks. Since that time I have grown to feel that the whole earth is my house, and the sun, the moon and the stars are all my own things. The training... is to take in God's love, which correctly produces, protects and cultivates all things in Nature and assimilate and unites it in our own mind and body."

—Morihei Ueshiba O'Sensei

such a moment with another person? With an animal? How many have experienced such exquisite balance in a moment of safety or peace? How many in moments of danger or intensity? How many of you have experienced a moment of profound balance while in nature? How many while at work? How many when you were very young? And how many when you were older?" Our poll has made it crystal clear that any time, any place, with the next step, or the next breath, we may tumble out of the chaos and confusion into the spiritual balance of grace.

In these precious and timeless moments, it is as though a key is turned, unlocking and opening a quality of being and experience that is both profoundly familiar and wondrously liberating. Something inside of us releases, lets go, and says yes in its belonging to the Mystery. These moments of grace have much to teach us about the true nature of balance. We learn about living more effortlessly, with a sense of flow and a joy that at times may be profoundly peaceful, though often intense beyond imagination. What emerges is an exhilarating sense that whatever this larger reality is, it is here in its wholeness with us in every moment.

What is unusual is not these moments of grace themselves—we are multidimensional beings, who live mostly unaware of the totality of ourselves. What is unusual is that we seem to live in a culture that, until recently, has been very shy about speaking openly of experiences that lie beyond the stifling confines of our status quo reality. Yet as the stress and pressures in our busy lives increase, and more and more people are feeling unbalanced, in ill health, or out of control, and as we watch our children and parents growing older, these instances are signposts reminding us of our deep belonging and the sense of profound inner peace that is only a breath away.

Moments of grace deepen our faith that it truly is possible to live in balance with the spirit of wholeness that is the source of all life. And they strengthen our aspiration to live our lives in a way that is likely to bring more balance into our turbulent world. As Brother David Steindl-Rast reminds us, "To those among us who have entered into this mystery through faith it need not be explained; to others it cannot be explained.... But to the extent to which we have given room in our hearts to gratitude, we all have a share in this reality, by whatever name we may call it.... All that matters is that we enter into that passage of gratitude and sacrifice, the passage which leads us to integrity within ourselves, to concord with one another, and to union with the very Source of Life."

When we touch times of profound balance we are given a glimpse of who and how we are at the core of our being. Even if only glimpsed for a few seconds, they may guide and inspire a lifetime that seeks to bring wholeness alive. "Everything is swinging: heaven, earth, water, fire, and the secret one is slowly growing a body." When we find ourselves in balance and see this, like Kabir, it makes us a servant for life.

REMEMBERING TO REMEMBER!

On the spiritual path there are three main steps to remember:

1. You never follow a spiritual path alone. Spiritual practice, by definition, is a path of deep relationships within the wholeness of your life. Begin each day, or even each activity, by pausing to remember a sense of belonging and connectedness, or by affirming your heartfelt relationships to the mentors, spiritual principles, and circle of spiritual friends who support you along the way.

2. Within this context of deep supportive relationships, do whatever you do wholeheartedly, with as much mindful, loving presence as you possibly can. Hold the intent or prayer that through your actions, your words, even your thoughts, you will move toward a greater balance and contribute to greater harmony in the world.

3. Reaffirm and celebrate your connection to all beings, and dedicate or share the potency generated through your actions. Imagine that as you breathe, you can gather the vital charge of all your good deeds into your heart, and convey it heart to heart to those you love, and to all living beings. Imagine streams of light or love flowing from your heart to the hearts of others. Or let it be like the light of a candle that is effortlessly reflected in the heart-jewels of countless beings in the vast constellation of your relationships. Let your love light up the lives of all who share your life. Let this light shine as an offering to the Source of All the Light in your life that it may continue to guide you and all others in a beautifully balanced way.

> "However young,
> The seeker who sets out upon the way
> Shines bright over the world.
> Like the moon,
> Come out from behind the clouds!
> Shine!
>
> —Attributed to The Buddha

Taken to heart, this simple framework will help you to weave your spiritual journey deep into the fabric of your daily life. Upon awakening, remember step one. During the day, recall step two. At the end of the day, take step three. At the beginning of a session of prayer or meditation, or at the beginning of a meeting or presentation, initiate step one. As you continue, remember step two. As you conclude and rejoice in your accomplishments, energize step three. Practiced in this way, a deeper core of balance will surely come alive through your life, no matter what else you do.

chapter eleven

Breathing Into Balance

IN THIS FINAL CHAPTER OF THIS SECTION, WE'LL WEAVE TOGETHER many of the key themes, images, principles, and teachings offered throughout this book. The loom of our weaving will be the natural flow of the breath which comes to us and flows through us approximately 21,600 times each day.

LESSONS FROM ARGON

Breathing in ... and breathing out.... We receive and we radiate, carried by a life-long rhythm of living in balance. For most people, most of the time, these breaths and moments flow by mindlessly, unnoticed, unlived, and irretrievable. But an alternative is available and we can learn, through practice, patience, and dedication to keep the light of our clear presence and great compassion aglow during more moments of each day.

If we were to hold in one hand all the moments when we are truly awake—when our wisdom eyes and compassionate presence are alive within us—and in the other hand, all the moments when we are mindlessly adrift, compelled by habit, and unaware, we would likely see that the balance is disappointingly skewed. As we mentioned in the Mindfulness chapter, most people are mindful only 1 to perhaps 20 percent of the moments of their lives, while the vast majority of the precious moments of their lives are forever lost to mindless distraction and inattention, as they sleep, walking through their busy lives.

Though such reflection may be humbling or even unsettling, it is heartening to realize how much potential we have for improvement,

"Since every particle in your body goes back to the first flaring forth of space and time, you're really as old as the universe. So when you are lobbying at your congressperson's office, or visiting your local utility, or testifying at a hearing on nuclear waste, or standing up to protect an old grove of redwoods, you are doing that not out of some personal whim, but in the full authority of your 15 billions years."

—Joanna Macy

and to realize that we can actually set our intention to improve the quality of our lives, to be more fully present, to wake up, live in balance, and presence the light of our compassion more fully and more often in our lives and world.

As we wake up to this limitless potential and engage in these practices, we can be assured of greater and greater success if we embrace this great work. And as we do, each precious moment, each precious breath, can become an affirmation and dedication of our compassionate spirit, reminding us that in each moment we truly breathe with and for all beings.

With each one of the 21,600 breaths of air and life you breathe today, oxygen and nitrogen—which comprise 98 percent of the air— are absorbed into your body to fuel the natural functions of your life. When you breathe out, you exhale carbon dioxide released from the body. One of the most interesting molecules in the air we breathe is the element argon, an "inert" molecule that doesn't react chemically with anything and therefore isn't absorbed into our body. Harlow Shapley, an American astronomer, once estimated that in *each* breath of air we breathe, there are 3×10^{19} molecules of argon (that's 3 followed by 19 zeros—which is a lot of argon molecules in each breath!)

So if we were to track the flow of argon molecules streaming through you in your next exhalation, it would diffuse into your immediate environment, perhaps flow in and out of the people or pets near you with a brief visitation, then flow out into your neighborhood and city, to then circulate in the air currents flowing around the globe. Shapley calculated that since the atmosphere is a relatively closed system, in one year—no matter where you might be on planet Earth—each breath you would breathe in would contain an average of 15 argon atoms from the original breath you exhaled a year earlier.

What this means is that with each breath we breathe in millions of atoms that have streamed through the bodies of countless beings of the past and that in a sense we truly do breathe with "all our relations" as the First Nations people would say. We breathe with the trees, with the birds and the bees, with the eagles and polar bears. We breathe with the salmon, and the whales who live on the earth today—and with all creatures great and small who have ever walked, or flew, or swam or crawled upon our earth in ages past. We breathe with the rich and the poor, the kind and the cruel, the greedy and the generous peoples of our world. We breathe with those living now, with all our relations from the distant past, and with those of countless generations to come. We breathe the same air that flowed through the lungs of the Buddha, Jesus, Joan of Arc,

"When you eventually see through the veils to how things really are, you will keep saying again and again, 'This is certainly not like we thought it was!'"

—Mevlana Jalaluddin Rumi

Mohammed, Gandhi, Martin Luther King, Jr., and Aung San Suu Kyi. Each breath, clearly seen, deeply felt, and taken to heart, is truly a gesture of balance, equalizing and humbling us to receive and to release, to share intimately the flow of energy and primal elements and atoms that weave our lives together.

In those moments when we expand our creative, intuitive wisdom and open our wisdom eyes to envision this, we behold the flow of the breath we share with all living beings, the two legged ones and the four legged ones, the creatures of the air and the seas, the noble and humble beings of all realms of being, and we realize that in a very real, deep, and intimate way, our lives are truly interweaving with each moment and each breath. For the First Nations people of the Americas this wisdom is reflected in the Thanksgiving prayers that are offered at the beginning of any gathering or ceremony. One refrain is often, "All my relations, let us join together, and as one heart, and one mind, give thanks," or the phrase, "... and now our minds are one."

Live in the present, launch yourself on every wave,

find eternity in each moment.

—Henry David Thoreau

"God has no body now on earth but yours
no hands but yours, no feet but yours.
Yours are the eyes through which he pours out,
compassion in the world, compassion in the world.
His are the hands, blessing me now.
All praise to the One.
Ring the bells that can still ring,
Forget your perfect offering,
There is a crack in everything,
That's how the light gets in."
— *Anthem*, by Leonard Cohen

HARMONIZING: ALIGNING AND ATTUNING

Taking our sense of balance even deeper, we find that we can go beyond merely "equalizing" ourselves with all the beings we share the breath with, to actually "harmonizing" ourselves in a deeper sense of harmony and balance. We do this by learning to align and attune ourselves to sources and forces of inspiration, strength, beauty, blessings, and healing that are available to us in our lives and world.

Can you remember how good it feels to come out of the cold and warm yourself by a glowing fire? Leaning in close, rubbing your hands above the flickering flames, you absorb that warmth and circulate it through your body, dissolving the sense of cold, and then naturally radiating your warmth back into the world around you.

In a similar way, guided and inspired by a myriad of teachings from the world's great wisdom traditions, we realize that we can gather and breathe in the light of the sun or the stars, and then offer or shine that light out into the world adding our light to the light of all beings. We can align and attune ourselves to these forces and sources, and breathe in the vitality, beauty, and freshness of our natural world and weave those streams of inspiration with our own inner elements to harmonize, balance, revitalize, strengthen, and renew ourselves.

We can also align and attune ourselves to the steadiness and strength of the earth, the fluidity and suppleness of the waters, the light and warmth of the sun, the vast spaciousness and openness of the sky. We can gather into ourselves with the breath the essence of all those elements, qualities of being available in or associated with those realms, and mix them with the countless subtle streams that nourish our inner, many-dimensional being. As we do, we realize that we can also radiate these positive qualities out into our world in balancing and harmonizing ways, and that we can add to and amplify this natural radiance through our heartfelt intentions and prayers, and our dedication of consciously offering this radiance in the spirit of blessings and inspirations we offer to the earth, to the plants, to the people we care for and who share our lives and our breath.

Such ways of living were discovered, taught, and practiced in millions of ways by the wisdom keepers of countless peoples who knew that the quality of their lives was deeply influenced by the depth of relatedness, connection, and harmony they cultivated in relation to the many dimensions of the mysterious and natural world. Such simple and profound ways of living, breathing, and moving through the world are in a sense truly "super" natural.

"Our individual well-being is intimately connected both with that of all others and with the environment within which we live. It becomes apparent that our every action, our every deed, word, and thought, no matter how slight or inconsequential it may seem, has an implication not only for ourselves but for all others too."

—The Dalai Lama

RECEIVING AND RADIATING

Expanding our view of living in balance still deeper, let's add another harmonic to this suite of practices for living in balance.

Resting in the easy natural flow of your breathing, reach up, touch your heart, and smile with a tender sense of deep connection and deep reflection. Give thanks for the blessings and the opportunities of your life and dedicate yourself to living ever more deeply in the compassionate spirit of balance that you sense is most essential to your true being. Allow your mindful awareness to blend more deeply now with the natural rhythms of your breathing and settle into this state of deep connection and flow.

As you sit here now, envision yourself sitting at this center of your universe, surrounded by all living beings. Holding this image in mind, pause for a moment to remember, invite, or sense the presence of those who have most deeply inspired you with their examples of compassion in action. These may be people you know, teachers, mentors, or family members, or people whom you have read about in scripture, books, or discovered on the web.

Reach out now from your heart, and with your hands, to these beings whose inspiring presence in your life is truly a blessing, a source of renewal, deep information and strength. Imagine that all of them are right here with you now, surrounding you and shining like a constellation of radiant compassionate suns. Or if you like, envision that these many sources of compassion merge into a single brighter star that shines a radiance of compassion and blessings into your life.

Imagine that with each breath you reach out to them, and they reach back to you. Envision yourself holding their hands, and that through your connection with them sense that you can draw strength and inspiration to deepen in your sense of wisdom, compassion, and balance. Notice how the stronger and more sincere your own aspiration, the deeper and stronger the flow of inspiration streaming to you and through you becomes. With each breath receive this light and inspiration, and radiate your gratitude back to each of them. Receiving... and radiating ... with each breath.

Imagine now that each of these inspiring people in turn reaches out to hold the hands of those to whom they look for guidance, strength, and compassion, and that they in turn reach out to those who have inspired them. Sense your teachers reaching out to their teachers who reach out to their teachers, who reach out to their teachers.... Envision yourself balanced within and receiving from this endless cascade of wisdom, compassion, and inspiration as it flows to you and through you from countless inspired ancestors of the far and distant past.

Sense this inspiration flowing to you as the light of wisdom, blessings, or compassion, soaking into you, illuminating and empowering you. It energizes the parts of you where your life force is weak. It balances whatever needs to be balanced, and heals whatever needs healing within you. This light floods, cleanses, and opens the spaces and places within you that are clogged or congested, and nourishes the seeds of your deepest potentials to blossom in your learning how to live in balance. Like sunlight filtering into a deep clear pool, sense these waves of

"Taken to heart, each breath becomes a breath of compassion, a gesture of balance, and an affirmation of your relatedness and caring, affirming your wholeness and freeing you from the illusion of separation."

—Joel and Michelle Levey

inspiring grace flooding your body-mind-energy-spirit. Every dimension of your being is illuminated, blessed, balanced, and renewed.

With each in-breath you are filled, saying silently to yourself, "*receiving*." Envision that with each exhalation you can *radiate* and expand this circle of gratitude, extending balancing and harmonizing energies with each out-breath. Receiving with each inhalation ... and radiating with each exhalation....

Breathing in, imagine the inspiration and blessings flowing into you, filling your heart, infusing your whole body and being. Breathing out, sense, imagine, or feel that your heart is silently radiating balancing and harmonizing qualities of being like a bright, shining star. Effortlessly offer the natural radiance to inspire all beings to live in greater harmony and balance. Allow it to shine out through the darkness within or around you. Allow the light of your influence to effortlessly illumine your inner and outer world. Let this be the light of your presence, the light of balance, the light of peace, the light of goodwill and compassion.

Now, as you sit here at this center of your universe, surrounded by all living beings, envision yourself reaching out to those who look to you as a source of inspiration, guidance, or loving support and imagine each of them reaching back to you. Reach out to your children, to your friends, to your family, to your students, clients or customers, to your patients, and to all those who look to you as they seek for greater balance, belonging, or well-being in their lives. Receiving compassion, inspiration, wisdom, and strength from those you draw guidance from, reach out with your hands and from your heart, and allow each exhalation to radiate harmony and balance to those who, in turn, look to you. Let each inhalation bring you inspiration from the sources of strength you are aligning and attuning to, and allow each inhalation to also gather the gratitude that streams back to you from those that look to you as a source of strength and inspiration. Receiving ... and radiating ... with each breath.

Envision each person you reach out to receiving the harmonizing and balancing influence you offer to them and taking the light of your love, strength, or compassion to heart. Sense that this deeply touches, strengthens, and inspires each of them. As your compassion reaches out to your children, envision them receiving and taking this light to heart and then passing it on to their children, who pass it on to their children, who pass it on to their children and to all whose lives they touch or ever will touch—directly or indirectly. Envision your students reaching out to their students who reach out to their students. Imagine that all those

"The call of this era for me is, BRING IT ON! Bring your gifts to the table and let them shine. We need all the light, the fierce light, we can muster. We need the vision, the energy, the enthusiasm of each and every one of us. NOW IS THE TIME. We need to bring our full individualism in all it's quirks and uniqueness out so that we can have the rich diversity we need to solve all the multiple converging crises of this era. AND, we need to harmonize, to work together, to bring this collective energy into focus so we can have tangible, real world results."

—Velcrow Ripper

to whom you reach out, take this light of your qualities of being and compassion to heart, and pass it on to those who will pass it on in an endless cascade of inspiration and blessings that reaches out into the world to help affirm and presence the light of compassion for countless generations to come.

In this way, receiving and radiating, sense yourself balanced in the infinite expanse of "deep time," surrounded by all beings, reaching out from this fleeting moment where all the experiences of the infinite past and all the potential for the boundless future converge. Viewed in this light, realize that your real life-work is to truly balance yourself in order to increase your capacity to reach out and realize your connectedness and wholeness, to increase your capacity to gather inspiration, wisdom and compassion, to take it to heart, and to then expand this circle of light, strength, love, compassion to all beings. As you rest in this contemplation, remember Einstein's famous words that once we have freed ourselves from the "optical delusion of consciousness" that leads us to feel separate from others, then our "task in life is to widen the circle of our compassion to embrace all living beings and the whole of nature in all of its beauty." With each breath, receiving, and radiating, expand your circle of harmony, balance, peace, compassion, and well-being for the benefit of all beings.

TRANSFORMING: THE BREATH OF COMPASSION

"Wisdom tells me I am nothing.
Love tells me I am everything.
And between the two my life flows."
— Nisargadatta Maharaj

Compassion is a natural response to the sufferings in our lives and world. It is an active response that emerges when we are balanced in the face of suffering and moved to alleviate that suffering. For our compassion to be effective and not create more problems it must be guided by wisdom, and for wisdom to deepen courage is required—the courage to keep looking ever more deeply into the web of complex, subtle, and meaningful interrelationships that weave the fabric of our lives and world. As you continue to explore and implement the principles and practices we have offered you in this book, a profound realization that there truly is no separation between us will deepen and grow. You will also come to appreciate that for compassion to flourish and be sustained, it must be fueled by heartfelt commitment, dedication, or devotion. The transformative practice that follows builds on the power of the previous ones in this chapter and fuels this fire of compassion with wisdom, love, and dedication. It too is woven on the loom of the breath. It is called *tonglen* in Tibetan, which means taking and sending. We also call it "the breath of compassion."

THE ESSENCE OF THE PRACTICE

As you breathe in now, gather the raw energy of any agitation or discomfort you may find in your body or mind, drawing it into the transformational vortex of your heart center like fuel for a furnace — and out of compassion, let it fuel the fire of transformation, giving you more light to radiate. With each breath, breathe in compost, and breathe out flowers and fruit. Breathe in fear, and let its energy be released into the radiance of confidence on the exhalation. Breathe in imbalance, and let it too fuel the radiance of your steadiness and resilience. Radiate the light of compassion out on the waves of your breath as a blessing of balance and peace in the lives of all those who share your world.

In this way, with practice, begin to understand that you can embrace any experience that comes to you as a vehicle to open your heart ever more widely and deeply to compassion. When you are faced with fear and suffering, let it fuel the radiance of your compassion for yourself and for others who "just like me" suffer in similar ways. Faced with beauty and the sweetness of life, let it intensify the radiance of your gratitude and joy. Imagine yourself as a light-bearer of wisdom, strength, and compassion illuminating and protecting the goodness of the world. Imagine the silent light of your innermost being blazing with radiant compassion in countless helpful ways. Holding your loved ones and friends in mind, radiate this light to them. Bring to heart and mind the leaders of the world, the children of the world, the beleaguered nations and species of the world, and radiate your heartfelt compassion and care to them.

Of all the contemplations that we know of, this breath of compassion practice is without equal in its universally practical applications and its profound implications for learning to live ever more deeply in the flow of dynamic balance. Taken to heart, this practice which rests in the natural rhythms of your breath, refines the balance of our sense of inner and outer, self and others, me and we, joy and sadness, pleasure and pain, peace and turbulence. The power of this practice helps us expand and affirm our intimate interrelationship with all of life, awakens our generative compassionate capabilities, and activates a genuine

"The whole idea of compassion is based on the keen awareness of the interdependence of all these living beings who are all part of one another and all involved in one another....The whole purpose of life is to live by love."

—Father Thomas Merton

"There are only two ways to live your life.

One is a though nothing is a miracle.

The other is as though everything is a miracle."

—Albert Einstein

heartfelt concern for the well-being of others, who just like you, want to be happy and free from suffering.

As a mother moved by compassion for the suffering of her child might wish to take in and transform her child's suffering and give back her love, strength, and healing energy, this practice of *tonglen* teaches us to embody this same gesture with regards to ourselves, our loved ones, and all suffering beings. It is widely regarded as the ultimate practice for opening our hearts fully to compassion and dissolving fear and separation. In our work we teach this practice widely, especially for people who work as caregivers or who offer protective services to others.

The practice of *tonglen* widens the circle of our compassion to reconnect us with a larger field of relationship and a vaster sense of the true dimensions of ourselves. Oftentimes we get out of balance and experience pain and suffering because we've become fixated and overly preoccupied with our own contracted, personal, and narrowly limited view. When we are suffering physically, emotionally, or mentally, there is a strong tendency to withdraw from the world and implode into a very self-centered and self-protective state. We lose perspective of the larger picture and identify too much with the dramas that we are immersed in at the time. This contraction cuts us off from feeling connected, and impedes our access to the healing and balancing energies we most need in those times. The greater our sense of isolation, the greater our suffering because self-isolation cuts us off from the flow of balancing and compassionate connectedness that is available to us.

DEEPENING THE PRACTICE...

As you begin, brighten the light of your clear presence with a gentle, heartfelt smile, and touch your heart to activate and affirm your connection with the light of compassion that shines from the true depths of your being. Then allow this clear presence and great compassion to flow with the natural rhythm, flow, and balance of your breathing.

Resting in the natural flow of your breathing, allow the area of your chest around your heart center to relax, open and soften, and establish a clear sense of inner spaciousness, like a vast open sky. Imagine or feel yourself as completely open and clear inside, like a big body balloon. Totally open and pervaded with the clear light of mindful awareness, there is a deep sense of being completely transparent inside and the sense that the space within you is continuous with the space around you. It is as though all the pores of your body are totally permeable to the flow of air and currents of energy that pass in and out through you,

"Transformation comes from looking deeply within, to a state that exists before fear and isolation arise, the state in which we are inviolably whole just as we are. We connect to ourselves, to our own true experience, and discover there that to be alive means to be whole."

—Sharon Salzberg

and you feel almost as if you can breathe in and out of all of your pores. Pause and rest here until you can clearly establish this feeling of open, clear, and unobstructed inner spaciousness.

Then, sense that within the region of your physical heart is a dimension of your true, pure, noble heart — your heart center or chakra. Sense or imagine this as a stainless dimension of deep inner strength, purity, and compassionate presence. Classically this dimension is symbolized as the sacred heart, or the pure heart jewel, whose light shines forth with the light of limitless lovingkindness and compassion embracing all beings. In this contemplation you can also envision this dimension of the heart as a transformational vortex, where you can draw in the fire of the suffering of the world, and turn it into the pure light of radiant compassion and well-being.

One of our teachers, Geshe Gyaltsen, often called this practice "Hoover vacuum cleaner meditation!" Powered by the motivation of compassion, use the "motor" of your inhalation to work like a "Hoover" suction, gathering up and drawing into the transformational vortex of this pure dimension of the heart any pain or negativity that might be present in your physical, mental, emotional, or spiritual continuum. If you don't feel any particular discomfort at the present moment, simply let your inhalation draw in any seeds or latencies that may be lying dormant in your body or mind — potentials of future suffering that could ripen if conditions became right. You can envision these as heavy, hot energy, or dark smoke.

Motivated by compassion — the desire to embrace, reduce or resolve suffering — as you inhale, imagine drawing any of these negative energies or potentialities into this pure dimension of the heart, and just as the darkness in a room disappears completely and immediately the moment the light switch is turned on, sense or imagine that any pain, suffering, or negativity is completely dissolved, resolved, and transformed. Breathing in heat or the fire of suffering and pain, let it dissolve into this pure dimension of your true heart, and sense that the suffering is completely dissolved and resolved, and then ride the waves of the out-breath to radiate back cooling waves of compassion, comfort, and ease back to where the suffering came from.

As you exhale, imagine that from your heart center waves of clear, radiant healing light pour forth. Imagine these waves filling your whole body and mind, healing, energizing, and transforming you. Allow the vortex at your heart to function as an energy transformer drawing in negativity, darkness, or pain, and transforming it into radiant light and healing energy. For example, drawing in agitation as you inhale, let it

On the journey of the warrior-bodhisattva, the path goes down, not up, as if the mountain pointed toward the earth instead of the sky. Instead of transcending the suffering of all creatures, we move toward turbulence and doubt however we can.

We explore the reality and unpredictability of insecurity and pain, and we try not to push it away. If it takes years, if it takes lifetimes, we let it be as it is. At our own pace, without speed or aggression, we move down and down and down. With us move millions of others, companions in awakening from fear."

—Pema Chödrön

dissolve into the pure dimension of the heart, and radiate peace back as you exhale; drawing in anger on the in-breath, let it dissolve, and radiate patience and compassion mounted on the waves of the out-breath. If you've taken the suffering of *fear in* with your breath, now send back *faith* and *strength* with your *out* breath. If the pain you breathed in was *tension*, let it dissolve, and breathe back *relaxation*, and so on. "Breathing in hot and heavy ... breathing out cool and light...."

With each exhalation send waves of compassion, healing, balancing energy or influence mounted on the out-breath to whatever region of your body or mind are calling for compassion. Using the movement of the breath as a motor and compassion as the motivator, direct whatever quality is needed to antidote, neutralize, or resolve the kind of suffering or pain you are embracing and transforming.

Some people find it helpful to visualize a color, texture, image, or sound that carries the feeling of the quality they are sending. Others prefer to simply ripple out a pure clear wave of intention. The key is to allow each breath to deepen and affirm your sense of being capable of this compassionate transformation in the pure dimension of our heart.

Continue in this way, embracing, gathering, sweeping and vacuuming, resolving and transforming, mounted on the waves of the breath, for as long as you like. Remember to keep your breathing gentle and natural, not forcing or holding the breath in any way. As you practice, you may find that the grosser, more noticeable discomforts dissolve or change. As this happens, allow your awareness to be drawn to subtler and subtler messages that call for your compassionate attention.

"Lord, make me an instrument of thy peace.
Where there is hatred, let me sow love;
Where there is injury, pardon;
Where there is doubt, faith;
Where there is despair, hope;
Where there is darkness, light;
Where there is sadness, joy.
O Divine Master, grant that I may not so much seek to be consoled as to console,
To be understood as to understand,
To be loved as to love.
For it's in giving that we receive, and it's in pardoning that we are pardoned.
And it's in dying—that we are born into eternal life."

—SAINT FRANCIS

The true power of this meditation comes alive as you begin to realize that the radius of your compassion can be vast and limitless in its scope, and that you are able to receive and transform the energies of others who share the larger body of life with you. The larger the field of connection and interrelationship that you acknowledge and participate in, the greater will be the reservoir of resource you have to draw from.

As you deepen in this practice, you realize that just as you wish to be free of the pain in your back, your loneliness, or heartache, so too does the person in the seat or house, the office, village, or country next to you, or across the world. And you also realize that it really doesn't take any extra effort at all as you breathe in, to hold the compassionate intention to embrace and transform their suffering at the same time as you're breathing in and transforming your own.

If you are tormented by anger or grief, imagine and affirm that with each breath, as your compassion transforms these energies or feelings within the sphere of your own personal, local body or mind, those same feelings shared by others can also be embraced and transformed by your compassion as well. Envision and affirm that the radiance of this compassion emanates out through you to be received by anyone who shares the same feelings, who suffers in the same way, or who even has the latency for such vulnerability in the future. Whatever the form of distress or suffering you find within yourself, embrace that in others or in the world at large. Mounted on the waves of the breath, receive and transform this discord with the balance of your heart of compassion and affirm the universality of your humanity and your kinship and heartfelt relationship to countless other beings who might share the same feelings, vulnerabilities, or concerns.

When it feels natural, allow the circle of your compassion to widen to embrace anyone else who comes to mind: a friend or loved one, a neighbor or coworker, a whole group of people who are living with fear, suffering, or danger. Breathing in, allow your heart to open, to touch, receive/embrace, and transform the fear, the distress, the loneliness, grief, or suffering. Allow these sorrows or distresses to dissolve and resolve completely within the pure, open, limitless dimension of your true heart. As this transformation naturally unfolds, allow the energy of your heartfelt compassion to also dissolve or explode the optical delusion of a separate self and expand your sense of identity and balance in the larger field of being that includes all life. As you feel the sensations of your out-breath, allow your heart to naturally open to send back waves of peace, patience, calm, protection, lovingkindness, and radiant compassion to all who suffer. Experience the openness and

"There is a light in this world, a healing spirit more powerful than any darkness we may encounter. We sometimes lose sight of this force when there is suffering, too much pain. Then suddenly, the spirit will emerge through the lives of ordinary people who hear a call and answer in extraordinary ways."

—Mother Theresa

connectedness that awakens as you expand the circle of your active, engaged compassion, caring, and balance in this way.

Continue to deepen into this meditation for as long as you like or have time for, allowing each cycle of breaths to further deepen and affirm your capacity to open your heart and expand the circle of your compassion.

This contemplation can be done in many different kinds of situations. First start with yourself, then let the circle of your compassionate awareness reach out to others yearning for the same quality of peace, harmony, and well-being that you're looking for, and keep expanding the circle of your compassion to individuals, groups, or other living beings who come to mind.

Taken to heart, this practice of *tonglen* can become a profoundly integrative practice for living in balance as you move through the world. In the Mahayana tradition it is said that once one begins to sense that their true life, identity, and purpose is intimately related to all living beings and one begins to cultivate this mode of higher-order relationship and balance in relation to all beings, one's capacity to engage in this meditation naturally and intuitively expands until in the moment of completely awakening to one's true nature and highest potentials, all that is left is a selfless quality of presence that exists in the mode of *tonglen* for the benefit of all beings.

Once you understand how this practice works, you can weave it into your flow of your daily life. Quietly and invisibly while you are waiting for or riding on public transportation, driving in your car; being present during a particularly tense meeting; while listening to or watching the news; sitting at home or walking through the busy city streets. (Of course, if you're operating a vehicle, be particularly attentive to your driving and keep your eyes open!) This mode of being is well suited for living in dynamic balance with a spirit of compassionate engagement in your world. It offers a glimpse of how it might be to become a beacon of inspiring, balancing, healing presence as you move through the world.

We once heard from a military leader that he had gone to a contentious meeting and had brought along an assistant adept in such practices to "work the field" and "generate good vibes" during the meeting. At one point in the meeting, when things were not going very well, the Colonel passed his assistant a note, saying "pump harder!"

Tonglen is a practice that we often do when we pull into a hospital parking lot to visit a patient or go to work. We've found the healing process begins before we even get into the elevator, and acts especially to balance the quality of mind and being that we carry with us!

When Joel was running the pain center at Group Health HMO, one of his most dear patients, "Jenny," was in remission from breast cancer and they worked together over many months to help her learn the life skills necessary to manage her stress, increase her strength, wellness, and resilience, and embrace her vulnerability. After some years, Jenny's cancer ultimately reasserted itself, and she found herself back in the hospital for treatment.

One day, after a particularly challenging and restless night, she called Joel's office at the medical center, and asked if he could make time for a consultation with her while she was still in the hospital. As Joel entered her room, Jenny said, "Please have a seat. I have a story to tell you…." Jenny went on to describe how the night before she was feeling miserable, alone, and imploded into her discomfort and self-pity. After some time, she became aware that the woman who shared her hospital room was crying. That recognition opened her heart to realize that there were two suffering people in the room and in that moment Jenny remembered the *tonglen* practice that she had worked with for years, and she began that meditation. Breathing in she gathered the fear, loneliness, helplessness, and despair that she was feeling along with the suffering of her roommate's, and envisioned those feelings of pain and suffering dissolving into the pure, open dimension of her heart, dissolving her sense of separate self, and affirming her compassionate, engaged presence in relationship and solidarity in suffering.

As the suffering dissolved it, it opened her heart to radiate waves of comfort, ease, and well-being to herself, and to the woman in the bed next to her. As she deepened in this contemplation, Jenny realized that there were other rooms on the oncology ward with other suffering patients and family members, and her heart opened to reach out to connect with and embrace their sorrows as well, and to radiate her loving-kindness and compassion to them all. She then realized that there were other floors of the hospital with others in need in cardiology, critical care, etc., and her contemplations expanded to embrace and include them as well. It then dawned on her that there were other hospitals in Seattle, filled with countless people who are anxious, uncomfortable, or suffering in countless ways … and that there were countless cities with hospitals and suffering people and loved ones watching over them filled with their own concerns, fears, and suffering. She then sensed the deep vulnerability of all living beings whose lives were certain to offer up fleeting joy and sorrows that would inevitably end in death.

As Jenny's contemplations expanded the sphere of her compassion to embrace more and more people, a deep peace, joy, sense of meaning

"You will suffer, not just from your own worries and fears, but because of your love for all beings. When you open yourself in this way, your companions will be other beings on the path of awakening who share your insight. They will work with you, side by side to alleviate the world's suffering."

—Thich Nhat Hanh

and purpose, well-being, and even a sense of great bliss came aglow within her. Finally, Jenny relaxed into a deep, restful, healing sleep, and when she awoke she felt a profound sense of peace and balance within her. As we sat together, listening to her story, Jenny reached out, took Joel's hand and said, "Joel, I know that long after I am gone you will be able to share my story with others, and that this will inspire them in appreciating the value and meaning of this profound practice for living in harmony and balance."

We've now taught this practice to tens of thousands of people from all walks of life, and of different philosophical and spiritual inclinations. to medical staff working in clinics and emergency rooms, to Special Forces troops facing untold dangers and fear, to children, corporate executives, clergy, and world-class athletes. For some, this practice makes immediate intuitive sense from what they know of the unobstructed flow of energy and information in the natural world. Others will translate this practice into a deeply personal participation in God's love or the compassionate presence of Quan Yin radiating and extending from the pure, sacred dimension of their heart out into the world.

As we have traveled and taught in Asia, we have found that this practice of *tonglen* is especially accessible for our Asian students who have grown up with a sense of relatedness to Quan Yin, "She Who Hears the Cries of the World." For those of us with the faith, intuition, or experience to know that there is a dimension of pure heartedness within us that is stainless and virtually invulnerable to any sort of discordant energies, the sense of offering the cries of the suffering world to the heart of your own inner Quan Yin can be as natural as breathing in and receiving, and breathing out and radiating compassion to all beings. One beloved Christian colleague who had practiced *tonglen* for many years, wrote a profound sermon for his congregation musing how likely it was that the final contemplation of Jesus on the Cross might have been in the spirit of *tonglen*, taking in and transforming the ignorance and sins of all beings who had "missed the mark" (the actual meaning of "sin") and dedicating all his love and compassion to their salvation — be they in the historical time of Jesus, or in future times when his teachings were still present in our world.

The universal spirit of this practice of "taking and sending" is as natural as the wish of a mother to take upon her self the suffering of her child and to offer all her strength, love, and joy to comfort them. Each of us will translate this potentiality in our own way. In this spirit, we invite you to take this sage advice to heart, to practice with it in your unique way, and see how it speaks to and lives through you.

"The holiest of all the spots on earth is where an ancient hatred has become a present love."

—A Course in Miracles

As you practice this method of living in balance, keep in mind that whether you are visibly able to transform the sufferings of others through this practice is secondary to transforming the illusion of your own sense of separateness and dissolving your own fear and narrow self-protectiveness. The real power of this practice lies in developing a deeper experience of kinship with the world, and in breaking free from our preoccupation with our own personal situation or limited personal identity.

The practice of *tonglen* is essentially a mind training that empowers your inner access to qualities of balance, and an immense source of compassionate transformational potential. *Tonglen* can awaken the wisdom and compassion necessary to free us from the anxiety, fear, imbalance, and exhaustion that come from trying to vainly protect the illusion of a separate self. It teaches us to live in harmony and balance within a more expansive, generative, and universal view of wholeness, and to honor and deeply respect the sacred mystery of interdependence by seeing how activating compassionate regard for others works simultaneously to heal our relationship with ourselves as well.

INTEGRATION: RECEIVING AND RADIATING COMBINED WITH *TONGLEN*

We come to naturally realize that with each breath, we can gather the light, strength, power, blessings of all creation, add our light to that, and offer it to all beings.

～

"Once you have adopted such an attitude of infinite interconnectedness, you naturally want to liberate not just yourself but all beings from suffering. The Buddha calls this 'the conception of the spirit of enlightenment.' It is the soul of the Bodhisattva, the person who dedicates himself or herself to helping all beings achieve total happiness. When you open to the inevitability of your infinite interconnectedness with other sensitive beings, you develop compassion. You learn to feel empathy for them, to love them, to want their happiness. You want to keep them from suffering, and you do so just as if they were a part of you....You don't congratulate yourself for helping others, just as you won't congratulate yourself for healing your own leg when you hurt it. It is natural for you to love your leg because it is one with you, and so it is natural for you to love others. You would certainly never harm another being. As...Shantideva wrote, 'How wonderful it would be when all beings experience each other as limbs on the one body of life!'"

—Robert Thurman

With each breath we can align and attune ourselves with all the sources of guidance and blessings available in our lives and world, back through endless time, and we can radiate, offer, and extend those streams of blessings and inspiration to those who look to us, and through them to all who look to them, and through them to all who look to them....

With each breath we can gather into the pure depths of our true heart the pain of all the fires of ignorance, greed, and aggression raging in our world, and we can transform, dissolve, and resolve those raging fires in the deep, clear pool of our heart, and radiate the cool, clear, radiance of compassion, balance and harmony into the hearts and souls of others.

Freed from the fear that breeds in the shadows of the optical delusion of consciousness that leads us to sense or view ourselves as separate from the world and all beings, we are ennobled and empowered to open our hearts and mind, our wisdom eyes and pure hearts, to become sacred vessels of transformation capable of embracing and transforming our relationship to the sufferings of the world.

And, in those inevitable moments where the darkness or complexity of our lives or world overwhelms us, we can also reach out to hold the hands, or draw into us the hearts of all the ennobling beings we receive and draw light and inspiration from, and we can blend those streams of empowering light with the torrents of grief, pain, or sorrow that we are tapping into.

Understood and taken to heart in this way, we realize that with each breath, 21,600 times a day we can balance ourselves, stand strong, shine bright, dispel fear, and connect with streams of sustaining and life-affirming strength, blessings, and inspiration, and that we can extend our light, love, and strength out to others. In this way we balance and weave together with each breath the practices of receiving, transforming, and radiating.

Expanding the Circle of Balance: Home, Play, Work, and World

"The first day or so we all pointed to our countries. The third or fourth day we were pointing to our continents. By the fifth day we were aware of only one earth."

—Sultan Bin Salman al-Saud,
Saudi Arabian astronaut

Now that we have gotten the basics of inner balance, it's time to expand the scope of our focus to include the world outside our individual selves, because, obviously, our interactions with others can either enhance or diminish the sense of wholeness we're seeking to cultivate. Though there are many different dimensions of relationship—parent-child; student-teacher; romantic and life partnerships; friends; siblings; playmates; and community relationships, to name a few—our intention is to focus on the aspects of balance that are common to all relationships. We'll be sharing ideas and methods that apply equally to people you know as well as people you don't know, and also present some specific guidelines for raising the balance quotient in some of your special relationships.

In the second part of this section, we'll examine the challenge of bringing our workaday world into greater balance with the rest of our lives. We'll start by appreciating the scope of the dilemma and then survey a variety of creative solutions for restoring life-work balance.

chapter twelve

All My Relations

When we seek for connection, we restore the world to
wholeness. Our seemingly separate lives become meaningful as
we discover how truly necessary we are to each other.

— MARGARET WHEATLEY

At its essence, to be in balance means to be a whole person in
relationship. That's because life is relationships — relationships between
the many subtle fields and flows of energy that weave the fabric of our
being; relationships with other people and with other living beings;
relationships between ourselves and the rest of the universe. If you look
deeply into any living being, a universe of intricate interrelationships
will be revealed. Life is all about relationships.

Balance in relationships can mean many things: the balance of giving and receiving; of speaking and listening; of being alone and being
together; the balance realized by resolving tensions or extending love
and caring. As paradoxical as it seems at times, the more deeply balanced we are within ourselves, the more sensitive, objective, empa-
thetically attuned we can be with others, and the more we can help
others move toward, rather than away from balance in their own lives.
That's why the work you have done so far in this book has been a crucial
preparation for interpersonal balance.

NETWORK OF SUPPORT

In recent times, advances in science have helped to expand our collective understanding of what ensures the health, vitality, longevity, and sustainability of an individual or a species. Our current understanding is that those most likely to survive and thrive are actually the ones who are the most cooperative, communicative, connected, and mutually supportive in relationship to the world.

This brings to mind the image of a bridge that spans a great chasm. The heavier the load it must bear, the more supportive elements are required to keep it from crumbling under the weight. As each of us struggles to manage the heavy load of pressures upon us, those of us who offer support and who are most supported by others stand a much better chance of holding up rather than caving in or suffering under the stress.

The bottom line is that to live a healthy, well-balanced life, it is essential to have a strong network of supportive relationships. Your network is made of all the people, places, or things that in some way nurture the quality of your life. It may include not only friends and family, but people at work or those we know through community, sports, or religious groups, professional associations, or special support groups that you join for a variety of reasons.

A growing body of research in clinical medicine and the social sciences affirms the vital importance of building a strong network of support. It has been consistently demonstrated that people with a strong support network live longer, are less vulnerable to getting sick, and tend to live happier, more fulfilling lives. In numerous studies, children who have strong, supportive relationships with their families were less prone to getting sick, and less likely to turn to drugs, get pregnant, or be involved in crime. Another study has shown that women with breast cancer who are in support groups have a life expectancy four times longer than women in the same situation who are not in support groups. In a study of men suffering with painful angina attacks, men who reported that they lived in supportive primary relationships experienced six times less chest pain than men who were not. And people who have suffered from a heart attack are far less likely to suffer a second if someone calls them once a week, even for thirty seconds, and lets them know they are cared about. Old folks who have a pet, or even a plant, to care for live longer than their counterparts who do not feel needed by others.

"If we think about it, we find that our life consists in achieving a pure relationship between ourselves and the living universe about us. This is how I 'save my soul'—by accomplishing a pure relationship between me and another person, me and a nation, me and a race of people, me and animals, me and the trees or flowers, me and the earth, me and the skies and sun and stars, me and the moon; an infinity of pure relationships, big and little.... this, if we know it, is our life and our eternity: the subtle, perfected relation between me and the circumambient universe."

—D.H. Lawrence

Especially as the pace and complexity of our life/work increases, the importance of support increases, though the time to develop and maintain it often seems to disappear. That's why it is crucial that you begin to see support as a vital component in the creation and maintainence of balance. We simply do not do well without it!

MAKE THE SUPPORT CONSCIOUS

Here's a way to enhance your support network and to articulate to others their importance to you. On a piece of paper make three columns. In the first column, list the names of the people who have most supported you over the past six months. In the second column, list the people who will be looking to you for support in the months to come. Finally, in the third column make a list of the people whose support you will most need in the next six months. Over the weeks to come, seek out each of these people. Thank them for the support they have given. Request continued support, or let people know you're ready to help them in the future. Then ask them, "How can I support you better as we continue our life or work together?" Talk openly about what you have learned from the past and what your hopes or concerns are for the future. Work together to come to the understanding necessary to offer greater support to help each other find more balance as your life continues.

The Support Map

In the center of a piece of paper, make a doodle that represents yourself. Now, around the "you" doodle in and write the names of everyone that makes up the network of support in your life. Surrounding you will be your friends, your parents, children, spouse or significant other, the members of your spiritual community or sports teams, your mentors and coaches, and perhaps your pets. Include here whoever offers support to you in your life in any way—materially, emotionally, morally, spiritually, informationally—doodle them in on this map of your network of support.

Then pause for a few moments to contemplate the unique role that each of these people plays in helping you to find balance and harmony in your life. Give each relationship two ratings. On a scale of one to ten, indicate how important each relationship is in your life—if it is very important, give it a ten; if it is not very important, give it a lower number.

" I am coming to believe that anything that promotes isolation leads to chronic stress and in time may lead to illnesses like heart disease. Anything that promotes a sense of intimacy, community and connection can be healing."

—Dean Ornish

"Spiritual practice is really about weaving a network of good relationships."

—Dhyani Ywahoo

In a similar way, give a rating for how strong that relationship currently is in your life: if it is very strong, or taking much of your time, give it a 10; if it is currently neglected or feels distant, give it a lower number.

Then step back and reflect on the balance or lack of balance revealed through this analysis. If you notice that your spouse is a "10" in importance and yet you only gave him/her a "5" in the strength of the connection you currently feel, what does that tell you? If you find that you are giving 9 points' worth of attention to a relationship that did not get a very high rating in its importance to you, then you may be well advised to seek for balance by resetting your priorities or talking with others to reset expectations.

If you are like many people, you may find as you do this rating that you have been neglecting some relationships that are deeply important to you. In fact, you may have drifted so far from some of them that you have actually lost track of people, or they have died without ever hearing from you how much you cherished them. If this is the case for you, harness the power of any grief you may feel to help you examine your values, and reset and reaffirm your priorities. Let this truth-telling strengthen your commitment to devote the quality of attention necessary for your important relationships. Make calls, send letters or gifts, say prayers, or plan a trip to let people know how much they really mean to you.

BALANCE IN THE FIELD OF RELATIONSHIPS

Now, let's expand your thinking about your field of relationships. In the center of a piece of paper, once again draw a symbol, or a circle, that represents yourself. Around your circle of self, draw other circles, or symbols, that represent all the people who are, or have been, most significant in your life—for better or for worse. If you feel close to a person, draw their circle close to you. If you feel distant from someone, draw their circle farther away.

Then, draw the quality of connection or relationship you have with each person. This may be a bold, strong, direct line connecting the two of you, or it might be a faint, broken, knotted tendril, or a telltale vestige of a once-deep bond. Some of these relationships may carry a positive or negative charge with them. To some you may feel physically drawn while toward others you prefer to keep your distance. Some relationships will reflect a true meeting of minds while others are more of a soul connection. Pause to reflect on this field of relationships:

- In which of these relationships do you experience the most harmony and balance?
- Which relationships seem most out of balance to you?
- What are the specific experiences, feelings, thoughts, desires, or assumptions that lead you to feel that this relationship is in or out of balance?

Stepping back to view the larger picture, think about what factors in your life are supportive of balance in those relationships that are working well, and what is getting in the way of finding balance and harmony in other relationships?

Focus now on two or three of your most significant relationships. Take some time to reflect upon and write down some insights regarding each of these relationships:

- What is working to create as much balance as there is in each of these relationships?
- What do you know in your heart, soul, or gut is needed to bring each of these relationships more toward balance?

To move toward a more mutually fulfilling balance in each of these relationships, meditate on what you are most grateful for in each relationship, that which you wish to carry forward into your future. What no longer serves in these relationships that it is time to let go of? What new ways of being together would you like to see emerge through these relationships?

Reflect also on what limits or boundaries need to be honored:

- What are you willing to do?
- What are you willing not to do?
- What are you not willing to do?

Next, consider your special roles in the different relationships of your life — as a friend, a lover, a spouse, a parent, a child, a peer, a professional, a leader, an employee. Ask yourself in which roles do you find yourself living most in balance? In which roles do you feel the most challenged to find or keep your balance? For example, do you sense yourself to be out of balance as a spouse, yet experience balance in your role as a parent? If you find yourself in the roles of both a parent and a child, in which role do you feel most in balance or out of balance? What

"Love for a person permits him to unfold, to open up, to drop his defenses, to let himself be naked not only physically but psychologically and spiritually as well. In a word, he lets himself be seen instead of hiding himself. In ordinary interpersonal relations we are to some extent inscrutable to each other. In love relationships, we become 'scrutable.'"

—Abraham Maslow

is the level of balance you currently feel in your professional role? At work, do you feel most in balance when you are in the role of a leader, a peer, or as someone who is being led?

It may also be revealing to notice which roles and relationships you have completely forgotten. Be honest with yourself and acknowledge those people and functions you have avoided writing down. Open your heart and mind to reflect on what this tells you about the issues you need to address in order to find greater balance within yourself and in relationships with others.

THE PATHS TOWARD AND AWAY FROM BALANCE IN RELATIONSHIP

By learning to recognize the many invisible patterns of relationship, you may come to a wealth of valuable insights regarding how to find more harmony with the people in your life. From our experience, it seems clear that we are more likely to find balance in relationships of all kinds — parent/child, life partners, friends, family, coworkers — when we:

- stay honest with ourselves and with others about what is really true for us;
- communicate what is true for us with authenticity and compassion;
- listen from the heart, and for the heart, in what is being communicated;
- make the invisible visible by recognizing and clarifying assumptions and expectations;
- know our options, and make conscious rather than compulsive choices;
- show respect by being willing to "look again" or "look more deeply" into ourselves and others;
- remain patient, tolerant, and keep our sense of humor;
- have confidence in ourselves and nurture trust in our relationships;
- treat ourselves and others with kindness, caring, and compassion;
- see our relationship as a mutually supportive vehicle for realizing our highest potentials and for discovering a wholeness greater than our individuality and;
- view the relationship as serving a larger sphere than just ourselves.

"... how few understand what love really is, and how it arises in the human heart. It is so frequently equated with good feelings toward others, with benevolence or nonviolence or service. But these things in themselves are not love. Love springs from awareness. It is only inasmuch as you see someone as he or she really is here and how and not as they are in your memory or your desire or in your imagination or projection that you can truly love them, otherwise it is not the person that you love but the idea that you have formed of this person, or this person as the object of your desire not as he or she is in themselves.

(continued)

The training ground of your relationships will continue to offer moment-to-moment feedback on the quality of balance in your life. Receive this feedback with a sincere wish to learn, and the quality of your relationships will noticeably improve over time.

CONSCIOUS RELATIONSHIPS

Most relationships are formed unconsciously through the interplay of our habits, mindless behaviors, and unacknowledged and unspoken expectations and assumptions. Is it any wonder that so many of our relationships seem so problematic and so far out of balance?

When you invite yourself and others to be more conscious in your relationships, you create the opportunity to let your relationship become more choiceful and creative. The artist Vincent van Gogh once said, "To live, to work, to play are really one. If you ask me, the most creative thing we can do is to love people." To turn our relationships into works of art takes a high level of honesty, objectivity, patience, and commitment. Mindful moment to mindful moment, the choice is always yours: succumb to the momentum of unconscious habits, or intensify mindful awareness to understand what is really going on and creatively, compassionately enhance it.

You can cultivate the artistry of any relationship even if your partners have no interest or inclination to raise their own level of consciousness, compassion, or creativity. Ultimately, this is work that only you can do on yourself. No one can do this for you, nor can you make changes in someone else's life without running a risk—at some level—of being disrespectful or of doing violence to them. Moment to moment, in every relationship you are in, you are making choices based on your habits, values, priorities, and the quality of awareness present. You can endure the situation as it is; you can withdraw from the relationship—physically, mentally, or emotionally—or you can search for ways to make that relationship a creative work of art.

Remember, learning is led by questions and fed by feedback. Questions organize and focus your attention. Feedback provides vital information necessary for learning: no feedback, no learning. Therefore, from time to time, it is helpful to check in with yourself and with the people you live or work with most closely. Ask yourself, and then ask others:

"The first act of love is to see this person or this object, this reality as it truly is. And this involves the enormous discipline of dropping your desires, your prejudices, your memories, your projections, your selective way of looking ...a discipline so great that most people would rather plunge headlong into good actions and service than submit to the burning fire of this asceticism. When you set out to serve someone whom you have not taken the trouble to see, are you meeting that person's need or your own?"

—Father Anthony de Mello

"You know there
are three kinds of
friends in the world.

An ordinary
person sees only
who you are;

for that you don't
need a friend.

Then there's a friend
who sees in you
what you can be.

And then there's
the real holy Friend,
and the presence
of this Friend you
are already."

—Reb Schlomo
Charlebach

- How are we doing in our relationship?
- What signs of balance or imbalance do you notice in how we are living or working together?
- What conscious or unconscious expectations or assumptions do we need to test, clarify, or reset to develop the quality of relationship that we both want to have?
- What is working well in our relationship that is worth celebrating?
- How are we feeling fulfilled or frustrated in this relationship?
- What do you think would help us to find greater harmony or balance in our relationship?
- To ensure the vitality and strength of this relationship, what seems like the next stage of our learning and growth?

Reflecting upon these questions will help you to bring more clarity and truth into your relationships. Sharing these reflections with those you live and work closely with can stimulate the dialogue and learning necessary to deepen your relationships. If you are honest with your self and others, you will recognize that there is often much to celebrate and much potential for further learning. Though this realization is seldom comfortable, neither is the buried dissatisfaction, frustration, and resentment that can come when we don't develop enough balance in our relationships to embrace and learn from the truth.

THE MIRROR OF RELATIONSHIPS:
WE ARE WHAT WE BEHOLD

"The only reason we
don't open our hearts
and minds to other
people is that they
trigger confusion
in us that we don't
feel brave enough or
sane enough to deal
with. To the degree
that we look clearly
and compassionately
at ourselves, we feel
confident and fearless
about looking into
someone else's eyes."

—Ane Pema Chödrön

The cardinal rule in bringing harmony to your relationships is to remember that your work is on yourself. It is not about changing, coercing, or manipulating others. Over the course of a lifetime, we have the opportunity to learn from and grow within the context of many different relationships. Lessons learned in one relationship will often offer valuable clues for other relationships. As we learn and grow, we change, and as we change, our relationships change. On the other hand, many of us have learned by now that though we may leave a relationship with someone, the same difficult issues we had with that person may keep showing up in other relationships until we work it out in a balanced way. If you have a lesson to learn and you don't learn it in one relationship, it will certainly keep resurfacing until you get it.

So it is crucial in all relationships that we ask ourselves again and again: What issues or qualities in my own life, attitudes, or beliefs are being reflected back to me in the mirror of this relationship? Is this relationship asking me to be more patient, more honest, more mindful, more loving, more lighthearted, more focused, more present, more caring, or more generous with my time and attention? Look, listen, and feel into the relationship for what is really being asked for in order to realize harmony and balance between you. Deepen your empathy to know and understand both what is true for you, and, as best you can, what is likely true for others. Balance both reasoning and intuitive intelligence to discover what is most alive in each relationship.

With this in mind, when certain themes arise in your relationships, if you are mindful enough, you can chuckle to yourself and say, "Oh, I get it. The irritation that I'm feeling around this person is asking me to look at and work with my impatience. The important message here is for me, not for them. Thank you for offering this mirror for me to recognize what I need to work on. Let's see how well I can do this time!" Or, "Ah, I get it, this isn't about your fashion preferences. You are really reflecting back to me valuable information about my own judgments and intolerance. I'm more comfortable focusing on what's wrong with you than taking a hard look at what could be working better in my own life." Or perhaps, "My withdrawal from the intensity of your love and caring for me is challenging me to open my own heart, to feel worthy of your love, and to accept myself, rather than rejecting you as I have tended to reject myself." You can see how, at the simplest, most basic level, our relationships are about teaching us how to deeply listen to, understand, befriend, and love ourselves, and then how to deeply listen to, understand, appreciate, and love each other.

In extending love to others, the key point to remember is this: Though the people with whom we live and work maintain an air of having it together and having their life in control, just like us they all carry deep wounds from previous experiences that lead them to act in ways that are difficult for us to understand, even if we think we know them. This simple yet challenging fact of life creates a learning laboratory in which we are constantly being invited to learn more about ourselves and one another as we dance together in life.

"I tell you one thing —if you want peace of mind, do not find fault with others. Rather learn to see your own faults. Learn to make the whole world your own. No one is a stranger my child, this whole world is your own."

—The last words of the Holy Mother Sri Sarada Devi

"When you see a man of worth,

Think of how you may emulate him.

When you see one who is unworthy,

Examine your own character."

—Confucius

INNER AND OUTER BALANCE IN COMMUNICATION

An important dimension of balance in action is how you communicate with others. As you practice mindfulness, you've probably begun to notice that, even as you engage in conversations with people throughout the day, you have a fair amount of background conversation going on in your own mind as you constantly interpret, evaluate, and judge your experience. Although this mental activity is useful in making sense out of your experience, it may actually be reducing the clarity of your experience itself. If we're talking together, for example, it'll be impossible for you to really hear what I'm saying if you're talking at the same time—and that includes thinking about what you're going to say next. Because so many of the breakdowns in our personal and professional relationships come about because people are not being listened to, or not feeling listened to, learning to listen better is really an important skill. Perhaps if people could calculate how much poor attention and listening habits cost us in rework, frustration, accidents, and heartache, we'd be more motivated to invest the time, energy, and attention necessary to improve the quality of our awareness and communication skills. Most breakdowns in communication could have been prevented if people were really listening to themselves as well as listening to each other. Begin listening to the listening as much as to what is actually being said. Understanding this, you might find some value in applying the following four principles to your communications with people.

Centering. Whenever possible, before you enter into a communication with someone, pause for a moment to get centered. Scan through your own circuits and, as you breathe, notice, loosen, and release any tensions that you may be holding. As you inhale, focus your attention right here in the moment, in the place where your power is, and as you exhale, let your awareness flow and open.

Intent to Stay Present. Generate the firm intention to be as fully present as you can with the person you're about to talk with. Imagine yourself using your breathing to stay present, open, and connected to them, and to simply listen wholeheartedly to what they're communicating. Think to yourself, Staying completely present, open, and connected with you, I breathe in ... staying completely present, open and connected with you, I breathe out....

Or simply, Present ... open ... connected....

Generous Listening. As you begin your conversation, listen attentively to what's actually being said. Be mindful of your own internal conversations about what others are saying, but quiet your thinking by gently saying to yourself, mentally, Listen. Use your breathing to help you stay focused and relaxed.

Active Listening and Feedback. Use active listening skills to briefly paraphrase for the person you're talking with what you've heard them say. If the message you are hearing from someone carries a strong emotional charge to it, remember to acknowledge that you have heard two important things. First, let them know that you understand the issue or concern that is important to them. Second, communicate that you are sensitive to their feelings about the situation. For example, "That's great that you made the finals in the competition. You must feel honored and proud to receive such recognition from your peers." Or, "It sounds like when your mom told that story about your first date, you were really embarrassed." Or, "I can understand how worried you were when your daughter wasn't home by 2 a.m. — I bet you were upset when she finally got home, and were grateful that she was all right." Keep in mind that people need to hear feedback that you understand their issues, their feelings, and their often unspoken needs. Use active listening to reflect back to them what you've heard and to check that you understood their communication to their satisfaction.

BEYOND WORDS

Balance in communication is about more than the interaction of what I say and what you say. Studies of effective communication have shown that 55 percent of the message is conveyed through body language, and 38 percent is carried by voice tonality. Nonverbal cues, then, account for as much as 93 percent of the total message that we receive, while only 7 percent comes from the words we hear or say! Taking this to heart, we come to understand that to improve our communications we must learn to listen carefully to numerous streams of information.

Let's look first at finding a balance between our internal dialogue and the actual words that we are hearing. It is helpful to understand that the speed of thought is many times faster than the speed of talk. Even a fast speaker would be lucky if they spoke 150 or 200 words per minute, while your thoughts zip by at nearly five times that speed. For every page of words you speak, I generate five to seven pages of my own internal script. It is as though we are communicating with modems that

> "It's so important that we have a conscious mind. How are we going to restore our relationships? If we are advocating for harmonious community, and we would love to have a sense of justice and prosperity, we cannot be using the same methods and the same tactics. Ends and means for me are the same."
>
> —Francisco 'Pancho' Ramos Stierle

> "Language is an old-growth forest of the mind."
>
> —Wade Davis

run at different speeds, which is measured in the number of bits of information that they can process in a second. The words we speak to each other flow relatively slowly, analogous to an old-model modem that could only send or receive information at a rate of 2,400 bits per second. In contrast, your thinking process is much faster, more like a newer model modem that is capable of processing 55,000 bits of information per second or faster. Given the heavy competition of our internal background conversation, is it any wonder that people so often do not feel heard or understood! Once again, mindfulness is the key. By learning to be mindfully attentive to both of these conversations at the same time, you'll be able to focus on what's really being communicated to you and to sort out your thoughts about what you have heard.

Here is a useful and fun exercise to apply mindfulness to finding balance in communications between yourself and others. Take a piece of paper and draw a line down the middle so that you have two columns. At the top of the right-hand column write, "What's actually being said." and at the top of the left hand column write, "What my internal conversation is saying about what's being said."

Once you get a sense for this exercise, you can expand your mindfulness in communication to include additional conversations that are going on simultaneously in every conversation. Add to the stream of words you hear, and the stream of thoughts that you think to yourself, the third stream of communications: the flow of nonverbal information generated by your partner. As they speak, "listen" attentively to the cues offered by their gestures, posture, facial expression, and the tonality of their voice, all of which carry valuable clues about the emotions associated with the words they are speaking.

Also be attentive to a fourth stream of communication, the message that you are communicating through your body. Be mindful of what you are saying in words and in silences, in your posture and gestures, and through your facial expressions, voice tone, and the energy of your presence.

The fifth stream of communications to monitor is your internal intuitive sense, which is active during the exchange of more tangible auditory and visual communication. Notice what you feel in your gut, what your body is telling you about this communication. Also be mindful of the mental images, emotions, and the clear intuitive insights that stream into your mind throughout your communications.

Remember that communication takes place on many different levels. As you learn to be mindful of how these five different streams of information weave together into your communications, your insight, intuition, and empathy will deepen. The ability to monitor your mental, emotional, and physical state while you're engaged in outer activities and interactions is the real key to finding balance in the midst of dynamic interaction with others. As you become more aware of these multiple streams of information and how they interact, you will recognize many opportunities to find more balance while you are communicating with others.

ALONENESS AND TOGETHERNESS

One useful measure of balance in your life is your level of comfort in relating to others versus being alone with yourself. These two aspects need to be in balance because the more you understand and are comfortable with yourself, the more authenticity and depth you will be able to bring to your relationships.

Some people are so uncomfortable just being with themselves that they are compulsively driven to be with others. They are afraid to be alone, so they call others or distract themselves with mindless activities or entertainment. We live in a culture that has invested heavily in trying to convince us that we are incomplete without being in a primary relationship or without being a parent. Although none of us can be fully complete outside of the network of our relationships, a healthy balance in our life is reflected by our comfort in being alone, that is, "all one," with ourselves.

Michelle really cherishes her quiet, alone time. She often says she must have been a Gypsy in a previous life, because she read once that Gypsies learned how to be together in such close quarters in their caravans by taking time every day — before eight o'clock in the morning — when they didn't talk to each other. She thought that sounded like a great idea! After thirty-two incredible years together, the two of us often say that one of the greatest strengths in our relationship is that we really know how to be "alone together." We love to do things together, and we work, write, spend time in retreat and in nature, and play intensively together! However, to maintain this intensity of relationship, it's essential for each of us to also have time to ourselves. It is not uncommon for us to walk, hike, or drive for miles together without saying a word to each other, or to sit and meditate or work around the house without interrupting each other for long periods of time. Then when we do reconnect, we bring a greater depth and insight to share with each other. We aren't disturbing and distracting each other out of our discomfort with ourselves, or out of our own sense of incompleteness.

"Grant me the ability to be alone;

May it be my custom to go outdoors each day among the trees and grasses,

among all growing things

and there may I be alone,

and enter into prayer to talk with the one that I belong to."

—Rabbi Nachman of Bratzlav

We are sharing insights, joys, discoveries, or questions that are really meaningful for us, and that may enrich each other.

Balance and wholeness in relationships depend on feeling whole both when we are alone and when we are with others. If you are comfortable being alone, but uncomfortable with others, stretch yourself to seek greater balance by increasing your social skills and comfort in relationships. If being alone is uncomfortable for you, move toward balance by gradually increasing your capacity to enjoy being with yourself. Begin with short periods of time, perhaps 10 or 15 minutes a day when you are undistracted by others. To accomplish this you may need to renegotiate your time commitments or reset the expectations that other people have of you. If you can help others understand that the quality of your time with them will be enhanced if you have time to find balance and wholeness with yourself, you will be more likely to enlist their support of your alone time.

In your own life, be mindful of what drives you to engage or disengage from others. Do you initiate conversations compulsively, or do you check in to see if your partner is in a mindset receptive to what you have to share? Do you withdraw into aloofness or take time to be alone out of fear, anxiety, shame, or frustration, or because you really do enjoy being by yourself? Are you in touch with what is really true for you and do you let others know what your needs and wishes are? Do you let others know when you would like to have some quality time together with them? Do you communicate that you really need time alone to find your own internal balance, time that will ultimately help you to be with them in a more complete and wholehearted way? Don't assume that your invisible thoughts, feelings, intentions, or needs are readily understood to people around you. It is necessary to both know what is true for you, and to communicate it!

Making time to simply be alone with yourself is actually an offering to everyone you live in relationship with. Only by understanding yourself—your inner thoughts, hopes, fears, aspirations, and spirit—can you know what is really true for you and convey that to others in a way that brings harmony and balance to your relationships. Though at first it may be awkward, begin to explore ways to create some alone time to develop a stronger, deeper, more intimate relationship with yourself. During your time alone you might:

- take a walk and just be with and discover the miracle of yourself
- sit quietly and mindfully explore what you sense and feel, what you

"To listen is very hard, because it asks of us so much interior stability that we no longer need to prove ourselves by speeches, arguments, statements or declarations. True listeners no longer have an inner need to make their presence known. They are free to receive, welcome, to accept.

Listening is much more than allowing another to talk while waiting for a chance to respond. Listening is paying full attention to others and welcoming them into our very beings. The beauty of listening is that those who are listened to start feeling accepted, start taking our words more seriously and discovering their true selves. Listening is a form of spiritual hospitality by which you invite strangers to become friends, to get to know their inner selves more fully, and even to dare to be silent with you."

—Henri Nouwen

think and want
- take time to write in your journal
- sit, stand, move, or dance in front of a mirror
- talk or sing to yourself, or play music
- meditate, deeply listen, feel and know what is true for you
- make a list of the questions that are important to you in your life
- spend time in nature exploring the mysterious boundary between yourself and the universe; see if you can find where you end, and the rest of the universe begins
- mindfully bathe or shower, brush your hair, or massage your body
- eat a mindful silent meal

Harmony in relationships is found in balancing the attention we give to ourselves with the attention we give to our loved ones, friends, and coworkers. If we invest too much attention outwardly and get out of touch with ourselves, we lose our balance and may end up feeling resentful, get into fights, or pull away. If we get too preoccupied with ourselves, we can fall into isolation, narcissism, or loneliness. Ideally each day—or at least each week—will reflect a balance of some time to be with ourselves and some time to be with others in a nourishing and quality way.

PLAY: THE GIVING AND RECEIVING OF LOVE

At a conference at the Menninger Foundation, we had the opportunity to watch a documentary about play behavior in animals that was made by a colleague of ours, Stuart Brown. One memorable bit of footage shows a hungry polar bear approaching a husky dog that was chained up in a yard on the outskirts of an arctic settlement. The bear approached, crouched down, with its ears back in a gesture that the dog recognized as an invitation: "Would you like to play?" Seemingly without fear, the dog assumed a responsive pose that communicated, "Sure!"

And play they did! Indeed, their play was so vigorous that the bear at one point actually tossed the dog way up into the air. They had great fun and played together until they were mutually fulfilled and exhausted. Panting and sweating, they concluded their playtime with gestures of completion and mutual satisfaction. Amazingly, the next day, the bear returned, and the dog and the bear continued to build their playful relationship with each other.

"When original play was abandoned,

life ceased to have meaning

and we discovered purpose.

When ethics arrived,

we played fairly—

to win at any cost.

When kindness dissolved,

we played for keeps."

—Fred Donaldson

Years ago, after one of many mass killings in Texas, the state government commissioned a study to identify the psychological profile of people who were most prone to acts of brutal violence. After extensive testing and interviews with the killers, their families, siblings, and former teachers, one factor stood out as most significant: as children, they had never really learned how to play with other children.

A play dysfunction can dramatically impair the quality of our health and relationships with others. Numerous studies suggest that societies who indulge in large amounts of play are healthier. Play is vital to the healthy development of our nervous systems, and it has been suggested that it brings balance to our waking life in the same way that dreaming and REM sleep does for us in our sleeping hours.

Genuine play is about giving and receiving love. It is about discovering the extraordinary within the ordinary. Play is found in the creative ways that emerge between infants or octogenarians. It can unfold between preverbal children and speakers, between people of different cultures, and between creatures of different species. Play is not about who is best or most skilled, and definitely not about winning or losing. Play is about mutual discovery, learning, and delight. In play there is no advantage to being big or small, old or young. Play is not about manipulation or deception. It is not about forcing your will or body on others or about causing discomfort for one of your playmates. Play is not about tickling, which is an excellent example of abusiveness masquerading as play, and which often leaves emotional scars similar to other forms of abuse.

At the heart of play is love and a deep sense of wonder and mutual discovery. Play is about balance, mystery, belonging, inclusion, trust, sacredness, fearlessness, touch, reciprocity, love, kindness, openness, and joy. It is about awareness, joining, blending, following, and contributing of energy. It is not about humiliation, rejection, competition, mocking, exclusion, admiration, defensiveness, or fear.

We can approach our lives with either a work ethic or a play ethic. The work ethic approach encourages us to be goal oriented, and to pursue "management by objective" approaches to work. Victory signals the end of the game. The play ethic takes a different approach to life, one that is about continuous inquiry and discovery that could go on forever.

Play is not about playing a game in which one person wins and another loses, it is not about one person dominating or imposing their will on another. Based in co-creative mutual discovery, play teaches us how to learn and explore relationships in mutually respectful ways. A measure of our success in playing with someone is that when we finish,

"Curiosity is a very important element of our soul, and one that is necessary for our inquiry.... Curiosity brings in a lighthearted playfulness, an ease and a flow, a purposeless engagement in life. This playful quality invites a sense of adventure and experimentation in the process of exploring and discovering the nature of reality. And all of these qualities are natural expressions of the heart's joy and delight in participating in the creative dynamism of the soul's unfoldment."

—A.H. Almaas

we feel a close bond, a deeper trust, and, given the opportunity, we'd welcome the opportunity to play together again. Play behavior, in its purest sense, is mutually fulfilling, self-fulfilling, noncompetitive, interactive exploration. It is essential to developing quality, balanced relationships.

Do you have enough play in your life? Do you play, really play as defined here, with your spouse, your children, your friends, your coworkers? One of our most inspiring friends and playmates, O. Fred Donaldson, author of *Playing by Heart*, is a true master of the high art of play. In his inspiring book, Fred offers the following six "Play Principles" you might want to consider in order to bring more play into your relationships:

1. Be not afraid of life.

2. Be quiet.

3. Touch is our primary language.

4. Be a beginner.

5. Smooth moves follow a clear heart.

6. Expect nothing, be ready for anything.

These six principles are actually six ways of beholding the unity of mind, body, and spirit. They are facets of the same jewel of balanced relationships. To understand one of these is to understand them all. To misuse one is to misuse them all. In the actual practice of play in relationships, these principles translate into action as follows:

1. Get down, touch the earth.

2. Be quiet.

3. Pay attention and be present.

4. Let go.

5. Release thoughts.

6. Be in touch.

As Fred reminds us, "We must feel it in our flesh and bones. We must touch and be touched. Then we will earn the integrity and wholeness of our lives by every act we do."

"What we free ourselves from is illusion, and what frees us from illusion is the discovery of truth. To make that discovery, we need to enlist the powerful intelligence of our own awake mind and turn it toward our goal of exposing, opposing, and overcoming deception. That is the essence and mission of 'rebel Buddha': to free us from the illusions we create by ourselves, about ourselves, and from those that masquerade as reality in our cultural and religious institutions."

—Punlop Rinpoche

In your own life, when were the times when you discovered the joys of true playfulness? During those precious moments, what actually happened that drew you into play? How were you left feeling during and after those encounters? How might you make yourself more available for such close and meaningful play encounters in the future?

In search of balance, invite yourself to consciously and intentionally seek out opportunities to play more in your life. Welcome the chance to learn from and play with children who still remember how to play — even if it's just for a moment in a checkout line at the market, or while standing at a street corner waiting to cross the street. Be ready for times when you can take a more playful stance and remind others of the joy to be found in living and working in a more creative, loving, open, and learningful way. Stretch yourself to assume a more playful attitude in at least some of the many situations you encounter. Remember, each encounter offers a treasury of extraordinary possibilities for you to choose from in weaving the balance of your life.

SHARED AWARENESS

Play offers us a glimpse of what it is like to give and be given undivided attention. Learning to play and to love expands our capacity to truly give our attention wholeheartedly to our lives. If we have learned these lessons well, being fully present in relationships comes easily. If not, we may have to apply more discipline to staying focused when we are with others.

Giving your complete attention to someone is a rare and precious gift. This next exercise provides yet another doorway that can open you to build this capacity and experience a deep connection, sense of balance, and flow with another person. We often teach this core practice when we work with caregivers, hospice volunteers, parents' groups, or other helping professionals. As you do this exercise, let your awareness hover equally within yourself and with the person you are attending to.

To begin, invite your partner to find a comfortable place to lie down while you pull up a chair or sit down next to them. The person lying down needs only to deeply relax and stay aware of the presence of their companion sitting by their side. When you are the person sitting close by, your role is to watch carefully and notice the breathing rhythm of your partner who is lying down. As you sit with your partner, tune in and become aware of their breathing, and observe the rise and fall of their abdomen or chest. Then begin to synchronize the

"Whenever the rabbi of Sasov saw anyone's suffering either of spirit or of body, he shared it so earnestly that the other's suffering became his own. Once someone expressed his astonishment at this capacity to share in another's troubles. 'What do you mean "share"?' Asked the rabbi. 'It is my sorrow; how can I help but suffer it?'"

—Martin Buber

rhythm of your own breathing with theirs. Each time that your partner inhales, you silently inhale. Each time he or she exhales, make a soft but audible "ahhh" sound. Inhale silently, exhale softly. Ahhhh.... The sounds you make let your partner know that you are completely there with and for him or her.

If you are the person who is lying down, let yourself simply receive the gift of this person's undivided loving attention. Do your best to stay receptive and feel the bond that grows between you. Patiently stay with this process through times of discomfort, self-consciousness, boredom, or distraction.

After 15 or 20 minutes, silently stretch, and then switch roles so that each of you has the opportunity to give and receive the gift of each other's complete attention. Then take some time to talk about how this experience has touched you.

- What did you learn about finding balance and flow in relationships through this experience?
- What insights have you gained about yourself in relationships through this exercise?
- Was it easier for you to be in the active or the receptive role?
- What feelings or thoughts did you notice?
- How was your perception of yourself or of your partner impacted through this exercise?
- What factors made this process easy or difficult for you?
- What did you learn about giving or receiving loving attention?

"Out of my experience ... one final conclusion dogmatically emerges: There is a continuum of cosmic consciousness against which our individuality builds by accidental forces, and into which our several minds plunge as into a mother sea."

—William James

This exercise provides a safe and often profound opportunity to experience without words what it is like to fully be present with another person, and to have someone be totally there for you. This experience may provide a fierce mirror for us to see how self-conscious, self-critical, or easily distracted we are. It also offers us a glimpse of a quality of connectedness, safety, intimacy, and caring beyond words that is deeply rewarding and affirming. As we develop our capacity to deeply listen to, care about, and give our full attention to ourselves and to others, we are more likely to discover what true balance in relationships can mean for the quality of our life.

BALANCING RITUALS FOR COUPLES

If you want to keep your intimate relationship alive, it's essential to give some time on a regular basis to connect deeply, even if it's only for a few wholehearted minutes each day! Here are some balancing rituals that can be easily integrated into your schedule. You can use these on a daily or weekly basis, and the time you give to them can be adapted to fit in with the changing rhythms of your lifestyle: if there is no time for it one day, that's okay. Just find what works best for you and keep trying.

Remember the fundamentals of balance: you will lose it, but you can always find it again! That is just as true for interpersonal relationships as for inner balance. The point is to mindfully notice that you haven't had time for deep connection and then return, forgiving of yourself and your partner, to deepen the connection once again.

Hair Brushing. One of our favorite quick ways to reconnect is to brush out each other's hair. Michelle particularly loves this. It seems to nourish the "roots" of balance in our joint psyche, linking us back to tribal days when people regularly shared moments of tender loving care through grooming each other. Bioenergetically, it also helps clear our energy field of accumulated static electricity, which is especially important after long days in front of a computer monitor.

Foot Rubs. In this same category of physical rituals that move us toward balance is the special gift of giving each other a foot rub. This is a great one for quiet moments after a hard day's work or play — or anytime! The soles of the feet have receptors connecting to all the organs and structures of the body. Foot rubs are one of the best ways to give and receive a balancing and revitalizing mini-massage, especially if you use some aromatic essential oil like lavender or juniper. You don't have to be an expert on reflexology to give your partner a deluxe treatment (though there are many guidebooks available on the subject, and even little cards that map out the terrain of each foot in detail). Just trust the inner guidance of your heart and let your hands "go for the sole."

Get Wet. Anything to do with water is a helpful strategy for balance — bathing or showering together, swimming, washing one another's feet, listening to the soothing sounds of a waterfall or ocean waves on recorded environmental music tapes, or even going for a walk in the rain, are all wonderful ways to reconnect in a balancing way.

Read to One Another. Two friends of ours experimented with unplugging their TV and reading poetry to each other in the evenings instead. Another couple we know are working their way through *The Hobbit* and can't wait to jump into bed to get to the next chapter.

"Nobody sees a flower—really—

it is so small—we haven't time—

and to see takes time.

Like to have a friend takes time."

—Georgia O'Keefe

"In love there's no pure identity because love involves two and yet the two become one. That's the great mystery."

—Father Bede Griffiths

Take a Walk. Friends of ours decided to go for a walk after work around the reservoir in their town as part of their daily routine. This strategy proved immediately beneficial, both for their own individual sense of health and vitality, and for their health, vitality, and balance as a couple. People with children can bring the kids along too!

Morning Tea and Meditation. Another couple we know found that reestablishing an old family custom of "morning tea and meditation" in bed made a major difference in the quality of their relationship and the energy with which their day got off to a start. For other couples, praying together in the morning or evening has become an integral element of staying balanced together.

The Four Rivers of Life. One couple with whom we worked started to incorporate a time of deep reflection and truth-speaking each evening. Using a simple process we'd introduced them to, which involves four questions as a tool to give structure to their contemplations, they each take turns listening and speaking deeply as they share what is true for them. Here are the four questions:

- Where today was I inspired by something or someone?
- Where today was I surprised?
- Where today did I find myself being challenged or stretched to grow or think in new ways?
- Where today was I touched or deeply moved by something that came into my life?

We first learned this series of contemplations from Angeles Arrien, who received them from her Basque ancestors. In the Basque tradition, these four questions honor the Four Rivers of Life: the river of Inspiration, the river of Surprise, the river of Challenge, and the river of Love. According to the wise elders of this tradition, it's impossible for us to truly stay in balance without jumping in and bathing in the rivers on a daily basis. We'll often expand the range of these rivers to include the river of Gratitude and the river of Learning. What other rivers might you want to add and "bathe in" in order to live more in balance?

RECOGNIZING EACH OTHER

Here's another practice to deepen your connection. Sit quietly across from one another. Like mirrors deeply reflecting each other, see in each other your parents, grandparents, and ancestors. See too the

"It happens all the time in heaven,

And

some day

It will begin to happen

Again on earth—

That men and women who are married,

And men and men who are

Lovers,

And women and women

Who give each other

Light,

Often will get down on their knees

And while so tenderly

Holding their lover's hand,

With tears in their eyes,

Will sincerely speak, saying,

'My dear,

How can I be more loving to you;

How can I be more Kind?'"

—Hafiz

generational cascade of traditions, attitudes, beliefs, customs, and habits that help or harm. See in yourself, and in each other, the miraculous moment of your conception. See yourselves swimming in the wombs of your mothers. See yourselves as tiny children, wide-eyed in a wonder-full world. See in yourself and in each other the potentials for becoming a wise old man or a wise old woman. See in yourselves and each other the seeds of influence that will bear fruit in the lives of others for countless generations to come.

Quietly, connectedly, come into harmony within this place where your two streams of being meet. See and feel the connection. Then, from this place, share your visions for the future, your hopes and your fears, your life's greatest joys, and your sorrows. Perhaps you might simply want to exchange the following: "What is true for me right now is…."

THE PRECIOUS MOMENT WE SHARE

Because it is so easy to get caught up in the business and busy-ness of life and forget how important the people in our lives are to us, the sudden death of someone we love can be one of life's most powerful teachers on living in balance. In the clear light of this stark reality, the preciousness of the moments we have to share with our loved ones becomes sharply etched in our hearts. The intensity and shock of losing a friend can also help us get clear on our values and our priorities, and can renew our commitment to giving more balanced attention to what really matters in our lives and relationships.

So if you are serious about finding balance in your life, consider using on a daily basis the following powerful reminder: In each encounter this may well be the last time you are together with this person. The winds of change are fierce and unpredictable. As you tuck your kids in, kiss your sweetheart good night, or lay thee down to sleep … who really knows what comes next?

Living half awake, our sense of false security dulls the keenness of our awareness, and leads us not to treasure as deeply as we might the extraordinariness of each "ordinary" encounter. As we begin to realize how tenuous our precious lives and relationships are, we discover a vivid clarity that wakes us up and brings us more alive. In the moments when we realize we have just been going through the motions of our lives, that we have been checked out more than checked in, and that we really haven't been loving as deeply as we are able, we touch a grief that can bring us wholeheartedly back to life. Thich Nhat Hanh offers a powerful antidote to such forgetfulness in relationships. He suggests that

"Walk around feeling like a leaf. Know you could tumble at any second. Then decide what to do with your time."

—Naomi Shahib Nye

"You cannot do a kindness too soon because you never know how soon it will be too late."

—Ralph Waldo Emerson

"Thus shall ye look on all this fleeting world: A star at dawn, a bubble in the stream, A flash of lightning in a summer cloud, A flickering lamp, a phantom, and a dream."

—Gautama the Buddha

when we are in the midst of a quarrel with our beloved ones, we take a time-out for a moment to look deeply into their eyes and consider where we will be in 300 years.

Let each encounter be the most important thing in your life at the time. For the few fleeting moments that you are together, exercise the discipline necessary to give this person your complete, undivided attention and love. When your attention wanders to memories of the past or fantasies of the future, smile to yourself, and reel yourself back into this precious moment alive together. Really listen. Really care. Be real. Let yourself love and be loved. Be with them in such a way that if they were never to see you again, they would be moved to comment how meaningful their time with you was. Be with them so that if you were to never see them again, you would know in your heart that those last precious moments of life that you shared were really good ones. Remember, when you deeply touch someone's heart, you change their life forever.

~∽

"Man comes from dust and ends in dust; he wins his bread
at the risk of his life. He is like the potsherd that breaks,
the grass that withers, the flowers that fade, the shadow
that passes, the cloud that vanishes, the breeze that blows,
the dust that floats, the dream that flies away."

—Hebrew Prayer

chapter thirteen

Life-Work Balance

No one else can tell you what your life's work is, but it's important that you find it. There is a part of you that knows — affirm
that part....

—WILLIS W. HARMAN

An important distinction for finding balance in your work-life is to
remember that your "job" is fundamentally different from your "Work":

- Your "job" is the set of roles and responsibilities that you need to
  fulfill in order to satisfy the terms of your employment.
- Your "Work" is the mission or purpose you feel most deeply called
  or guided to fulfill in the course of your life.
- True life-work balance can be realized when you learn how to get
  your Work done while you are doing your job!

For example, perhaps your job is to create websites, sell a product,
or offer services of some kind—and your "Work" is to live in harmony
and balance, or to become ever more fully present, kind, compassionate, creative, or helpful in how you live your life. Experiment with
holding the intention to pay attention to this higher purpose in your
life as you do your job talking to clients, writing code, giving a presentation, teaching yoga, running a business, serving lattes to customers, editing, or whatever you do for employment, and simultaneously

holding the intention to pay attention to being helpful, kind, or creative in the process. The buoyancy that this will offer to you in living your life and doing your job will be profound in terms of learning to live and work in balance.

STRESSFUL TIMES

We live in a strange and stressful time, when about one-third of us are overworked and looking to cut back, and another third of us are looking for meaningful employment. Although some economists say that we are addicted to work and that people want to work more hours, many others understand that in today's highly competitive work environment people are working long and hard due to increased pressure, higher expectations, and greater uncertainty for people who do have jobs.

It's difficult to feel we are living our lives in balance if we feel overworked and burned out. Yet for many of us, this is a fact of life. Among full-time employees, most say that their employers expect an unreasonable amount of overtime, and with increasing numbers of unemployed, highly educated people, many people with jobs are anxiously overworking themselves at the cost of finding balance in their life and work. Working long hours, especially in jobs that we don't find fulfilling, leaves little time or energy to spend quality time with our families and friends, or to do things that renew, revitalize, and develop ourselves. As a result, many people feel frustrated, depressed, or resigned to just hang in there until some major wake-up call — an illness, accident, a threatened marriage, or life catastrophe — amplifies the internal screams: Help! Let me out of here; there must be a better, wiser, kinder way!

Many factors motivate us to strike a better balance between the personal and professional dimensions of our lives. For nearly half of the people we've asked, a wish to give more quality attention to their children is a key motivating factor. One man described how he had made a major shift in his work habits 17 years ago when his second grader came home from school with a picture he drew of the family. "There were four of us in the family," he said, "but there were only three figures in the picture — mommy, daughter, and son, the artist. When my wife asked, 'Where's Daddy?' my son replied, 'He's at work!' In response to this wake-up call, this man got off the fast track he was on at the telecom he worked for and avoided taking jobs with extra hours and lots of travel. Though he says that the decision dashed his dreams of having a big house or driving a Tesla, he has no regrets about having rearranged his priorities to spend more time with his family.

> "The minute you begin to do what you really want to do, it's really a different kind of life."
>
> —Buckminster Fuller

Contrast this decision with the situation in Japan where the second leading cause of death after cancer is called *karoshi*: "death from overwork." Estimates are that 10,000 workers per year drop dead at their desks as a result of 60-hour workweeks in Japan. In Tokyo there is a hotline, set up by a group of lawyers to help victims file compensation claims with the government. The most common victims of *karoshi* are between 34 and 61 years old. They often die at their desks or commuting to work, after a blood vessel in their heart or brain explodes. In Japan, time for anything besides work is so extremely limited that many people in young families don't have the time to go visit their elderly family members. To meet this need, an ingenious business has emerged called "Rent-a-Family," that hires actors and sends them out to visit lonely parents. The company is so popular that it has a waiting list of nearly one thousand people—elders are so lonely that they are profoundly grateful for the opportunity for seemingly meaningful interaction with other people, even if they are only actors paid to "really care for them."

In Japan, there's a popular TV commercial with a jingle that says, "Can you battle 24 hours a day?" We're told that everyone in Japan knows it, and that some companies sing it together every morning. While younger generations are more quick to say, "My time after five," older corporate warriors are more likely to stay out late drinking because to come home early is a sign that something must be wrong at work. To combat these trends, unions are actively promoting a shorter workweek with the slogan, "Let's have a Japan where families can eat dinner together." They are also seeing an increasing number of young Japanese who frown on overtime and prefer reduced time at work over increases in pay.

In the United States, the problem may not be as severe as in Japan, but it is still a huge issue. The amount of paid vacation time is rapidly dwindling, and many people are afraid to even take the vacation time they do have. In the United States, workers take only an average of 57 percent of their vacation days, while last year 64 percent of people actually cancelled their vacations. For those who do actually take their vacations, 25 percent say they check into work hourly while on vacation, and 59 percent say they check during traditional holidays like Christmas and Thanksgiving.

In these times of downsizing, we are afraid of being seen as replaceable or expendable, or our department has been so downsized that there is no one to cover for us. Many people admit that they are now doing not only their own job, but have taken on responsibilities from one or two other people who are no longer employed in their organization. For the increasing numbers of people who are self-employed, time off is often directly equated with money lost, challenging the self-employed to make tough and tangible boundaries to establish or maintain some semblance of balance in their lives.

The following data reflects the extent of stressful, unbalancing trends in our workplaces:

- 80 percent of people are dissatisfied with their jobs.
- The average person spends 90,000 hours at work over their lifetime.
- Couples in which one partner spends 10+ hours more than usual at work divorce at twice the average rate.
- There isn't much job security. On average, Americans hold seven to eight different jobs before age 30.
- 25 percent of employees say work is their main source of stress.
- More than 13 million working days are lost every year because of stress-related illnesses. (41 million absent days in 2008 were on account of these crises, which led to 3.9 billion euros in lost production costs in the E.U.)
- Women make only 77.5 cents for every dollar that men earn.
- 15 percent of director-level women have slept with their bosses — and 37 percent of them got promoted for it.
- Nearly half of America has gained weight at their current job; 28 percent have gained more than 10 pounds; 13 percent have gained more than 20 pounds.
- The rate of deaths from suicide now exceeds the number of deaths from violence and environmental disasters.

"We live in a world where ideas and innovation are paramount. But people can't be creative if they are exhausted. And when people work when they are tired, they make mistakes. If we have learned anything from the quality movement, it is that the cost of finding and fixing mistakes is greater than the cost of preventing them. So, give people time off."

—Jeffrey Pfeffer

Other indicators of the scope of the problem: stress-related workers' compensation claims in the United States continue to skyrocket, and a vast majority of people experience some sort of stress-related illness. Ninety percent of private sector workers say their job is either "very" or "highly" stressful. As many as 80 percent report suffering from work stress — induced exhaustion, insomnia, depression, muscle pains, ulcers, and other stress-related disorders. Add to this the startling finding that most heart attacks occur between eight and nine o'clock on Monday mornings, and you have a graphic picture of just how our work is killing us!

WOMEN AND WORK

When it comes to life-work balance, it seems that women are particularly suffering. Indeed, it is heartbreaking to see so many working women drained and depleted by the stress of trying to maintain not only their own sanity and balance, but also to promote the well-being and success of their families, households, careers, coworkers, and oftentimes their bosses' sanity and success as well! The toll is often telling and quite costly in terms of compromised health, strained relationships, emotional exhaustion, and spiritual starvation. Once in a while one of them breaks free, like Beth, who recently quit her well-paying job as an information technology specialist to realize her lifelong dream of opening a bed-and-breakfast in Martha's Vineyard, or Janice, who joyfully made a career change in mid-life to study horticulture and begin a small landscaping business.

However, most of our female friends and coworkers continue the ongoing battle with fatigue and the life-work pressures that assail them daily. Some keep at their stressful jobs purely for financial reasons in hopes that they will be able to discover a way to balance it all one day. Others truly enjoy the challenges and opportunities of their work, and view the benefits as far outweighing the perils.

A survey by the Families and Work Institute shows that 55 percent of employed women bring in half or more of their household income, and that 53 percent say they don't want to cut back on any of their responsibilities at work or at home. Surprisingly, 48 percent of the women surveyed say they would choose to work even if they already had enough money to live as comfortably as they like, indicating that employment affects self-esteem, and that women who work full-time are more likely to feel valued at home. Forty-six percent of women cite work-family balance as something they worry about "a great deal." Though life-work balance and other family concerns are viewed as peripheral issues by many corporate managers and politicians, these are core issues to many women. More than a quarter of women report lack of time together with their family as their greatest family concern, even more than neighborhood crime and safety.

Polls show that the top concern is having enough time and energy to get everything done that needs to be done. Women juggle their time among household, family, career, and community volunteerism. Fifty-six percent of the women polled by Lake Research said that they worry about balancing and juggling work and family very often or often. Their next major concern was retirement security, followed by "making ends

"Women need to define success differently than men. If you don't learn to unplug and recharge, you're not going to be as good a leader. Look at the price we're paying. Look at the increase in heart disease and diabetes for career women. If success continues to be defined as driving yourself into the ground and burning out, it will be disastrous for our families, our companies, and our world. We have so many people making terrible decisions, despite the fact that they have high IQs and great degrees. If success doesn't include your own health and happiness, then what is it?"

—Arianna Huffington

meet." Moving ahead was much less on the minds of women than men. Lake's results suggest that most women are feeling challenged to make time for all the things they have to do now, without looking ahead to a better job.

Although 43 percent of those polled said that women are better off than they used to be, with job options and choices about work outside the home, half of those polled said that women don't necessarily have more choices, because economic necessity dictates women's work. As the labor market has restructured and many men have lost jobs because of downsizing and layoffs, women's earnings have become more important. More and more women are the sole support of their families, and many are the primary wage earner.

The only women we've seen who really seem to thrive and keep their spirits alive, despite the barrage of demands at work and at home, are the ones who have supportive relationships, are doing something they really love to do (at work or outside of work), and stay committed and connected to nurturing their physical and spiritual needs in healthy ways. Although most would appreciate a lighter and more balanced load, they enjoy their work and want to continue to grow in and through it.

In a study examining career women who successfully balanced career and relationship demands, Dr. Luann Linquist found that:

- no woman was willing to give up her career entirely;
- self-esteem appeared to increase with career success;
- they knew how to delegate;
- they found relief from stress by getting involved in their work;
- if they were in an intimate relationship, they tended to have supportive significant others; and
- they tended to see their career success as enhancing themselves and their significant-other relationships.

Sustained success in balancing career and relationships is a creative and dynamic process. It requires at least three primary elements: 1) a high degree of personal honesty and self-awareness; 2) skill and willingness to communicate what is true for you to others; and 3) a willingness to creatively collaborate, explore possibilities, and reach mutually satisfactory compromises with others.

If you are a working woman, pause here to look back over the ideas in this section and underline the key points and questions that speak most directly to your situation. Ask yourself what shifts you need to

"Because work addiction keeps us busy, we stay estranged from our essential selves. An aspect of that estrangement is that we cease asking ourselves if we are doing our right work. Are we actually doing our true work, performing tasks or pursuing vocations that are good for us, for our families, for the universe?"

—Diane Fassel

"Work is an essential part of being alive. Your work is your identity. It tells you who you are. It's gotten so abstract. People don't work for the sake of working. They're working for a car, a new house, or a vacation. It's not the work itself that's important to them. There's such joy in doing work well."

—Kay Stipkin

make to find a greater balance among work, family, and the rest of your life. What unspoken needs and requests for action do you have that you can communicate to others, to increase their understanding of your search and struggles to find balance in your life?

If you live or work closely with a working woman, take these ideas to heart and consider talking with your partner to see how you can help her to be more successful at finding balance in her life work.

THE TOLL ON OUR CHILDREN

Fortune magazine ran a provocative cover story entitled, "Is Your Family Wrecking Your Career? (and vice versa)." The article paints a disturbing picture of the conflict between corporate values and family values, and highlights the devastating impact on many of the children of dual-career parents. It includes statistics from a report by the Carnegie Council on Adolescent Development, which found that kids spend significantly less time in the company of adults than they did a few decades ago. About one-third of all adolescents have contemplated suicide; half are at moderate or high risk of abusing drugs, failing in school, getting pregnant, or otherwise seriously damaging their lives. The report stated, "In survey after survey, young adolescents from all ethnic and economic backgrounds lament their lack of parental attention and guidance." Elementary school teachers are debating whether they should quit assigning homework because working parents are too tired or busy to handle it. Add to this the "digital family divide" that leaves many families in the same room, same car, or dinner table, with each person totally absorbed in their own digital universe with no meaningful dialogue and connection with each other in physical space.

Because travel has become a critical component of many jobs in global companies, one parent—or both—may often be gone from home on short notice, and the family dinner has regularly disappeared in many homes as parents work late hours. In addition, many households have unstable childcare situations, with a vast array of babysitters and parents needing special apps to keep it all straight. One elementary school teacher said her students seem needier than those in years past; they are more easily distracted and more often fatigued. "Just as adults get scattered, children get scattered," she commented.

The criticality of the current situation demands our collective creative thinking, action, and investigation. What are the effects on our children and future society if families continue to require two wage

"(Being a parent) is an immovable object in my life ... it's like a 140-character limit... it forces balance."

—Evan Williams, Twitter

"The work will wait while you show your child the rainbow, but the rainbow won't wait while you do the work."

—Patricia Clafford

earners to make ends meet? What role can government play to bring about a workplace transformation that would promote a saner society? What role can you play in modeling strategies for greater inner and outer balance? These are just some of the vital questions that we need to be asking as we contemplate life-work balance.

One tip we'd like to offer is that if you have children, are concerned about these issues, and would like to see your family live more in harmony and balance, seek out Daniel Siegel's insightful books, *Whole Brain Child*, and *Brainstorm: The Power and Purpose of the Teenage Brain*. These are essential primers for raising children with the attuned quality of relationship, neural integration, and mental coherence needed for growing and living in balance.

FAMILY LIFE AND SUCCESS

If you need still more incentive to create a healthier life-work balance for yourself, then consider an important study conducted by professors at the Wharton School of Williams College, who set out to determine whether people pay a price in workplace success if they give priority to family concerns. Taking a unique approach, it looks at data collected from the same people at two stages in their lives. It begins with responses offered by the participants when they were high school seniors from across the nation, at which time they responded to a series of "life interest" questions. These were then compared with the respondents' earnings fourteen years later.

What the researchers found was that men who had placed high importance on building a good marriage and having a strong family life earned more than those who didn't, after accounting for educational differences, tenure with current employer, and total job experience. Women in the study showed a similar trend, though less consistently. The researchers also found that placing an emphasis on success in work, or having money and steady work, really had no effect on earnings.

The researchers concluded that time invested in family life actually makes workers more, not less productive, and enhances overall health, well-being, and corporate performance. On the other hand, it was clear that having a poor family life creates more stressful demands on an employee's time and attention, causing enormous negative consequences in the workplace. Developing a good family life seems especially important early in careers, which is the time when many problematic relationship patterns are set up. The people who didn't build a strong

"I tried to teach my child with books,

He gave me only puzzled looks.

I tried to teach my child with words,

They passed him by, often unheard.

Despairingly, I turned aside, 'How shall I teach this child?' I cried.

'Come,' he said, 'Play with me!'"

—Anonymous

"Let us take care of the children, for they have a long way to go.

Let us take care of the elders, for they have come a long way.

Let us take care of those in between, for they are doing the work."

—Traditional African Prayer

foundation for their family life often paid the price for years, spending considerable time "putting Band-Aids on family problems."

The Wharton study suggested that employers who are authentically concerned about life-work balance, and the quality of work that people offer to their businesses, would be wise to give their employees as much support as possible to spend time with their families. Though this may require allowing for extra time out of the office, supporting people in finding life-work balance that works for each person's unique situation will pay significant dividends for employees, their families, their employer, and likely for those they serve.

But even if your employer doesn't share these values, the Wharton study should help you see that in the long run, you can have a productive, successful work life even if you make your family a top priority.

MIXED SIGNS OF PROGRESS

Despite all the setbacks, stresses, and cutbacks, many companies are beginning to re-evaluate the stressful demands that they put on their employees. In recent years we have seen a mixed valuing of life-work balance. For a while, interest in the topic was in vogue, with many companies valuing such policies for reasons of employee satisfaction and retention. As the economy has become increasingly unpredictable, some companies have backed off on their commitment to work-life balance, while others have given it much more attention. Note: work-life balance is a term often frowned on as indicating a priority toward work over life. One factor that is consistent is that when we do exercises on values with corporate teams and executives in vastly differing industries, the number one value we see emerging over and over again is — you guessed it — balance.

Alternative work styles and schedules that promote greater balance and satisfaction in employees' lives have been shown to pay off both business-wise and health-wise. There is abundant data that correlates supportive, satisfying conditions at work and good health, while low job satisfaction, a perceived lack of support, and a sense of "joyless striving" are recognized as major health-risk factors. Dr. Suzanne Couellette Krobasa, professor of psychology at the Graduate School of the City University of New York, found that people who felt they had the backing of their boss were half as likely to get ill as people who lacked that support. One enlightening study of 3,200 people at Boeing showed that workers who stated that they "hardly ever" enjoyed their job were two-and-a-half times more likely to report a back injury than

"Though organizational development is a huge and profitable business, studies show that more than 70% of organizational change efforts fall short of their intended goals. Why? Because most change efforts fail to take an integral approach to the complex whole system change. In order to develop agile, resilient, thriving organizations, we need to continually monitor and manage across both the inner and outer dimensions of our work, while investing attention to optimizing the personal, 'me,' and collective, 'we' dimensions that are critical to our well-being and success in every moment and interaction."

—Joel & Michelle Levey

subjects who "almost always" enjoyed their job. The study also showed that the most important factor in determining an employee's successful rehabilitation and the length of time it would take for him or her to return to the job was the employee's perception of the company's empathy for them.

In a business world where people are stressed, reactive, and not prone to deep reflection or clear thinking, it is not uncommon to hear statements like, "We're in business to make money, not to run a social center or a playground!" when such ideas are first presented. Though there is some validity in such a statement, hopefully the results of these and many other studies will temper this with the deeper recognition that creating a work environment where people feel valued and cared about, enjoy their work, and are excited about coming to work is not only tremendously practical and rewarding, but it is also likely to be profoundly profitable.

Study after study shows that companies with cultures that nurture trust and empower their employees by giving them proper leadership, support, and all the information that they need to make wise decisions, are actually far more likely to outperform competitors who function in a more top down, autocratic, "command and control" manner.

THE LIGHT AND SHADOWS OF LEADERS

In our work with leaders around the globe, one of the most useful quotes we have found is this one from Parker Palmer, which echoes and affirms many of the views and values we've shared thus far. Dr. Palmer, author of *Healing the Heart of Democracy: The Courage to Create a Politics Worthy of the Human Spirit*, is regarded as one of the thirty "most influential senior leaders" in higher education and one of the ten key "agenda-setters" of the past decade.

> "A leader is a person who has an unusual degree of power to project on other people his or her shadow or his or her light. A leader is a person who has an unusual degree of power to create the conditions under which other people must live and move and have their being — conditions that can either be as illuminating as heaven or as shadowy as hell. A leader is a person who must take special responsibility for what's going on inside him or her self, inside his or her consciousness, lest the act of leadership create more harm than good.

"As winning companies find they must engage workers' hearts as well as their minds, the increasingly emotional aspect of business is destroying the old corporate machismo that once allowed us to keep our feelings hidden and our inner lives mysterious, even to ourselves.... To the degree that individuals are successful at plumbing their depths, those people should be better off, and the companies that employ them may gain competitive advantage. In fast-shifting markets, the unexamined life becomes a liability."

—The Learner Within, *Fortune Magazine*

"Our prevailing system of management has destroyed our people. People are born with intrinsic motivation, self-esteem, dignity, curiosity to learn and joy in learning."

—W. Edwards Deming, Father of Total Quality Management

The problem is that people rise to leadership in our society by a tendency toward extroversion, which means a tendency to ignore what is going on inside themselves. Leaders rise to power in our society by operating very competently and effectively in the external world, sometimes at the cost of internal awareness.

I've looked at some training programs for leaders. I'm discouraged by how often they focus on the development of skills to manipulate the external world rather than the skills necessary to go inward and make the inner journey."

At this point in our human history we are witnessing an unprecedented shift in human values around the globe. Millions of people all over the world are fed-up, frustrated by the misguided actions and inactions of their leaders and the deteriorating state of the world and their lives. They are taking a strong stand demanding that their voices be heard, not just in how our nations are governed, but also in how our organizations are run, and how communities organize to become wiser, resilient, compassionate, and thriving. People are asking for equality, fairness, transparency, truth, and justice; they want to be responsible and accountable for the choices they make in their lives and the impacts their decisions and actions have on others. They also want to be able to admire and trust their leaders, have pride in their organizations, communities, nation, and society, and they want to feel supported by these institutions in living in harmony, health, and balance while meeting their basic needs and fulfilling their highest aspirations.

When we look with disbelief at the actions, and inactions, of leaders whose decisions shape our lives, our organizations, and our world, it is helpful to understand what is driving them. Research in social psychology tells us that leaders who rate high on what is called the Social Dominance Orientation (SDO) scales tend to seek out roles and positions of power within institutions that maintain and increase social inequality, and that they tend to be highly concentrated in the upper levels of many powerful organizations. Leaders with high SDO also tend not to live in balance, and suffer greatly from high levels of stress, anxiety, and depression. These leaders typically demonstrate extremely low levels of empathy and compassion toward others, and are actually fearful of showing compassion to others or receiving compassion from others, or even showing compassion toward themselves. Such high-SDO leaders tend to set policies and have leadership styles that inhibit sharing, avoid transparency, discourage humane, holistic, egalitarian

"The outward work can never be small if the inward one is great, and the outward work can never be great or good if the inward is small or of little worth."

—Meister Eckhart

values and ways of working that would be more likely to encourage the flourishing of balance within their organizations.

These leaders also rate high on the activation of the drive and self-protection systems in their brains, and psychologically they tend to be overachievers, who are hyper-conscious of their status and fearful of rejection. As they gravitate toward the top of powerful, hierarchical organizations, these leaders often play a stifling role in promoting policies that undermine standards for life-work balance, environmental protection, employee well-being, philanthropy, or the emotional health of their employees.

ENTROPIC ORGANIZATIONS

In addition, such leaders are likely to have positions of power in what Richard Barrett calls "entropic organizations." Barrett, former assistant to the vice president for Environmentally Sustainable Development at the World Bank, and founder of the World Bank Spiritual Unfoldment Society, defines "'Cultural Entropy" as "a measure of the level of anxiety/fear/unhappiness/frustration that people feel about being able to meet their basic needs and satisfy their growth needs (to get, have, or experience what they value) in the environment and context in which they live."

According to Barrett, "non-mindful organizations or societies" are characterized by "high cultural entropy": flourishing of hierarchy, bureaucracy, corruption, dominance and victimization, blame, uncertainty and apprehension regarding the future, wasted resources, materialism, high crime/violence, unemployment, conflict/aggression, military dominance, surveillance, and disrespect for privacy.

In contrast, "mindful organizations or societies" are characterized by "low cultural entropy" and are characterized by balance and integrative states of: equity and mutual respect; continuous learning and

"The current global threats to human survival and well being are actually symptoms of our individual and shared states of mind. The state of the world reflects the state of our mind; our collective crises mirror our collective consciousness. The same consciousness which both created and was created by our millions of years of evolution now stands threatened by its own remarkable, though incomplete success."

—Roger Walsh, M.D.

〜

"Ed Deming used to say that 97% of what matters in an organization can't be measured. Only maybe 3% can be measured. But when you go into most organizations and look at what people are doing, they're spending all their time focusing on what they can measure and none of their time on what really matters—what they can't measure. Why would we do this? We're spending all of our time measuring what doesn't matter. In fact, it's part of avoiding a lot of the really difficult and important issues, like virtue."

—Peter Senge

improvement; environmental protection; strong, sensible, and equitable moral codes; political rights; education; information availability; shared values and vision; contentment and happiness; gender equity; nature conservancy; and spirituality (rather than religion).

The degree of cultural entropy present within an organization or a society is a reflection of personal entropy and lack of balance modeled by current leaders in our organizations and by the entropic legacy of past leaders, which has been institutionalized within the organizations' policies, processes, systems, and structure.

A PROFOUND SHIFT

It is becoming increasingly clear that living in balance is a global affair that makes no real sense in isolation, and applies at every level of our human society. In today's increasingly complex and interconnected world, decisions we make and actions we take ripple out and create consequences around the globe in ways we can seldom anticipate or imagine. The high stakes of this present age ask us all to contemplate more deeply what living in balance means for us individually and collectively in these complex times.

Some years ago, during our work at the World Bank, we had the good fortune to meet with Mieko Nishimizu, one of the most gifted executives at the Bank. As one who has lived a privileged life while working in some of the most impoverished regions of Asia, she has a rare insight to offer. At a conference some years ago Mieko poignantly said, "The future appears alien to us. It differs from the past, most notably in that the earth itself is a relevant unit with which to frame and measure that future. Discriminating issues that shape the future are all fundamentally global. We belong to one inescapable network of mutuality — mutuality of ecosystems; mutuality of freer movement of information, ideas, people, and goods and services; and mutuality of peace and security. We are tied, indeed, in a single fabric of destiny on planet Earth. Policies and actions that attempt to tear a nation from this cloth will inevitably fail."

In these complex times, one of the most evident design flaws that impairs the capacity of modern human beings to live in balance is being illuminated. This is that while our neuroanatomy is finely tuned to register sudden, dramatic changes in our environment, we are lacking in capacity to register and respond wisely to threats and changes that emerge slowly in our lives and world. Loud noises, flashes of light, and sudden movements in the world around us call for our immediate

"The every-man-for-himself model cuts against what all of our great religions have taught us; it also goes against what our great scientists are teaching us, and it denies what we know in our hearts. It's time for compassion to come front and center in our public discourse. We need to get away from worshipping at the altar of profit and markets as if they were flawless deities. If we care about each other, invest in each other, and put the well-being of human beings first, we will soften the rough edges of the market system and we all will profit more."

—Congressman Tim Ryan

attention. Yet, as we focus on our immediate circumstances, needs, and problems, we fall prey to the illusion that what is most noticeable is the most real or most important. After millennia of being highly conditioned to identify with our personal, immediate needs, those of our family, tribe, or social unit, we are lacking in the neurological wiring or the cognitive, emotional, and intuitive skills necessary to adequately conceive of and prepare for the multiple, looming, slowly approaching crises that are present in these times.

Sanjay Khanna, global macro trends expert at Massey College in the University of Toronto, observes that many senior global leaders find it tremendously challenging to align short-term business and innovation realities with the dire societal implications of accelerating global climate change. "These leaders may shut down because accelerating change is by its very nature overwhelming," he says. "That's exactly why professional education should teach how to perceive clearly and function optimally amidst massive change."

Here is a powerful example of this that was described to us by a colleague. He had brought a group of senior leaders from British Petroleum (BP) for a flight over the Alberta Tar Sands region where they were supporting oil extraction. During the flyover, a number of these leaders became physically ill upon witnessing first-hand the devastating impact that their work and policies—done back at corporate headquarters—were having on the natural environment. They were simply unable to fathom or cope with the damage they had done and the impact they were having on destroying the earth.

In a brilliant essay titled *Creating Desired Futures in a Global Economy*, Peter Senge, director of the Center for Organizational Learning at the MIT Sloan School of Management, noted that humanity is stuck in a "Catch-22," saying, "Systemic imbalances fail to compel our attention because we simply do not see them in the same way we see more immediate and local problems. And, we fail to see the systemic issues because we define urgency by what is immediate. We are victims of a self-reinforcing crisis of perception—a crisis of our own making. If it persists, we doom ourselves to continued passivity. Only catastrophe will compel action, which, given the growing social divide that distributes problems like global warming unevenly between rich and poor, is likely to manifest as social and political disruption—not unlike what we are already seeing around the world."

Senge goes on to reflect that, "My view is that nothing short of a profound shift in the Western, materialistic worldview is likely to dislodge this crisis of perception. How can diverse people from around

"The first revolution was women getting the vote, the second was getting an equal place at every level of society...The third revolution is changing the world that men have designed. It's not sustainable. Sustainability is not just about the environment, it's personal sustainability."

—Arianna Huffington

the world come to a fuller sense of the whole—that is, the social, economic, and ecological systems we share? Perhaps that will begin when, together, we start to appreciate the exquisite web of interconnectedness that enables life in the universe, wherever we stand, and the role of our own consciousness in that web."

INSPIRING LEADERS

Creating the conditions for life-work balance to flourish within an organization is closely linked with the depth of wisdom, caring, and commitment of an organization's leaders. With the theme of living in balance in mind, the leaders who stand out to us from our work around the globe are the ones who, through their own personal epiphanies and tragedies, bounced back to dedicate their lives to creating organizations, communities, and circumstances in which others might thrive:

David, a plant manager for a leading technology company, nearly died of a stress-induced heart attack in his mid 30s. With two small children and a lot to live for, David returned to his work to become one of the most innovative, successful, and compassionate plant managers in the world.

After nearly dying from cancer, Suzanne courageously came back to work at her IT department in a major insurance company, only to realize that if she didn't radically change the work culture there that many others would likely get sick or die from their driven stressful norms at work. She dedicated herself to working with us to create a program called, "Taking Care of Ourselves, Taking Care of Each Other," which completely transformed her organization into a resilient, mindful, high-tech, high-touch department that inspired many other departments to follow her lead. Talking with members of her team years later, we've often heard comments that what they learned during their time on that team gave them the wisdom and skills to stay resilient through many other changes that followed in their lives and work.

Jon Dunnington's vision of developing the capacity of R&D managers from Weyerhaeuser's different divisions to tap into the field of their collective wisdom and intuitive intelligence to source breakthrough innovations, drew a group of us together for two years of deep, inner, transformational work that not only brought more balance to people's lives, but opened a portal to the treasury of the most refined human resource—collective wisdom—that few organizations ever succeed in tapping. The lessons learned there have inspired our work in dozens of other organizations.

"The arising conversation is not about how much money we make or how senior our job title, but is instead on what it means to live wisely and purposefully. It is about what will truly matter on our deathbeds when all is said and done.... It is how we live these qualities that is gathering enormous interest in our culture... ways to experience deeper meaning and connection. It is a rising community that is not likely to go away, and who are fueled not by standing against technology or modern culture, but for a way of living that is aligned with what they most value."

—Soren Gordhamer, Founder, Wisdom 2.0

At Hewlett-Packard one of the most inspiring GMs we've ever met was shaped by major life challenges and losses that opened his heart and mind to lead with tremendous compassion, wisdom, and strength. He came into his position after a major upheaval in the organization and we worked together to transform the largest, most profitable division of H-P into one of perhaps the first explicitly mindful organizations in the world, where thousands of people at every level of the organization worked together with the guiding value of mindfulness in their day to day work.

An Intuit software vice president was motivated by his own personal struggles and a strong altruistic wish to use his power to create a legacy of personal and professional development for his people that they would look back on and say, "That was the most meaningful and enriching time in my career." We supported him and his team to transform their organization's mission and business with outcomes in terms of increased customer satisfaction, quarterly returns, and employee delight that were off the charts.

Not only did these leaders and organizations succeed in creating organizations that were supportive of their people living and working in balance — but many also funded programs related to wellness, resilience, and life-work balance for the families of their employees and for community organizations such as public schools and medical centers. Having the privilege to work closely with these leaders and their teams has given us great confidence that it truly is possible for a toxic, dysfunctional, and highly stressful workplace to become balanced, life-affirming, successful, and radically transformed.

NEW METRICS FOR BALANCE AND SUCCESS

In recent years, we've been inspired by the highly visible and far-reaching personal, organizational, and global transformation story of Arianna Huffington, founder of *The Huffington Post* and one of the most influential media moguls on the planet.

Leading a bold, new, crusade for living in balance as a key success strategy for business on a global scale, Huffington recognizes the heartbreaking cost to society from imbalances of merely focusing on money and power as measures of success. In her widely viewed commencement address to Smith College's graduating class of 2013, she said, "I want to ask you, instead [of climbing the ladder of success], to redefine success."

Arianna's redefinition of success says that in addition to our society's notion of success as money and power, a "third metric" is vital

"The most important trait of a good leader is knowing who you are. In our industry very often we don't have time to think. You have to do all your homework, but then you have to go with your intuition without letting your mind get in the way.

We all have the fantasy that we control what happens to us in our lives—and this is especially true of CEOs. But in fact none of us have that kind of control. Meditation helps me with that, giving more confidence that I can let go of the feeling that I have to control everything and things will still turn out all right."

—Ed McCracken, CEO, Silicon Graphics

for us to begin to attend to. For her, this metric is a fusion of four vital factors: well-being; wisdom; wonder; and giving back. She explains that the point is really about finding a wise, healthy, and meaningful balance in our lives, and that in order for our lives and our society to truly be successful, these factors must balance our drive for more money and power.

Six months later at the World Economic Forum on "The Reshaping of the World: Consequences for Society, Politics and Business" in Davos, Switzerland, Huffington moderated a plenary session titled "Health Is Wealth," expanding on her Third Metric principles and making it clear that there is no tradeoff between our well-being and the well-being of our companies and our countries.

Huffington's mission has been described as shifting attitudes from macho, stressful, driven norms toward greater wisdom, wellness, and balance. She sees women leading the charge because they are more sensitized to have clarity on the really vital issues that are essential for personal, organizational, and societal success and thriving. "The first revolution was women getting the vote, the second was getting an equal place at every level of society," she said, noting that this revolution is still underway. The third revolution is changing the world that men have designed. It's not sustainable. Sustainability is not just about the environment, it's personal sustainability.... Ironically, when we succeed at making these changes, not only are we going to have a lot of grateful men because they are paying too heavy a price, but we're going to have a lot more women at the top. Many women currently leave the workplace because they don't want to pay the price."

Huffington's Third Metric epiphany came to her in 2007 as a proverbial slap in the face. As she describes, "I learned this the hard way. Five years ago, I fainted from exhaustion. It was still the early days of building *The Huffington Post.* I'd just returned home from a college tour with my daughter, where I'd agreed not to be on my BlackBerry while we were looking around. We stayed in hotels where she would go to sleep and I'd start working. When I got back to my office, I fainted, hit my head on my desk, broke my cheekbone, and had to get five stitches around my right eye. It got me thinking about what kind of life I was leading. I was getting four to five hours of sleep a night. I had to slow down and reevaluate the choices I was making."

'When I look back, it really was an incredible gift because who knows what would have happened to me if I had not course-corrected and learnt to prioritize sleep? It also sensitized me to what was

"The price of anything is the amount of life you pay for it."

—Henry David Thoreau

"When you're faced with a decision under pressure: pause, reflect on core beliefs."

—Padmasree Warrior, Cisco

happening all around me in the workplace — heart attacks, high blood pressure, diabetes.'

After reprioritizing her own life to include more sleep and exercise, meditation and yoga, she began the work to enroll her staff in shifting the culture, priorities, and norms within her 850-employee organization at *The Huffington Post*. Weekly meditation and yoga classes were introduced and instructions communicated that any work-related emails sent out during "off hours" were not expected to be replied to. "We have a phrase at *The Huffington Post*: 'Unplug and recharge.' In just the same way we must plug in our devices to recharge them, we need to unplug ourselves in order to recharge." Beds and sleep pods were installed in the New York offices of *The Huffington Post*. 'At first, people were nervous to use them, but now they are booked solidly,' she says.

Huffington's Third Metric meme has continued to expand as *Huff Post* devoted a major editorial initiative to this emerging global trend, and has hosted an expanding series of global conferences tapping into a widespread desire among readers to redefine success and live the lives we want, not just the lives most people have settled for, and to move beyond exhaustion, sleep deprivation, and burnout.

In June of 2013, at her apartment in New York, Arianna hosted the first Third Metric Conference which was so well received that it was followed shortly thereafter by similar events in Munich, London, and Hawaii. Generating an expanding global dialogue with many leaders in the arts, high tech, health care reform, government, and contemplative science communities, she continues to call for a deeper consideration of the need for leaders around the globe to wake up to the realities of these times and expand the definitions of reward and success to include our well-being, wisdom, capacity to wonder and to give.

This shift is accelerating as thousands of business leaders around the globe hit the wall, crash and burn, and wake up to embrace and affirm the value of their personal and organizational mindfulness and living in balance initiatives. Fueling the trend toward mindful living, this growing movement is predicted to shape the decades to come. With more than 35 percent of large American corporations now offering some kind of stress-reduction program for employees, and 25 percent offering mindfulness-related training, it's clear that we no longer need to speculate on the evidence-based benefits of living a more balanced and sustainable life and creating workplaces in which people can thrive. As Huffington says, "Science has finally caught up to ancient wisdom, and the results are overwhelming and unambiguous. And

"The individual is forcing the change. People are shopping around, not only for the right job but for the right atmosphere. They now regard the old rules of business as dishonest, boring, and outdated. This new generation in the workplace is saying, 'I want a society and a job that values me more than the gross national product. I want work that engages the heart as well as the mind and the body, that fosters friendship and that nourishes the earth. I want to work for a company that contributes to the community."

—Anita Roddick, Founder of the Body Shop

since the problem is universal and transcends geographic boundaries, so is the solution."

In search of balance on a global scale, many economists, political leaders, and communities are redefining the measures of success. Scientists are telling us that in order to slow down disastrous climate change effects, wealthy countries need to reduce their CO_2 emissions by 8 to 10 percent per year. While the impacts on quarterly profits and the economy will be severe, the consequence of inaction, or lack of political will, are likely to be dire for generations to come.

One of the most widely accepted sensible strategies to bring greater balance to the environment, the economy, and to people's lives is to reduce the "normal" working week to 21 hours. Economists tell us that the higher the average hours of work in a nation are, the greater is the poverty, while in countries with shorter work hours, there is less poverty. Not only are there benefits for families and societies, but shorter hours of work are also strongly related to reducing global greenhouse gases and reducing eco footprints. Households who have more time do things in more ecological ways, as seen in the contrast between the highly wasteful practices in the United States as compared to France and Germany, where work time and resource consumption are much lower. Changing the way we use our time patterns also gives us more time for family, community, and spiritual practice.

In many global forums the ecologically devastating practices associated with defining national success by Gross National Product (GNP) are being challenged and a shift toward more eco-friendly, sustainable growth models like the GPI (General Progress Indicator) are being seriously considered. This movement is inspired by Bhutan's Gross National Happiness system, which measures the total average per capita levels of economic, environmental, physical, mental, workplace, social, and political wellness. Following Bhutan's example, similar initiatives have been launched in more than eighty countries around the globe seeking to reassess their standards for success.

In a famous speech by Senator Robert Kennedy, he reminded us, "Too much and for too long, we seemed to have surrendered personal excellence and community values in the mere accumulation of material things....Gross national product counts air pollution and cigarette advertising, and ambulances to clear our highways of carnage. It counts special locks for our doors and the jails for the people who break them. It counts the destruction of the redwood and the loss of our natural wonder in chaotic sprawl. It counts napalm and counts nuclear warheads and armored cars for the police to fight the riots in our cities …

and the television programs which glorify violence in order to sell toys to our children. Yet the gross national product does not allow for the health of our children, the quality of their education or the joy of their play. It does not include the beauty of our poetry or the strength of our marriages, the intelligence of our public debate or the integrity of our public officials. It measures neither our wit nor our courage, neither our wisdom nor our learning, neither our compassion nor our devotion to our country. It measures everything in short, except that which makes life worthwhile."

A PROTOTYPE FOR A MINDFUL WORKPLACE

One of our favorite ways of having leaders and work teams experience how a workplace can effectively be transformed to be more conducive to balance and mindfulness is through what we call an "urban workplace mindfulness retreat." These intensive, integrative urban retreats offer an accessible format for people to learn, practice, and develop a robust suite of life skills and confidence, for streaming mindful awareness in a more balanced way continuously during their busy days at work — and beyond.

A very successful example of this was a program we offered at corporate headquarters in the heart of an upscale shopping district in Beverly Hills where we guided an urban mindfulness retreat for fifty-five of the two hundred people on site. We needed to limit the number of participants for this session to fifty-five as that was the capacity of the largest meeting room they had available. Delivering benefit for participants, the hosting business, and all the stakeholders of people's lives, the goals of this dynamic, shared learning experience were to "experiment with living and working on-purpose, with greater awareness and self-mastery, and explore the possibilities for increasing our capacity to live with greater mindful clear presence, dynamic balance, change resilience, wisdom, and creative compassion amidst the ever-changing circumstances of our lives, our work, and our world."

This program ran for five days, with the first half-day offering an introduction to basic skills, strategies, principles, and practices for integrating mindful presence into every activity and interaction of daily life and work. Following this initial introductory session, we sent people back to their desks with clear guidelines for how to engage in every meeting, conversation, and activity in a mindful manner.

Then, at the end of each day, we gathered again as a whole group for an hour of mindfulness practice, mindful dialogue and reflection regarding the insights, applications, implications, and challenges of

"As long as we operate within this old paradigm, we are separated from our heart and values and feel powerless. We cannot suspend our values during the workday and think we will have them back when we get home. We're all interconnected. There is a spiritual dimension to business just as to individuals."

—Ben (Cohen) and Jerry (Greenfield)

"There is an important link between deep change at the personal level and deep change at the organizational level. To make deep personal change is to develop a paradigm, a new self, one that is more effectively aligned with today's realities. This can occur only if we are willing to journey into unknown territory and confront the wicked problems we encounter."

—Robert Quinn

their experimentation, and harvested the highlights of their day of mindfulness at work. In anticipation of the commute home and the evening to come, we also offered guidelines and encouragement for deepening in the continuity of mindfulness as they made their commute, went shopping, and spent the evening with family, friends, or by themselves. As additional steps along a journey of mindfully balanced life-work that was fully integrated and whole, participants received guidelines for how to begin each day in a mindful, intentional way, and for making the journey back to work the next morning in the spirit of continuous mindfulness practice.

Each morning that week, we gathered at corporate headquarters for an hour or two of mindfulness practice and reflection on insights from the evening and morning of practice. Then, with clarified intention, each person embarked into the day's work ahead, holding the intention, attention, and attitudes most optimal to engaging in their work and progress with their goals for the day in a mindful and extra-ordinary manner. We also offered an optional session each day to share a silent, mindful lunch together and an opportunity for interactive Q&A. Then, at the end of the day, we'd gather again for some time to return to the sweet territory of mindfulness as a group practice, feel the reverberations of the day, deeply reflect together on the gifts, learnings, and challenges of the day, and set clear intentions for carrying the momentum of the practice on into the evening's commute and activities.

As the week progressed and the practice deepened, people were amazed at the quality of presence, insight, ease, and heightened productivity they were able to bring to their work. Perhaps our greatest challenge was how to deal compassionately with the disappointment of the other 145 people on site who weren't able to participate directly in the program due to a lack of space! Within even a few hours, people were able to see the direct, immediate benefits of individually and collectively showing up at work in an intentionally mindful way. Each meeting on site that week began with a few moments of quiet focusing, centering, and setting clear intentions for the goals and purpose of the meeting, and a few moments of check-in with each person present to get a "pulse check" on the collective consciousness available in the room. Awareness and connectivity grew stronger with each day, the quality of communications improved, meetings were more productive, interactive, inclusive, fun, and people were inspired by how much they could enjoy being at work in this novel, natural, curious mode of creative experimentation and discovery. A large number commented on insights regarding meaningful and productive encounters they had had with colleagues or clients, reflecting on the quality of connection, the mindful flow of communications, and greater ease in speaking to and resolving challenging issues.

Sharing insights, highlights, and best practices from each workday, evening, morning, and commute, people's stories and personal examples began to really inspire each other and they began to share best practices. One mid-level manager spoke about how instead of waking up, checking email, and turning on his TV first thing in the morning as he usually did, he instead made a cup of coffee and went out on to his patio to just be fully present, quiet, and mindful, to watch the sun rise, listen to the birds sing, and sense the neighborhood awaken. He said he felt such a deep sense of peace and connection, serenity and wholeness, in such a simple, yet profound way. In the days to come other people commented on how, inspired by his sharing, they too, in their own way, had spent some time in their garden, on their balcony, or in the park on the way to work, connecting with themselves … their natural world … sourcing guidance and inspiration for a new day of life and work.

Many really enjoyed the challenge that we gave to notice the first moment of the day that they were "awake that they were awake" and then in that moment to wiggle their toes, or touch their heart, pause for a few moment of gratitude for all the gifts, opportunities, or blessings of their lives, and then to pause to listen deeply for their own inner guidance for what was most important for them to remember and stay true to throughout the day.

Then at work, at random moments, someone would ring a "wake-up chime," or "bell of mindfulness," to invite everyone within earshot to "wake-up," remember whatever they had set their intention to stay true to during the day, take a few mindful breaths, in … and out … and then to stream their mindful, clear presence on into whatever conversation or activity was next for them. When the bell chimed, if people were on the phone, or talking with someone who wasn't part of the retreat group, they'd simply continue on with a renewed mindfulness. We also encouraged everyone to download apps for their devices to chime at random times as a "ping" or wake-up bell to reboot and refresh the screen of their mindful presence.

For some in the urban retreat group, the daily commute was transformed into a time of renewal, deep reflection, and meditation. They discovered that they could rest in the mindful flow of the breath, the sensations of the steering wheel, or the movement of cars and scenery as they cruised the L.A. freeways on the way to work. Others would reach out from their heart and wish people driving beside them a good day,

"Finding the right work is like discovering your own soul in the world."

—Thomas Moore

"And in all of my experience,

I've never seen lasting solutions to problems,

lasting happiness and success,

that came from

the outside in."

—Stephen Covey

"Mindfulness can help us slow down enough, and pay attention enough, to see clearly the basic human truth Darwin stated. We're not going to get this from the business talk shows: they will tell us that if we buy the right stock, we'll flourish. We won't get it from the news channels: they'll tell us that if we have a certain political view, we'll vote the right people into office, and then we will flourish as never before. We won't get it from the commercials telling us that the latest product will bring us deep satisfaction. We'll get it by slowing down and seeing how powerful compassion can be."

—Congressman Tim Ryan

or that they might safely arrive at their destination and find happiness and fulfillment there.

Many of the people in the office who were not able to attend this session asked how soon we could schedule another session, and reported that just through their interactions with their colleagues who were being more disciplined about doing their work in a mindful way, and from their readings of some of the program materials that we posted and made available to everyone on site, that they were getting great value and learning a lot about how to be more balanced and mindful, and less stressed and anxious in their workday interactions.

As this week of workplace mindfulness practice progressed, people discovered a natural sense of ease and continuity of mindful presence. They were inspired by how effortless it could be for them to simply flow from one conversation, meeting, phone call, or time of focused work, with a continuity of mindful awareness like a surfer riding an endless set of waves that washed through their lives. Our colleagues also noted that their connections with other people were more at ease, interactions had less strain, tension, or compression, leaving each person with a greater sense of worth, value, recognition, confidence, and sense of self-mastery. This was supported by the realization that each moment could be welcomed for what it was, with Recognition, Acceptance, Investigation, and Non-Identification (RAIN), clearly seen, deeply felt, skillfully and efficiently responded to, leaving minds clear and open, bodies at ease, and hearts happy and peaceful. By the end of this week's immersion in mindfulness at work in the heart of the city, people were amazed by how quickly the time had passed, how much excellent, productive work was accomplished, how deep and nourishing their interactions with each other had been, and how generally balanced, energized, and peaceful

~~~

"Compassion is observed in the quality of service and attention that the organization is giving to all of its stakeholders: Clients, employees, stockholders, suppliers, the larger community, and the environment. Another expression of this is 'ethical business' which makes good business sense ... but learning via compassion means more than that. Whereas routine interaction in the workplace drives us to see each other only in our work-related roles, looking at each other with compassion lets us see the whole being, the mystery behind the familiar faces. An organization advancing on this path can establish an atmosphere of trust, solidarity and mutual learning that results in a workplace with high levels of commitment."

—George Por

they felt in flowing back and forth between their life at work and beyond. This integrative training really demonstrated how to approach work in a "chaordic" way that flowed with the integrative balance of Flexibility, Adaptability, Coherence, Energy, and Stability (FACES) as a natural and fulfilling way of life-work.

The metrics and reviews from this program were heartening with 88 percent of the attendees agreeing that, "I have learned skills that help me to live more in balance." (The other 12 percent were neutral.) Nearly everyone agreed that they had made positive, health enhancing lifestyle choices, gained greater clarity regarding their personal values and priorities, increased their skills for recognizing and mastering stress, were more effective in their communication with others, were better listeners, and more empathic in working with others.

HUBS

One inspiring innovation in the life-work balance movement is the emergence of a worldwide network of urban Hubs offering a common space, suites of services and technology, and a creative, dynamic, diverse community of professionals. The Hubs provide a sphere of social interaction, professional sharing, and networking in addition to their tech services — an actual non-virtual professional social network allowing people to have both a sense of community and autonomy in where and how they get their work done. The Hubs create an enriching environment 24/7 that gives people more options for where and how they get their work done, as well as a range of options that promote greater autonomy, community, freedom, choice, and support, while also providing a vibrant learning environment with many personal and professional development opportunities.

"The brain is a wonderful organ. It starts the moment you get up and doesn't stop until you get to the office."

—Robert Frost

WORKCATIONS

The rapidly expanding global network of Impact Hubs offers a brilliant example of a multi-focused innovation lab, business incubator, and social enterprise community center where new ways of living, working, connecting, and innovating are emerging. Their novel approach has inspired us to experiment with prototyping another creative form of life-work balance: "workcations." Combining both "work" and "vacation," this inviting model encourages a balanced experience of productive work time as well as relaxation, adventure, nature, and community.

The workcations that we've hosted can be engaged in a number of formats, and offer an opportunity for diverse groups of people to come together in a beautiful, natural setting to bring their projects, be in the company of an inspiring group of professionals, and have the opportunity to learn and practice new approaches to working more mindfully, creatively, and resiliently. Our workcation setting creates a "green Hub" with technology and networking services in a nurturing and serene natural environment, with close proximity to beautiful beaches, stunning hikes, cozy tea and coffee shops, galleries, restaurants, and villages offering the novelty, beauty, solitude and community conducive to deep creative reflection, rest, renewal, focus, and inspiration necessary to recover from the trauma and stress of "business as usual" burnout.

Workcations provide the supportive conditions for making progress on a creative project, such as designing a new product or app, putting together a special presentation, workshop, or class, composing music for a new CD, working on a book, or editing a new film, to name just a few examples of projects that have emerged from our workcation model. The products of these workcations have won awards at Indy film festivals around the globe, generated inspiring new courses for universities, brought forth some jammin' new CDs, and served to clarify the vision, sense of direction, values and priorities needed to give new meaning and direction to people's life-work and creative expression.

Group workcations can also provide an opportunity to bring together a working team seeking to advance the action on their team projects, while living and working in balance in a more relaxed and mutually supportive setting. This kind of format and setting provides a novel approach for a geographically dispersed team to come together in a neutral yet nurturing environment, or for a group of people who work together in an office every day to bust out into an extraordinary setting with new degrees of freedom for how the team works together. This kind of intensive living and working in balance experience also sets the tone of a mindful environment with times of individual and group "centering" or mindfulness practice, yoga, periods of silent focused individual work time, and plenty of time for mindful dialogue and deep reflection on the shared work at hand, as well as preparing and sharing delicious and healthful meals together. In such a setting, slowing down to the speed of life, the progress of work can accelerate to breakthrough levels, and sometimes months of work can be accomplished in a week. Plenty of opportunities are made available for hikes in Nature, outings to the beach, dancing or playing music together—all in a peaceful and relaxing setting supportive of experimentation and prototyping new models for how they can upgrade the quality of their working relationships and develop more creative synergy.

Through creating and hosting these short term, relaxing yet intensive, living and working in balance workcations hubs and learning laboratories, we've seen people discover or remember how to increase their skills in personal energy management, strengthen their mindfulness, and learn how to connect more deeply and meaningfully with themselves, others, and the natural world, to source the inspiration, guidance, renewal, strength, and deep human resources needed to be creative, innovative, productive, and to thrive at work and beyond. We see these workcations as an experiment in progress and a creative incubator prototype that can be easily scaled and adapted to a myriad of nurturing, natural, and creative settings around the globe, and we look forward to seeing this meme expand and engage many people to do good work in a deeply life-affirming and balanced way.

TECHNOLOGY SABBATHS

Living in balance with digital devices is a transformational art form. Though people often say that their technology is essentially neutral, our devices do exert an influence on us that can be either balancing or unbalancing. Just as we suggested in the section on physical balance that you experiment with mindful eating and being mindful of how you feel before, during, and after eating or drinking, we encourage you to bring this same quality of mindful curiosity and experimentation into the use of your personal devices. Here are some simple, yet powerful guidelines to experiment with. To bring a deeper sense of balance, curiosity, discovery, or even playfulness to the following experiments, we encourage you to keep an inner smile with you as you try these out:

1. Be mindful of how many times a day your check your devices. Published reports indicate that the average person checks their devices between 25 and 150 times a day. Highly addicted people check as often as every six seconds! Begin a written or mental log to simply note how often you check.

2. Remembering that "choice follows awareness"—when the impulse arises to check your device or send a communication—make a mental note of the feeling that is most present for you. Curiosity … anxiety … boredom … agitation … concern…. Whatever it is, in one word, actually name the feeling that is most strong for you at that time.

"When Thoreau considered 'where I live and what I live for,' he tied together location and values. Where we live doesn't just change how we live; it informs who we become. Most recently, technology promises us lives on the screen. What values, Thoreau would ask, follow from this new location? Immersed in simulation, where do we live, and what do we live for?"

—Sherry Turkle

3. Before you answer your phone or reach for your device, pause ... and balance yourself with one or two mindful breaths. Ahhh))) And then, if you like, check to see who is reaching out to you.

4. When you touch or pick up your device, bring your mindfulness to the actual sensations of physical contact with it. Be mindful of the sensations of warmth or coolness, heaviness or smoothness, and ground yourself with the mindfulness of making physical contact with your device. Mentally note a word that describes the sensation you are experiencing.

5. As you interact with your phone, pad, or laptop, smile to yourself and be mindful of the narrative or internal dialogue that is present as you reach for your device, or after you send a message. What is the storyline that is running through your mind? What is your storyline about your storyline?

"But when technology engineers intimacy, relationships can be reduced to mere connections. And then, easy connection becomes redefined as intimacy. Put otherwise, cyberintimacies slide into cybersolitudes. And with constant connection comes new anxieties of disconnection,"

—Sherry Turkle

6. From time to time throughout the day or the week, as an experiment in freedom and digital sovereignty, just turn off your devices, or leave them home. Float free as you launch out into the world unleashed from your digital tether. Enjoy a face-to-face conversation without digital intrusion. Take a mindful walk and enjoy the sights ... the sounds ... the smells ... that stream to you and through you. As you float free of the digi-sphere, open your senses, your mind, and become aware of what is streaming to you and through you live and unfiltered, viscerally and mentally free without wireless or roaming charges! If this is an unsettling proposition, begin with just a short time — 30 minutes or an hour, then expand this to a couple of hours, half a day, a whole day, or even ... a weekend.

Just after our first book came out — our first CD was released and our career was on the rise — we had the opportunity to participate in a year-long silent meditation retreat, during which time we were completely off-line. Disconnected from technology, we were at the same time experiencing a deeper connection with our selves, each other, and the world around us than we had ever experienced before. Our message systems responded to incoming contacts saying, "Thank you for contacting us. We are away, working on an important, intensive project. We'll be back in a year. IF your inquiry is still relevant at that time, please contact us again. Do not leave a message. All the best!" At the end of the year, when we surveyed our colleagues who also participated in this retreat and who had been similarly unplugged for the year, we all agreed that the time had flown by more quickly than any other year in our lives. Re-entering the techno-verse with fresh eyes, we appreciated the wonders that technology offered, while savoring the freedom and independence that we knew was available whenever we wanted it.

CULTURAL CREATIVES

Another inspiring trend toward living in greater balance and wholeness in the economy and workplace is the rising number of Cultural Creatives, who currently comprise more than a quarter of the population in the United States and nearly twice as many estimated in the European Union. First identified by Stanford sociologist Paul H. Ray and psychologist Sherry Ruth Anderson, trend trackers say that the Cultural Creatives are on the rise by an estimated 3 percent per year. Their values include:

- Authenticity, actions must be consistent with words and beliefs
- Engaged action and whole process learning; seeing the world as interwoven and connected
- Idealism and activism
- Globalism and ecology
- The importance of women
- Altruism, compassion, self-actualization, and spirituality

"You don't get to choose how you're going to die or when.

You can only decide how you're going to live."

—Joan Baez

If you are a Cultural Creative, you are likely to agree with ten or more of the following statements:

- You love nature and are deeply concerned about its destruction.
- You are strongly aware of the problems of the whole planet (global warming, destruction of rain forests, overpopulation, lack of ecological sustainability, exploitation of people in poorer countries) and want to see more action to address these problems coming from the private sector as well as government agencies.
- You would pay more taxes or would pay more for consumer goods if you knew the money would go to clean up the environment and stop global warming.
- You give a lot of importance to helping other people and bringing out their unique gifts.
- You volunteer for one or more good causes.

- You see religion and spirituality as important in your life.
- You want more equality for women at work, and more women leaders in business and politics.
- You are concerned about violence and the abuse of women and children around the world.
- You want politics and government spending to put more emphasis on children's education and well-being, on rebuilding our neighborhoods and communities, and on creating an ecologically sustainable future.
- You are unhappy with both the left and the right in politics, and want to find a new way that is not in the mushy middle.
- You tend to be rather optimistic about our future and distrust the cynical and pessimistic view so often supported by the media.
- You want to be involved in creating a new and better way of life in our country.
- You are concerned about what big corporations are doing in the name of making more profits: downsizing, creating environmental problems, and exploiting poorer countries.
- You have your finances and spending under control, and are not concerned about overspending.
- You dislike all the overemphasis in modern culture on success and "making it," on getting more and spending more, on wealth and luxury goods.
- You like people and places that are exotic and foreign, and like experiencing and learning about other ways of life.

Cultural Creatives play an active role in our planetary immune system by helping with our recovery from the complex web of global crises that have emerged largely due to a deficit in the critical factors listed above.

In his book *Karma Queens, Geek Gods and Innerpreneurs*, Ron Rentel was the first to identify the Cultural Creative subculture in entrepreneurship. Rentel named entrepreneurial Cultural Creatives "innerpreneurs." Innerpreneurs share the defining characteristics of any entrepreneur:

- high need for achievement
- high need for independence
- low need for conformity
- internal locus of control

> Self-organizing chaos is integral to the movement building process and essential to its success."
>
> —David Korten

- love of ambiguity
- propensity for risk-taking
- obsession with opportunity

While entrepreneurs use their business for monetary gain, "inner-preneurs" dedicate their work-life to realizing personal fulfillment (creatively, spiritually, emotionally) and creating social change. Many involved in charting economic and business trends for the decades to come agree that being creative and inventive will be the key to business success in the 21st century and that the success of any economy will be determined by the ability of leaders to mobilize, attract, inspire, and retain creative, talented, committed individuals.

Innerpreneurs are putting their values to work in order to find greater balance in their own minds, bodies, and families while creating new business models, new economies, and non-profits that are rede-fining and broadening the meaning of "success." By adding measures of environmental sensibility, social equity, health and happiness of all stakeholders, they are demonstrating that a more soulful and bal-anced approach to life and work can offer value for everyone, and for the planet as a whole.

Given that two-thirds of the economic activity in America is related to consumer purchases, it is clear that even a small shift caused by this demographic will make a tidal wave of reverberations throughout the whole economy. In recent years, whole new industries have been emerging to support the ecologically minded, health-conscious, and spiritually oriented. Look at the explosion of consumer concern for safe, healthy, green, sustainable, ethically produced and manufac-tured products, such as the shifts toward healthier diets that rely on fresh whole organic foods, rather than processed, genetically modified "foods" or antibiotic-riddled animal products and their devastating health and environmental consequences. As more and more people shift from yearning for balance to actively making the changes that cre-ate it, both the game and the paying/playing field will also change.

"To live content with small means;

to see elegance rather than luxury,

and refinement rather than fashion;

to be worthy, not respectable,

and wealthy, not rich;

to listen to stars and birds, babes and sages

with open heart;

to study hard;

to think quietly, act frankly, talk gently,

await occasions, hurry never;

in a word, to let the spiritual unbidden and unconscious,

grow up through the common—

this is my symphony."

—William Henry Channing

SIMPLER LIVING

Simple living has been preached as a wise way of life for thousands of years. Jesus urged his followers to get their priorities straight and advocated the virtues of a simple life. Likewise, the Buddha recom-mended a middle way that avoided problems caused by overindulgence or by extreme deprivation or asceticism. The Taoist sage Lao Tzu observes that "He who knows he has enough is rich." In recent times, Gandhi reminded his followers, "Civilization, in the real sense of the term, consists not in the multiplication, but in the deliberate and voluntary reduction of wants. This alone promotes real happiness and contentment."

The ideal of simple living is not new even to American culture. It dates back to the self-reliant lifestyles of the Puritans, the Shakers, and to Henry David Thoreau in his two-room cabin at Walden Pond. In this century, the concept of "voluntary simplicity" was first introduced by Richard Gregg in 1936. A Harvard graduate, Gregg was inspired by his time with Gandhi and defined voluntary simplicity in this way: "Voluntary simplicity involves both inner and outer conditions. It means singleness of purpose, sincerity and honesty within, as well as avoidance of exterior clutter, of many possessions irrelevant to the chief purpose of life. It means an ordering and guiding of our energy and desires, a partial restraint in some directions in order to secure greater abundance of life in other directions. It involves a deliberate organization of life for a purpose."

In more recent decades this notion has been expressed in various ways, as "down-shifting," "right-sizing," or just plain simple living. The Trends Research Institute, a think tank in Rhinebeck, New York, named "voluntary simplicity" as one of the top ten trends of the 21st century. Evidence from other polls and from experts in the field shows a mushrooming of the movement of people toward a simpler and more balanced lifestyle. This is due to many factors, some of which we have been exploring in this chapter.

A classic survey commissioned by the Merck Family Fund entitled "Yearning for Balance" showed that 72 percent of people age forty to forty-nine agree with the statement, "I would like to simplify my life." A full 28 percent of all the respondents in the study reported "making voluntary changes in my lifestyle that resulted in making less money" — not including those who had taken a regularly scheduled retirement.

Such people are sometimes described as "downshifters" or "domos" — downwardly mobile professionals — who are typically under fifty and who have abandoned a successful or promising career to pursue a life of greater purpose or spiritual focus.

The downshifters offer many reasons for making this shift in their lives. The most frequently mentioned reasons are:

"To laugh often;

to win the admiration of intelligent people

and the affection of children;

to earn the respect of honest critics

and endure the betrayal of false friends;

to apprehend beauty;

to find the best in others;

to leave this world a bit better

whether by a healthy child,

a garden patch

or a redeemed social condition;

to know that even one life

has breathed easier

because you have lived

that is said to have been successful."

—Ralph Waldo Emerson

- wanting to live a more balanced life (72 percent of moms, and 74 percent of dads)
- wanting more time (60 percent)
- wanting a less stressful life (70 percent of moms, and 58 percent of dads)
- wanting to spend more time caring for their children (87 percent of moms, and 72 percent of dads)

Would you guess that people who have downshifted are happy with their decision, or that they regret their decision? The study shows that those who have chosen to downshift are overwhelmingly happy about the changes they have made in their lives. Only 6 percent of the women and 13 percent of the men say they are unhappy with their decision, while 81 percent are happy with their decision and believe that lifestyle simplification leads to more balance and joy in life.

These findings are not isolated. Numerous polls show that many people are beginning to shift toward a more balanced way of life. These polls agree in their reports that 75 to 80 percent of the public is saying, "We need to make major changes if we are going to live in a sustainable way on this earth." The recent International Worklife Values Survey tells us that 65 percent of the people interviewed from around the globe have experienced a major transformation in their lives in the past five years. Add to this that about 60 percent say, "Not only do we need to change, we want to change." Though for many this notion is still in the realm of ideal, most people really are sympathetic to the changes needed to live a more balanced and sustainable way of life.

According to the Merck Poll, people commonly say that three things will bring their lives more into balance and make their lives more satisfying: 1) spending more time with family and friends; 2) reducing stress; 3) doing more to make a difference in their communities.

People are not only aware of what will bring their lives more into balance, but many people are actively making changes in their lives to bring this about. Some "pro-balance" life-work strategies that are being promoted include:

- flex time;
- job sharing;
- working at home;
- telecommuting;
- early retirement;

"I am done with great things and big plans, great institutions and big success. And I am for those tiny invisible loving human forces that work from individual to individual, creeping through the crannies of the world like so many rootlets, or like the capillary oozing of water, yet which, if given time, will rend the hardest monuments of human pride."

—William James

- simple living;
- co-housing;
- "urban village" industries;
- sabbaticals;
- exploring what has meaning and purpose for you in your job.

Getting Started

So, what can you do to begin making changes toward greater balance in your life? Some clues can be gained by rethinking how you spend your money and time. The following three exercises can be helpful to organize your thinking.

1. Make a three-column form on a piece of paper. In the first column, record each purchase you make, and in the second, note how much you spend on it. In the third, note the level of satisfaction you gain from that choice. If you like, you can use a scale of −10 to +10, indicating the level of dissatisfaction or satisfaction that you experience. For example, if you spend $10 to go to a movie that you didn't enjoy, your level of satisfaction might be −8. If you buy a jacket that you really enjoy and that keeps you dry and warm, perhaps your return on that investment will be a +9. Make similar notations for every purchase you make.

2. Keep a similar log of how you spend your time, noting the quality of satisfaction you gain from experiences that you have that don't really cost any money. For example, watching the sunset, talking with a friend, playing with your child, holding a loved one in your arms. How much fulfillment do you gain from how you spend your time in these ways? (This is a great exercise for finding more time in your life for things you want to do — it's amazing how much time we fritter away on things we really don't care about.)

3. Take some time to figure out your hourly earnings, after taxes and other deductions. Once you've done this you will know how much your "life-time" is really worth. With a clearer sense of what your "life-time" is worth to you, you will be in a better position to evaluate how you invest your time, energy, and attention. For example, if you make ten dollars an hour, then a movie ticket or a meal out for $10 is equivalent to investing one hour of your life. Remember, the choice is always yours, and to the degree you are aware of what

"The key to our inner resources is self-knowledge. Self-knowledge is gained by personal development—that is, by collecting experiences out of which new insights and wisdom are born....This comes close to being the meaning of life. Consequently the raison d'être for a company is to supply an environment in which personal development of human beings involved in the company can best take place... What a precious gift to humanity and our planet it would be if the remarkable knowledge we have achieved should be united with wisdom. Then our planet would be the paradise it is meant to be. Business life has the opportunity to bring that gift forward."

—Rolf Osterber, Founding Member of World Business Academy

the real costs are, you will be more likely to create balance in your life by spending your time in more fulfilling ways.

Stepping back to analyze how your investments of time, energy, attention, and money create balance or imbalance in your life can offer valuable insight into how your choices create or detract from the quality of life you want to live. Many people notice that as the cost of maintaining their lifestyle falls, the amount of free time in their lives increases. The decision to slow down and simplify often adds quality time to your life. With more time you will be more likely to discover and explore what truly satisfies you in your life. It gives you the opportunity to improve and strengthen your relationships, and to focus on the values and life priorities most near and dear to your heart.

THREE DIMENSIONS OF BALANCE: SUSTAINABILITY, SATISFACTION, AND SOULFULNESS

We are at a critical turning point as a global culture. If we as individuals, families, communities, and societies are to learn to live in balance, we must learn to assume a more ecological view of life. To do this, we need to seek balance within and among three primary ecologies — the physical, social, and spiritual. Duane Elgin, 30-year senior staff member of a joint Presidential – Congressional Commission on the American Future and author of *The Living Universe* and *The Promise Ahead*, reminds us that these three spheres are related to the three S's of sustainability, satisfaction, and soul or spirit.

The path of the first S leads us to live a more sustainable way of life by learning to live in harmony with the physical ecology of our world. Pausing to reflect on how you relate to the physical world, ask yourself the following questions:

- How often do I consider the impact of my shopping habits and my lifestyle on the sustainability of the physical environment?
- What are three things I can begin to do today to improve my impact on the environment?
- What reminders to do this can I create for myself?
- What are some food choices for the benefit of the planet and my own physical well-being that I can make three times a day?

"The biggest (and hardest) lesson I've learned in life is that the external world is just a reflection of the world within."

—Tony Hsieh,
  Zappos CEO

The path of the second S leads us to consciously cultivate a more satisfying way of life. This is one that helps us to learn and discover how to live in harmony with our social ecology, that is, our relationship with other people, organizations, and communities, as well as with people of other countries and cultures, different races, genders, and mindsets. Again, pause to ask yourself:

- What do I most enjoy about my life? About my work?
- Who are the people whose presence and support I am most grateful for in my life? Who are the people who most look to me for inspiration and support? Who are the people or groups of people I am most comfortable with? Most uncomfortable with?
- What are some steps I might take to expand my comfort zone in order to enhance my social ecological wisdom, and cultivate more satisfying relationships?

The path of the third S invites us to discover how to live a more soulful or spiritual way of life — one that seeks to build harmony and awareness with the spiritual ecology of ourselves in relation to the larger, more mysterious and multidimensional Whole, however we might describe it. Pause again now to reflect or to write down your answers to the following questions:

- How do I nourish and inspire myself spiritually?
- Who are the people whose examples most inspire me as the embodiments of my spiritual ideals? Who are the people who most support me in my spiritual growth?
- What literature, media, or scripture do I find spiritually uplifting and inspiring?
- What would it mean for me to bring more soul and spirit into my daily life? How can I deepen my spiritual understanding and express that wisdom, compassion, love, and creativity in my life and work?

Balance is found in wholeness, not fragmentation. Taken to heart, these three paths braid together in a balanced and beautiful way. Remember that living in a way that honors our wholeness is truly the path of balance, and discover how these three paths to wholeness actually merge into one.

THE LAW OF PROGRESSIVE SIMPLIFICATION

From his analysis of the rise and fall of twenty civilizations, the great historian Arnold Toynbee offers us insights into our search for a balanced lifestyle, and a larger perspective on the current shifts in values and ways of life. Summarizing the principles of civilization growth, Toynbee formulated the Law of Progressive Simplification, which provides some clues to the shift needed toward greater balance in our civilization as a whole. The law reminds us that the growth and vitality of a civilization is not a function of power over land or power over people, and it is most certainly not related to how much we sell or how many resources we buy, sell, or consume. Rather, the measure of a civilization's growth is in its ability to transfer increasing amounts of energy and attention from the material side of life to the psychological, cultural, aesthetic, and spiritual side of life.

This startling and profound idea has much to teach us about finding life-work balance that is truly satisfying and meaningful. What it means is that the more mature a civilization is, the more people will invest their time, energy, and attention in activities and relationships that offer not merely material goods and gratification, but the satisfaction gained by a high quality of relationships, authentic and meaningful communication, the sharing of valuable information, and by the sublime satisfaction of authentically inspiring spiritual experience.

If we take this principle to heart, it is clear that our civilization is still early in its evolution. Hopefully the strain we feel, and the multiple signs of burnout, distress, and imbalance we witness, will be viewed in retrospect as growing pains that are helping us to individually and collectively wake up, and to shift our priorities and commitment toward living life in a way that is truly in balance.

You can call yourself a cultural pioneer to the degree that you take this wisdom to heart, and begin to increase your ability to transfer your own energy and attention from preoccupation with the things of your life, toward the more sublime fulfillment offered by developing quality relationships, and by nurturing the creative, aesthetic, compassionate, and spiritual dimensions of your life. Perhaps this could be said to truly be your real work.

"If diversity is a source of wonder, its opposite—the ubiquitous condensation to some blandly amorphous and singularly generic modern culture that takes for granted an impoverished environment—is a source of dismay. There is, indeed, a fire burning over the earth, taking with it plants and animals, cultures, languages, ancient skills and visionary wisdom. Quelling this flame, and re-inventing the poetry of diversity is perhaps the most important challenge of our times."

—Wade Davis

chapter fourteen

Finding Yourself in the World

Within each of us, in the ground of our being, powers reside
for the healing of our world. These powers do not arise from
any ideology, access to the occult, or passion for social activism. They are inevitable powers. Because we are part of the web
of life, we can draw on the strength—and the pain—of every
creature. This interconnection constitutes our 'deep ecology':
it is the source of our pain for the world as well as our love and
appetite for life.

— JOANNA MACY

OUR SEARCH FOR BALANCE IS NOT A SOLITARY AFFAIR, NOR ONE THAT
we need to work out solely with family members or other intimate
relationships, nor even just between our work and home life. For the
sense of belonging to a larger whole is a fundamental force in the
search for balance, one that begins in our need for connection to a
larger community, extending out to encompass the entire human family and, ultimately, to all of nature. Acknowledging our place in the
greater whole helps us round out our experience, fostering our ability
to see our part in the wheel of life and ultimately, creates a deep sense
of balance and peace.

GLIMPSES OF COMMUNITY

It is only natural that we yearn for a sense of community. As bio-psycho-social creatures, we long for recognition, mutual support, and shared interest with other people—beyond the need for family ties. The fulfillment, in the sense of belonging, that one may find in being a member of a high-performing team, a spiritual community, or even a street gang can be immeasurable.

For millions of years we primates have faced the chaos of our world by taking refuge in community. Just as our ancestors huddled together for warmth, banded together for protection, teaching the young, gathering provisions, we gather today to seek out warmth, nourish ourselves, and find safe passage and clear direction in the company of others. From recent research in the natural sciences it is clear that cooperation is a more cogent force for balanced survival and sustainability than competition. Feeling ourselves as members of a community seems essential to our well-being and our health. As former health care providers and medical researchers — and corporate consultants for many years — we can assure you that the "disease" of loneliness is one of the most common and devastating illnesses of our time and culture.

People are starving for meaningful, nourishing, supportive relationships. In a culture where more than 75 percent of the population do not know their neighbors, people are longing for connectedness, belonging, and for the assurance and fulfillment that comes from being in the midst of a circle of deeply committed friends. The malaise seems largely due to a lack of knowing people more deeply, and failing to discover a common sense of purpose, meaning, vision, and values that are vital to community life. Remember, the root meaning of community implies "with unity!"

Communities may develop intentionally, as in intentional housing developments, or in membership in organizations and clubs. Or a sense of community may emerge more informally, by sharing interests in a neighborhood, or having kids on the same soccer team or carpool. As the pressures on individuals and families continues to increase, and as people spend such large amounts of time on their job, we hear increasingly frequent comments about the importance of developing a sense of community both at work and beyond. For example, a recent *Industry Week* survey of business managers from around the globe suggests that people in business feel a deep sense of isolation, and over two-thirds

"The Way is long—
let us go together.
The Way is difficult—
let us help each other.
The Way is joyful—
let us share it.
The Way is
ours alone—
let us go in love.
The Way grows
before us—
let us begin."

—Zen Invocation

"A too highly developed individualism can lead to a debilitating sense of isolation so that you can be lonely and lost in a crowd.... 'Ubuntu' is not easy to describe because it has no equivalent in any of the Western languages.... *Ubuntu* speaks to the essence of being human and our understanding that the human person is corporate. The solitary individual is in our understanding a contradiction in terms. You are a person through other persons. *Ubuntu* speaks about the importance of communal harmony... speaks about warmth, compassion, generosity, hospitality, and seek to embrace others."

—Archbishop Desmond Tutu, Nobel Peace Prize Laureate

of them, 69 percent, expressed an interest in having a greater sense of belonging in the workplace.

These days many of us are nourished and affirmed through participating in on-line social networks and virtual communities that span the globe. Many of the connections developed in virtual space lead to real time, face to face encounters in members from around the globe. For us, when we actually meet colleagues with whom we have developed relationships online, we already have a deep recognition and bond established.

The roots of community are basic to life balance. In terms of humanity, remember that our bodies were shaped through countless generations of tribal communal living. The templates for our body, mind, and language were shaped by moving, touching, and living in close connection with others. We were born not merely to work, but to dance, to sing, to create art, to find, prepare and eat food together, to tell and listen to stories, to care for each other, and to be close to those we love, to ponder, to discuss, and to commune together with the awesome mysteries of life that we associate with the spiritual reality that extends beyond the horizons of our ordinary knowing. The pulse of our lives weaves us together into a larger circle of community with those we walk, dance, and pray with, those we eat and sleep with, those we work with and for, and those we learn from.

As the millennia passed and social groups increased in size and complexity, the need for community has become increasingly fulfilled through relationships with people at work and play, and through political parties, religious communities, clubs, sports teams, or neighborhood groups. As the fabric of our society continues to unravel, many of us still struggle to find a sense of community and belonging. Often, we are too busy for it, too tired, or too cynical to even look for it. Or we honestly have no sense of where to begin if we were to mount the search.

"We are visitors on this planet. We are here for ninety, one hundred years at the very most. During that period, we must try to do something good, something useful with our lives. Try to be at peace with yourself, and help others share that peace. If you contribute to other people's happiness, you will find the goal, the true meaning of life."

—The Dalai Lama

In the absence of close family, the drive for belonging and community in many of our children may be satisfied through loyalty to local gangs. Countless lonely, exhausted adults alienated from their families and neighbors settle for the illusion of community by pledging allegiance to a sports team with which they may have virtually no direct contact. Others adopt a media community populated by characters whose flickering fantasy lives assume great, but unfulfilling importance. Our displaced need for nurturing leads Americans to own more stuffed animals than any country on earth and to spend a fortune on our pets.

Speaking from years of community building, Starhawk, permaculture designer and teacher, global justice eco-activist and author of *The Fifth Sacred Thing*, reminds us of the felt sense of community: "Somewhere there are people to whom we can speak with passion without having the words catch in our throat. Somewhere a circle of hands will open to receive us, eyes will light up as we enter, voices will celebrate with us whenever we come into our own power. Community means strength that joins with strength to do the work that needs to be done. Arms to hold us when we falter. A circle of healing. A circle of friends. Someplace where we can be free."

While Phil Jackson was head coach of the Chicago Bulls, they were the winners of three NBA championships prior to breaking the all-time record for the number of season's victories. Speaking to the heart of their success as a team, Jackson offered an insight into community in his book *Sacred Hoops* when he said, "Working with the Bulls, I've learned that the most effective way to forge a winning team is to call on the players' need to connect with something larger than themselves. Even for those who don't consider themselves 'spiritual' in a conventional sense, creating a successful team—whether it's an NBA champion or a record-setting

∽

"...right relationship means right relationship with the elements, the land, the sacred directions...The seed of pure mind is within all people. It is always there. It is not made impure. Our actions may be impure and set up a stream of reactions, but always we can come again to the seed of pure mind and right relationship...it is time now for people to choose. The first step is to see the power of your own consciousness...The common kernel is care for all beings, good relationship, cycles of reciprocity, generosity, giving of oneself, being an empty bowl so you can know what is."

—Dhyani Ywahoo

"The community stagnates without the impulse of the individual.

The impulse dies away without the sympathy of the community."

—William James

"It is possible that the next Buddha will not take the form of an individual. The next Buddha may take the form of a community—a community practicing understanding and loving kindness, a community practicing mindful living. This may be the most important thing we can do for the survival of the earth."

—Thich Nhat Hanh

sales force — is essentially their self-interest for the greater good, so that the whole adds up to more than the sum of its parts."

So, in your search for balance, be sure to include the element of community. Think about the presence or absence of community in your life, and ask yourself:

- What have been the most fulfilling experiences you have had?
- What communities welcome you with the greatest sense of belonging?
- What gifts do you bring to these communities?
- What do you find most fulfilling in participating in these communities?
- How would involvement in community best play in bringing greater balance into your life?

The complex relationships formed in community offer us the opportunity to draw inspiration from a larger whole. As Anne Hillman, author of *The Dancing Animal Woman: A Celebration of Life*, perceptively explains: "As we weave our own stories into the tapestry of life around us, we begin to develop a wholly different perception of what it means to be human. This larger identity is formed in a group. It cannot be formed in isolated nuclear families, as our first identity was. We need the combined energy and wisdom of larger numbers. 'So many are required for the truth!' Perhaps this is the strong pull to community and group life that many of us feel in these last decades of the twentieth century. Perhaps a new archetype of the group is coming into being....This resonance is a presence that may become a kind of 'knowing together,' (consciousness). Might then some higher intelligence begin to move our species as a group so that each of us becomes an instrument, attuned to the whole flock?"

On the path of balance, remember that you are never alone. Continue to seek out kindred souls and allies with whom your journey can be truly shared in a mutually fulfilling way.

GLOBAL FAMILY

While attending a conference in India, our friend Joan took some time to visit some of the outlying villages. Seeing the poverty around her, she felt self-conscious of her fine clothing and jewelry. In one particularly poor village, she encountered an old woman with a peaceful gaze who, though dressed in a tattered sari, carried herself with great dignity. "Is it really true," the old woman asked, "that in your country people live in large buildings close to each other and that they don't know each other or talk to their neighbors?" "Yes," Joan said, "This is true."

"And, is it true that in your country, people pay strangers to care for their children?"

"Yes, I'm sorry to say this is also true in my country," Joan replied.

"I have also heard that in your country," the old woman went on, "your old people are taken away and banished to live isolated with other old people, living far distant from their children. Is this true too?" Joan quietly nodded, "yes."

"Oh, my dear," the old woman said. Eyes brimming over with tears, she reached out and took Joan's hand, "This is what I have heard but I have never been able to ask a Westerner if this was actually so. I want you to know that I pray for you poor people every day."

We have become so inured to the decline of real community in our own culture, that sometimes it takes a vastly different, and more balanced, perspective of another culture's values to wake us out of our insensitivity and forgetfulness. It's sobering to realize that what was viewed as unthinkably tragic in this woman's poor rural village is accepted as commonplace in most modern cities. What will it take for us to look and care deeply enough to appreciate how the social and spiritual poverty in our own lives rivals, or even dwarfs, the material poverty of a people whose dignity and compassion are clothed in tattered saris?

We were talking with a friend recently, who had been on a medical mission that gave immunizations to thousands of children in Africa. "How did that experience touch you?" we asked. "It was amazing," she said, "Those people had nothing. Absolutely nothing. And they were so very happy. Their children had no toys. They barely had enough to eat and hardly any shelter, but they had a sense of heritage, community, and connectedness to their environment. They really knew how to laugh and cry, how to live and love. And they really knew how to sing and dance. They were so very happy and they were the most generous and giving people I have ever met, even though they had so little to give." Returning home after two months away, and after flying sixteen hours to return to the States, her husband picked her up at the airport. It was Monday evening and he had tickets for the football game, so they stopped for fast food and went to the stadium. What a lesson in balance that must have been!

During the course of our lifetimes, the image of a global village is growing from metaphor to reality. Linked by webs of light-speed communication, the diverse people of the planet communicate, travel, and

What we are creating is completely unknown. It is everywhere. There is no center. There's no one spokesperson. It's in every country and city on Earth. It is within every tribe, every race, every culture and every ethnic group in the world. This is the first time on Earth that a powerful, non-ideological movement has arisen... This is where salvation will be found. We know that as biologists, we know that as community organizers, we know that as ecologists. It's found in diversity. This movement is humanity's immune response to resist and heal political disease, economic infection and ecological corruption caused by ideologies."

—Paul Hawken

"Adam Kahane shared a story of when the apartheid regime coming to an end in South Africa, people who had been killing one another were struggling to form a new democratic government: 'A popular joke at the time said that, faced with the country's daunting challenges, South Africans had two options: a practical option and a miraculous option." The practical option was that everyone would 'go down on their knees and pray for a band of angels to come down from heaven and fix things for us.' The miraculous option was that people would 'talk with one another until we found a way forward together.' Fortunately, South Africans opted for the miraculous option— talking with one another and discovering their interconnectedness to their common homeland, to their future, and to one another."

—Adapted from an article by Peter Senge

exchange information and energy in countless ways. The following image offers a profound and sobering insight into the relationships among the many people of the earth.

Imagine all of the people of the earth as a village made up of 100 people. Fifty would be men and fifty would be women. Of the 100, five would be LGBQT (lesbian, gay, bi, queer, transgender). Sixty-one live in Asia, fifteen in Africa, ten in Europe, five in North America, and nine in South America. Five speak English and could read this book. Seven would have a college degree and twelve cannot read or write. Forty-eight people live on less that 2 USD per day. Thirteen do not have safe water to drink. Half seldom, if ever, see the night sky and have lost their sense of connection to the vastness of the starry sky. The richest one in our village actually owns 40 percent of the entire wealth. Half of the village's wealth would be in the hands of only six people, and most of them would be citizens of the United States. About sixty families live on only 10 percent of the land while only seven families own 60 percent of the land. Seventy families have no drinking water at their homes. Seven families consume 80 percent of all of the available energy. Envision the conditions, the struggles and tensions in this village where there are seven mansions and an airport on one side, and where there is no drink-ing water, little comfort, and much suffering on the other. Try to com-prehend how the activities of both the rich and the poor are destroying the life-support systems for the entire planet so that they can survive, feed their families, or profit in this lifetime.

Now imagine that something radical changes. People begin to wake up, to better understand themselves, and to respect and love one another. Can you envision what our world looks like and how we would live if we were to find true balance and harmony among all of the

"In a real sense all life is inter-related. All persons are caught in an inescapable network of mutuality, tied in a single garment of destiny. Whatever affects one directly affects all indirectly. I can never be what I ought to be until you are what you ought to be, and you can never be what you ought to be until I am what I ought to be. This is the inter-related structure of reality."

—Rev. Martin Luther King, Jr.

people of this tiny, fragile world? What courses of development would we continue? Which ones would we change? What new ways of living and learning together in balance would need to emerge?

Then ask yourself, "What choices can I make and what actions can I take to bring greater harmony and balance to all members of our human family? What actions will I take and what investments will I make to build a better world?"

REMEMBERING OUR BIO-PALS

Waking up high on the slopes of Haleakala Crater in Maui, Hawaii, one cold morning, the two of us encountered our friend Stan, who came over to greet us with a warm cup of chai tea. "Hey, you want to meet my new neighbor?" "Neighbor?" We looked questioningly at each other, and then out across the remote windswept pastures that Stan had homesteaded for twenty years. "We didn't know you had a neighbor," Joel said. Stan smiled, and said somewhat mischievously, "Oh, he's new here and lives just over there." Stan pointed to a hillside with no visible dwelling above an old ranch road. "Follow me. I'll introduce you." We scrambled up the hill behind Stan. Stan's pace slowed to walk very quietly and mindfully through the grass. Raising his finger to his lips, Stan turned and gestured for us to be quiet and to crouch down. He reached gently forward and pulled back a clump of tall grass. Two huge, bright yellow, saucer-shaped eyes peered out from a nest in the hollow.

"And whoooo are you?" the eyes of this baby owl seemed to say. It appeared to have no fear, only a penetrating sense of presence, strength, and objective curiosity. It was clear from the striking presence of this being that someone was home here: balanced, awake, present! We'd seen the look before in the clear presence of wise old elders, or in the deep eyes of some infants, but to encounter such a strong sense of being in a nonhuman was a bit disarming. We've caught a glimpse of it swimming with the dolphins in Kealakekua Bay, and from time to time in a special cat whose presence calls for attention.

We two-leggeds have incredible influence in assuring or destroying the lives of other beings on this planet. Yet how often do we think about, listen for, and truly hear their voices? Who speaks for wolf, salmon, and the other critters at the policy roundtables of the world?

A recent meeting on the Onodaga Reservation brought together representatives of the Six Nations of New York state. Speaking impassionedly to those gathered, Chief Oren Lyons said, "We see it as our duty to speak as caretakers for the natural world. Government is a process

"Hard material necessity and human evolutionary possibility now seem to converge to create a situation where, in the long run, we will be obliged to do no less than realize our greatest possibilities. We are engaged in a race between self-discovery and self-destruction. The forces that may converge to destroy us are the same forces that may foster societal and self-discovery."

—Duane Elgin

"One thing to remember is to talk to the animals. If you do, they will talk back to you. But if you don't talk to the animals, they won't talk back to you, then you won't understand, and when you don't understand you will fear and when you fear you will destroy the animals and if you destroy the animals, you will destroy yourself."

—Chief Dan George

of living together, the principle being that all life is equal, including the four-legged and the winged things. The principle has been lost; the two-legged walks about thinking that he is supreme with his man-made laws. But there are universal laws of all living things. We come here and say they too have rights."

This sensitivity to all the creatures of the earth needs to be a part of each of our lives. Matthew Fox reminds us that when Jesus commanded people to follow the golden rule and to "love your neighbor as yourself," he didn't just say to love your two-legged neighbors. In search of balance, how can we open our hearts and minds to all those living beings who share the earth? According to Jewish midrash, both Moses and David were chosen to lead the nation of Israel because of their compassion toward animals. What criteria for choosing a national leader! Saint Francis, it is said, was once so moved with concern for the fate of a lamb that when he met the shepherd on the way to the market he traded the cloak off his back for the sheep so that the lamb might live. It is also said that Saint Francis could listen to and talk to the animals, and he would even preach to them in a way that they could understand. His love for animals was so great that they would follow him everywhere, even going into buildings with him.

If we are to truly learn to live in balance and harmony in this world, we must find room in our hearts and minds for all beings: the two-legged, the four-legged, the birds of the air, the fish in the seas, the critters that live in the ravines behind our apartment houses, the countless creatures inhabiting the rainforests who may have much to teach us about cooperation and healing, and all the countless beings whom we are unaware of. This life is truly a laboratory to learn about relationships and that includes our relationship to the other beings who inhabit the planet with us. The more conscious and caring we become about all God's creation, the more our lives will reflect that balance.

In our neighborhood, near the heart of Seattle, we have the company of squirrels, raccoons, opossums, eagles, hawks, the seasonal songs of migrating birds, buzzing insects, streams and lakes full of fish — and of course various pesky rodents and a herd of domesticated felines and canine friends. When we sleep out on our roof deck, we can hear the voices of the lions, elephants, and monkeys who now live at our local zoo. Keeping an eye out for your neighbors can help you to remember and restore your balance in relationship to the larger web of life in which you live.

Traditionally, Hawaiian families each had three *aumakua* or guardian protectors: one for the earth, such as mo'o the lizard, one for the

"Man has the capacity to love, not just his own species, but life in all its shapes and forms. This empathy with the interknit web of life is the highest spiritual expression I know of."

—Loren Eiseley

"One day we were eating roast lamb. It was the lambing season so there were all these beautiful young lambs gamboling around the fields surrounding our house, running and playing together. We looked at the lambs playing and we looked at the lamb on our plates and we realized we were eating leg of lamb. We looked at them running around outside again and saw a leg of lamb running and playing. And that was it, the great turning point: if it has a face, don't eat it!"

—Paul McCartney

sky, like pueo the owl; and one for the sea, the shark or dolphin, for example. Members of that family would show special respect to these protectors, and would consider seeing them as auspicious. They would never kill one of their *aumakua*. By carefully observing the habits and characteristics of these creatures, the people gained many insights for how to live a balanced life.

People with the roots of deep relationship still intact in their lives regard the four-legged, the winged ones, the swimming beings, and crawling beings as their brothers and sisters, embodying a unique and special gift from the Creator. They honor the swiftness of Hawk, the clear seeing of Eagle, the playfulness of Dolphin, the craftiness of Raccoon. They live with respect for the unique gifts and qualities that each creature offers to the world and to humanity. Each encounter with a moose, or bear, or eagle, or crow, or any other living being is considered a meaningful revelation. And when the medicine gifts of a specific animal are required, the wise ones often fast, pray, and seek guidance from the spirit of these creatures. Our relationship with animals can open a portal to mythical and archetypal dimensions of our lives. Take a moment to consider:

- What animals appear most frequently in your dreams or in your waking visions?
- What qualities or strengths do they represent to you?

Through the ongoing experiment of evolution our planet has seen countless creatures come and go. Yet in the past hundred years, one species—humans—has obliterated tens of thousands of species who will never be known again upon the earth. And each year, millions of living creatures are brutally tortured, maimed, or killed in research centers. Estimates are that each year 65 to 100 billion cows, chickens, pigs, ducks, turkeys, rabbits, goats, water buffalos, and camels and over a trillion fish are slaughtered. Meanwhile, hundreds of billions more languish in intolerable circumstances while also generating a tremendous amount of waste and pollution that poison our waters and air.

In your journey toward balance, remember to keep the animals, our "bio-pals," in mind as you make choices in the products that you buy, the clothing you wear, and the food you eat. Keep asking yourself, "What would living in balance with all of the creatures of the earth look like for me? And how are my choices creating more balance or imbalance, more joy or sorrow, in the lives of others?"

"The ethics of reverence for life makes no distinction between high and low, more precious and less precious lives. It has good reason for this omission... How can we know what importance other living organisms have in themselves and in terms of the universe?...To the truly ethical man, all life is sacred."

—Albert Schweitzer

"If you listen carefully enough to anything, it will talk to you."

—George Washington Carver

"If I spent enough time with the tiniest creature—

even a caterpillar—

I would never have to prepare a sermon.

So full of God is every creature."

—Meister Eckhart

As we come to a wider, deeper sense of ourselves, we discover a natural connectedness, belonging, and intimacy with all living beings and with all of creation. This naturally expresses itself as living with kindness and relating to others in a nonviolent way. As Gandhi said, "The rock-bottom foundation of the technique for achieving the power of nonviolence is the belief in the essential oneness of all life."

"Ethics is how we behave when we decide that we belong together," Benedictine monk David Steindl-Rast reminds us. It seems clear that any action, however small, that devalues any form of life is a dangerous symptom that we are losing our balance and forgetting our place in the circle of life. For, as Chief Seattle's famous words remind us, "What we do to the animals we do to ourselves."

Self-Compassion

In the last decade, a growing body of research on self-compassion has emerged that confirms the profound value and power of learning to open our hearts to ourselves in a more balanced way. This groundbreaking research is largely inspired by the work of Dr. Kristin Neff, Associate Professor in Human Development and Culture, University of Texas at Austin. Among the many findings of this research related to living in balance is that as we cultivate compassion for ourselves, we also increase our mindfulness, compassion for others, and life satisfaction, and decrease depression, anxiety, stress, self-criticism, rumination, thought suppression, and the impact of trauma in our lives.

Among the many guidelines for strengthening our self-compassion are these four core contemplations that honor the universality of suffering and our capacity for generating compassion:

> This is a moment of suffering:
> The first phrase helps us to be mindful and open to the sting of physical or emotional pain. (You might also just say "this is really hard right now" or "this hurts.")

> Suffering is a part of life:
> The second phrase normalizes your experience and reminds you that suffering unites all living beings and reduces the tendency to feel ashamed and isolated when things are difficult in our lives.

May I be kind to myself:
The third phrase begins to open our hearts to kindness toward ourselves, rather than judgment or self criticism.

May I give myself the compassion I need:
The final phrase reinforces the idea that you both need and deserve compassion in such difficult moments in your life.

These phrases can help us to have a more open hearted, realistic, and balanced regard for ourselves, and greater empathy and compassion toward others.

Widening Your Circle of Compassion

All great wisdom teachings and scientific traditions tell us that we—and all beings—are part of a great wholeness that we call the "Living Universe." Our experience of ourselves as something separate is, as Einstein reminds us, merely "an optical delusion of consciousness." The good news is that we can actually free ourselves from this delusion! And the liberating method is to widen the circle of our compassion to embrace ALL living creatures (i.e., not just human beings) and the whole of nature in all of its beauty.

How can we widen the circle of our compassion? One powerful clue comes to us from Stanford University's Center for Compassion and Altruism Research and Education program (CCARE), where an essential meme in the emerging new curriculum of "Compassion Cultivation Training" is to regard all living beings with the sense that "Just like me …this person longs to be happy …just like me, this person wants to be healthy, etc."

In this spirit of cultivating a practice of regarding others as "just like me," it is mind-expanding to contemplate that comparative genomic research indicates that while genetically we are 99.5 percent similar to any other human being, we are 96 to 98 percent similar to chimpanzees (depending on how it is calculated); 90 percent similar to cats; and 80 percent genetically similar to cows. About 60 percent of chicken genes correspond to a similar human gene, and even the tiny fruit fly (Drosophila) shares about 60 percent of its DNA with humans. As our wisdom eyes open and our circle of compassion grows, we begin to sense that all living beings are indeed intimately related.

As you move through the world today, open your wisdom eyes to see beyond the blinders of your optical delusion of consciousness to

"All things have this essence, all life does. Some people interpret this as unconditional love. Everyone has the capacity to be loved. And it's up to each one to discover their capacity of what that is."

—Kumu Raylene
Ha'alelea Kawaiae'a

"The more you are motivated by love,

the more fearless and free

your actions will be."

—The Dalai Lama

"If we learn to open our hearts, anyone, including the people who drive us crazy, can be our teacher."

—Pema Chödrön

sense the underlying wholeness of all things and all beings. Widen the circle of your compassion, as you behold "others" as "another myself," "just like me...!" Contemplate:

> "Just like me," you want to be happy and successful in your life, work, and relationships....

> "Just like me" you want to get to work on time....

> "Just like me," you want to feel valued and listened to....

> "Just like me" you want your children, family, and friends to be safe, nourished, healthy, have clean water to drink, a good education, and opportunities to flourish in their lives....

> "Just like me" you yearn to live in harmony and balance....

Building on this contemplation, another simple yet potent practice you can do on a daily basis to revitalize your interconnectedness at a deep level is the practice of lovingkindness. We especially like to do this one at the end or start of a day, or to celebrate and share the joy of a job well done or a moment well lived. The essence of this prayer and meditation is the wish that we and all beings enjoy happiness and well-being. Here's how it goes:

Begin by touching your heart, if you like, breathe deeply, and smile to yourself a smile of tender appreciation and care. Holding the sincere wish to be of benefit to yourself and others, heartfully repeat the following phrases mentally, first to yourself, several times, and then expand the radius of your lovingkindness successively out to wider and wider circles. Go for the meaning and the feeling behind the words:

> May I be happy and peaceful.
> May I be free from fear and pain.
> May I live with love and compassion.
> And may I fully awaken and be free.

Next, reach out with your heart/mind to embrace your loved ones and friends with the energy of lovingkindness in the same way and radiate these thoughts of well-being to them:

"Put away all hindrances, let your mind full of love pervade one quarter of the world, and so too the second quarter, and so the third, and so the fourth. And thus the whole wide world, above, below, around and everywhere, altogether continue to pervade with love-filled thought, abounding, sublime, beyond measure, free from hatred and ill-will."

—The Buddha

"Some day, after we have mastered the winds, the waves, the tides, and gravity we shall harness the energies of love. Then, for a second time in the history of the world man will have discovered fire."

—Father Teilhard de Chardin

May you be happy and peaceful.
May you be free from fear and pain.
May you live with love and compassion.
And may you fully Awaken and be free.

As you hold the image of your beloved ones and repeat these phrases, sense or imagine that they are actually touched by the love radiating out from your heart and that it is truly helpful for them.

Next, hold in mind someone or some group of people toward whom you feel neutral, perhaps some of the neighbors whom you really don't know, or folks you see on the way to work. As you repeat these phrases, bring them into your heart and wish for them:

May you be happy and peaceful.
May you be free from fear and pain.
May you live with love and compassion.
And may you fully Awaken and be free.

Sense or imagine that these wishes and prayers really do support them.

Now, having primed your heart pump, turn your attention toward someone, or ones, toward whom your heart is closed with pain, resentment, or negativity. Remembering that this person or group of people may in the past have actually been kind to you, and that, in their own way, they too are searching for happiness and hoping to avoid suffering in their own lives, let your heart open to them. As best as you are able, wish for them:

May you be happy and peaceful.
May you be free from fear and pain.
May you live with love and compassion.
May you fully Awaken to your greatest potentials, and be
    free of any ignorance and confusion that leads you to act
    in unskillful ways.
May you fully Awaken and be free.

As you hold them in mind and radiate these thoughts of lovingkindness, be merciful with yourself. Let your own heart open to free you from the prison of imbalance that you may have created for yourself out of

"If you want to stop being confused, then emulate these ancient folk: join your body, mind, and spirit in all you do. Choose food, clothing, and shelter that accords with nature. Rely on your own body for transportation. Allow your work and your recreation to be one and the same. Do exercise that develops your whole being and nor just your body. Listen to music that bridges the three spheres of your being. Choose leaders for their virtue rather than their wealth or power. Serve others and cultivate yourself simultaneously. Understand that true growth comes from meeting and solving the problems of life in a way that is harmonizing to yourself and to others. If you can follow these simple old ways, you will be continually renewed."

—Lau Tzu, Inner Chapters, Hua Hu Ching

your own anger, fear, or resentment toward this person with whom you are having a hard time, or whose relationship you would like to heal.

Visualize yourself surrounded now by all your circles of supportive relationships, and invite into your loving awareness all the networks of support, visible and invisible, known and unknown, near and far, that make up the whole circle of living beings, the web of life. Expand your love and care equally to this larger field as the sun shines its life-giving rays equally to all. In this way, with great equanimity to all living beings, extend the radius of your lovingkindness to all your loved ones and friends, to all the strangers or neutral people in your life, to all the people toward whom your heart has been closed, to all the humans and nonhumans who search for happiness, harmony, and balance on their fleeting journey through life. And, imagining that this vast circle of relations joins you as you open your heart to include and embrace all beings, extend the waves of lovingkindness out now in all directions:

> May all beings (or, may we all) be happy and peaceful.
> May all beings be free from fear and pain.
> May all beings live with love and compassion.
> And may all beings fully Awaken to their true nature and
>   potentials and be free!

Let these wishes radiate to all beings to the east: To all beings to the west, to all beings to the south, to all beings to the north. Let these wishes reach out to all beings above you and below you. To all beings in this world, or in all worlds. In this time and in all times.

Then, with your hands, imagine that you can gather the energy and the light you have generated through this series of contemplations. Imagine that you can bring this all to focus as one intensely bright light of love and compassion like a clear shining jewel. Bring this light of lovingkindness and compassion into your heart. Let it shine there like a luminous loving sun that bathes the world and all beings within it in the light of love that radiates through you as a blessing for the world. Carry the natural radiance of this love with you wherever you go. When your awareness of it fades, re-energize it by using the phrases and images offered here, and let the light of your love light up your world.

RESTORING THE WORLD TO WHOLENESS

As the wish for balance not just for ourselves but for all beings awakens in our hearts, we participate in a profound teaching from the

"We are not so different from all the peoples of this world, yet the message which has come through us is special and unique. To discover, express, and expand our uniqueness, as individuals, and as a People, supports *tikkun haolam,* the completion of creation, to which we are called. With gratitude, then, we reach into the heart of our uniqueness. Not to best another, but to better understand ourselves."

—Rabbi Ted Falcon

kabbalah on restoring balance. This is called "*tikkun ha-olam*" in Hebrew, which means, "repairing the world." *Tikkun* means to mend or repair. Outwardly, *tikkun* is associated with social action that has the goal of improving the world. But inwardly, in the esoteric traditions, *tikkun* is the sacred innerwork of mending a broken world and restoring it to wholeness and balance through spiritually developing the love that carries us beyond our separate self. *Tikkun* is regarded as the highest, most profound purpose of our life.

This activity to restore balance and harmony in our world is closely akin to the Buddhist notion of *bodhichitta*, "the spirit of awakening," which holds that at the heart/core of every living being is a universal impulse to fully awaken to the wholeness of its potentials and to serve others in their awakening. This is the universal yearning to reduce suffering, cultivate harmonious relations, and find dynamic balance.

The work of repairing, rebalancing, and awakening is an inside-out job. It is said that every tiny bit of restoration of wholeness within ourselves directly contributes to the restoration and awakening of all beings and of the whole world. The impulse of every movement toward healing, every moment of mindfulness, every act of kindness we generate within ourselves, is directly shared or transmitted to support the emergence of that potential within each and every living being.

That's because the more deeply and completely we are balanced within ourselves, the better equipped we are, and the more natural it is, for us to reach out and nurture the emergence of greater harmony in our world. As our awareness and sensitivity increase, we recognize that certain situations in our life or world are intolerably unproductive, toxic, or destructive. This helps to strengthen our resolve to get healthier; resolve conflicts; put a stop to abusive violence in our relationships; and become an advocate, activist, or celebrant of noble causes that expand the sphere of balance and harmony to our world and to the lives of others.

Imagine that you are standing on a mountaintop on a still, clear, dark night. In the sky around you are an infinite number of jewels linked together in a subtle network of light. Imagine now that as you light a little candle, instantly its light and warmth are reflected in each and every one of the jewels surrounding you. Not only that, but each of the jewels is also illumined by the light that is reflected in it from all the illuminating jewels. It is a fantastic and inspiring sight. Now imagine that as you light up a moment of mindfulness within you, the light of that mindfulness "lights up" all living beings. Likewise, if within yourself you awaken or light up a moment of love, gratitude, wonder, joy, or

"...right relationship means right relationship with the elements, the land, the sacred directions... The seed of pure mind is within all people. It is always there. It is not made impure. Our actions may be impure and set up a stream of reactions, but always we can come again to the seed of pure mind and right relationship... it is time now for people to choose. The first step is to see the power of your own consciousness... The common kernal is care for all beings, good relationship, cycles of reciprocity, generosity, giving of oneself, being an empty bowl so you can know what is."

—Dhyani Ywahoo

"The emptying of self and repairing the world with love are two sides of the same spiritual practice. We are not seeking to escape the world, we are seeking to transform it."

—Reb Yerachmiel Ben Yisrael

forgiveness, that impulse immediately lights up within all others. The transmission is effortless, immediate, heart to heart. Each of the jewels in the net is lighting up all of the other jewels, giving rise to waves of excitement, waves of sympathy, waves of gratitude, love, or blessings.

In each moment that we are awake, we can feel what is reverberating within ourselves and we can respond in a way that lights up the world in either a weird or a wonderful way. Mindful moment to mindful moment, from the very core of our being, we contribute to the balancing and rebuilding of the world in wholeness, or contribute to the fear and confusion. In moments of distraction, when mindlessness sets in and we lose our balance, the momentum of habit and countless impinging forces propels us. In moments of self-remembering, when we awaken to mindfulness, we at least have a choice.

As we learn to recognize and repair the rifts and imbalances in our own life we reestablish wholeness within ourselves. As our internal repair work deepens, we are better able to reach out—inwardly and outwardly—and repair the world around us. As we focus the flow of our dynamic being more into balance, and dissolve the rigid boundaries that separate us from our wholeness, we restore the world to balance. These aren't just nice ideas, this is descriptive of the way things are. Our journey toward balance is one of awakening in order to bring more lucid, loving, radiant, presence into our world. This is very deep *tikkun*.

"Love is that flame that once kindled burns everything,

and only the mystery and the journey remain."

—Mevlana Jalaluddin Rumi

section four

Reclaiming Our Balance, Embracing the Whole

> *"Transformation comes from looking deeply within, to a state*
> *that exists before fear and isolation arise, the state in which*
> *we are inviolably whole just as we are. We connect to our-*
> *selves, to our own true experience, and discover there that to*
> *be alive means to be whole."*

—Sharon Salzberg

In this final section, we'd like to offer a unifying framework in which the synergy of all these different strategies can be seen and understood. You'll learn ten key principles that will give you more leverage for living your life and approaching your work with greater harmony and resilience. To celebrate the many paths we've walked to come home to our wholeness and reclaim our essential balance, we'll also take a guided walk in the four directions—north, south, east, and west—where you'll receive some important reminders to help you continue in wholeness on the balancing Way.

We hope you've begun to realize that this search for balance is truly a spiral path—as our inner balance grows, it flows out into the world in ways that improve the harmony and balance in our outer lives and relationships, and this supports the refinement of our inner harmony and balance. The fruit of quality relationships is mind/body harmony and peace of mind. The fruit of peace and clarity of mind is increased mindfulness. The fruit of mindfulness is deeper insight and understanding. The fruit of insight is a wisdom that is inseparable from effectiveness, compassion, and lovingkindness. These, in turn, ripen as the fruits of greater kindness and right relations. The central harvest of all these paths and qualities woven together

as a spiral of learning, is confidence in yourself and faith and devotion to the Mystery in which all things and all beings find their wholeness.

Like facets of a jewel-like balanced life, each of these themes is an inseparable aspect of the whole. Wherever you focus steps onto this path, you will find the benefits of your efforts will be reflected in each of the other facets of this jewel. Growing in harmony and health, peace and power, insight and understanding, creativity and compassion, each step along the spiral brings the spirit of balance and wholeness more alive in your life.

chapter fifteen

Principles for Resilience

If you feel that you are living in a time of disintegration, your activities will be fearful and violent. If you feel that you are living in a time of reintegration and evolutionary emergence, your activities will be more open and filled with hope and wonder.

—William Irwin Thompson

In this chapter we'd like to present another set of lenses to illuminate your pathways toward balance. This framework is drawn from the results of numerous studies, conducted over the past forty years that have searched for clues to the quality of lifestyles most conducive to balance and "optimal health." Research shows that when faced with major life changes, 5 to 10 percent of the population actually breaks down, gets sick, or dies. At the other end of the change resilience continuum, however, are a very interesting 5 to 10 percent of people who actually come more alive and thrive when confronted with significant life changes. Considerable attention has been given to studying these fortunate people who actually thrive on change, and this research reveals a number of common factors that help them to maintain their health and balance.

CHANGE RESILIENCE CONTINUUM

Foremost among these studies are the pioneering works of Dr. Krobasa at the City University of New York, and a five-year "Sound-Mind,

"Wisdom is the harmony between our mind and the laws of reality.

Morality is the harmony between our convictions and our actions.

Concentration is the harmony between our feelings, our knowledge and our will,

The unity of all our creative forces in the experience of a higher reality."

—Anagarika Govinda

Sound-Body" research project conducted by Kenneth Pelletier, M.D., former director of Stanford University's Corporate Health Program. This groundbreaking research project, funded by the Rockefeller Foundation, identified the central characteristics that are the basis of optimal health.

From these and related studies, seven key principles emerge for living in balance. You'll find that we have touched on these issues throughout the book, for each of these elements reflects a high level of conscious awareness or mindfulness, a more "whole-systems" way of relating to the world, and a spiritually and socially attuned "altruistic" inclination. These seven principles are: attitude, accountability, commitment, supportive relationships, service, personal mastery, and faith.

Attitude

Do you view the stressful changes of your daily lives as a threat, or as a challenge and opportunity? People who are able to take change in stride and respond in a balanced way tend to hold a personally empowered and self-encouraging attitude. They have the confidence and trust that they can handle challenging situations and positively affect the course of their lives. They view change as an opportunity, not as a threat.

A reporter once asked Albert Einstein, "Dr. Einstein, if you could ask the universe a single question and receive a direct reply, what would you ask?" His reply came swiftly, as though he had pondered the question for a long time: "Is the universe friendly?" Pause for a moment to reflect upon Einstein's question. What do you think? How would you live if the universe were truly friendly and supportive of you?

Moment to moment, the attitudinal lenses that you choose to wear color your world for better or for worse. Experience the difference between being appreciative or being critical, or between viewing yourself as a victim or holding a more empowered attitude. Adopting an optimistic attitude toward the universe at large and the immediate challenges you face allows you to tap into a greater reservoir of creative energy potential that helps you maintain an even keel. The first step is to recognize the attitude you are holding, and notice whether it diminishes or enhances your energy and effectiveness. Then, without sacrificing realism, experiment with embodying a more positive outlook that will keep you buoyant and balanced on the sea of constant change.

Accountability

Folks who live generally in balance focus on what they can do and don't lose energy spinning their wheels or getting tied up in knots over what is outside their control. At the same time, they hold a strongly accountable point of view, don't avoid problems, and are willing to own the part they play in a situation.

To get a sense for this, draw three concentric circles on a piece of paper. Label the inner circle "control" and in this circle write or think about all the things in your life that you have direct control over. Next, label the second circle "influence." Here identify all the things in your life that you don't have total control over, but that you can influence by your actions. Now, label the third and largest circle "appreciate" or "learn from." Within this circle, pause to note all the factors and forces in your life that are too large, complex, or distant for you to feel much of a sense of influence over. Many of these forces, such as the powerful realities of the weather, taxes, or organizational bureaucracy are beyond your direct control or even your influence. Yet many people exhaust themselves struggling against, worrying, or complaining about these large and unwieldy forces.

A wiser, more balanced approach is to focus attention on those aspects of our life/work/environment/relationships that we can better learn from, influence, or even control, and allow ourselves to better understand and appreciate the large mysterious forces that are too complex to feel much control over. Saint Francis expressed this balanced awareness in his prayer: "God, Grant me the serenity to accept the things I cannot change, the courage to change the things I can, and the wisdom to know the difference."

In our own work as coaches, facilitators, and trainers with individuals, teams, and organizations, we often remind people to focus on those factors that they can really get some leverage on. Understanding that we can't cover the thorny earth with leather, we concentrate our efforts to make shoes. Realizing that the bureaucracy in our organizations is difficult to change, we mobilize people at a grass roots or team level, and identify ways that we can improve things in the department or area that we do have some control or influence over. Adopting an "accountable" approach to change means being mindful of where we can expand our circle of control and our circle of influence. This also means being mindful of our often unconscious beliefs, assumptions, or attitudes regarding the larger forces in our lives and finding more balanced,

"People are always blaming their circumstances for what they are. I don't believe in circumstances. The people who get on in this world are the people who get up and look for the circumstances they want and if they can't find them, make them."

—George Bernard Shaw

learningful, or appreciative ways to relate to them. "Remember, when we are aware we have a choice. Holding an accountable point of view brings our life more into control and balance by focusing on where we can get leverage and where we can make a difference.

Commitment

Balanced people live and work with a strong and clear sense of purpose. They view themselves as having a meaningful role to fulfill and hold a strong inner belief in its importance.

George Bernard Shaw exemplified the passion and spirit of this when he declared: "This is the true joy in life . . . being used for a purpose recognized by yourself as a mighty one . . . being a force of nature instead of a feverish, selfish little clod of ailments and grievances complaining that the world will not devote itself to making you happy. I am of the opinion that my life belongs to the whole community, and as long as I live it is my privilege to do for it whatever I can. I want to be thoroughly used up when I die. For the harder I work the more I live. I rejoice in life for its own sake. Life is no brief candle to me. It's sort of a splendid torch which I've got to hold up for the moment and I want to make it burn as brightly as possible before handing it on to future generations."

Commitment brings balance by giving more focus and clarity of purpose to your life. It operates like a plumb line, helping you stay tuned to what has meaning and importance, increasing your energy and attention while reducing distraction. When you know what you are committed to, you'll be better able to set and stick to priorities, to recognize and honor limits, and to live with integrity.

Supportive Relationships

At the core of our being, we are social creatures who thrive on meaningful, caring, and affirming contact with others. Although finding a balance of personal time and social or family time is crucial, the importance of social contact for assuring life balance is a key element not to be overlooked.

One striking example of the importance of supportive relationships in our lives is that the fact that risk factors for a person who is lonely are far greater than for a person who smokes, drinks, eats a poor diet, and doesn't get any exercise! We've already talked about the health-enhancing effects of support networks in Chapter Ten and community in Chapter Twelve. The main point here is that people who have supportive

"When you are inspired by some great purpose, some extraordinary project, all your thoughts break their bonds; your mind transcends limitations; your consciousness expands in every direction; and you find yourself in a great, new and wonderful world. Dormant forces, faculties and talents become alive and you discover yourself to be a greater person by far than you ever dreamed yourself to be."

—Patanjali

"There is a whole other journey that goes on, and that is internal. It's one that tests you to do things you can't do in your normal life. Much of navigation is this internal journey. It's a commitment that comes from, I don't know, some place that is very deep inside. I think from the spirit or soul of those who take this challenge."

—Nainona Thompson

networks of close relations and friends are happier, healthier, more resilient to change, and do much better in handling life's stresses than those who feel alone, isolated, and unsupported.

Service

We all know how good we feel when we do something to help others. Each time we do, we tap the energy of love and compassion that is fundamental to life. Highly change-resilient people view service as their true mission in life, and hold material wealth and success as secondary to helping others. They have a strong sense of belonging and understand the value of nurturing relationships with family, friends, coworkers, and community.

Many people have discovered that making time in their lives to be of service to others provides a quality of joy and satisfaction that is deeply renewing. We continue to learn more and more about balance by realizing that in serving the needs of others from a selfless place of caring and connectedness, many of our own deepest needs can also be fulfilled.

Personal Mastery

People who understand the importance of personal development and who have cultivated a high degree of self-mastery are the ones most able to sail through challenging times with confident balance. They've learned to deeply listen and respond skillfully to the subtle whispers that warn them when they are drifting out of balance. As a result, they are more likely to eat when they are hungry, and to rest and renew themselves when they are tired. By recognizing and reducing the harmful accumulations of stress, they are able to live in a more balanced and more disease-resistant way. In the process of developing the mindfulness necessary to recognize and master stress, we can also deepen our mind-body-spirit connection as a whole. This allows us to gain the inner strength and understanding necessary to meet every situation in a more balanced, centered way.

One sign of effective personal energy management is that people are able to maintain optimal energy levels throughout the day without dependence upon the use of such stimulants as caffeine, sugar, and nicotine. As we have already discussed, although stimulants appear to offer us free energy, they actually drive the system out of balance at our expense. As a result, the body has to expend more energy to restore the imbalance caused by them. Instead of relying on counterproductive

"The only ones among you who will be truly happy are those who have sought and found how to serve."

—Albert Schweitzer

"Give of your hands to serve and your hearts to love."

—Mother Teresa

"As human beings, our greatness lies not so much in being able to remake the world... as in being able to remake ourselves."

—Mahatma Gandhi

stimulants, "balance masters" choose options such as frequent exercise and practicing self-renewing and revitalizing skills that prevent the accumulation of stress, and bring a higher degree of self-confidence, self-control, self-acceptance, and self-respect. Like skills in any domain, such personal skills are developed gradually over time through discipline, practice, coaching, and proper instruction.

Faith

A spiritual outlook toward life is common among people who live in balance. Holding a spiritual frame of reference, or reverence, develops our faith, confidence, and trust, and reduces the intensity of toxic, worrisome emotions and destructive behaviors. People with a deep spiritual perspective often say that it is their faith that helps them to see their lives within a larger perspective and gives them a sense of belonging to a greater whole. For many, their spirituality is anchored in the fellowship, community, and worship associated with their church, synagogue, temple, mosque, or meditation group. For others, the spiritual grounding of their lives may be found in communion with nature, or through their love for family and friends, or through service to others.

Faith allows us to reach out and take refuge in our connectedness to a larger, deeper reality and Source than our tiny personal selves. By remembering to open our hearts and minds to affirm the link in spirit between our personal identities and our universal nature, we shift the center of gravity in our lives more toward authentic balance.

Compassionate Awareness

These studies on change resilience reveal a number of interesting findings about living in harmony and balance:

* Attention to diet, exercise, rest, and stress management alone will not assure optimal well-being.
* Living with a strong self-centered preoccupation with individualistic and narrowly narcissistic concerns seriously compromises the quality of health, life balance, and performance, and reduces our adaptability and change resilience. The more rigid, chaotic, or out of touch or unfeeling we are (regarding ourselves, our relationships, society, or environment), the more we diminish our happiness, health, longevity, and effectiveness and put ourselves at dangerous risk.

"Faith is the opening of all sides and every level of one's life to the Divine in-flow."

Martin Luther King Jr.

"The divine beauty of heaven and earth,

All creation, members of one family."

—Morihei Ueshiba O'Sensai

"My religion is kindness."

—The Dalai Lama

- Learning to quiet one's body and mind, and to raise or deepen the quality of our mindful awareness, is the essential first step toward living in balance, realizing optimal health, and gaining the deep guiding insights that nourish our lives with inspiration and meaning.

What stands out as we consider these seven elements is that they each speak to living with both a high degree of mindfulness and a deeper sense of compassion and caring. When we lose our balance and become overwhelmed by the stressful demands and complex circumstances of our lives, the higher order "executive functions" of our brains literally shut down, shunting control of our critical decision-making to more primitive and emotionally reactive brain centers that increase our tendency for panic and mental paralysis. These responses only further reduce our ability to move toward balance and exacerbate already desperate circumstances. When we are overwhelmed by stress and lose our physical, emotional, and mental balance, our level of functioning is as impaired as that of someone who is heavily intoxicated. This is confounded by the common response to stress that is to lapse into mindless reactivity and denial, to distract ourselves with media or business, or to rely even more heavily on the consumption of alcohol and a host of other mind-numbing substances as a faulty strategy of denial and retreat. Is it any wonder that VUCA circumstances in our lives and world tend to escalate in their criticality and become ever more complex, overwhelming, out of control, and out of balance?

As we become mindful of the tendency to implode and constrict, we can choose instead to more quickly relax, center ourselves, and actually expand our thinking and awareness to encompass and see clearly the reality of the whole situation that we are in the midst of.

Reflection

Pause now for a few moments to reflect on the following questions:

- Which of these seven principles of living a balanced life are presently strong in your life?
- Which of these principles would it be wise for you to pay more attention to in order to give you more leverage for living your life and approaching your work in a more balanced way?

"We are accustomed to the phrase Homo sapiens, but our full designation is 'Homo sapiens sapiens.' To be 'sapient' is to be wise or knowing. We humans describe ourselves as being more than sapient or wise, we are sapient sapient and have the unique potential of becoming "doubly wise" or 'doubly knowing.' It is often remarked that where animals 'know' only humans 'know that they know.' Our highest potential as a species is our ability to achieve full self-reflective consciousness or 'knowing that we know.'... Through humanities awakening, the universe acquires the ability to look back and reflect upon itself—in wonder, awe, and appreciation."

—Duane Elgin

It is always heartening to see how deeply impactful these seven principles are when we explore these with our corporate clients. People generally recognize their wisdom and feel that their own inner intelligence and their core personal and spiritual values are deeply affirmed and renewed by these findings. With awareness they can begin to shift their priorities to incorporate more of these principles into their lives.

Given that the price we pay for not practicing them is so high, and the benefits are so great, many we work with have begun to explore how they might practice these principles more conscientiously within their circles of friends, family, and colleagues. Self-organizing groups have come together for community service projects like Compassion Games International, or to share a healthy meal, take a mindful walk, meditate together, or even Skype or Google Group into a group meditation or discussion of articles or research studies that offer insight and inspiration.

In our community in Seattle, after offering a very warmly received workshop for the medical school faculty at the University of Washington, we started the Meditation and Medicine Professionals Circle that has been running strong for over ten years now with monthly meetings, annual retreats, and trips to conferences on Contemplative Science and Clinical Practice. Hearing that a Mindful Lawyers group had also started meeting in town, we initiated a larger Contemplative Professionals group that brings together hundreds of colleagues working in education, health care, law, the arts, business, government, high tech, and sports, to deepen their practice, develop their social networks, and inspire each other with best practices for living in balance at work, and beyond. As we have shared these stories with colleagues around the world, other groups have organized drawing together people for community, study, and practice. As people learn more about these principles and practices for living in balance in nurturing and supportive settings, many realize that their networks of support have been neglected and they take a more active role in contacting old friends, and strengthening friendships of kindred souls and colleagues in their professional lives and beyond.

People also take these principles home to share with their spouses, kids, significant others, church, or community groups. Again and again, we hear that this shared dialogue is a very meaningful forum for helping families come up with strategies to develop a healthier, more balanced lifestyle by clarifying priorities and identifying tangible ways to bring greater harmony and balance alive.

Who are the people in your life with whom you would like to have this conversation? Remember, health, harmony, and balance in our lives is not a solitary pursuit—self-centered and isolated people cope poorly with change and stress, and are in great danger of having the quality of their health, work, families and relationships disintegrate.

Now that you have learned these seven factors, you can use them regularly as reference checkpoints to monitor how you're doing on the course to balance. Like a compass, they will give you reliably clear directions to guide your way home.

THREE KEYS TO RESILIENCY

Living in balance helps us to develop resilience in responding to the inevitable changes and challenges of our lives. Here are three useful principles to keep in mind to increase your resilience in order to live in balance in the midst of change:

1. Increase your capacity to have an eyes-wide-open acceptance of reality.

   With mindfulness, curiosity, and courage, we are able to stay fully present in order to see and accept what is happening within and around us.

   Do you embrace and accept challenging life experiences in a realistic way — or are you more prone to denial, rationalization, or wishful thinking?

   What can you learn from this to help you prepare for living in balance with greater resiliency in the future?

2. A deep belief that life is truly meaningful.

   Our worldview plays a huge role determining the meaning we find in our life experience.

   Can you remember a time when you were able to find deep meaning in a life-experience that could have overwhelmed you?

   What can you learn from this to help you prepare for living in balance with greater resiliency in the future?

3. A creative spirit that makes do with what is available to innovate and improvise.

   Your resourcefulness plays a key role in your resiliency.

   Can you remember a time when you were able to tap your creative spirit in order to respond to a challenging situation?

   What can you learn from this to help you prepare for living in balance with greater resiliency in the future?

"No revolution in outer things is possible without prior revolution in one's inner way of being. Whatever change you aspire to in your affairs must be preceded by a change in heart, an active deepening and strengthening of your resolve to meet every event with equanimity, detachment, and innocent goodwill. When this spiritual poise is achieved within, magnificent things are possible without."

—I Ching Hexagram 49, translation by Brian Browne Walker

chapter sixteen

Earthwalk: Essential Reminders For a Balanced Life

Grandfather, Great Spirit ... You have set the powers of the four quarters of the earth to cross each other. You have made me cross the good road, and the road of difficulties, and where they cross, the place is holy. Day in, day out, forevermore, you are the life of all things.

— BLACK ELK, OGLALA SIOUX

EACH MOMENT AND EACH DAY OF OUR LIVES, WE ARE CALLED ON TO acknowledge and find harmony with a larger sphere of relationships and forces in our world. Living in dynamic interdependence with the world, it is becoming increasingly clear that in order to find happiness, harmony, and balance in our busy, personal lives, it is essential for us to learn to expand our personal concerns to include a more global, whole-systems view.

In this spirit, the elders of the Seneca nation traditionally encouraged their people to reflect on four essential questions in order to determine if they were living in balance with their world. We have found these questions to be helpful in our own lives, and often share them with those with whom we work. These questions are especially relevant for us on our modern-day "earthwalk," as we look at our lives, set our priorities, weigh our choices, and gauge our progress toward our most cherished goals. As you read each of these four questions, pause to reflect and honestly answer each one:

1. Are you happy living how you are living and doing what you are doing?

2. Is what you are doing adding to the confusion?

3. What are you doing to further peace and contentment in your own life and in the world?

4. How will you be remembered after you are gone — either in absence or in death?

If you are happy doing what you are doing, what brings you the greatest joy? What is your next frontier for satisfaction and fulfillment? If you aren't happy living the way you are living, is balance to be found in changing what you are doing, or in changing your mindset or attitude toward what you are doing?

If you find that what you are doing is actually adding to the confusion and creating more problems or imbalances in your life, say "whoa," and ask yourself, "what is driving me to act in these ways?" Often, the forces that drive us into self-defeating or destructive ways of living are unconscious to us. When we are able to look and listen deeply into our hearts and minds, and to look squarely into the eyes of our own "inner enemies," we are better able to shine the light of our compassion, forgiveness, or wisdom into these aspects of ourselves in order to heal our wounds, and restore our balance.

These four essential questions offer us a powerful tool for helping us to bring greater awareness and accountability to creating the quality of life that we want to create for ourselves, for others in our lives, and even for generations to come. If upon reflection you find that you could be doing more to bring greater peace and contentment into your life, listen deeply for what a step in that direction might be for you. Is greater balance for you to be found in taking more time alone, or in spending more quality time with your loved ones and friends, or helping others in your community? Is balance for you at this time in your life to be found in taking on more activity, or creating more quiet time? Listen deeply, pray, reflect, do whatever it takes for you to know what your next step is!

"With Beauty before me, may I walk

With beauty behind me, may I walk

With Beauty above me, may I walk

With beauty below me, may I walk

With beauty all around me, may I walk

Wandering on a trail of beauty, lively, I walk."

—Navajo blessing

Compare how you would like to be remembered with the realities of the legacy that you have created thus far. Ask yourself, "If I were to die next week, what would I be most proud of? What wounds would I most like to heal or forgive? What words do I need to speak, and what actions most need to be taken for me to leave this world, or this job, or to complete my watch at this station of my life with integrity, dignity, and balance, as a true pilgrim on the path of wholeness?" Within the laboratory of your own mindbody and relationships, experiment with refining and distilling what is most essential, most powerful, and most beautiful in your life.

These compelling and poignant reminders call our attention to how much there is to learn from people who for centuries lived in harmony with one another and with the whole of Nature in all of its beauty. On the journey, according to the elders of the Seneca tribe:

- Self-knowledge is the need,
- Self-understanding is the desire.
- Self-discipline is the way.
- Self-realization is the goal.

Take some time to ponder these ideas ... to take them to heart ... and see how these simple but profound principles can help you to live in greater balance.

THE PAUSE THAT TRULY REFRESHES

Remember, life is all about learning, and learning brings balance. Without feedback and self-reflection, there is no learning. In each of our lives it is necessary to regularly take time out to check our bearings and honestly ask ourselves, "Am I living on purpose?" Often we don't make time in our lives for this kind of self-assessment. We are too busy attending to what is urgent, and have little time or attention for what is truly most important. Living in this way, the subtle "whispers" of warning signs are easily overlooked until they become dangerous screams demanding our attention. All too often we wait till a major crisis arises before we pause to look and think deeply about our lives. When we do pause for reflection, often what we find is that, for many reasons, we have strayed from our ideal path. We find that we have neglected people or pastimes that are really important to us and have squandered our precious time with people or activities that are not really so important to us.

In moments of honest self-reflection, there arises a bittersweet sense of three special qualities. One is a quality of profound grief that can shake us to the core, and often leave us sobbing with deep regret. This grief is often mixed with a second quality, that of deep gratitude for what we really cherish in our lives, be it our health, a loved one, or an ability we have or had that we are thankful for. Third is a fierce determination, fueled by both our grief and our gratitude, to live our lives with true integrity in a way that honors what is essential in and to us. This brings about a greater congruence of our innermost beliefs and values with our way of life.

Tumbling on fast-forward, driven by expectations, burdened by responsibilities, and feeling overwhelmed, we are easily distracted and lose our balance. That's why, in your lifelong journey of balance, it's wise to pause often to determine if you have wandered off track. By stopping often to check in with yourself and with those who share the journey with you, you can save valuable time and energy. Remember that each moment of your life is precious and irretrievable. If you are unclear on what direction to go, then take some time to reflect again on these questions, and let your answers offer insight with regard to the next stage of your own journey. Detours can be lengthy, drain you of vital energy, and lead to serious regrets downstream.

Our friend, the poet David Whyte, often tells the story of a woman manager from AT&T who participated in one of his corporate workshops. When invited to reflect upon the ways that her personal life vision and dreams had been sacrificed for career advancement, she wrote, "Ten years ago … I turned my face for a moment, and it became my life."

How does that resonate for you? Ten years ago I … launched onto a career path … got married … had kids … was divorced.… I started a business that grew faster than I would have dreamed.… I went unconscious trying just to cope. Now, richer or poorer, grayer or balder, with or without kids and aging parents, something in you says, "Whoa! Who am I now?" and "How do I want to live the rest of my life?" These fierce moments of awakening to the call for balance are worthy of celebration.

When you wander from your path — as you certainly will — reflect on the forces, inner and outer, that drew you off course, and use those learnings to actually accelerate your progress as the journey continues. What cues did you overlook or misinterpret? What assumptions or expectations blinded you from seeing the actual path? What learning can you take from the last "mistake" to build your wisdom, skills, and confidence as you embark on the next stage of the journey? Mistakes are only mistakes if we don't learn from them. With a learningful attitude we

"The inhabitant or soul of the universe is never seen; its voice alone is heard. All we know is that it has a gentle voice, like a woman, a voice so fine…that even children cannot become afraid. And what it says is "Sila ersinarsinivdluge,' 'Be not afraid of the universe.'"

—Inuit teaching

can say to ourselves, "Yep, missed that turn, fell into that trap, crashed and burned, and I have learned a few things along the way. I don't need to invest more time in repeating those mistakes!"

Remember that the word sin means literally to "miss the mark." If the mark you are shooting for is to learn greater balance for yourself and your world, then regularly asking yourself the re-clarifying questions of the Seneca elders can truly be a lifesaver.

COMING FULL CIRCLE

What is "the note" that you are called to hold and "true to" in the great symphony of living in balance, harmony, and wholeness? Is it to be kind, to be helpful, to be fully present, to grow food, to steward a sanctuary, to mentor young people, to be a healer, an advocate, to deliver the best possible goods or services needed, to raise healthy, wise, resilient children, or to be a fiercely compassionate warrior for social justice?

Returning to the vision of the Great Turning that we began this journey together with, we draw further clarity and inspiration for living in balance from the advice and shining example of our beloved friend and teacher, deep-ecologist Joanna Macy, who encourages all of us to engage in three dimensions of action that are essential to bring to our Earthwalk at this pivotal time. These are:

Take action to slow the damage to Earth and its beings. These are the most visible responses that include all manner of political, legislative, legal, and economic actions including: lobbying; documenting and publicizing corruption and dangers; whistle-blowing; vigils at places of ecological destruction or injustice; and civil disobedience with great love. These kinds of actions buy time, save lives, and can offer protection, but these alone are insufficient to create societal change.

Analyze and understand the dynamics of the old systems and create wise new alternatives. This second dimension of action stretches us to expand our collective courage and creativity in order to bring forth new, life-affirming, lower carbon footprint and sustainable new ways of living. Examples of some emerging models include: alternative energy systems; alternative economies, local currencies, and gift economy; independent media; restorative justice; holacracy; permaculture and natural farming; cohousing, ecovillages, and pocket neighborhoods; community gardens and community-supported agriculture; watershed restoration; teach-in's; and Transition Towns.

> "Peace is not weak. Standing up to a tank is harder than dropping a suicide bomb."
>
> —Matthieu Ricard

Raise consciousness and deepen in the wisdom and creative compassion we bring to life. Ultimately, the most important shift that needs to take place is within our beliefs, worldview, and identity. As Joanna describes, "The insights and experiences that enable us to make this shift are accelerating, and they take many forms. They arise as grief for our world, giving the lie to old paradigm notions of rugged individualism, the essential separateness of the self. They arise as glad responses to breakthroughs in scientific thought, as reductionism and materialism give way to evidence of a living universe. And they arise in the resurgence of wisdom traditions, reminding us again that our world is a sacred whole, worthy of adoration and service." Strategies in this dimension include explorations into: deep ecology; mindfulness and other forms of contemplative practice; contemplative science; general living systems theory; ecopsychology; ecofeminism; complexity theory; interspiritual movement; creation spirituality and liberation theology; social justice movement; the resurgence of shamanic traditions; and the simple living movement. We once attended a seed exchange in a neighboring community and Michelle mentioned that we steward a small permaculture farm and learning center on the northern tip of the Big Island of Hawaii. "Oh, that's wonderful," said one of the vendors there, "What do your raise on your farm?" she asked. Michelle smiled, and simply said, "Consciousness!"

ONE STEP AT A TIME

In walking a path, the only step you can find balance on is the one on which you are standing. You can work only on yourself, and you can take a step forward only from where you stand on the path. Keeping the whole in mind and being honest with the current state of affairs in your life are the crucial keys to balance. If you are in ill health, make efforts to regain your health. If you are feeling alienated and alone, explore ways to develop more of a sense of belonging and community. If you are resentful or feel guilty about something, explore ways to resolve your situation. If you are stunned by the glory of the universe in which you live, deepen your capacity to commune with the source of life through prayer and meditation. Keeping the whole in mind, knowing where you stand, take one mindful step at a time to deepen and expand your balance.

"...Grasses are blooming, grandfathers dying, consciousness blinking on and off; all of this is happening at once. All of this, vibrating into existence, out of nothingness. Every particle foaming into existence, transcribing the ineffable. Arising and passing away, arising and passing away, 23 trillion times per second. When Buddha saw that, he smiled. 16 million tons of rain are falling every second on the planet. An ocean, perpetually falling, and every drop is your body. Every motion, every feather, every thought is your body. Time is your body. And the infinite, curled inside like invisible rainbows folded into light... Let our lives be incense burning like a hymn to the sacred body of the universe."

—Drew Dellinger, excerpt from *Hymn to the Sacred Body of the Universe*

The Circle of Wholeness

We have devoted our lives to studying and teaching many systems of higher-order thinking, knowing, and learning that have been developed in many fields of science and philosophy. These systems invite us to look at the patterns of relationship that weave any system together: beginnings and endings, what is developing and dissolving, what is manifesting and what are the system's potentials. Where is there movement and flexibility? Where is there "stuckness" and resistance to change? This is what is referred to as systems thinking. Weaving together a variety of ancient and modern approaches to systems thinking, we'd like to introduce you here to a physical practice that can help you discover the balance among the many parts of the whole.

Begin by orienting yourself to the four directions: east and west, north and south. (If you're not sure of the directions, simply hold for now that the direction you're facing is the east, and then at a later time when you get your bearings, repeat this technique facing each of the actual directions.)

Turn first to face the east—that place of dawning, sunrise, and new beginnings, the place of inspiration where what was hidden by the night is revealed and becomes clear. The east—where insight crosses the threshold into light that illuminates your world. That place that the earth forever turns and returns to. The east.

Next turn to face the south, that place of the brightest light, that noontime sky when the sun is most high, and the light is warmest and brightest. The south ... the place where everything is manifest, full blown, and full grown, and, in being in its fullness, is sure to wane from here.

Now turn to face the west. Behold that place of sunsets and completions, the time and place where the last rays of light, the last waves of breath disappear across the threshold into night. The place of transformation and unification of light and darkness, day and night.

Turning again, face the north, home of the north star—that one still unchanging point in the spinning universe that seems always to be there. That dark place where there is infinite potential for the light of new potentials to emerge.

Returning now to the rising light of a new dawn, face the east, restoring your faith that again out of the deepest darkness, light will surely come, that out of the coldest winter will come a new spring, that out of the darkest night will come a new bright dawn, a new birth, and a new beginning.

"Grandfather
Great Spirit

All over the world
the faces of living
ones are alike.

With tenderness
they have come up
out of the ground.

Look upon your
children that
they may

face the winds and
walk the good road
to the Day of Quiet.

Grandfather
Great Spirit

Fill us with the Light.

Give us the strength
to understand,

and the eyes to see.

Teach us to walk the
soft Earth as relatives
to all that live."

—Sioux prayer

Return again to face the south.

And return again to face the west.

And return again to face the north.

Each breath carries you round this wheel and through every phase of the cycle. Exhaling completely, you arrive at the north, empty, open, receptive. As the inhalation begins, you turn to and through the east to reach your fullness at the top of the inhalation facing the south. Then exhaling, turning toward the west, releasing and letting go of your fullness, trusting to release and let go, returning again and again to the still point of infinite potentials in the north.

Turning again, growing, sprouting, gestating toward a new birth and new beginnings and emergings in the east. Contemplate the meaning of east—spring equinox, inhaling, creativity, blossoming, filling, becoming in your life.

Turning again, reflect upon the meaning of south—summer solstice, full inhalation, ripe fruit on the trees, the prime of life. Growing, strengthening, expanding to the fullness in the south.

Turning again toward the west, contemplate the meanings behind the experience of crossing the threshold into night, autumn equinox, leaves falling from the trees, getting colder, darker, older, endings, deaths, wanings, diminishings, deepenings, dissolvings, exhaling toward the west.

And turning toward the north, ponder midnight, winter solstice, exhalation, receptivity, and emptiness soon to be filled, that plenum void of unmanifest potential waiting ... to be expressed in a new dawn. North, you old friend, you've been here before, no need for fear of stillness or frozenness, knowing that spring, inspiration, and the seeds of new beginnings are enfolded in potential here. Here you know winter as the womb of spring, darkness as the womb of light, and death as the womb of birth.

You can use this process in your daily life to step into the center of a question or a project in order to see how all the complex forces and phases fit together in search of balance. For example, turning toward the east, metaphorically or in actuality, ask yourself, "What is beginning and emerging here? What has yet to fully emerge into clarity? What is being born that needs to be developed and brought through to fruition? What is the potential for breakthrough in this breakdown?"

To the south ask, "What is clear here? What has reached its peak, fullness, or maximal extension and is about to wane?"

"Everything we do—our discipline, effort, meditation, livelihood, and every single thing we do from the moment we're born until the moment we die—we can use to help us to realize our unity and our completeness with all things."

—Pema Chödrön

"Walking alone in the
Path Way of
the Ancients
Upheld by a Faith
empty of all Beliefs.
My Treasure is the
White Cloud drifting
aimlessly across
The vast Blue Sky
The full Moon rising
Pearl over gently
rolling hills.
I journey like a Leaf
Floating with
No-mind
upheld by the
gracious
Breeze as it carries
me hither and yon.
My heartbeat
is content
And walking is at ease
for body and mind no
longer run toward
this True Horizon
beneath my feet.
Without care
Not-knowing
where I go
Wandering yet never
leaving my
True Home."

—Andrew Shugyo
  Daijo Bonnici

To the west you ask, "What is passing or coming to completion in this process? What seeds are being sowed into the earth now and what is being composted to feed the next cycle?"

And to the north you ask, "What remains unchanged? What are the possibilities that are latent here but have not yet been recognized? Where am I stuck or withdrawn, and what seeds of potential are frozen that must thaw or be released for the next cycle to begin?"

Use the basic truth of the natural cycle to organize your attention and focus your thinking. With each cycle of the process, a clearer and deeper sense of wholeness emerges. With each iteration, you deepen your wisdom of balance by seeing how each part is included in the whole, and how the whole is inseparable from its many parts. Each circle defines a whole: a whole breath, a whole day, a whole lunar cycle or year or lifetime. Understanding this, contemplate how the insights you come to may apply across many dimensions of wholeness, many cycles of time, many relationships, situations, or projects in which you seek for balance. This quality of multidimensional, whole systems thinking will help you to focus on the many elements of your life and weave them into a balanced whole perspective.

Ultimately, your greatest wisdom is in learning to hold all of these perspectives and points of view simultaneously, to behold a global vision of the whole system in all of its phases and stages at the same time. When you have learned to do this you come to stand in that witnessing wisdom and creative intelligence that is the essence of mindfulness.

As Robert Frost once wrote, "We dance round in a ring and suppose, but the Secret sits in the middle and knows." The great Chinese poet Chuang-tzu shared similar wisdom when he said, "When we understand, we are at the center of the circle and there we sit, while Yes and No chase each other around the circumference."

As you begin to think deeply about the unique aspects of each phase of the cycle, you begin to see a complete view of the whole system. You begin to recognize that the rhythms of energy and change within you and around you are deeply related. In each phase of the cycle, you begin to see every part of the system in its balanced relationship to a larger wholeness, and you begin to feel that the same forces that are alive within you are alive and unfolding in the world around you.

RETURN TO WHOLENESS

We began this book with the question, "What does it mean to live in balance and wholeness in our world today?" Through the course of the journey you have been making through the many methods and ideas that have been presented here, you have, no doubt, been expanding your sense of what this means for you. As you continue to integrate what you've found of value here, you may find that the journey of this book is truly a never-ending story. Each time you return to these pages they will reveal a deeper reflection of the possibilities for balancing your life. And as you grow in balance and wholeness, everything else in your life will continue to teach you.

Ultimately, balanced living comes from remembering, affirming, and experiencing in an ongoing way the essential wholeness of your being. The pathway into this experience comes from staying tapped into your connection to a much larger Wholeness whose very nature is always in dynamic balance. Knowing that you are intrinsically, inseparably embedded within the matrix of this fundamental field of Wholeness, that you are intimately a part of it, and it of you, is the most vital wisdom key you can have to access the reservoirs of inner strength and confidence you need to meet life's challenges with balance.

In our own lives, we call this remembrance the practice of "taking refuge." It is something the two of us do on a daily basis, often several times a day, as a way of anchoring ourselves in the ultimate Source of balance, blessing, and guidance. What is it that steadies you? What or who, for you, can be a reliable source of refuge? Here is a meditation you can do to remember.

"And what does it mean to 'take refuge?'

It means we can't do it alone."

—Natalie Goldberg

Receiving and Radiating

As you sit here now, envision yourself sitting at the center of your universe, surrounded by all living beings. Holding this image in mind, pause for a moment to remember, invite, or sense the presence of those who have most deeply inspired you in your life. Reach out now with your heart and hands to these beings whose presence in your life is truly a blessing, a source of renewal, deep information, and inspiration. Imagine that all of them are right here with you now, surrounding you and shining like a constellation of brilliant suns. Or if you like, envision that these many sources of light merge into a single brighter sun that shines a radiance of blessings and inspiration into your life. Imagine that with each breath you reach out to them and hold their hands, and that through your connection with them you can draw strength and inspiration. In fact the stronger and more sincere your own aspiration, the deeper and stronger the flow of inspiration becomes. Imagine that each of these inspiring people in turn reaches out to hold the hands of

"With each true friendship, we build more firmly the foundation on which the peace of the whole world rests."

—Gandhi

those whom they look to for guidance, strength, and inspiration, and that they in turn reach out to those who have inspired them. Sense your teachers reaching out to their teachers, who reach out to their teachers. Envision yourself balanced within and receiving from this endless cascade of wisdom and love as it flows to you and through you from countless inspired ancestors of the far and distant past.

Envision this inspiration as knowledge and energy, soaking into you now. It energizes the parts of you where your life force is weak. It balances what needs to be balanced. It floods, cleanses, and opens the spaces and places within you that are clogged or congested, and nourishes the seeds of your deepest potentials to blossom beautifully. Like sunlight filtering into a deep clear pool, sense these waves of inspiring grace flooding your body-mind-energy-spirit. Every dimension of your being is illuminated, blessed, and renewed. With each breath you are filled, silently thinking, receiving. With each breath you release what you no longer need to hold on to, thinking inwardly releasing. Receiving ... releasing.... Receiving ... releasing.... Plugging into this renewal circuit, you are revitalized, calmed, and energized, and move toward balance between your inner and outer worlds.

Having cleared your circuits, charged your batteries, and filled your tanks, begin now to radiate and expand this sense of peace and well-being within you. With each inhalation, shift to receive, and then with each exhalation, radiate. Breathing in, imagine the inspiration and blessings converging and spiraling into you, filling your heart. With each out-breath, imagine that your heart is silently radiating like a bright shining star. Effortlessly offer the natural radiance of your innermost being to the world. Allow it to shine through the darkness within or around you. Allow it to light up your inner and outer world effortlessly, immediately. Let this be the light of your love, the light of your peace, the light of your presence, the light of your goodwill and positive regard.

Now, having enhanced and expanded your radiance, begin to direct your attention and energy to the world around you. Reach out now to those who look to you as a source of inspiration, guidance, and support. Reach out to your children, to your students, to your patients, clients, and customers, and to all those who look to you as they seek for balance and belonging in their lives. Receiving inspiration, wisdom, and strength from those you draw guidance from, reach out with your hands and from your heart, and let each exhalation become an inspiring gift that you offer to those who, in turn, look to you.

"To be truly happy in this world is a revolutionary act because true happiness depends upon a revolution in ourselves. It is a radical change of view that liberates us so that we know who we are most deeply and can acknowledge our enormous ability to love."

—Sharon Salzberg

Envision each person you reach out to taking your gift to heart: Feel that it truly inspires and awakens greater wisdom, balance, and strength in their lives. As you reach out to your children, envision them receiving and taking this gift to heart and then passing it on to their children, who pass it on to their children, who pass it on to their children and to all whose lives they touch. Envision your students reaching out to their students who reach out to their students. Imagine that all those whom you reach out to take these gifts to heart, and pass it on to those who will pass it on in an endless cascade of inspiration and blessings that reaches out into the world to help nurture harmony and balance for countless generations to come. In this way, receiving and radiating, sense yourself balanced here reaching out from this fleeting moment where all the experiences of the infinite past and all the potential for the boundless future converge. Viewed in this light, understand that your real life-work is to realize your connectedness and wholeness, to deepen in balance, to increase your capacity to gather inspiration and wisdom, to take it to heart, and to pass it on as far and wide as you possibly can.

Now, as you breathe, gather the raw energy of any agitation or discomfort into your heart, like raking coal or wood into a furnace, and let it fuel the fire of transformation, giving you more light to radiate. With each breath, breathe in compost, and breathe out flowers and fruit. Breathe in fear, and let its energy be released into the radiance of confidence. Breathe in imbalance, and let it, too, fuel the radiance of your steadiness and resilience. Radiate the power of equanimity out on the waves of your breath as a blessing of balance and peace in the lives of all those who share your world.

In this way, with practice, begin to understand that you can utilize any experience that comes to you as a vehicle to deepen your inner strengths, and tap you into a greater sense of connectedness. If you are faced with fear and suffering, let it fuel the radiance of your love and compassion. Faced with beauty and the sweetness of life, let it intensify the radiance of your gratitude and rejoicing. Imagine yourself as a light bearer, illuminating the world. Imagine the silent light of your innermost being blazing with exquisite clarity and radiating out to fill your body. Imagine it radiating out into the world around you now, as you yourself act as a radiant source of inspiration for the world. Holding your loved ones and friends in mind, radiate this love to them. Bring to heart and mind the leaders of the world, the children of the world, the beleaguered nations and species of the world and radiate your heartfelt care and prayers to them.

"Having been brought up in a mythical culture...archetypes are primordial encapsulated stories or mythologies and they are in the form of a seed in consciousness. When you plant that seed in consciousness, that archetypal seed, that mythical journey, then that seed starts to sprout. And as it sprouts, the patterning forces creates the situations, circumstances, events, and relationships for the unfolding of the story. I say select two or three heroes or heroines in mythology, or religion, or history and then ask these mythical beings to incarnate through you. And then don't be surprised when your see situations, circumstances, coincidences, synchronicity, and relationships finally show up that actually are part of the story you have been seeking to express."

—Deepak Chopra

In this way receiving … radiating … each breath affirms your deep relationship with the whole of creation, and with all beings in time past, present, and future. In this way, each blessed breath becomes a gesture of balance, a gesture of receiving from and offering to all.

CLOSING THOUGHTS

It is humbling for us to reflect on the state of the world and our positions and freedoms within it. Those of us writing or reading this book likely belong to a tiny minority of people who have adequate, or even luxurious, living conditions compared to most of humanity. We live with relative safety and peace of mind, free from much of the frightening unrest and danger in the world. We are educated and have many freedoms that others will never know. Many of us have the privilege and power to affect the lives of thousands of people and to help create the conditions for them to achieve a greater quality of life. We also have the privilege to develop and improve ourselves. If we choose, we can give time and attention to cultivate the paths of transformation, and work with others who share our freedom and inclination to create more balance and a better world for all.

In closing, we ask that you take this good fortune to heart. Utilizing the many methods and principles in this book has saved our life, our health, and our marriage many times, and it has served equally well for thousands of people we've worked with. We have confidence that it can help you in similar ways. Now it's up to you to put these guidelines to the test and make greater balance a living reality in your life.

We hope that your insights in reading this book will continue to ripen over time, and inspire an inquiry that opens you to live and work with greater balance, greater freedom, and a deeper kind of wisdom, caring, and wonder. The closing of this book is an opening into the rest of your life, as the circle of wholeness turns, bringing all things into balance. In this spirit, we will end with a beginning—the first verse of Genesis. In the Hebrew language, each letter of the alphabet has a meaning in itself. Understanding this, Stan Tenen's beautiful rendition of this verse translates the original Hebrew words one letter at a time to reveal an inner vision of wholeness. We invite you to read each line out loud and to be mindful of whatever imagery or feelings arise as you do. May the deep meaning of these uplifting words remind you of the ever-present wellspring of balancing energies available deep within you and in the heart of all of Creation at all times.

"Each time a person stands up for an ideal, or acts to improve the lot of others.... he sends forth a tiny ripple of hope, and crossing each other from a million different centers of energy and daring, those ripples build a current that can sweep down the mightiest walls of oppression and resistance."

—Robert F. Kennedy

"Blessings and Balance,

Balance and Blessings,

For from Balance comes all Blessings."

—Grandmother Keewaydinoquay, Ojibway Medicine Woman

"Breaking Open, Inside Outside
Rushing, Radiating, Reaching

All Life
Shining Source-Light
In Inner Being
Itself Recurring In Itself

Breaking Open, Inside Outside
Rushing, Radiating, Reaching
All-Life

All-Life
Blooming, Kindling, Inside Lighting
Looking Open, In with Out
In Inner Being
Golden-Flowing, Moving Outward, In Itself

All-Life
Itself Recurring In Itself

Looking Open, In with Out
Shining Source-Light
Inside Dividing
In Inner Being
Golden-Flowing, Moving Outward, In Itself

Doing, Living, Co-Evolving
All-Life
Itself Recurring In Itself

Looking Open, In with Out
All-Life
Rushing, Radiating, Reaching

Treetop, Upright; Bearing Wholeness, Carrying Light!"

"We shall not cease
from exploration,
and the end of all
our exploring will
be to arrive where
we started and
know the place
for the first time."

—T.S. Elliot

"As you practice these
precious teachings,

slowly the clouds of
sorrow will melt away,

and the sun of
wisdom and true joy

will be shining

in the clear sky

of your mind."

—Kalu Rinpoche

Our Invitation to You

Rumi once said:

> "The secret of my song though near none can see and none
> can hear, and oh for a Friend to know the sign
> and mingle all their soul with mine."

Has reading *Living in Balance* activated your curiosity, passion, or a thirst to learn more and explore the many realms of living in harmony and balance more deeply?

Would you like to connect with other kindred souls who share this interest and thirst to study, share, reflect, and support one another in learning how to live in balance?

Would you be interested in opportunities to study more closely with us in person, or on-line, to bring these principles and practices for living in balance more fully alive in your life, your work, your relationships, your organization, your community?

Would you like to develop the capacity of your organization or community to thrive in these complex, VUCA times?

If these questions resonate for you with a "Yes!" we invite you to engage with us to realize these potentials. We will post these emerging opportunities at:

http://WisdomAtWork.com/Balance

We invite you to check back to this site frequently for updates and inspirations.

Our vision is to develop, post, and host a wealth of resources that will inspire and support your continued explorations of ways to live in greater harmony and balance. We also welcome your invitations to offer special programs for your circles of friends, communities, and organizations who hear the call and understand the importance of learning to live in balance.

Permissions

Acknowledgments

OUR HEARTFELT THANKS AND DEEPEST APPRECIATION TO:

Michael Wiese, whose deep recognition of the call to balance was the visionary spark that birthed this new edition into being, and to everyone else at Divine Arts who has shared in weaving these words together into the beautiful book you now hold in your hands.

In particular, we'd also like to acknowledge the special contributions of: David Wright, for your masterful copyediting, patience, precision, and good humor in going through the laborious and painstakingly detailed process with us so carefully; John Brenner, for your amazingly beautiful cover design; Howie Severson for your inspired creativity, support, and skillfulness in laying out the handsome interior design of this book; and finally, great gratitude to Ken Lee and Travis Masch for your encouragement and help, being there to answer our questions, meet the challenges, and coordinate the many different collaborative dimensions that bring a book into being.

Steven Sieden for your inspiration to introduce us to Michael Wiese and Divine Arts.

Mary Jane Ryan, who initiated and skillfully edited the first edition of *Living in Balance*.

Our Hawaiian a'ina and ohana, for the gift of aloha, and for balancing our busy urban life with nature's healing power and beauty in joyous Island splendor.

Our deep respect, appreciation, and admiration to all our many extraordinary and inspired teachers, living in memory and presence, who have shared with us their wisdom, and the wisdom of their teachers. And, especially, a very deep bow to Nobel Peace Laureate Tenzin Gyatso, the Dalai Lama, for his kindness in offering the Foreword for this book, for his loving support, guidance, and blessing in our lives and work, and for his incredible embodiment of balanced living amidst the most challenging of circumstances. Despite the ongoing genocide of the Tibetan culture over the past sixty years of brutal Chinese occupation, he has inspired the people and the leaders of the world with the possibility of a wise and nonviolent way of life that actively seeks justice while showing compassion and respect for all. May we too exemplify such capacity for balance in our own lives.

Michelle's parents, Ida and Benjamin Gold, for helping her take her first steps in the direction of balance.

Our many colleagues and clients around the globe, for encouraging and supporting our work of bringing greater balance and mindfulness to the workplace—and beyond!

Joanna Macy; Daniel Siegel; Wade Davis; Congressman Tim Ryan; Jon Kabat-Zinn; Otto Scharmer; Jack Kornfield; Peter Senge; Robert Thurman; Pema Chödrön; Thich Nhat Hanh; Duane Elgin; Arianna Huffington; and Kumu Raylene Ha'alelea Kawaiae'a—who have inspired our understanding of living in balance and whose quotes are woven into this book.

We honor and give gratitude to all the guiding and supportive forces of the universe that are truly at the heart of this work, and through whose grace the miracle of this book has come into being and into your hands. May we learn to look, listen, and feel ever more deeply, to discover how profoundly interwoven all things and beings are within the mysterious balance of our lives.

Also, a hearty woof to our beloved canine companion Maitri (which means "unconditional friendliness") who has taught us so much about living in balance, took us for long walks, and kept us laughing through many long days and nights of writing this book.

Finally, we acknowledge you, the reader, sincere enough in your yearning for balance to invest yourself in reading this book. As you read, we will touch hearts and minds. We invite you to hold this book as a basket containing many seeds and jewels of wisdom that we have gathered through our encounters with many remarkable people.

Through your connection with us you will meet many of our friends and teachers, and in meeting them you will encounter their teachers. In this way, may the wisdom stream of our teachers flow into your life. As you read these pages, and as you test or take these ideas to heart, may your own wisdom and faith in the potentials of your life grow. Through your own increasingly balanced way of living, may you, in turn, inspire others, who will inspire others, who will inspire others for generations to come, so that this living source of wisdom and compassion will continue to nourish the spirit of balance in our world in ever more wonderful ways.

About the Authors

© 2014 Barbara Li Photography

DR. JOEL AND MICHELLE LEVEY HAVE DEVOTED THEIR LIVES TO STUDY-
ing, researching, and teaching disciplines related to how to live and
thrive in greater harmony and balance. They have been pioneers over
many decades in developing extra-ordinary capacities of leaders,
teams, organizations, and communities through the emerging fields of
mindfulness, mindbody medicine and contemplative science; integrative health care; change resilience; neurofeedback, cyberphysiology,
interpersonal neurobiology; collective wisdom and intelligence; systems thinking; and the global compassion movement.

Michelle and Joel have worked with hundreds of leading organizations and communities around the globe to inspire people to deepen
their capacity to bring a deeper wisdom, compassion, resilience, and
creative intelligence to life, work, and relationships. Their clients
include: NASA; Google; N.I.H.; Intel; M.D. Anderson Cancer Research
Center; World Bank; NOAA; The Clinton Global Initiative; U.S. Army
Special Forces; West Point Military Academy; Earthsave; Forest Ethics;
Compassionate Action Network International; Stanford Research
Institute International; U.S. Surgeon General's Office; Washington
Athletic Club; St. Francis Hospice; M.I.T; and World Business Academy.
They served as chairpersons for the Center for Corporate Culture &

Organizational Health at the Institute for Health & Productivity Management, and on the Board of Advisors for the International Campaign for Compassionate Cities; The Art Monastery Project; The International Working Group on Compassionate Organizations, and participated in the All-Party Parliamentary Group on Mindfulness.

The Dalai Lama, an advisor on a number of their projects, encouraged the Leveys in their work, saying: *"You are presently engaged in work that has great prospects for bringing the Dharma to a very wide section of people who may not under ordinary circumstances come into contact with the Dharma. I am very pleased about the work that you are doing and send you blessings and prayers for your success."* Joel and Michelle have studied closely with many of the world's most respected teachers in the mind science and contemplative science traditions, and were fortunate to participate in a year-long silent contemplative retreat.

The Leveys are co-founders of Wisdom at Work; the International Institute for Mindfulness, Meditation and MindBody Medicine; InnerWork Technologies Inc.; and SportsMind, Inc. They serve as clinical faculty at the University of Minnesota Medical School's Center for Spirituality and Healing, and Bastyr University where they teach special programs on Mindfulness, Compassion, Meditation, and Mindbody Medicine. They have also developed and taught special graduate programs for Mahidol University in Thailand; Indian Institute of Management; Antioch University; and University of Texas Center for Spirituality and Health. The Leveys were honored by the Institute of Noetic Sciences as leading "teachers of transformation." Joel and Michelle directed clinical programs related to mindfulness, resilience, stress mastery, and biofeedback for Group Health and Children's Medical Centers, and developed advanced biocybernautic training for the U.S. Army Special Forces' Jedi Warrior Program, which was described by leaders in the military and human potential movement as "the most exquisite orchestration of human technology we have ever seen," and "the most intensive and advanced leadership and human development program to be offered in modern times."

Their published works include: *Living in Balance: A Mindful Guide for Thriving in a Complex World; Mindfulness, Meditation, and Mind-Fitness; Wisdom at Work; Luminous Mind: Meditation and Mind Fitness; The Fine Arts of Relaxation, Concentration, and Meditation: Ancient Skills for Modern Minds; Corporate Culture and Organizational Health; Learning Organizations; Community Building in Business; Intuition at Work; The New Bottom Line;* and *VUCA Savvy Leadership: Thriving in Complex Times.* They also blog for *Huffington Post* (Spirit and Wellness).

Joel and Michelle live in Seattle and the Big Island of Hawaii, and work with communities and organizations around the globe. To extend an invitation, or learn more about their lives and work, please contact Balance@WisdomAtWork.com or visit:

WisdomAtWork.com/Balance/
WisdomAndCompassion.us
MeditationAndMedicine.ning.com
KohalaSanctuary.com

Like us on Facebook:
www.facebook.com/pages/Joel-and-Michelle-Levey/184438048260908

Follow us on Huffington Post:
www.huffingtonpost.com/joel-michelle-levey

Follow us on Twitter: WisdomAtWork

Children - 76

104 - Neuroplasticity - cycle of
mental & physical transformation

The moment you change your perception
is the moment you rewrite the
Chemistry of your body - Bruce Lipton

105 -11 - mindful of: